Employment Law and Human Resources Handbook 2010

• •

Edited by Alex Davies

Workplace Law Group
Second Floor, Daedalus House
Station Road, Cambridge CB1 2RE

Tel. 0871 777 8881
Fax 0871 777 8882
info@workplacelaw.net
www.workplacelaw.net

ISBN 978-1-905766-68-0

Published by
Workplace Law Network
Second Floor
Daedalus House
Station Road
Cambridge CB1 2RE
Tel. 0871 777 8881
Fax. 0871 777 8882
Email info@workplacelaw.net
www.workplacelaw.net

Design and layout by Workplace Law Group and Amnet Systems Ltd.
Printed and bound by Oriental Press, Dubai.

Cover design by Gary Jobson

© Copyright in the *Employment Law and Human Resources Handbook 2010* is the property of the publishers or relevant content providers. Neither the publishers of nor the contributors to this book are responsible for the results of any actions or omissions taken on the basis of information in this publication. In particular, no liability can be accepted in respect of any claim based on or in relation to material provided for inclusion.

All rights reserved. No part of this publication may be reproduced, stored in a retrieval system or transmitted in any form or by any means electronic, mechanical or otherwise without the prior permission in writing from the publishers. Although great care has been taken in the compilation and preparation of the *Employment Law and Human Resources Handbook 2010* to ensure accuracy, neither the publishers nor the contributors can in any circumstances accept responsibility for errors, omissions or advice given in this publication. Readers should be aware that only Acts of Parliament and Statutory Instruments have the force of law and that only the courts can authoritatively interpret the law.

The views expressed in the *Employment Law and Human Resources Handbook 2010* are the contributors' own and not necessarily those of the publishers.

Contents

Comment from the editor 7

The contributors 10

Absence management 30
Agency and temporary workers 35
Comment: A pyrrhic victory for agency workers' rights 40
Alcohol and drugs 43

Comment: Taking the heat out of business regulation 46
Bullying and harassment 49

Carers 54
CCTV monitoring 59
Childcare provisions 65
Children at work 68
Contract disputes 71
Contractors 74
Criminal records 78

Data protection 84
Directors' responsibilities 89
Comment: Disability – Agreeing to disagree 95
Disability legislation 98
Disciplinary and grievance procedures 106
Discrimination 110
Comment: Believe it or not 121
Dismissal 124
Dress codes 129
Driving at work 133

Employee benefits 138
Employee consultation 142
Employment contracts 146
Employment disputes 150

Contents

Employment status	154
Employment Tribunals	158
Comment: Crunching the numbers	**164**
Equal pay	167
Comment: Equality doesn't happen overnight	**174**
Expenses	177
Facilities management contracts	180
Family-friendly rights	182
Fixed-term workers	187
Flexible working	190
Foreign nationals	194
Freedom of information	208
Health surveillance	212
HIV and AIDS	215
Holiday	219
Homeworking	222
Human rights	226
Intellectual property	229
Internet and email policies	236
Interviewing	240
IT security	244
Jury service	250
Leave	252
Medical records	257
Mental health	261
Migrant workers	269
Minimum wage	273
Comment: Ten years of the National Minimum Wage	**276**
Money laundering	279
Monitoring employees	292
Night working	299

www.workplacelaw.net

Contents

Notice periods 301

Occupational health.. 304

Part-time workers 308
Pensions 312
Personnel files... 317
Pregnancy.. 324
Private life 327
Probationary periods... 332

Recruitment and selection... 335
Redundancy 339
Comment: There's no other way – alternatives to redundancy 344
References 347
Restrictive covenants and garden leave....................................... 350
Retirement... 353

Self-employment 357
Sickness benefits 361
Comment: Going the whole hog – coping with swine flu.................... 366
Smoking.. 369
Staff handbooks 375
Stress 381
Strikes 388

Trade unions 391
Training 395
TUPE... 399

Unlawfully procuring information.. 403

Confidential waste... 410
Whistleblowing... 414
Work experience, internships and apprentices................................ 417
Working time 423
Comment: UK wins latest battle over 48-hour working week 428

Workplace Law Network
www.workplacelaw.net

Contents

Young persons. 430

Directory of information sources 432

Index 436

Comment...

Comment from the editor

Alex Davies is the Project Editor at Workplace Law Group. She has a wide range of experience in publishing, having completed a BA (Hons) Publishing degree in 2001, and worked on many business titles in a freelance capacity. This is her third year as Editor of the *Workplace Law Handbook*.

The 'credit crunch'. The 'downturn'. The 'current economic climate'. Whichever euphemism you prefer, it's clear the UK is in recession, and avoiding the grim reality isn't the way to get through it. Apart from avoidance of the 'R' word, you won't find many euphemisms in this book. Workplace Law Group's consultants and affiliates believe in telling it how it is, in jargon-free, no-nonsense language, so that by looking at the worst case scenario a realistic and suitable solution can be found.

'Redundancy' is another 'R' word people are trying to avoid – yet over the past six months the number of redundancies has topped the half-million mark. The redundancy process is stressful and time-consuming – for both employer and employee – and is a potential minefield in terms of legal action if the proper process isn't followed. There has been a dramatic increase over recent months in Employment Tribunal cases, with redundancy and unfair dismissal in the top ten types of claim.

In a tough economic market, employees are determined to hold on to their jobs, and know their legal rights. It is therefore imperative that, should the difficult decision to make redundancies become unavoidable, organisations follow the correct procedures, get good advice, and do everything by the book.

The *Workplace Law Handbook 2010* is here to help you get to grips with the seemingly endless stream of legislation that governs working practices. Taking the advice and feedback from many of our members and readers, we have made the decision this year to split the (increasingly weighty) *Handbook* into two. The edition you are holding in your hands contains all the information you need to know on human resources and employment law, whilst its sister title details everything to do with health and safety, premises management and the environment.

Splitting the *Handbook* into two will, we feel, provide a more cost-effective and relevant information service to our members. We recognise that in an information-rich society it is often preferable to receive only targeted, relevant and pertinent information, tailored to an individual's specific needs.

It's something we have been putting into effect over the past 12 months on our

Comment from the editor

website – www.workplacelaw.net – with a selection of significant and related news feeds, gathering all the latest workplace law news in one place, and in our award-winning magazine, which is also now more subject-oriented, split into the separate disciplines of employment law and health and safety. Over the next few months we will be giving the website similar treatment, to make all the information that Workplace Law supplies accessible, manageable and easy to navigate.

Employment law is more complex than ever, and the number of Employment Tribunal claims being made against employers is continuing to rise to record levels. Employment law affects every aspect of running a business, from initial recruitment right through to termination of employment: and the cost of getting it wrong for employers has never been greater. How can you possibly gain the expertise – and find the time – to keep on top of it all?

The Workplace Law HR Support Contract provides you with total support, 365 days of the year, regardless of how many people you employ. Since every organisation is unique, so is our support contract – tailored to meet the specific needs of your business, your people, and the sector you operate in.

The *Handbook* is just part of that support, and is offered as your first port of call. At 440 pages, with 79 chapters and ten topical comment pieces, written by 66 experts from 30 firms, it's, statistically, the most comprehensive reference guide on the market. We're big on statistics this year. You'll find over 300 facts and figures within these pages, in handy, easy to use, fact boxes. Every chapter also features key points for each subject, helping you navigate your way around the book even more easily.

During difficult economic times there tends to be a 'rapid and sustained increase,' in the words of ACAS' annual report, in the number of unfair dismissal claims, and that is reflected in the statistics for 2008/09, which show the figure rose from 40,941 in 2007/08 to 52,711 in 2008/09. Only time will tell as to when the UK will get back to its feet, and the downturn's effects on unemployment statistics will be negated by a rapid recruitment drive.

It is hoped that with the help of Workplace Law's complete Human Resources Support Package, your organisation will be a legally-compliant and fair place in which to work. I'd love to hear your comments and views on the *Employment Law and Human Resources Handbook 2010*. Please get in touch at alex.davies@workplacelaw.net.

A. Davies.

About Workplace Law Group

Established in 1995, Workplace Law has grown to become one of the UK's leading providers of legal information and advice. We specialise in delivering plain-English advice and information to suit your needs.

The Workplace Law Network is a membership organisation keeping over 50,000 professionals, including facilities managers, health and safety officers, and personnel managers, up to date with the legal issues affecting the workplace.

Premium members have access to an extensive range of in-depth guidance and case reports, updated daily, on all areas of health and safety, building management and employment law. Premium members also have exclusive access to a panel of top solicitors and experts who can answer specific queries about legal issues in the workplace.

Workplace Law is also now one of the UK's leading health and safety and HR training and consultancy firms, providing public and in-house training in accredited qualifications such as IOSH Managing Safely, IOSH Directing Safely and the NEBOSH National General Certificate, as well as the CIPD Certificate in Personnel and Practice and Certificate in Employment Relations Law and Practice. We also undertake general risk assessments, fire risk assessments, health and safety audits and project work, and on the employment side, provide employers with practical HR and legal support.

Workplace Law is dedicated to helping businesses get to grips with the requirements of the law. Please let us know how we can help you and your organisation.

www.workplacelaw.net

T. +44 (0)871 777 8881
F. +44 (0)871 777 8882

Workplace Law Group
Second Floor, Daedalus House
Station Road
Cambridge
CB1 2RE

The contributors

Anderson Strathern LLP is a dynamic and progressive full service law firm. The firm is focused on its clients' needs and achieving excellence in terms of the quality of advice and its overall service. Anderson Strathern's impressive client base includes commercial, heritage and public sector clients.

The firm has recognised strengths in all aspects of property, corporate services, dispute resolution, employment, discrimination and private client management. Its parliamentary and public law team provides a unique service and is relevant to many areas of business. The firm has the largest number of Accredited Specialists of any Scottish law firm and was the only new appointment to the Scottish Government Legal Framework Agreement Panel. Anderson Strathern is a member firm of the Association of European Lawyers. While much of its client work has a Scottish focus, a significant number of the firm's solicitors are dual qualified in England as well as Scotland and the firm acts on behalf of clients in transactions throughout the UK, while the firm's Employment Unit represents employer clients in Employment Tribunals in Scotland, England and Northern Ireland.

www.andersonstrathern.co.uk

Lizzy Campbell
lizzy.campbell@andersonstrathern.co.uk

Lizzy Campbell is a Senior Solicitor in the Employment Unit. Lizzy advises both employer and employee clients on a wide range of employment issues including unfair dismissal, TUPE and performance management as well as negotiating Compromise Agreements. Lizzy is also involved in representing clients in the Employment Tribunal. Lizzy regularly delivers training on employment law topics, including, most recently, sessions on performance management and managing disciplinary / grievance investigations. Lizzy is currently working towards obtaining the CIPD Certificate in Training Practice.

Debbie Fellows
debbie.fellows@andersonstrathern.co.uk

Debbie Fellows is an Associate in the Employment Unit. She has experience advising both employers and employees across a wide range of employment issues, including unfair dismissal, redundancy, TUPE, contracts of employment, service contracts and discrimination, as well as representing clients at Employment Tribunal. Debbie regularly provides interactive training to clients on employment and discrimination issues and through this is committed to working with clients to ensure their compliance and understanding of employment law.

Chris McDowall
chris.mcdowall@andersonstrathern.co.uk

Chris McDowall is an Associate in the Employment Unit. He deals with all aspects of employment law and advises a wide variety of clients on issues that are both individual and collective in nature. Chris has designed and delivered in-house training sessions to the HR teams of clients as well as training for their managers, including a practical guide to employment law as part of an induction-training programme for new line managers. He has also tutored at the University of Edinburgh and is a member of the Employment Lawyers Association and the Scottish Discrimination Lawyers Association.

The contributors

*berwin leighton paisner

Berwin Leighton Paisner is a leading law firm based in the City of London. We pride ourselves on our superb client base including many leading companies and financial institutions. We strive to lead the market in the excellence of our service delivery.

We are well known for our extraordinary success in developing market leadership positions within the real estate, corporate and finance areas. We distinguish ourselves by working with our clients in creative and innovative ways to achieve commercial solutions.

www.blplaw.com

Fiona Clark, Associate
fiona.clark@blplaw.com

Fiona is an Associate at Berwin Leighton Paisner specialising in employment law. She advises on both contentious matters, including unfair dismissal, discrimination and restrictive covenants, and non-contentious matters such as drafting contracts of employment and staff handbooks.

Ian De Freitas, Partner
ian.defreitas@blplaw.com

Ian is a Partner in the Intellectual Property Group. His practice splits into three main areas: all forms of intellectual property disputes; media and crisis management; and technology and outsourcing disputes. He is best known for his work in the technology and new media sectors, but he also acts for a number of clients in the financial services, publishing and hotels sectors.

He is a regular contributor of comments on legal issues to the broadcast and print media.

Ian also deals with public relations and crisis management issues. This has involved work across a broad spectrum, including investigative broadcast and print journalism; pressure groups; shareholder activists; foreign governments; hate websites; and harassment of directors and employees. Ian is a partner in the firm's Crisis Management Team and has close links with professionals in the PR industry.

Nicole Hallegua, Senior Associate
nicole.hallegua@blplaw.com

Nicole advises on a broad range of employment matters, both contentious and non-contentious, including wrongful dismissal, unfair dismissal, and high profile discrimination claims. She frequently advises clients on the application of TUPE in corporate finance, property and PFI/PPP transactions. Nicole has particular expertise in PFI/PPP transactions, including Retention of Employment model procurements, where she acts for both public and private sector clients on the employment law aspects of such transactions.

Toby Headdon
toby.headdon@blplaw.com

Toby specialises in contentious and non-contentious aspects of all intellectual property law. This includes advising on the protection, enforcement, acquisition, disposal, and exploitation of all types of intellectual property rights. Toby has considerable experience in negotiating IP licences and advising on IP ownership strategies. He has worked on a number of complex acquisitions, disposals and licensing arrangements, which have involved tracing ownership and intra-group restructuring of IPR for tax-driven purposes. He also has considerable experience in advising on avoiding IPR infringement and enforcing IPR against infringers (including in relation to software), including the conduct of court proceedings to full trial.

The contributors

Mark Kaye, Senior Associate
mark.kaye@blplaw.com

Mark advises on a broad range of employment matters with a particular emphasis on non-contentious corporate finance and PFI transactions, including frequently advising in relation to the application or otherwise of TUPE.

Lizzie Mead, Junior Associate
lizzie.mead@blplaw.com

Lizzie advises in all aspects of employment law. She has experience in a wide range of areas including preparing cases for the Employment Tribunal and High Court, involving discrimination, whistleblowing and post-termination restrictions, drafting service agreements and contracts of employment, advising on TUPE issues, unfair dismissal and employment status. Lizzie advises a range of clients across various industries but is experienced within the financial services, retail and recruitment sectors. Lizzie regularly presents at seminars, provides in-house training and writes articles and chapters for leading legal and personnel publications on a wide range of employment law issues.

Jackie Thomas, Assistant Solicitor
jackie.thomas@blplaw.com

Jackie specialises in all aspects of employment law, and advises on both contentious and non-contentious employment law issues, including executive service contracts, discrimination and issues arising from the termination of employment.

The contributors

BIRD & BIRD

Bird & Bird is an international commercial law firm which combines leading-edge legal expertise with an indepth understanding of chosen industry sectors including aviation and aerospace, banking and financial services, communications, electronics, information technology, life sciences, media and sports. In each of these sectors we provide a full range of legal services and have full service capability from all our offices.

We work with some of the world's most innovative and technologically advanced companies and have a long established reputation for providing cutting-edge legal advice to clients operating at the forefront of their sectors. With offices all over the world we are strategically placed to offer local expertise within a global context helping our clients to realise their business goals both domestically and internationally.

www.twobirds.com

Rhian Hill, Associate
rhian.hill@twobirds.com

Rhian joined Bird & Bird's Commercial Group in September 2006, having joined the firm as a Trainee Solicitor in 2004. She provides general commercial and technology advice in the public and private sectors. Rhian provides general data protection compliance advice including drafting and reviewing data protection policies and employee monitoring policies, and advises on a variety of Freedom of Information and Data Protection compliance issues.

Elizabeth Upton, Senior Solicitor
elizabeth.upton@twobirds.com

Elizabeth is a Senior Solicitor working in the Commercial Department at Bird & Bird. She advises clients on a wide range of IT matters including the licensing of software, agreements for the provision of internet services, online terms and conditions and other legal implications of ecommerce. In addition, as a member of Bird & Bird's Information Law Group, Elizabeth regularly advises on data protection and privacy issues for all types of business and has recently been involved in a data protection audit for a large group of UK companies. Elizabeth has particular experience of advising on the use of personal data in the online environment.

The contributors

Solicitors

Law firm BPE is based in Cheltenham, and clients range from private investors, to dynamic entrepreneurs, high street chains, public institutions, blue chip multi-nationals, and a foreign Government. Legal services supplied range from corporate, company commercial, commercial property, commercial litigation, insolvency, employment, tax / trusts and wills, PI for Insurers and volume residential property.

www.bpe.co.uk

Sarah Lee, Associate
sarah.lee@bpe.co.uk

Sarah trained at Eversheds LLP, qualified in 2004, and joined BPE in October 2008. Well versed in all aspects of employment law, Sarah has advised companies, educational establishments and individuals on contentious and non-contentious matters. She also has experience in regulatory litigation, having represented organisations in health and safety, food safety and trading standards investigations and prosecutions.

Lisa Norman, Associate
lisa.norman@bpe.co.uk

Lisa has over 12 years' experience in employment law. Working with businesses in retail, manufacturing and financial services, and the public sector, she regularly defends complex and high value discrimination claims, and has offered strategic advice on business restructuring and TUPE. She is also experienced in trade union and collective issues.

The contributors

CMS Cameron McKenna

CMS Cameron McKenna is a full service international law firm, advising businesses, financial institutions, governments and other public sector bodies. The firm has about 200 partners and employs over 1,600 people. CMS Cameron McKenna has a strong network of offices throughout the UK, CEE and Western Europe. Our lawyers have strong expertise in many legal areas including facilities management, construction, health and safety, projects and project finance, real estate, environment, financial services, corporate, energy and natural resources, insurance and reinsurance, technology, life sciences, intellectual property, human resources, pensions, competition, European law, arbitration and litigation.

www.law-now.com

Amy Bird, Solicitor
amy.bird@cms-cmck.com

Amy graduated from King's College London with first class honours in Law and completed her legal practice course at BPP, obtaining a distinction. After training with CMS Cameron McKenna LLP, she qualified as a solicitor into the firm's employment team in August 2007.

She has worked with clients across a wide range of sectors in formulating service agreements and negotiating severance arrangements, drafting staff handbooks, advising on individual disciplinary and dismissal issues, and advising on TUPE issues and other employee aspects of corporate transactions.

Her litigation experience includes handling Employment Tribunal claims for unfair dismissal, discrimination and whistleblowing. She also has experience of High Court litigation, including seeking injunctive relief for misuse of confidential information.

Rupert Choat, Partner and Solicitor Advocate
rupert.choat@cms-cmck.com

Rupert is a Partner and Solicitor Advocate at CMS Cameron McKenna LLP. He has specialised in facilities management and construction for 12 years.

Originally an Atkin Chambers barrister, Rupert often appears as advocate; for a non-confidential example see the High Court judgment in the much reported *Ringway v. Vauxhall* (Nos one and two). Rupert has made numerous programmes for the Einstein Network and often speaks at seminars and other events. He is widely published in journals from the UK to Australia and regularly contributes to *Building* magazine and RICS Journals as well as CMS' market leading Law-Now alert service.

Independent directory, *Chambers UK* 2008, says that Rupert is "a gifted intellectual and good manager of a team'.

The contributors

GREENWOODS
SOLICITORS LLP

Greenwoods Solicitors LLP is a commercial law firm providing top quality legal advice and pragmatic solutions to our local, national and international clients. Whilst not one of the largest regional firms, we have been successful in identifying the market in which we are best placed to operate. By knowing who we want to work for and having the right lawyers we have been able to focus and develop our strengths to give those clients the very best service. We know the importance of building strong working relationships with our clients. We seek to understand their objectives, the commercial environment within which they operate and their need for practical legal advice. We are proactive, we look for solutions (rather than just problems) and adopt a 'can-do' attitude. We are committed to drafting legal documents in plain English and to communicating with our clients in a straightforward way.

www.greenwoods.co.uk

Robert Dillarstone, Director
rdillarstone@greenwoods.co.uk

Robert is Greenwoods' Managing Director. He has acted in cases both before the Court of Appeal and the House of Lords. His strength lies in his commercial, practical and personable approach to delivering solutions to clients. The 2006 edition of *The Legal 500* states that Robert 'heads a two-partner team that has an excellent reputation as far afield as the City' whilst Chambers and Partners' *A Client's Guide to the Legal Profession 2007* states that 'the Peterborough-based team is headed by the "talented and effective" director, Robert Dillarstone, who "never ducks an issue".' Robert delivers training on a wide range of employment law topics at public events and in-house.

Kathryn Gilbertson, Director
kgilbertson@greenwoods.co.uk

Kathryn heads Greenwoods Solicitors LLP's nationally renowned Business Defence team advising on all aspects of regulatory law, including corporate manslaughter; health and safety issues; food safety and trading law matters. Kathryn, with the support of her team, has represented numerous companies in trials and inquests concerning fatal accidents, major workplace incidents and safety issues. A recognised leader in her field, she has a reputation for an innovative approach to regulatory compliance issues and for her astute commercial awareness.

Lisa Jinks, Associate
ljinks@greenwoods.co.uk

Lisa has substantial experience in all aspects of employment law, having qualified in 1992. Her all-round expertise includes corporate immigration advice, an area that Lisa built up since joining Greenwoods Solicitors LLP. One of Lisa's key responsibilities is employmentlaw@work, Greenwoods' up-to-the minute email update service which has been a great success since its launch in 2002.

John Macaulay, Director, Head of Employment and Employee Benefits
jmacaulay@greenwoods.co.uk

John has specialised in employment and discrimination law since qualifying in 1991 and has a wealth of experience in advising on all aspects of employment law, including spending significant time 'at the sharp end', arguing clients' cases at Tribunal. The 2006 edition of *The Legal 500* states that John is 'highly regarded by clients'.

The contributors

A substantial commercial law firm with offices in Birmingham and London offering a full range of legal services – both nationally and internationally. The number of people in the firm ensures that it has strength in depth with a dedicated team of people who pride themselves on their ability to give advice to clients which is prompt, technically correct and commercial. One of Martineau Solicitors' strengths is an ability to think creatively and constructively with a view to solving problems and enabling transactions to be completed to its clients' maximum advantage. The close working relationship between departments enables the firm to provide an efficient and effective specialist service. With accreditations in ISO9001 and Investors in People, its commitment to both quality and people is clearly demonstrated, whilst it constantly looks for ways to improve its service delivery and reduce costs by means of technology.

www.martineau-uk.com

Michelle Billingsley, Solicitor
michelle.billingsley@martineau-uk.com

Michelle is a Solicitor in the Employment and Pensions Group at Martineau. She joined the Group as a Solicitor on qualification in September 2008, having completed her training contract with the firm. Michelle spent eight months in the Group prior to qualification and during that time she gained experience in a variety of contentious and non-contentious employment matters. Her non-contentious experience includes drafting and advising on employment contracts, compromise agreements and policies and procedures, advising on immigration queries, drafting articles and carrying out training sessions for employers. Her contentious work involves preparing claims for Claimants and defending claims on behalf of Respondents.

Jo Bradbury, Solicitor
joanne.bradbury@martineau-uk.com

Jo is a Solicitor in the Employment and Pensions Group at Martineau Solicitors. She joined the group in September 2005 having completed her training contract with the firm. Jo undertakes a broad range of contentious and non-contentious employment work, acting for both claimants and respondents. Jo also has experience in defending discrimination claims in respect of access to membership of public sector pension schemes.

David Browne, Solicitor
david.browne@martineau-uk.com

David is a Solicitor in the Employment and Pensions Group at Martineau Solicitors. He joined the group in September 2007 having completed his training contract with the firm. David undertakes a broad range of contentious and non-contentious employment work, acting for both claimants and respondents. David is also a member of the Employment Lawyers Association.

Nicola Cardenas-Blanco, Solicitor
nicola.cardenas-blanco@martineau-uk.com

Nicola is a Solicitor in the Commercial Disputes Management team, specialising in regulatory issues and representing both corporate and educational clients. Nicola has been involved in matters concerning workplace fatalities, asbestos exposure and related issues, product liability and a variety of other workplace health and safety concerns. Nicola deals with claims involving negligence, contract and breach of statutory duty, and additionally in relation to educational clients, human rights and judicial review.

The contributors

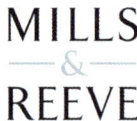

Mills & Reeve is amongst the UK's largest full service law firms with offices in Birmingham, Cambridge, London and Norwich. The firm provides a full range of commercial legal services and focuses on providing quality, pragmatic, commercial advice to businesses, institutions and individuals in the UK and internationally. The firm has a national reputation for its advice to clients across a range of sectors including: property, private client, higher and further education, healthcare, insurance and technology. Mills & Reeve was recognised as one of the top three firms in the UK in *The Lawyer*'s annual awards. The firm has more recently been listed in *The Sunday Times* Top 100 Best Companies to work for and has also been recognised as one of the country's top employers by the Corporate Research Foundation.

www.mills-reeve.com

Anna Youngs, Solicitor
anna.youngs@mills-reeve.com

Anna is a Solicitor at Mills & Reeve, specialising in Employment Law in the Birmingham office. She works for a range of private companies and public sector bodies. Her recent work includes advising on collective redundancy procedures, including collective redundancy litigation, advising on the implications of a recent merger and the subsequent restructuring process, acting on complex disability claims and advising on the TUPE implications of transfers from the public sector to the private sector. Anna carries out advocacy at the Employment Tribunal and prepares a wide range of training materials for clients.

The contributors

Pinsent Masons LLP is one of the most highly regarded property law firms. The firm's strategy is to be recognised as the pre-eminent legal advisor serving the needs of the energy and utilities, financial services and insurance, government, infrastructure and construction, manufacturing and engineering, real estate, technology and facilities management industries. The team was a finalist in the category of Real Estate Team of the Year at The Lawyer Awards 2008. The firm ranks in the UK top 15 law firms and is one of Europe's leaders. Clients benefit from the depth of industry knowledge of the firm's teams of specialist lawyers who provide a comprehensive service in health and safety, employment, PPP/PFI projects, dispute resolution (property and commercial), commercial property, planning, environment and sustainability, corporate and commercial, data protection, pensions, insolvency and taxation.

www.pinsentmasons.com

Leonie Power, Senior Associate
leonie.power@pinsentmasons.com

Leonie is a Senior Associate in the Outsourcing Technology and Commercial Group at Pinsent Masons LLP, with specialist experience in relation to both online and offline data protection issues and other information law issues. Leonie has acted for a wide range of companies including in the retail, premiership football, telecommunications and financial services arena and has been involved in a considerable number of projects involving cross-border transfers of employee data.

Michael Ryley, Partner
michael.ryley@pinsentmasons.com

Michael joined Pinsent Masons as a Partner in January 1998. He heads the firm's Employment Group and is based in the London office. Save for a period spent working in Tokyo, Michael has spent his entire career to date in the City of London, advising a wide range of clients on all aspects of employment law and human resources strategy. Although his practice includes advice in contentious matters, Michael spends the bulk of his time advising on the employment law aspects of mergers and acquisitions, outsourcings, PFI schemes and facilities management contracts. As such he is recognised as an expert on TUPE and is well known as a writer on the employment law issues which arise in such projects.

Louise Townsend, Senior Associate
louise.townsend@pinsentmasons.com

Louise is a Senior Associate in the Outsourcing, Technology and Commercial Group at Pinsent Masons. She specialises in data protection and freedom of information compliance and speaks regularly at seminars and workshops on data protection and freedom of information. She advises both public and private sector clients on information law issues, including subject access requests, employee monitoring and FOI requests. She is recognised as an 'Associate to Watch' in *Chambers 2009*.

The contributors

Taylor Wessing is a powerful source of legal support for organisations doing business in or with Europe and is based primarily in the UK, France and Germany, with further offices in Brussels, Alicante, Dubai and Shanghai. A market leader in advising IP and technology-rich industries, Taylor Wessing boasts a strong reputation in the corporate, finance and real estate sectors alongside indepth experience across the full range of legal services including tax, commercial disputes and employment.

www.taylorwessing.com

Naomi Branston, Associate
n.branston@taylorwessing.com

Naomi is an Associate in the firm's Employment and Pensions group. She has experience in all aspects of employment law. Naomi's non-contentious experience includes the drafting of contracts of employment, consultancy agreements, secondment agreements, employee handbooks and compromise agreements. She also assists in corporate transactions, outsourcing and company restructuring exercises requiring advice on transfers of undertaking, and redundancy procedures. Contentious experience includes the conduct of Employment Tribunal proceedings (principally defending employers) and High Court injunction proceedings.

Naomi mainly advises corporate entities although she also represents executive-level employees. She has advised clients such as Enterprise Rent-A-Car and Specsavers for a number of years and her clients range from small companies to multi-national businesses.

Naomi has been described in the *Legal 500* as having a "swift appreciation of commercial issues". She is a member of the Employment Lawyers Association and the European Employment Lawyers Association. She speaks fluent German and as well as having been seconded to our German offices, she also advises German-speaking clients.

Mark McCanney, Associate
m.mccanney@taylorwessing.com

Mark is an Associate in the Employment and Pensions Group. Mark has advised corporate clients and individuals on a number of day-to-day employment issues, such as unfair dismissal, maternity and parental leave, disciplinary and grievance procedures, redundancy and employment policies. He provides ad hoc employment advice to a number of European and international clients who require accurate, commercial advice often within short timeframes.

Recent work has included advising a large corporate client in defending a race discrimination claim, preparing for an Employment Tribunal for a large US client and reviewing the handbook and employment contracts of several US start-up and technology companies.

Mark is also part of the cross-firm Immigration Group and has advised on work permits and other immigration status issues. Mark has assisted the Group in preparing for the implementation of the new Points Based System in the UK and the effect this is having on clients who rely on employing non-EU workers. Mark trained with the firm and qualified into the Employment and Pensions Group in September 2007.

Tania Revell, Associate
t.revell@taylorwessing.com

Tania is an Associate in the Employment and Pensions group, specialising in UK employment law. She advises both employers and employees on a wide range of contentious and non-contentious employment issues.

The contributors

Tania graduated from the University of Manchester in 2005 and completed the LPC at Nottingham Law School. She qualified at Taylor Wessing in September 2008, having trained with the firm.

Dana Shunmoogum, Senior Associate
d.shunmoogum@taylorwessing.com

Dana is a Senior Associate in the Pensions Group. She qualified in September 2001 and joined Taylor Wessing's Pensions Group in London in July 2006 having previously practiced in the Mayer Brown International pensions group. Dana advises both sponsoring employers and trustees of pensions schemes in all areas of pensions law and practice. Her experience ranges from general scheme advisory and documentation work arising from the administration of occupational pensions schemes, and the winding up of such schemes, to litigation. Dana is a member of the Association of Pension Lawyers (APL) and is a regular speaker on the APL Introductory Course. She has also had a number of articles published.

Andrew Telling, Professional Support Lawyer
a.telling@taylorwessing.com

Andrew is a Professional Support Lawyer. He focuses on analysing the latest legal and market practice developments in corporate law and their impact for our clients and the transactions we advise on. He also organises and updates our corporate legal know-how resources, prepares bulletins for clients and provides internal legal training for our lawyers.

He worked for many years in the corporate departments of Linklaters and Allen & Overy, and draws on extensive transactional and advisory experience in public takeovers, private M&A, reverse takeovers, joint ventures, leveraged transactions, full list and AIM IPOs and secondary listings, demergers, members' and creditors' schemes of arrangement, capital reductions, rights issues, B share schemes, statutory transfer schemes, company rescue restructurings, group reorganisations and corporate governance.

He has spent periods on secondment at Smiths Group and a government department in the UK and at two leading law firms in Rome and Milan. Educated at Cambridge University and The College of Law, Andrew was a partner at Allen & Overy LLP before joining Taylor Wessing LLP in 2007. He speaks French and Italian to a good standard.

Emma Tracey, Associate
e.tracey@taylorwessing.com

Emma is an Associate in the Pensions Group. She joined the group on qualification in September 2006, having trained with the firm. She has recently become an associate member of the Association of Pension Lawyers (APL) and speaks regularly at APL seminars. Since qualification, Emma has gained experience on a variety of pensions law matters. These include Pensions Ombudsman complaints, corporate transactions and advising trustees on matters relating to winding up. Emma has also helped advise trustee boards on scheme documentation and the administration of occupational pension schemes.

The contributors

Other contributors

Ashurst: Marc Hanson
www.ashurst.com

Ashurst's specialist construction and facilities management team is a widely recognised market leader. It has been involved in many facilities management and construction projects ranging from procuring standalone maintenance contracts to major PFI / PPP infrastructure contracts.

The team is responsible for the drafting of the two standard form contracts produced for the facilities management industry, the Chartered Institute of Building Standard Form of Facilities Management Contract and, for the Property Advisers to the Civil Estate, the PACE Government Contract / Works / 10 Standard Form of Facilities Management Contract along with relevant volumes of Guidance Notes for the contracts.

Marc Hanson is Head of the Facilities Management Team specialising in all aspects of facilities management law, from contract drafting to dispute resolution. He has extensive experience of advising property owners, contractors, institutions and public authorities in connection with major domestic and international projects.

Marc is well known in the industry and is author of the Chartered Institute of Building Standard Form FM contract, the government PACE GC / Works / 10 standard form of FM contract and *Guide to Facilities Management Contracts* (3rd Edition) published by Workplace Law Network. Marc is described as 'leading' lawyer in the *Chambers Guide to the Legal Profession*, and is a member of the British Institute of Facilities Management.

Bond Pearce: Dale Collins
www.bondpearce.com

Bond Pearce LLP is a leading business law firm providing commercial, corporate, real estate and dispute resolution services to some of the UK's pre-eminent corporate and public sector organisations. The firm advises in excess of 40 FTSE 350 companies, making it one of the leading FTSE advisors outside of London.

Bond Pearce is a national leader in energy, retail, real estate and insurance and is also recognised for having one of the largest dispute resolution practices in the country, a heavyweight property, planning and environment team and full service corporate, finance and commercial capability.

Dale Collins is a Solicitor-Advocate and is recognised in the legal directories for his experience and expertise in the field of health and safety law. He has been a criminal advocate for over 22 years and has extensive advocacy experience in the criminal courts and before other tribunals, both from a prosecution and defence perspective, having dealt with everything from pollution of watercourses to corporate manslaughter. Dale also has an MA in Environmental Law and is an experienced lecturer.

Butler & Young Group: Dave Allen and Steve Cooper
www.byl.co.uk

The Butler & Young Group of companies provides professional, practical advice and support on a wide range of construction projects. Its development has seen it grow to a company with over 150 professional staff in all disciplines and over 15 offices nationwide. Building on its success, the Butler & Young Group now has a family of companies providing a multi-disciplined construction consultancy, comprising building control, fire engineering, health and safety, DDA auditing, environmental engineering and asbestos surveys through to structural design and party wall surveying. The Butler & Young Group provides an effective and efficient service with experts in all fields of the building industry. This enables it to provide completed schemes, which are on budget, on time, and satisfy all statutory obligations.

The contributors

Dave Allen is the Head of Quality and Standards at Butler & Young Group and is responsible for setting technical policy in the group and ensuring a quality service is maintained through technical and procedural auditing. He has 25 years' experience in Building Control, dealing with projects as diverse as towers in Canary Wharf and listed barns in Herefordshire. He is actively involved in national building control working groups and has recently been involved in the implementation of a new IT system at Butler & Young.

Steve Cooper is the Standards and Warranty Manager for Butler and Young Group and is a member of the Association of Building Engineers. He has over 20 years' experience in the construction industry having spent most of that time in Building Control. During this time he has been employed in both the private and public sector and has experience in dealing with the full spectrum of building work from the refurbishment of historic buildings to modern methods of construction. Recently the Government has placed a great deal of emphasis on reducing carbon emissions in Building Regulations and they are likely to be used as the driver for the move to the Code For Sustainable Homes. Steve has been providing training on this subject.

Charles Russell: Carolyn Haddon and Susan Thomas
www.cr-law.co.uk

Charles Russell's 242 years of diligent client service has given it a unique position as a firm which successfully combines traditional values with the progressive practices of a modern commercial firm. The result is a firm which enjoys a refreshing diversity of work. Through the quality, intelligence and commitment of our staff, we have achieved a balance which offers real benefits to our clients whether they are seeking legal advice for themselves, their family, or on behalf of their business.

We increasingly find that clients require a full range of legal services and so we are committed to providing legal services to both commercial and private clients. After all, where there is commerce there are people.

Carolyn Haddon joined Charles Russell as a trainee solicitor in September 2001 and qualified into the Employment and Pensions Service Group in September 2003. She is now an Associate and specialises in all aspects of employment law, both contentious and non-contentious, acting for a wide range of corporate clients.

Susan Thomas qualified in September 2005 and primarily advises corporate clients and not-for-profit organisations on all aspects of employment law, both contentious and non-contentious, including business reorganisation and transfers, discrimination, employment policies and procedures, parental rights and grievance and disciplinary issues.

Clarion Solicitors LLP: Joanna Downes
www.clarionsolicitors.com

Joanna Downes is an Associate Solicitor in Clarion's Employment Law Team, within the Corporate and Commercial Department. Joanna deals with all areas of employment law and frequently assists Clarion Solicitors LLP's Corporate Team on the employment related issues involved in corporate transactions. Joanna has a particular expertise with employee information and data protection and recently presented to a Marketing industry summit in London. Joanna was educated at Durham University and the College of Law, York, before joining the firm in September 2004.

Cripps Harries Hall LLP: Roger Byard
www.crippslaw.com

Cripps Harries Hall LLP is a leading law firm based in the South East providing a wide range of legal services. We advise many high-profile clients including plcs, financial institutions, private companies, local and national government, charities and individuals.

The contributors

Our simple and effective strategy of concentrating resources in a single regional centre of excellence has enabled us to provide the maximum benefit to clients, including being highly competitive on cost. Our core values of being Distinctive, Open and Committed underpin all that we do to provide the highest quality of service to our clients.

Roger Byard is a recognised leader in his field and has substantial experience in handling a wide range of employment issues, acting for both employers and employees. He advises on the appointment of senior executives, the management of grievance, disciplinary and dismissal proceedings, the reorganisation of businesses (including redundancy programmes), and discrimination. He has considerable experience of the Transfer of Undertakings (Protection of Employment) Regulations particularly in connection with changes in service provision.

Davies Arnold Cooper: Daniel Cotton and Andrew Workman
www.dac.co.uk

Daniel Cotton is an Employment Law Specialist and advises clients on the full range of employment issues, including both contentious and non-contentious matters. Daniel acts for clients from a wide range of sectors including charities, finance and the medical profession.

Daniel speaks fluent French and German. Prior to qualifying as a solicitor, Daniel worked for the market information company TNS, now part of the WPP Group, where his clients included several FTSE 100 companies.

Andrew Workman joined the Employment Group at Davies Arnold Cooper in April 2009. Andrew is an employment law specialist and an experienced Tribunal advocate. Originally qualifying as a barrister, he has developed particular expertise in representing employers in unfair dismissal and discrimination cases, and has experience at appellate level. Andrew also has substantial experience as an adviser to high net worth individuals and senior executives.

Dundas & Wilson LLP: Mandy Laurie
www.dundas-wilson.com

Dundas & Wilson is a leading UK corporate law firm with over 80 partners and 200 other lawyers across our offices in London, Edinburgh and Glasgow. The core of the firm's strategy is its commitment to clients – and the firm has an enviable UK client base. D&W offer clients an integrated UK capability in the key areas of its practice and is continually expanding its London capabilities to further support this. D&W recruit and retain top quality personnel – not just lawyers, but at all levels throughout the firm – and this has played a large part in strengthening our client proposition and our position in the marketplace.

Mandy Laurie is a Partner in D&W's employment team and has considerable experience in representing both Private and Public Sector clients in Employment Tribunals throughout the UK. Mandy regularly gives advice on potentially contentious issues and problems with an international focus. She has particular interest in discrimination and equality and has presented a number of seminars in this area.

Freeth Cartwright LLP: Vanessa di Cuffa
www.freethcartwright.co.uk

Freeth Cartwright LLP is one of the UK's leading regional law firms. Our solicitors operate from offices in Nottingham, Birmingham, Derby, Leicester, and Manchester, and our client base reflects not only our regional strength but also our nationwide service delivery. We are committed to continuous improvement and our increasing success as a business is built on achieving success for our clients. We work in close partnership with clients, providing positive, practical solutions and clear, comprehensive advice.

Vanessa di Cuffa heads up the employment law practice at the Birmingham office of Freeth Cartwright LLP. She has extensive experience in dealing with Employment Tribunal claims,

The contributors

including unfair dimissal claims, breach of contract claims, redundancy and all aspects of discrimination claims. She works for a wide range of private companies and public sector clients and she has advised in all aspects of employment law, contentious and non-contentious. Some of her recent advice includes advising on a collective redundancy situation for a local authority and TUPE issues. She has defended complex disability and sex discrimination claims and many age discrimination claims. She has also defended on some very complex constructive dismissal claims. She has a particular expertise in the equal pay claims in the public sector and she regularly appears in Tribunal doing advocacy. Vanessa regularly reviews policies and contracts and advises on the technical implications of TUPE transfers and re-structuring of companies. Vanessa delivers seminars and bespoke training and regularly produces articles for publication.

Greta Thornbory, Occupational Health Consultant
www.gtenterprises-uk.com

Greta Thornbory is an Occupational Health and Educational Consultant with 30 years' experience in OH practice and teaching. During that time she has worked with government departments, professional bodies, pharmaceutical, educational and other companies, including several multi-nationals, on a variety of occupational health and safety projects. She also worked for the Royal College of Nursing for 12 years as a senior lecturer and programme director of both occupational health and continuing professional development, during which time she was responsible for many of the 95 Nursing Update programmes for the learning zone on BBC TV and was the RCN representative on the UN Environment and Development Round Table on Health and Environment.

She is now Consulting and CPD Editor of *Occupational Health* and is responsible for commissioning and editing the monthly multidisciplinary CPD articles and resources for professional updating purposes. She is the co-author with Joan Lewis of *Employment Law and Occupational health: a practical handbook* first published in 2006 (new edition out early 2010) and edited *Public Health Nursing*: a textbook for health visitors, school nurses and occupational health nurses, published in July 2009. Greta also authored Workplace Law Group's Special Report: *Occupational Health – Making the Business Case*.

Hempsons Solicitors: David Sinclair
www.hempsons.co.uk

Hempsons is one of the UK's leading law firms in the health sector, acting for both the NHS and private sector businesses providing healthcare services or products to the UK health sector. The firm also has a reputation as a leading charities practice, acting for many health, medical or research-related not-for-profit organisations.

David Sinclair is a dual-qualified Solicitor and safety practitioner, who was amongst the first practitioners in the UK to achieve Chartered Health and Safety Practitioner status. Trained originally as a mining engineer, David has a BSc Honours degree in Occupational Health and Safety and a Durham University postgraduate diploma in Environmental Management.

Kennedys: Catherine Henney, Hayley Overshott and Philippa Skrein
www.kennedys-law.com

Kennedys is known primarily as an insurance-driven commercial litigation practice, although the firm is also recognised for skills in the non-contentious commercial field, particularly within the insurance, construction and transport industries. Kennedys has a fast-growing reputation for its work in employment law and the healthcare and insolvency sectors.

Kennedys' approach in all matters is recognising that the 'product' required by clients is the economic resolution of the claim, not merely the legal services necessary along the way. The firm looks at the commercial issues relevant to each case. All Kennedys' fee earners work with this philosophy in mind. Having acted for individuals and organisations involved in many of the major cases in this area, including the trial resulting from the Hatfield rail crash, Kennedys' Health and Safety team is widely recognised as a leader in its field.

The contributors

Catherine Henney is a Solicitor in the Health and safety Group. She has expereicne of advising and defending large and small companies in regulatory matters, including health and safety, environmental and trading standards prosecutions. Catherine also advises clients in preparation for and attending PACE interviews with the HSE and other regulatory bodies.

Hayley Overshott advises on health and safety law and assists in defending companies and individuals in police / HSE / ORR investigations and prosecutions. Hayley advises companies and individuals on a variety of employment litigation matters including discrimination and unfair dismissals, reviewing employment contracts and policies, and advising and representing clients in relation to commercial disputes.

Philippa Skrein is a Solicitor in the Employment Group. She has experience of a variety of claims including unfair dismissal, discrimination, breach of contract, unlawful deductions, flexible working and equal pay. Philippa advises HR Managers and in-house legal departments on employment issues, negotiates compensation packages representing both employers and employees, and drafts and advises on compromise agreements.

Loch Associates: Pam Loch
www.lochassociates.co.uk

Founder of Loch Associates, Pam Loch is a dual qualified lawyer with extensive experience in contentious and non-contentious employment matters, having acted for employers and employees, advising on all aspects of employment law. She has advised fully listed plcs, AIM listed plcs, private companies and individuals. Her sector experience is extensive but includes manufacturing, media, advertising, financial institutions, technology and leisure, including advising football clubs. The matters she has advised on include:

- All forms of documents governing relationships in the workplace, including service agreements, contracts, handbooks, policies and procedures;
- The termination of senior executives and other workers and enforcing restrictive covenants and confidentiality obligations;
- Discrimination in the workplace;
- Dealing with disputes with workers and industrial disputes involving trade unions;
- Information and consultation in the workplace;
- TUPE and cross border issues;
- Pension disputes;
- The employment and pensions implications of restructuring businesses; and
- Mergers and acquisitions.

As well as conducting her own advocacy in Employment Tribunals, she has also acted for clients in proceedings in the Employment Appeal Tribunal and the High Court. Pam is an Associate of the Chartered Insurance Institute and a member of the Employment Lawyers' Association; she is also an accredited mediator.

MacRoberts: David Flint, Derick MacLean, Lynsey Morris and Valerie Surgenor
www.macroberts.com

As one of Scotland's leading commercial law firms, MacRoberts prides itself on being highly-attuned to clients' needs. Over many years, a huge range of leading British and international businesses, banks and other financial institutions have continued to trust MacRoberts' lawyers to lend a clear insight to the commercial and legal issues that face them. MacRoberts has the experience, the range of contacts and the specialist disciplines to help clients, large or small, individual or corporate, cut through extraneous matter and make the right decisions. In an increasingly frantic world there is no substitute for a commercial partner on whom you can

The contributors

rely. With offices in Glasgow and Edinburgh, staffed by partners who feature consistently in Scotland's legal *Who's Who*, MacRoberts is a firm that meets that essential client requirement.

David Flint is a Partner in the firm's Intellectual Property and Technology Law Group and specialises in all aspects of non-contentious intellectual property, with particular emphasis on computer-related contracts and issues. David is acknowledged as a leading expert in Intellectual Property Law, Computer / IT law, and European Law.

David has played a key role in a number of major commercial contract projects and on IP issues relating to the privatisation of British Energy plc. He advises a major Scottish University on IP and Technology matters and is engaged in advising a major Scottish company on IP issues arising out of the use of the Internet as a worldwide marketing medium.

David is a recognised authority on restrictive practices and competition law, and, with qualifications from both Glasgow and Amsterdam Universities, also advises extensively on all aspects of EU Law including agency and distribution. He is a member of the CBI Competition Panel and the Joint Working Party on Competition Law of the UK Law Societies and Bars. David writes and lectures extensively in the UK and internationally in relation to his specialities.

Derick MacLean is a Solicitor in the Employment Law Group. Derick has experience of advising employers and employees across a range of employment law issues, including redundancies, severance packages, TUPE, disciplinary and grievance matters and discrimination. He is also experienced in drafting and revising contracts of employment and policies.

Lynsey Morris is currently a trainee at MacRoberts and has a keen interest in technology law.

Primarily practicing in non-contentious intellectual property and information technology matters, Valerie Surgenor has a keen interest in the areas of information security and data protection / freedom of information with particular experience in the carrying out of European and UK-wide Data Protection Compliance Audits, and regularly provides advice to public bodies and commercial entities on compliance with and utilisation of data protection and freedom of information legislation.

She has considerable experience in drafting and negotiating of contracts for the exploitation and protection of intellectual property and regularly advises on the drafting and negotiation of a wide range of IT and commercial contracts.

Matthew Arnold & Baldwin LLP: Rebecca Fox and Adam Fuge
www.mablaw.com

Rebecca Fox is a Solicitor in the employment department at Matthew Arnold & Baldwin LLP. Rebecca qualified as a solicitor with Matthew Arnold & Baldwin in 2008 having undertaken her training contract with the firm and having worked in the employment department for the final 12 months of her training contract.

Rebecca provides advice on all aspects of employment law including advising and drafting employment contracts and HR policies, advising on employer and employee disputes relating to unfair dismissal, all forms of discrimination and redundancy management. She also advises employers and employees in relation to all matters arising from termination of the employment relationship.

Adam Fuge is a Principal and Head of Employment at Matthew Arnold & Baldwin LLP. He has expertise in executive severance and board disputes, unfair / wrongful dismissal, discrimination, general HR advice on issues such as maternity and other family-friendly rights, sickness absence and the Working Time Regulations, TUPE, redundancy and relocation programmes, restrictive covenants and confidentiality, breaches of fiduciary duties, information and consultation procedures, disciplinary and grievance procedures, employment contract issues and harmonisation of terms and conditions, agency workers, whistleblowing and data protection issues arising in relation to employees.

The contributors

Peters & Peters: Dr Anna Odby
www.petersandpeters.co.uk

Peters & Peters specialises in Fraud and Regulatory Litigation, Commercial Fraud Litigation and Compliance. Key practice areas include asset recovery, commercial litigation and alternative dispute resolution, competition regulation including cartels and price fixing, regulatory and financial services compliance including money laundering and financial sanctions compliance, extradition and mutual legal assistance, corruption, corporate risk and fraud prevention, financial crime and tax investigations.

Dr Anna Odby is an Associate in Peters & Peters' Fraud and Regulatory Department. She specialises in business crime and regulatory advice, with particular expertise in money laundering regulation and compliance. A former university lecturer in Public Law and Human Rights Law, Anna holds a Doctorate in anti-money laundering law. She joined Peters & Peters in 2005 where she trained in civil and criminal fraud before qualifying.

Rochman Landau: Howard Lewis-Nunn
www.rochmanlandau.co.uk

Howard Lewis-Nunn qualified as a barrister in 1994 and has practised in law firms in the City and West End since 1997. He has extensive experience in all aspects of employment law including executive contracts, dismissals, discrimination claims, injunctions, advising on employment issues on transactions, data protection issues, and executive service agreements. With a background as a barrister, Howard has particular expertise in advocacy. He also gives presentations to clients and external organisations on employment issues. Howard's clients include retailers, professional service companies, employment agencies, manufacturers and individuals. Howard is a member of the Employment Lawyers' Association.

Shoosmiths: Rebecca McGuirk
www.shoosmiths.co.uk

Shoosmiths is amongst the UK's largest national law firms offering you great value and a readily accessible, personal service through a network of eight offices.

We can help you with advice on legal areas including construction, health and safety, environment, crisis management, employment, pensions, property, dispute resolution, corporate, commercial, insolvency and taxation.

Rebecca McGuirk is a Partner within the employment team, specialising in the not-for-profit sector, providing a full range of employment advice, representation and assistance to registered social landlords and local authorities. Experienced in handling both contentious and non-contentious matters, Rebecca has significant experience in TUPE, be it creating or flattening group structures, mergers, large scale voluntary transfers and outsourcing from other organisations, including primary care trusts. She deals with a high volume of contentious matters on all aspects of employment law, and in particular discrimination.

Steeles Law: Elizabeth Stevens and Louise Westby
www.steeleslaw.co.uk

Steeles Law is a modern and vibrant top 200 UK law firm with offices in London, Norwich (HQ) and Diss, employing over 100 legal and support staff.

The firm provides a wide range of legal services for a diverse mix of national and international PLCs, Limited companies, small to medium-sized enterprises, corporate organisations, institutions, public sector bodies, charities and individuals.

We recognise that delivering professional legal services in an increasingly competitive marketplace requires us to be dynamic, flexible and, above all, client-driven. Every individual

The contributors

working at Steeles Law is committed to delivering a personal, accessible service, with straightforward legal advice upon which you can rely.

Elizabeth Stevens has specialised in employment law since qualifying in 2000 and now works as a professional support lawyer in the employment team at Steeles Law. Her role includes keeping track of employment law developments, writing client bulletins and articles for publication, and producing seminars for clients.

Louise Westby is a trainee in the firm who worked in the employment team for six months as part of her training contract.

Tyndallwoods Solicitors: Aliya Khan
www.tyndallwoods.co.uk

Tyndallwoods is a Birmingham Legal Practice undertaking a wide range of contentious and non-contentious work. Our Immigration Team, while undertaking a very wide range of advice and advocacy has in the past mainly focused on human rights. We have now launched a tailored business unit within the Immigration Team, Migration for Business – MfB. Our highly experienced and specialist team has provided immigration services for more than 25 years and we are regularly cited as one of the leading firms in this area. The law relating to migrant workers changed in 2008/09 when a new type of relationship between employer and employee rolled out by the Government in tandem with a points-based objective qualification system. The system assesses applicants against a wide range of criteria and brings significant additional responsibilities for those involved in migration which, if not complied with in full, can have serious consequences.

Aliya Khan is a Legal Executive and a senior caseworker in the Migration for Business unit – MfB. She has been working with Tyndallwoods since 2003. She undertakes various applications and reviews such as Skilled Migrants under Tier 1 and Tier 2 Sponsorship, Work Permits for Romanian and Bulgarian nationals, Tier 1 Post Study Workers, student applications and EEA nationals. Her main focus of work is with those who wish to seek employment in the UK or who are already working in the UK.

Veale Wasbrough: Gemma Cawthray
www.vwl.co.uk

Veale Wasbrough is a regional firm with a national presence. We act nationwide for clients in the corporate, education and charities, public, real estate and healthcare sectors. Regionally, we offer a dedicated service to private clients. We also manage two distinctly branded divisions, Augustines Injury Law and Convey Direct. Our staff of over 250 operate regionally and nationally, from our modern office in the heart of Bristol city centre – a vibrant and growing business community. We also have a small London office in Chancery Lane, which enables us to respond to our clients' needs and ensures that we are easily accessible in the city. Our goal is to help our clients succeed, through high standards, technical expertise, a creative approach, and our commitment to our people.

Gemma Cawthray is a Solicitor at Veale Wasbrough Lawyers who specialises in employment law. Gemma advises on a wide variety of contentious and non-contentious employment law issues acting for a broad range of clients within both the public and private sector.

Absence management

Anna Youngs, Mills & Reeve

Key points
- Keep accurate absence / attendance records.
- Monitor absence data.
- Consider whether the Disability Discrimination Act applies.

Legislation
- Access to Medical Reports Act 1988.
- Disability Discrimination Act 1995 (as amended).

Absence problems
Although employers expect a certain amount of absence, high levels of absence can be disruptive, and expensive. Absence-related dismissals or disciplinary sanctions can lead to expensive Tribunal claims and therefore it is important that employers handle absence carefully. The treatment of absences will depend on a number of factors including whether the absence is:

- persistent, frequent, short-term absence;
- long-term absence;
- sickness related; and/or
- unauthorised absences (including lateness).

Employers are liable to pay employees' statutory sick pay for certain periods. There may be an underlying cause for the absence, which could be sickness related, related to the employee's personal or domestic circumstances, or could be due to a problem in the workplace. Establishing the cause may enable employers to work out a solution and manage absence more effectively.

The following gives a brief overview of some of the issues that arise in this complicated area of employee management.

Monitoring absence levels
Monitoring absence will assist in assessing how much working time is lost, and whether there are particular employees who have more time off than others. Monitoring also assists the employer to get to the cause of absences, and highlight any problems in any particular department or relating to any type of work.

Monitor absence by keeping detailed attendance records, showing when, and why, any individual employee has been absent and the duration of the absence (this will include a record of whether the absence was authorised).

Reducing absence levels
Employers should implement an absence management policy, which sets out how they will monitor absence, and what will happen as a result of employee absenteeism.

Most employers have trigger points for different stages of the absence management procedure. Some employers calculate 'working time lost'; others use the 'Bradford Factor', which is a long-standing HR tool.

The triggers and the procedure should be applied consistently, and at each

Absence management

stage the employee should be given an opportunity to explain their absences.

One tool that many employers have found to be effective in reducing absence levels is a return to work interview, where some gentle quizzing of the employee about the reason for the absence, how they are feeling, what support they may need etc. is undertaken. It is not clear why this is so effective but some speculate that the reduction in absenteeism may be because some employees fear having to face a manager on their return to explain about their absence.

Other steps that can be taken to reduce absences include:

- induction and training for employees;
- training managers and supervisors to manage absence effectively;
- ensuring that the absence policy covers the provision of medical or self certificates to cover sickness absence;
- involving occupational health as appropriate, especially if there is no medical certificate to support self-certified absences;
- undertaking risk assessments in respect of any recurring causes of absence (including stress risk assessments if applicable); and
- keeping in contact with absent employees and throughout any process consult with the employee.

In all cases of sickness absence the employer should have an up-to-date report on the employee's medical condition. This may be a GP report, specialist advice, an Occupational Health report etc. The employer should not just

Facts

- In 2007, levels of absence fell from eight days per employee per year to 6.7 days.
- The latest CBI / AXA Absence Survey showed that average absence levels across the public sector stood at nine days, which is 55% higher than the 5.8 day average of the private sector.
- Long-term absence (20 days or more) accounted for half (50%) of all time lost in the public sector, but under a third (31%) in the private sector.
- Of the 172 million days lost to absence in 2007, more than one in ten (12%) are thought to be non-genuine, costing the economy £1.6bn.
- In 2006, on average, 46% of absence-related dismissals were justified on the basis of capability. Just under a third of such dismissals were argued on the grounds of conduct and only 9% are justified by some other substantial reason.
- In 2006, the average cost of sickness absence remained almost static at £598 per employee per year, compared to £601 in 2005.
- The number of employers reporting an increase in stress-related absence continues to increase – 46% reporting an increase in 2006, compared to a 39% increase from 2005.
- Employees working between 16 and 30 hours a week and between 31 and 45 hours a week were more likely to take sickness absence than employees working fewer than 16 hours a week or over 45 hours a week.

Source: CBI / AXA Absence Survey 2008, CIPD and National Statistics.

Absence management

ask for a 'report' but ask specific questions on diagnosis and prognosis in the employee's / employer's circumstances.

ACAS recommends that in all cases the employee should be told what improvement is expected and be warned of the likely consequences if no improvement occurs. If there is no improvement, ACAS recommends that employers take into account the following factors before deciding upon appropriate action:

- Performance;
- Likelihood of change in attendance levels;
- Any improvement already made;
- The availability of suitable alternative work (if appropriate); and
- The effect of past and future absences on the business.

Historically, an employee's length of service has been taken into account with their employment history when looking at appropriate sanctions for absenteeism, but this should not be a major factor given that the Employment Equality (Age) Regulations 2006 may render this discriminatory on the grounds of age.

Disability Discrimination Act 1995 (DDA)

Where the reason for absence is ill heath, employers must consider whether the DDA is applicable. This is not just the case for long-term absences, as a disability within the meaning of the DDA could result in an employee taking frequent short periods of absence.

Employers must consider whether there are any reasonable adjustments that can be made for a disabled employee. This may include adjusting the way in which a sickness absence policy is applied to a disabled employee.

The DDA is one of the most complex areas of law. Many employers shy away from dismissing or disciplining an employee who has a disability, fearing a claim of disability-related discrimination. This depends on the facts of the case, but currently if the same sanction would be given to an employee in the same circumstances (e.g. with the same absence record) but without a disability, then the sanction will not amount to discrimination. However, given the complexities of the law under the DDA, employers should tread carefully and be able to 'justify' their decisions as set out in the DDA. In any event, adjustments must have already been considered prior to any sanction being carried out and, where reasonable, adjustments should be made. Employers are advised to consider a wide range of adjustments and keep a record of those considered. Where an adjustment is not made, the employer should keep a note of why that adjustment was not considered to be reasonable. For more on this subject see '*Discrimination*,' p.110.

Dismissals in this context are hard to get right, but that does not mean that it cannot be done. If monitoring absence reveals an underlying medical condition, employers should:

- get an up-to-date medical opinion to determine the extent of the condition, its likely duration and whether the levels of absence are likely to decrease to an acceptable level;
- consider, in light of any medical report(s) and other information whether the illness may amount to a disability under the DDA; and
- if the employee may be disabled, look at what reasonable adjustments can be made.

Note: Dismissal or disciplinary action in respect of maternity-related absence is highly likely to amount to sex discrimination.

Absence management

Additional points to note when dealing with unauthorised absence or lateness

Where absence is unauthorised and is not sickness-related, absence should be treated as a conduct issue. The Tribunals will look at the very least for the following steps to have been taken (as well as compliance with the new statutory ACAS code on disciplinary and grievance procedures and the employer's own policy) before dismissal:

- A fair review of the attendance record and reasons for absence;
- An opportunity for the employee to have made representations; and
- Targets for improvement and warnings of dismissal if attendance does not improve.

If an employer believes that an employee has extended their annual leave through sickness absence, rather than actually being sick, a reasonable investigation must be carried out before taking disciplinary action.

Additional points to note when dealing with short-term certified sickness or uncertified absence

Short-term sickness absence can be dealt with as a capability issue. Special care must be taken if the employee could have a disability (as set out above).

If considering dismissal, check and consider the following:

- Employee's prognosis and whether absence levels are likely to decrease and if so in what time-frame;
- Whether the employee's attendance record has improved; and
- The effect of the absences on the business, and whether temporary cover can address this.

Additional points to note when dealing with long-term sickness absence

If an employee has been off on long-term sickness absence, the risk that they are covered by the DDA is increased. Particular points are:

- The employee's prognosis and whether absence levels are likely to decrease and if so in what time-frame;
- Employee consent will be needed to get a medical opinion from a doctor appointed by the employer or the employee's own GP. If the employee refuses permission, employers must take action based on the information available to them;
- Consider reasonable adjustments to the job or working arrangements, which may include finding an alternative role, or a phased return for the employee;
- Whether the absence is caused in whole or in part because of a failure to make reasonable adjustments. If the employer has failed to meet the duty to make reasonable adjustments, dismissal is likely to be unfair and discriminatory. Employers may need to seek advice as to what adjustments would be reasonable and what can be taken into account when determining whether an adjustment is reasonable;
- Consider whether the job can be covered by other employees or temporary replacements and how long the job can reasonably be kept open;
- Be clear about sick pay arrangements and keep the employee informed; and
- A thorough investigation will be required before dismissal.

Ill health retirement may be an option, but this would not prevent an employee from making a Tribunal claim, so consultation is again key.

The ACAS Advisory Booklet, *Managing Attendance and Employee Turnover*, gives further detailed advice about how to manage different types of sickness absence.

Absence management

See also: Disciplinary and grievance procedures, p.106; Leave, p.252; Medical records, p.257; Occupational health, p.304; Sickness benefits, p.361.

Sources of further information

ACAS Code of Practice on Disciplinary and Grievance Procedures: www.acas.org.uk/CHttpHandler.ashx?id=1047

ACAS guide – Discipline and grievances at work: www.acas.org.uk/index.aspx?articleid=2179

ACAS: Managing attendance and employee turnover: www.acas.org.uk/index.aspx?articleid=1183

EHRC: www.equalityhumanrights.com/advice-and-guidance/information-for-employers/

HSE: www.hse.gov.uk/sicknessabsence/index.htm

Agency and temporary workers

Fiona Clark, Berwin Leighton Paisner

Key points

Usually, agency workers are supplied by an agency to a client business for temporary assignments. The agency and the client will enter into a contract for the supply of the named worker, and the worker will enter into a contract with the agency.

Usually, the agency will pay and have the right to discipline the worker, but the client will give the worker day-to-day instructions.

The main legal issues concerning an agency worker are whether he is self-employed and, if not, whether he is the employee of the agency or the client. These issues will determine the worker's entitlement to statutory employment rights and status for taxation purposes.

Temporary employees (i.e. those people directly employed with organisations on short-term contracts) will not be entitled to claim unfair dismissal, redundancy pay or certain maternity rights if they do not have sufficient continuous service.

Legislation

- Employment Agencies Act 1973.
- Fixed-term Employees (Prevention of Less Favourable Treatment) Regulations 2002.
- The Conduct of Employment Agencies and Employment Businesses Regulations 2003 (the Regulations).

Overview

Many employers use agency workers on short-term projects or to meet surges in demand. The most common agency arrangement is for the agency to supply temporary staff to clients, for which the agency charges a weekly fee. The worker submits his weekly timesheets to the agency, which pays the worker at an hourly rate.

In the case of more permanent positions, an employment agency may offer the client a different service, whereby the agency introduces potential candidates to the client, following which the successful candidate contracts directly with the client. Because the agency drops out of the picture, this is a standard employment relationship between the client and the worker.

Employed or self-employed?

It should be emphasised that there are, at present, no hard and fast rules as to whether the worker is employed or self-employed. Tribunals have reached different conclusions in cases with similar facts.

In general, workers find it difficult to establish that they are employees of the agency because the agency lacks sufficient day-to-day control over them. However, if the agency does exercise

Agency and temporary workers

considerable control, a Tribunal may determine that the worker is its employee for either the whole relationship (known as an 'umbrella contract') or in relation to a particular assignment.

Agency workers also find it difficult to show that they are employees of the client, because there is no contractual relationship between the parties. Recently, several cases suggested that it may be possible to imply a contract of employment between the client and the worker (particularly in the case of long-serving workers). However, several EAT decisions in 2006 and 2007 moved away from this approach and now an employment contract will only be found to exist between the client and the worker where it is necessary to give effect to the reality of the relationship. As a result, it is now much less likely that an agency worker will be an employee of a client, particularly if there is a contract between the worker and the agency and there has been no change in circumstances since the initial supply of the worker by the agency.

Why an agency worker's employment status is important

In employment law terms, the main advantage of engaging an individual on a self-employed basis is that many employment rights do not apply. Unfair dismissal, redundancy payments and maternity rights, for example, may be claimed only by employees.

Additionally, if an individual is self-employed, he will pay income tax on trading income (formerly Schedule D) and pay National Insurance contributions at the self-employed rate. Business expenses may be set off against the individual's tax liability.

Importantly, whether or not an agency worker is deemed to be an employee of the client, they are likely to be a 'worker' (thereby acquiring rights under other legislation such as the Working Time Regulations and anti-discrimination legislation) and the client is likely to be vicariously liable for any tortious actions committed by the worker while at work,

Facts

- There are some 1.7 million temporary workers in the UK, who make up about 7% of the workforce.
- Around 82% of union reps have reported that the number of people employed on temporary contracts in their workplace has increased in the last ten years. These include fixed term contracts, agency, casual and seasonal.
- Only 28% of agency workers positively choose agency work over a permanent job and around 40% are temping because they cannot find a permanent job.
- The most common form of temporary work is a fixed-term contract that accounts for nearly half (46%) of all temporary employees.
- Temporary agency staff are mainly employed by the private sector (81%).
- 33% of agency workers have been assigned to one workplace for fewer than three months.
- 83% of agency workers aged 18-25 have been placed with their current employer for fewer than 12 months.

Sources: LFS 2004, TUC and Unison.

Agency and temporary workers

mainly because it will exercise day-to-day control over the worker. It may also be liable to the worker for any claim by him for personal injury.

Standards for employment agencies

The Employment Agencies Act 1973 and subsequent Regulations impose certain standards on employment agencies. These include the requirement to obtain and provide certain information to workers and clients and to agree certain terms with them before providing any services.

Temporary workers

Employers of employees on temporary contracts should be aware of the Fixed-term Employees (Prevention of Less Favourable Treatment) Regulations 2002. They should also be aware that temporary employees will not be able to claim certain statutory rights if they lack sufficient continuity of service. Unfair dismissal requires one year's continuous service (in most cases); the right to receive a redundancy payment requires two years' continuous service; and statutory maternity pay is only payable where the woman, on the 15th week before her expected week of childbirth, has worked continuously for 26 weeks. However, a worker need not have acquired any length of service to make a discrimination claim.

Recent cases

Consistent Group Ltd v. Kalwak (2008)

The claimants were Polish nationals. The defendant recruitment agency was involved in the provision of staff to work principally in the hotel industry, but also in food processing factories. The claimants had arranged for the agency to place them in work before they entered the UK. Upon their arrival in the UK, the agency accommodated them in a house where other Poles were already living. Money was deducted for accommodation and cleaning charges.

The contract that the claimants entered into with the agency was entitled 'Self employed sub-contractor's Contract for Services'. Under an 'Obligations' term of that contract it provided that:

- the claimants should provide services on an ad hoc and casual basis;
- the claimants were not employed by the agency;
- there was no obligation upon the agency to provide work; and
- there was no obligation upon the claimant to accept work offered by the agency.

However, under a 'Substitution' term, the agreement provided that where the claimants were assigned to a job, they were to perform those services personally, unless they could not, and that if a claimant was unable so to perform, suitable substitute cover was to be provided by the claimant. The Employment Tribunal found that the claimants were employed by the agency. That decision was upheld by the Employment Appeal Tribunal but the Court of Appeal allowed an appeal by the agency and found that there was in fact no contract as any implied terms would be inconsistent with the express 'obligations' term.

James v. London Borough of Greenwich (2008)

James worked for the Council through an employment agency from 2001. In 2003 she left that agency and joined another agency, which paid a better hourly wage. She had a contract with the agency, and the agency had a contract with the Council, but there was no express contract directly between Ms James and the Council. After a period of sickness in August and September 2004 she was told that she was no longer required and that the agency had sent a replacement.

Agency and temporary workers

The Employment Tribunal found that the applicant was not an employee of the defendant under a contract of service and rejected her claim for unfair dismissal. That decision was upheld on appeal by the Employment Appeal Tribunal. The applicant appealed, contending that the Employment Tribunal should have considered whether there was an implied employment contract between her and the defendant, particularly in the light of the fact that she had been employed with the defendant for a number of years.

The Court of Appeal dismissed the appeal as, whilst the defendant had provided work to the applicant for several years, the mere passage of time did not generate a legal obligation on the part of the defendant to provide her with work any more than it generated a legal obligation on her to do the work.

Recent developments

CBI and TUC Agreement
In May 2008 the CBI and TUC reached agreement on how fairer treatment for agency workers in the UK should be promoted, while not removing the important flexibility that agency work can offer both employers and workers. Agreement was reached that after 12 weeks in a given job there will be an entitlement to equal treatment with permanent employees. It was also agreed that equal treatment will be defined to mean at least the basic working and employment conditions that would apply to the workers concerned if they had been recruited directly by that undertaking to occupy the same job.

EU Temporary Agency Workers Directive
On 9 June 2008, the draft Agency Workers Directive was discussed at the European Employment Council. At the Council, political agreement was reached on the Agency Workers Directive. This broke six years of deadlock on this issue.

The Council of the European Union adopted a Common Position on the proposal in September 2008 and this was adopted by the European Parliament shortly afterwards. The final version of the Directive was published on 5 December 2008 and member states have until 5 December 2011 to implement its provisions.

The main points of agreement in the Temporary Agency Workers Directive are:

- The basic working and employment conditions of temporary agency workers (remuneration, paid holiday, overtime, maternity and anti-discrimination provisions and, arguably pension contributions) should be no less favourable than if they had been recruited by the company directly.
- Entitlement to such equal treatment will start after the temporary agency worker has been employed for 12 weeks.
- Possibility to derogate from this through collective agreements and through agreements between social partners at national level.
- Temporary agency workers to be informed about permanent employment opportunities in the user enterprise.
- Equal access to collective facilities such as a canteen, childcare facilities and transport service.
- EU Member States have to improve temporary agency workers access to training and childcare facilities in periods between their assignments so as to increase their employability.
- Member States have to ensure penalties for non-compliance by temporary agencies and enterprises.

Agency and temporary workers

The Government recently published a consultation paper on the Directive, seeking views on who should be covered by the Directive; the implementation of the 12-week qualifying period; how the principle of equal treatment should be established; how pay should be defined; who should be liable for compliance; and the means of dispute resolution. The consultation closed on 31 July 2009 and the Government will publish its response before undertaking further consultation on draft Regulations.

Withdrawal of VAT staff hire concession

The VAT concession was withdrawn from April 2009. Since that date, employment businesses have been required to charge their clients VAT on the full amount of the value of the supply (including salary and other payments and benefits provided to agency workers). As a result, the cost of using agency workers has considerably increased. For more on this, and the new Directive, see '*A pyrrhic victory in the battle for agency workers' rights,*' p.40.

> *See also*: Employment status, p.154; Fixed-term workers, p.187; Self-employment, p.357.

Sources of further information

Agency workers FAQs: www.berr.gov.uk/employment/employment-agencies/faq/page23965.html

Workplace Law Group's **Working with Contractors 2008: Special Report** defines the difference between an employee and a contractor, and is essential reading for those involved in the appointment of contractors for work activities. It is designed to provide workplace managers with everything they need to know to ensure they, and the contractors they employ, meet their duties under health and safety and employment law. For more information visit www.workplacelaw.net/Bookshop/Special Reports.

Comment...

A pyrrhic victory in the battle for agency workers' rights

Rebecca McGuirk is a Partner within the employment team at Shoosmiths, specialising in the not-for-profit sector, providing a full range of employment advice, representation and assistance to registered social landlords and Local Authorities. She deals with a high volume of contentious matters on all aspects of employment law, and, in particular, discrimination.

The age-old conflict between capital and labour, exploited to devastating effect by Messrs Lenin, Mao et al, has seen a more recent incarnation in the battle to secure enhanced rights for agency workers in the UK.

As Marx predicted, it took unity at a European (if not World) level to secure a win for the workers. After years of wrangling and resistance from the UK, a new Temporary Agency Work Directive 2008/104/EC (the 'Directive') was finally approved by European ministers in June 2008. It has to be implemented in the UK by the end of 2011.

Prior to the agreement on the Directive, the UK Government had brokered a deal between trade unions and the CBI, under which agency workers in the UK could only secure equality with their permanent colleagues after 12 weeks in the job. The terms of that deal, unenthusiastically described by employers' groups at the time as the 'least worst option,' may in time come to be regarded as a tactical blunder by the capitalists.

Why is that? The answer lies in the fact that the long-fought campaign for agency workers rights had became entwined with that other shibboleth of the business lobby, the UK's opt-out from the 48 hour working week imposed by the Working Time Directive.

Although the UK Government and business groups fought doggedly over the years to preserve the status quo, they were forced into a compromise at a European level: in return for agreeing to the Directive they could keep the opt-out provisions of the Working Time Directive.

This might have looked like a fair price at the time, but the battle lines were redrawn when, ironically, the amended Working Time Directive was never finalised; it stalled when the European Parliament and Commission failed to agree on a re-worked text. Undoubtedly this is not the end of attempts to amend the Working Time Directive, but when this project is resurrected by Europe, will anyone remember, let alone give credit for, the concessions on agency workers made by UK employers?

There has long been a tension between employers' desire for a flexible (i.e. cheap and easy to get rid of) labour force and

Comment: Agency workers' rights

trade unions' demands for fairness and job security. Business leaders believe it is flexibility that makes the UK such an attractive environment for enterprise and ultimately creates jobs and prosperity for all.

In the pantheon of employment rights, 'workers' come somewhere in the middle – not as unprotected as the genuinely self-employed but far less looked after than employees. For example, they have no right to family-friendly benefits such as maternity leave and pay, no right to a redundancy payment and no right to claim unfair dismissal.

Agency workers, placed with an 'end-user' client of the agency, and often working alongside and performing exactly the same duties as employees directly employed by that client, have long been perceived as getting a raw deal as a result of their employment status.

For example, there was outrage in February 2009 when BMW terminated the engagement of some 850 long-serving agency workers at the Oxford factory that makes the Mini. This was clearly a result of the financial crisis engulfing the car industry and demonstrated precisely why employers need to use agency workers; so that they can respond quickly to changing circumstances and, ultimately, protect the jobs of permanent employees. However, the public perception was that the agency workers in this case had been treated unjustly.

Agency workers have tried to use the Courts to extend their legal rights, creatively arguing that where they had been on assignment with the same end-user for a significant period of time a contract of employment should be implied between them and the end-user.

In *James v. London Borough of Greenwich* the Court of Appeal called a halt to this line of argument, but not before Lord Justice Mummery effectively challenged the Government to do something for agency workers, saying:

"This is a matter of controversial social and economic policy for debate in and decision by Parliament informed by discussions between the interested parties…

"The questions for discussion, negotiation and decision are not legal questions susceptible to adjudication or appropriate for comment by a court or tribunal…

"Policy decisions have to be taken by others about what changes (if any) to make, what rights to confer on whom, what qualifying periods to set and so on. The increasing amounts of money, time and effort spent on litigating this issue in tribunals and on appeals might in some cases be invested more productively in making representations to and through bodies which can pursue the debate on policy or even reform the law."

So, what will the new Regulations implementing the Directive in the UK look like? We are at the start of the consultation process and many questions as to how this will all work in practice remain – the devil will certainly be in the complex detail. From the current consultation paper a broad outline is now emerging.

It is clear that the new legislation will not formally change the employment status of agency workers in the UK or their entitlement to existing rights that are available only to employees, for example the right to claim unfair dismissal.

The new Regulations will introduce the principle of equal treatment so that agency

Comment: Agency workers' rights

workers will be entitled to terms and conditions during an assignment that are at least as favourable as if they had been recruited directly by a hirer to do the job.

This means that it will be necessary to compare the agency worker's terms with a comparable worker doing broadly similar work in the same organisation. However, the principle of equal treatment will apply in relation to basic working and employment conditions only. Basic working and employment conditions will include terms relating to working time, holiday entitlement and pay.

Pay would include both basic pay and other contractual entitlements linked to work such as overtime, shift allowances and bonuses related to personal performance. However, it is proposed that other payments linked to service and loyalty such as profit-sharing schemes would not be caught.

It is not proposed that agency workers will have to be allowed to participate in company pension schemes. However, from 2012, agency workers will have to be automatically enrolled in any personal pension account.

Other points to note are:

- Primary liability for breach of the equal treatment principle would be with the agency and not the hirer;
- An agency would have a defence in the event that it had taken reasonable steps to obtain accurate information from the hirer regarding the equal treatment package. Liability would pass to the hirer if they provided the agency with incomplete or inaccurate information;
- Agency workers who believe they are not receiving equal treatment would be able to ask their agency for written details and these would have to be supplied within 21 days. Ultimately, agency workers would be able to pursue a claim in the Employment Tribunal; and
- The question of remedies for agency workers who bring a Tribunal claim has not yet been outlined, but will be covered in the second consultation on the Regulations themselves.

There are some additional rights that agency workers will be entitled to from day one of their assignment with an end user. These include being given information about permanent vacancies at the hirer and access to on-site facilities such as a canteen and childcare (unless any difference in treatment can be objectively justified).

A CBI survey showed 65% of agency worker assignments last longer than six weeks while 17% last longer than 12 months, so clearly this new law is going to have a real and dramatic impact for employers who use agency workers (not least on legal fees as businesses get to grips with the new requirements and their impact).

The worst case scenario is that employers vote with their feet and give up on agency workers as their use becomes increasingly less attractive. While the passing of the Directive could have been seen as a defeat for business, the end of the flexible workforce would be a pyrrhic victory for the forces of labour.

Alcohol and drugs

Mandy Laurie, Dundas & Wilson

Key points
- There are legal obligations on employers to ensure a safe and healthy workplace for their employees.
- Employees have a right to work in a safe and healthy workplace and they have responsibilities for their own wellbeing and that of their colleagues.
- Ensuring health and safety in the workplace necessitates the regulation of the use of alcohol and drugs.
- Having clear guidelines regarding the use of alcohol and drugs in the workplace will assist employers in achieving regulation in this area.

Legislation
- Misuse of Drugs Act 1971.
- Health and Safety at Work etc. Act 1974.
- Disability Discrimination Act 1995.

Legal obligations on employers and employees

The Health and Safety at Work etc. Act 1974 and the Management of Health and Safety at Work Regulations 1999 place a general duty on employers to ensure, so far as is reasonably practicable, the health, safety and welfare of employees.

If an employer knowingly allows an employee under the influence of alcohol or drugs to continue working and this places the employee and/or others at risk, the employer could be prosecuted.

The Misuse of Drugs Act 1971 makes it illegal for any person knowingly to permit drug use on their premises except in specified circumstances (e.g. when they have been prescribed by a doctor).

Regulation of alcohol and drugs in the workplace

It is important that employers regulate the use of alcohol and drugs in the workplace because failure to do so can lead to:

- poor performance and reduced productivity;
- lateness and absenteeism;
- accidents and therefore health and safety concerns;
- low morale and poor employee relations; and
- damage to the company reputation and customer relations.

The detrimental effects of drug and alcohol misuse in the workplace can be seen in the following statistics:

- A study by Norwich Union Healthcare found that 77% of employers consider alcohol to be the number one threat to employee wellbeing and that it plays a large role in sickness absence.
- In early 2004 the HSE published a report into the scale and impact of illegal drug use by workers, which found that, overall, 13% of working respondents reported drug use in the previous year.
- In a survey conducted by Norwich Union Healthcare, 32% of those surveyed admitted being at work with a hangover and 15% said they had been drunk at work.

Alcohol and drug misuse by employees are two problems that increasing numbers

Alcohol and drugs

of employers face. It is therefore essential that employers have policies and procedures to deal with such problems.

Employment policies and procedures

Policies on alcohol and drugs in the workplace should:

- set out the legal obligations behind the policy and summarise the aims of the policy;
- be clear as to whom the policy applies;
- make clear what will be considered to be alcohol and drug misuse and any specific rules/exceptions, e.g. in relation to prescription medicines;
- set out the disciplinary action that will be taken following a breach of the policy;
- provide advice as to where help can be obtained and details of any support that the employer will provide; and
- assure staff that any alcohol or drug problem will be treated in strict confidence.

The ACAS guidelines on 'Health, Work and Well Being' provide information on producing alcohol and drug policies.

In addition to ensuring that there is a drug and alcohol policy in place, employers should:

- consider putting in place procedures to find out if an employee has an alcohol- or drug-related problem, e.g. alcohol / drugs screening or medical examinations;
- seek to support the employee in the event that medical advice determines that they have an alcohol- or drug-related problem;
- ensure managers receive appropriate training to implement the policy and to ensure that it is applied consistently;
- consider placing the employee on alternative duties until they have combated their alcohol- or drug-related problem;
- consider the application of the Disability Discrimination Act 1995. Alcohol and drug addiction are not classified as disabilities (other than where addiction is a result of a substance being medically prescribed); therefore there is no requirement on an employer to make reasonable adjustments. The symptoms of alcohol and drug

---

Facts

- Around one in five (19%) workers is classified as a heavy drinker outside of work (four or more drinks in one day in men and more than three in women). A further 8% are classified as frequent drinkers (some alcohol on five or more days of the week) outside of work, and 11% are classified as drinking at work.
- A survey of British men has found 96% experience work-related stress, and 37% use alcohol as a way to put work behind them.
- Victims of actual or threatened violence at work said that the offender was under the influence of alcohol in a third (31%) of incidents, and drugs in a fifth (21%) of incidents.
- 17 million working days are lost to alcohol-related sickness absence every year, which equates to a £6.4bn annual alcohol-related output loss to the UK economy.

Sources: Alcohol Policy UK, Alcohol Concern, CIPD and Home Office.

Alcohol and drugs

addiction may, however, be classified as disabilities as the cause of the impairment is irrelevant. Therefore, depression or liver disease caused by alcohol dependency would count as an impairment;
- consider disciplinary action where an employee under the influence of alcohol or drugs places either himself or others at risk in the workplace;
- consider dismissal on grounds of capability or for some other substantial reason, where there is an ongoing problem and there appears to be no other alternative. A dismissal on capability grounds may be fair where an employee's performance falls below an acceptable standard, or where an employee is absent through ill health because of an alcohol- or drug-related problem. A fair procedure should always be followed; and
- consider reporting any criminal activity to the police. However, there is no obligation for an employer to do so.

In all cases of dismissal, employers should ensure that they follow the ACAS Code of Practice on Disciplinary and Grievance Procedures.

See also: Mental health, p.261; Monitoring employees, p.292; Private life, p.327; Smoking, p.369; Stress, p.381.

Sources of further information

As an employer, you are committed to providing a safe working environment for your employees. You are also committed to promoting the health and wellbeing of your employees. Alcohol and substance misuse can be detrimental to the health and performance of employees and may pose a potential risk to safety in the workplace and the welfare of other employees. Workplace Law Group's **Drug and Alcohol Policy and Management Guide v.2.0** policy is designed to help protect employees from the dangers of alcohol, drug and other substance misuse and to encourage those with a drug or alcohol problem to seek help. For more information visit www.workplacelaw.net/bookshop/policiesAndProcedures.

Comment...

Taking the heat out of business regulation

Founder of Loch Associates, Pam Loch is a dual qualified lawyer with extensive experience in contentious and non-contentious employment matters, having acted for employers and employees, advising on all aspects of employment law.

In the midst of an economic downturn, British businesses are bracing themselves for a difficult journey ahead. With the current recession being compared to the Great Depression in the early 1930s, small businesses are at the centre of the crisis with many having to surrender to increasing financial pressures.

The British Chambers of Commerce's aptly named '2009 Burdens' Barometer' has revealed that the survival rate of small businesses is set to rapidly fall as a result of the cumulative cost of new business regulation.

To date, the cost of regulatory changes for businesses is believed to have risen to £76.81bn. This includes over £10bn since 2008. Research carried out by the BCC found that almost half of small business employers claimed they experienced problems navigating through the voluminous employment regulation as well as struggling with a fall in demand, cash-flow issues and a loss of investment confidence.

Regulations

Three key Acts – the Regulatory Enforcement and Sanctions Act 2008 Legislative, the Regulatory Reform Act 2006 and the Regulatory Reform Act 2001 – were designed to try to reduce regulatory impact on businesses. However, this does not appear to be the case. Instead, businesses have had to try to cope with a situation that has been exacerbated by the sheer amount of new legislation affecting businesses in recent years.

In 2008, 57 new or amending Regulations affecting businesses were implemented, with a similar number expected in 2009. Employment law changes and other regulatory measures are some of the most costly burdens faced by small businesses. Some question whether or not this is the right time to impose more regulations on businesses.

In the last 12 months the number of changes to employment law have been significant and, arguably, have been too costly for businesses and potentially unnecessary. For example, statutory holiday entitlement was increased from 24 days to 28 days. While unions argue this was necessary to protect employees, many businesses will disagree. The cost of implementing this change for some businesses has been very significant.

The impact of accommodating extra days' holidays can necessitate a requirement for changes in the way work is undertaken

Comment: Business regulation

in a business and/or on the number of employees required to carry out the work. In difficult financial times the impact can be magnified. It is anticipated that this could cost businesses up to £4.4bn per year.

Another regulatory change that has been questioned was the introduction of the new ACAS Code of Practice on Discipline and Grievances, which came into force in April 2009, replacing the statutory dispute resolution procedures. While many businesses welcomed the change in approach, there are still costs being incurred during difficult times as businesses have to adapt their procedures, knowledge and understanding of employment law.

The Business, Enterprise and Regulatory Reform (BERR) and the Department for Innovation, Universities and Skills have also been recently merged together, to become the new Department for Business, Innovation and Skills (BIS). Only a few years ago BERR superseded its predecessor, the Department of Trade and Industry. Unlike BERR, BIS' remit is to focus on current and developing global issues which the recession has highlighted as a major factor in the UK economy. It will be responsible for the development of higher and further education and the Government's ambitious plans to expand apprenticeships. Some employment experts, however, warn that the merger will further complicate the skills system, which many employers say is already too confusing.

In the middle of a potentially deep recession, questions have been raised about the benefit of such a merger and the merit of additional costs being incurred to implement it. Many businesses are also sceptical about the impact of the merger, and are unable to appreciate the benefits of such changes. It is of course too early to be able to assess the merits (or the negative impact) of all these changes.

Changes are still afoot. After many years it is anticipated that legislation will come into force increasing the rights of temporary workers. Many businesses have relied heavily on temporary workers to fill gaps in their workforce. The impact of giving a temporary worker the right to become a permanent employee after 12 weeks of temporary employment could be huge. Nevertheless, it is anticipated that this will happen in the not too distant future.

Moratorium

The impact of recession, together with the impact of regulatory changes, is believed to have led some businesses to reach a decision to delay expanding their businesses and recruit new employees.

There are calls being made for a freeze on regulatory changes, to compel the Government to take account of the burden of new legislation on businesses. In April 2009, just under 4,000 members of the Institute of Directors signed a petition urging the Government to do this. The British Chamber of Commerce has also called for a three-year moratorium on new employment legislation, to enable businesses to fully focus on their survival through the downturn.

A moratorium is likely to cost nothing but it could make a huge difference to businesses. David Frost, Director General of the British Chambers of Commerce believes:

"It will be business that leads the UK out of recession. For this reason it is vital that companies are given the freedom to create jobs and wealth ... a moratorium on harmful extra legislation would be good

Comment: Business regulation

news in what are exceptionally difficult times."

By implementing a freeze on business regulation, attitudes could change, resulting in businesses being more willing to recruit. The challenge for the Government is ensuring it introduces regulation and changes that can make a positive contribution to help businesses, while protecting employees, particularly the vulnerable ones. By putting in place onerous or costly changes though, the impact on businesses can result in decisions being made to reduce their workforce or, worse still, deciding to close or move their businesses overseas. Many businesses are hoping a temporary moratorium will be put in place to avoid that happening and instead achieve a positive expansion going forward.

Bullying and harassment

Debbie Fellows, Anderson Strathern

Key points
- Ensure that a formal statement or policy exists and is supported by senior management.
- Issue a clear statement that bullying and harassment is totally unacceptable.
- Investigate alleged incidents thoroughly and immediately.
- Provide access to counselling and advice for recipients, where practicable, or consider giving time off for these activities.
- Make appropriate use of grievance and disciplinary procedures, or introduce a harassment procedure.
- Train your managers to increase knowledge and awareness.

Legislation
- Sex Discrimination Act 1975 as amended by the Sex Discrimination Act 1975 (Amendment) Regulations 2008.
- Race Relations Act 1976.
- Disability Discrimination Act 1995.
- Protection from Harassment Act 1997.
- Employment Equality (Sexual Orientation) Regulations 2003.
- Employment Equality (Religion or Belief) Regulations 2003.
- Employment Equality (Age) Regulations 2006.
- Offences (Aggravation by Prejudice) (Scotland) Act 2009.

It should be noted that the relevant law is currently set out in many different statutes and sets of Regulations. The Government is planning to consolidate the legislation into a single Equality Act, which is expected to be introduced in Spring 2010 (see '*Equality doesn't happen overnight*,' p.174).

What is bullying and harassment?
Bullying is an abuse or misuse of power that may be characterised as offensive, intimidating, malicious or insulting behaviour intended to undermine, humiliate, denigrate or injure the recipient.

Harassment, in general terms, involves unwanted conduct that has the purpose or effect of violating a person's dignity or creating an offensive, intimidating or hostile environment. It is unlawful if it is related to age, sex, sexual orientation, disability, religion or similar philosophical belief, nationality, ethnic origin, race or any personal characteristic of the individual, and may be persistent or a single incident. Further, if the individual can show that the conduct has created a hostile and degrading environment for them, it will not matter that the harassment related to another individual. An example of this could be where somebody has been offended by sexist remarks made about or to another person.

The key element is that the actions or comments are viewed as demeaning and unacceptable by the recipient.

In Scotland, the perpetrators of harassment may face increased penalties for harassment offences under the criminal

Bullying and harassment

law, which may be treated as aggravated where the harassment is on grounds of disability, sexual orientation or transgender identity in terms of the Offences (Aggravation by Prejudice) (Scotland) Act 2009, once in force.

How can bullying and harassment be recognised?

It is good practice for employers to give examples of what is unacceptable behaviour in the workplace. These may include:

- spreading malicious rumours or insulting someone (particularly on the grounds of race, sex, disability, sexual orientation, religion or belief, or age);
- ridiculing or demeaning someone – setting them up to fail;
- copying memos that are critical about someone to others that do not need to know;
- exclusion or victimisation;
- unfair treatment;
- unwelcome sexual advances – touching, standing too close, displaying offensive materials even generally;
- making threats or comments about job security without foundation;
- deliberately undermining a competent employee by overloading and constant criticism;
- blocking or refusing promotion or training opportunities; and
- threatening behaviour, violent gestures or physical violence.

Why do employers need to take action?

Not only is bullying and harassment unacceptable on moral grounds, but it could cause serious problems for an organisation, including:

- poor morale and poor employee relations;
- loss of respect for managers and supervisors;

Facts

- The Government has estimated that employers' failure to tackle the root cause of bullying in the workplace costs the UK economy £13.75bn a year.
- According to HSE reports, bullying costs employers 80 million working days and up to £2bn in lost revenue every year.
- Workers experience psychological symptoms as a result of bullying; e.g. anxiety, irritability, depression, withdrawal, lowered self-esteem etc. and physical symptoms such as disturbed sleep, lethargy, stomach disorders and headaches.
- The Chartered Institute of Personnel and Development (CIPD) reports that a third of employees have witnessed some form of bullying and harassment against others in their organisation in the last year.
- According to HSE reports, 87% of employees have taken sick leave as a result of bullying.
- The CIPD reports that mediation skills are not widely used in training to manage bullying at work (17%), although this rises to 25% in the public sector.
- 44% of smokers report an increase in smoking as a result of bullying and 20% of drinkers reported an increase in drinking alcohol.
- The Chartered Management Institute (CMI) reports that a lack of management skills is the factor most commonly cited as contributing to bullying in the workplace.

Bullying and harassment

- poor performance;
- lost productivity;
- absence;
- resignations;
- damage to company reputation; and
- tribunal and other court cases and awards of unlimited compensation.

The legal position

Employers are generally responsible in law for the acts of their employees, unless it can be shown that the employer took such steps as were reasonably practicable to prevent the employee carrying out the bullying and harassment ('the reasonable steps defence'), which has proven to be a high test to meet.

Since the implementation of the Sex Discrimination Act 1975 (Amendment) Regulations 2008, which came into force on 6 April 2008, employers are now liable for acts committed by third parties. An employee who has been subjected to harassment by a third party on two or more previous occasions, with the knowledge of her employer, will be able to bring a claim against her employer if the harassment happens again. The employer will be liable unless they can successfully rely on the reasonable steps defence referred to above. The third party can be different on each occasion but the employee can only raise a claim if she herself has been harassed on three occasions. Therefore, employers will not be able to ignore acts of harassment, simply because they are due to the actions of customers or other non-employees. It remains to be seen whether the liability of employers for acts committed by third parties contrary to the Sex Discrimination Act 1975 will be extended to other areas of discrimination legislation.

Employees who suffer bullying and harassment in the workplace may bring a variety of claims against an employer, including:

- A claim of unfair constructive dismissal (based on the employer's breach of the implied terms of trust and confidence).
- A claim for harassment under discrimination legislation (i.e. a claim that the harassment is on grounds of sex, race, disability, sexual orientation, religion or belief, or age).
- In more extreme cases, including personal injury, a claim can be brought in the civil courts based on either negligence or a breach of a statutory duty, such as the duty to provide a safe place and system of working under the Health and Safety at Work etc. Act 1974.
- Employers can be vicariously liable under the Protection from Harassment Act 1997 for bullying by their employees, if it constitutes harassment under this Act and it satisfies the appropriate tests. In order to bring a successful case under this Act there must be a course of conduct consisting of two or more instances, the conduct must constitute harassment (e.g. cause harm to others) and the perpetrator must have known / ought to have known that the conduct amounted to harassment. According to the judgement of the Court of Appeal in *Sunderland City Council v. Conn* (2008), what crosses the boundary between unattractive and even unreasonable conduct and conduct that is oppressive and unacceptable, may well depend on the context in which the conduct occurs. What might not be harassment on the factory floor or in the barrack room might well be harassment in the hospital ward and vice versa. The touchstone for recognising what is not harassment for the purposes of the Act will be whether the conduct is of such gravity as to justify the sanctions

Bullying and harassment

of the criminal law. In respect of a claim under this legislation there is no 'reasonable steps defence' available.

What should employers do?
- Ensure there are in place up-to-date equal opportunities / harassment policies, coupled with commitment from senior management.
- Supplement policies with training for managers and employees.
- Set a good example.
- Maintain fair procedures.
- Ensure complaints are handled confidentially, fairly and sensitively.

Formulating a policy
- Include in the policy a clear statement that bullying and harassment will not be tolerated.
- Give examples of unacceptable behaviour.
- State that bullying and harassment may be treated as disciplinary offences.
- Outline the steps you will take to prevent bullying and harassment.
- Outline the responsibilities of supervisors and managers.
- Give reassurance of confidentiality for any complaint.
- Ensure protection from victimisation.
- Refer to grievance procedures (informal and formal), including timescale for action.
- Refer to disciplinary procedures, including timescale for action.
- Include provisions for counselling and support.

How should employers respond to a complaint?
There are four basic options:

1. *Informal approach.* In some cases, people are unaware that their behaviour is unwelcome. Sometimes a 'quiet word' can lead to greater understanding and an agreement that the unwelcome behaviour will stop.
2. *Counselling.* This can provide a vital and confidential path for an informal approach and sometimes the opportunity to resolve the complaint without the need for formal action. Other options include employee assistance programmes funded by the employer.
3. *Grievance procedures.* If the employee does not wish his/her complaint to be dealt with informally (or the informal approach has failed) the complaint should be fully investigated and dealt with in terms of the grievance procedure.
4. *Disciplinary procedures.* Where the outcome of the grievance procedure is that the complaint of bullying and harassment is upheld, the employer may consider disciplinary action against the perpetrator in accordance with the disciplinary procedure.

It is important to follow a fair procedure with regard to both the complainant and the person accused. See '*Disciplinary and grievance procedures,*' p.106, for more information.

What should be considered when imposing a penalty?
Action taken must be reasonable in the circumstances. In some cases, counselling or training may be more appropriate than disciplinary action. When a penalty is imposed, consider the employee's general disciplinary record, action in previous cases, any explanations or mitigating circumstances, and whether the penalty is reasonable.

Written warnings, suspension or transferring the bully or harasser are examples of suitable disciplinary penalties. Suspension or transfer can only be used if permitted in the employee's contract of employment, so check it carefully before imposing this.

Bullying and harassment

When gross misconduct has occurred, dismissal without notice may be appropriate.

Finally, review your harassment and bullying policy on a regular basis to ensure that it remains effective.

See also: Disciplinary and grievance procedures, p.106; Discrimination, p.110; Employment disputes, p.150; Mental health, p.261; Stress, p.381.

Sources of further information

Equality and Human Rights Commission: www.equalityhumanrights.com

Employers should have a clear record of the policy and procedures for disciplinary matters to provide clear guidance to employees on the procedure that will be followed by their employer. Workplace Law Group's **Non-contractual Disciplinary and Grievance Policy and Management Guide, v.4.0** helps employers comply with their obligations, with a view to minimising allegations of unfair treatment. For more information visit www.workplacelaw.net/bookshop/policiesAndProcedures.

Carers

Gemma Cawthray, Veale Wasbrough

Key points
- Caring has an important role in society and workplaces need to accommodate carers.
- Current law does not provide adequate support and assistance to working carers.
- It is in employers' interests to help carer employees.
- Caring can be difficult and stressful and there is evidence to suggest that one in every five carers has to give up their paid employment to be a full-time carer. Becoming a carer can often happen overnight; for example, if a relative is injured in an accident, or is diagnosed with a serious illness. Therefore, the nature of caring is unpredictable and changeable.

Legislation
- Disability Discrimination Act 1995.
- Employment Rights Act 1996.
- Maternity and Parental Leave Regulations 1999.
- Employment Framework Directive (2000/78/EC).
- Employment Act 2002.
- Work and Families Act 2006.

Definition of a carer
A 'carer' is usually defined as someone who, without pay, looks after and provides help and support to a partner, child, relative, friend or neighbour, who could not manage without their help or support. This caring responsibility could be necessary due to age, physical or mental illness, addiction, sickness or disability.

Providing support for employee carers
It is increasingly important for employers to be aware of the difficulties carers face and provide support to employee carers. Employee carers have to juggle their work commitments with their other responsibilities. Many employers need educating in the issues working carers face and how they can assist them. The question of why employers should work to assist carers is easy to answer. Most carers tend to be over 30 and consequently are in their prime employment years. Employees in this age range are often the most experienced and valuable. Organisations derive benefit from retaining their existing staff, as it reduces the need to recruit and retrain and provides stability. There are many other benefits to providing such support, including lower turnover of staff, reduced absence rates, higher levels of morale and greater productivity.

Carers and the law

Flexible working
The right to request flexible working was initially introduced in 2003 under the Employment Act 2002 and has since been modified and extended by various regulations. Originally only carers of children under the age of six (or disabled children under the age of 18) qualified for the right. The Work and Families Act 2006 extended the right to carers of adults. In April 2009 the right was further extended to those responsible for children up to and including the age of 16.

Carers

Only certain employees qualify under the legislation. The right applies to employees who have been continuously employed for 26 weeks and who fall into one of the following categories:

- Have a child under 17 or a disabled child under 18 and are responsible for the child as a parent / adoptive parent / guardian / foster parent or holder of a residence order, or are the spouse, partner or civil partner of one of the categories listed or are applying to care for the child; or
- Are a carer who cares, or expects to be caring, for a spouse, partner, civil partner or relative who lives at the same address and who is over the age of 18.

Many carers do not fall within the statutory definition of those who are entitled to apply for flexible working. The application to work flexibly must be made in writing and the employee may request a change to the hours they work, a change to the times they are required to work and to work from a different location. These three categories enable a wide range of possible working patterns. Upon receipt of the application, the employer has a legal duty to consider the request seriously and objectively and it can only object on specified business grounds. The following procedure must be followed:

1. The employee submits a written application.
2. The employer and employee must meet within 28 days of receipt of the application to discuss the matter.
3. The employer must provide the employee with written notification of its decision within 14 days of the meeting.
4. If the employer accepts the request, both parties will need to meet again to consider what arrangements will need to be put in place. An accepted request normally amounts to a permanent variation to the employee's contract of employment.
5. If the request is rejected, the employee has the right to appeal in writing within 14 days.
6. Within 14 days of receiving the written appeal the parties must again meet and the outcome should be notified to the employee within 14 days of the meeting.

This process can take up to 14 weeks but it should be noted that an employee can only make one request a year under the legislation. The employee is entitled to be accompanied at all meetings by a workplace colleague. There are limited circumstances in which an employee may lodge a claim in the Employment Tribunal for failure to follow the procedure but such cases are rare. Employers should also note that employees have a statutory right not to be subjected to detriment or

Facts

- It is estimated that there are approximately six million carers in the UK, of which three million are employees.
- This equates to one in seven of the workforce having some form of caring responsibilities in addition to their employment.
- It is estimated that over the next three decades the total number of carers in the UK will increase from six million to nine million and this will obviously impact on the workforce.

Workplace Law Network
www.workplacelaw.net

Carers

be dismissed for making, or proposing to make, an application for flexible working.

Emergency time off

The Employment Rights Act 1996 gave employees the right to 'reasonable time off' to deal with any unexpected emergencies that arise in relation to 'dependants'. A dependant is classified as a husband, wife, partner, child or parent of the employee. It also includes someone living with the employee as part of the family. In the case of illness or injury, it also includes a person who relies on the employee for assistance. It is unlawful for an employer to penalise an employee for taking time off for genuine reasons. The right is intended to cover genuine emergencies only and is unpaid.

There is, as yet, no limit set on the number of times an employee can be absent from work exercising this right. However, it should be noted that this right is generally for unforeseen circumstances. If an employee knows in advance that he/she will need time off, he/she should ask for leave in the usual way. This could involve the employee taking annual leave, or some other type of leave, e.g. compassionate leave, if the employer provides it (see 'Leave', p.252).

This right is available for all employees regardless of length of service.

An employee can make a complaint to the Employment Tribunal if he/she considers that he/she has been unreasonably refused time off, suffered a detriment for taking or seeking to take time off, or been dismissed for taking or seeking to take time off.

Parental leave

Parental leave is available to employees who have one year's continuous service and have, or expect to have, parental responsibility for a child. Employees can take 13 weeks' unpaid leave in total for each child and the leave must be taken before the child's fifth birthday or before the fifth anniversary of the date of placement in respect of an adopted child. Parents of disabled children can take up to 18 weeks in total and must be taken before the child's 18th birthday.

Parental leave should only be used for the purpose of caring for a child. Leave may be taken in short or long blocks. Employers and employees can agree their own procedures for taking parental leave and the legislation encourages this. However, the legislation does provide a default scheme that will apply automatically where there is no other agreement in operation. Employees have the right to bring a claim in the Employment Tribunal if their employer prevents or attempts to prevent them from taking parental leave and they are also protected from victimisation, including dismissal, for taking it.

How employers can help

It is evident from the above that only certain employees are entitled, under law, to request certain types of leave and flexible working. Carers who look after friends and families who do not live at the same address are often excluded. Accordingly, employers should consider going beyond the statutory minimum. There are a variety of actions employers can take to help carer employees. An easy first step would be to consult with employees and produce a carer-friendly policy. Employers should investigate a full range of flexible working options, including part-time work, job sharing, flexi-time, homeworking etc. It may be that employees who do not fall within the statutory definition, or those that do not have any caring responsibilities, become resentful towards those who work flexibly and therefore employers should consider

Carers

whether it would be appropriate and practical to allow all employees to request to work in a flexible manner.

In particular, employers should try and act promptly in responding to any requests. The use of a trial period may also be a sensible option, to allow both parties to decide if a variation is workable. In addition, some carers may only need to work flexibly at certain times, depending on the circumstances, and employers should aim to be as accommodating as possible. The rights to emergency time off work and parental leave do not carry with them any right to payment, but employers may consider it appropriate for this to be paid. In addition, employers may want to investigate introducing measures such as planned leave for situations where people may need to provide nursing care for a short period, or allow a longer lunch break to enable a worker to visit the person they care for.

Other practical support would be to allow the employee access to a telephone or give him/her parking near work to allow him/her to get in and out of work easier.

National Carers Strategy

In June 2008 the Prime Minister launched the National Carers Strategy. The Strategy sets out a ten-year vision, including a set of commitments on some of the important issues surrounding carers. It proposes a number of measures to be undertaken by 2011. Many consider the Strategy to be an important step forward in recognising the needs of carers and it includes a focus upon carers in employment. In relation to employment matters the Government has stated that it will be funding an awareness campaign to ensure that both employers and employees are aware of their rights. Furthermore, the Government will be undertaking a review of who is entitled to request flexible working rights, due to the fact that many carers do not fall within the statutory definition of a carer and therefore miss out. The Strategy has also committed £38m of additional funding to support carers in returning to work.

Discrimination and *Coleman v. Attridge Law* (2008)

On 17 July 2008 the European Court of Justice (ECJ) handed down a potentially far-reaching decision in *Coleman v. Attridge Law*. Ms Coleman was a secretary at a law firm and the principal carer for her disabled son. She resigned and claimed unfair constructive dismissal and less favourable treatment due to her son's disability. In January 2008 the Advocate General gave his opinion, saying that he considered 'discrimination by association' to be illegal. He concluded that subtler forms of discrimination should be caught by the anti-discrimination legislation as the aim of the legislation was to combat all forms of discrimination on the grounds of disability, the principle of equal treat did not apply to a specific category of people.

The ECJ followed the Attorney General's opinion and ruled that the ban on employment discrimination is not limited to disabled people but also extends to those responsible, their carers, or those with close connections. After the ECJ's ruling, the case returned to the Employment Tribunal where, at a pre hearing review, it was held that the Disability Discrimination Act 1995 could be interpreted so as to prohibit associative direct discrimination and harassment. Accordingly, Ms Coleman's claim could proceed to a full hearing for a decision to be made on the facts. Attridge Law has appealed against the Tribunal's decision; as yet the appeal has not been heard. In light of the ECJ's ruling, the forthcoming Equality Act is set to remove any ambiguity and clearly prohibit direct discrimination and harassment by association.

Carers

The ECJ's ruling is significant and dramatically strengthens the employment rights of carers as they now cannot be treated less favourably in connection with their caring responsibilities. Employers will need to be careful that they do not discriminate against employees who care for either disabled or elderly people, or they could risk facing a disability or age discrimination claim. There is no limit on the amount of compensation that can be awarded if discrimination is proven.

> *See also*: Childcare provisions, p.65; Discrimination, p.110; Family-friendly rights, p.182; Flexible working, p.190; Homeworking, p.222; Leave, p.252; Pregnancy, p.324.

Sources of further information

National Carers' Strategy: www.carersuk.org

Department for Business, Innovation and Skills: www.berr.gov.uk

Direct Gov: www.directgov.co.uk

CCTV monitoring

Elizabeth Upton, Bird and Bird

Key points
- Workplace managers should note that most CCTV systems will be covered by the Data Protection Act (the Act). They should therefore familiarise themselves with the Information Commissioner's CCTV Code of Practice.
- Before installing a CCTV system, an impact assessment should be carried out to assess whether the use of CCTV is justified or whether another, less privacy-intrusive, solution (e.g. improved lighting in a car park) could achieve the same objectives.
- Workplace managers should put in place a policy regarding use of the CCTV system by camera operators and retention of images.
- Warning signs should usually be posted, and the organisation must ensure it is able to comply with a data subject access request for images.

Legislation
- Data Protection Act 1998.
- Human Rights Act 1998.
- Regulation of Investigatory Powers Act (RIPA) 2000.

CCTV in the UK
Increasingly, CCTV has become the principal method of carrying out surveillance of areas that may be accessed by the public. Whilst many members of the public are not concerned, others are troubled by increasing levels of routine surveillance. The main benefit claimed for CCTV is that it provides protection for both the public and property. However, there is much debate as to whether CCTV schemes have an effect on overall crime rates.

A 2008 Home Office report suggested that CCTV had a modest effect on crime, being most effective in car parks to detect and prevent vehicle crimes. It should also be acknowledged that it is possible for CCTV to be misused as a means of covert observation. Although many people do not object to the use of CCTV in public places, as they recognise that there are benefits to the community that may override any concerns of a 'Big Brother' approach to policing, this attitude does not extend to the use of CCTV cameras in the workplace. Employees are suspicious of any form of surveillance by their employers at work. The Information Commissioner has recognised that special considerations apply in the workplace, and has produced guidance to assist employers to comply with the law.

Dummy and non-operational CCTV
The Data Protection Act applies to images captured by CCTV. If no image is captured, no personal data is processed; therefore the Data Protection Act would not apply, additionally it would be difficult to argue any infringement of an individual's privacy. Therefore, the guidance in this chapter does not apply to the use of dummy or non-operational cameras.

Data Protection Act 1998
The Data Protection Act 1998 is the major legal control over CCTV surveillance. The Data Protection Act requires data

CCTV monitoring

controllers to process personal data only in accordance with the principles set out in the Act.

'Personal data' is defined in the Data Protection Act as "Data which relate to a living individual who can be identified (a) from those data, or (b) from those data and other information which is in the possession of, or is likely to come into the possession of, the data controller".

A record of a person's appearance captured on CCTV images is clearly therefore personal data within the meaning of the Data Protection Act, as a person can be identified from his or her appearance. This personal data is processed by automatic means via the CCTV system.

Information about people that is derived from CCTV images such as vehicle registration numbers will also be caught by the definition of personal data in the Act. In fact, most uses of CCTV by organisations will be covered by the Act, regardless of the number of cameras or the sophistication of the systems.

Note: The Information Commissioner has changed his view as to what will be caught by CCTV images. Previous guidance suggested that only the most sophisticated CCTV systems with the ability to zoom in on individuals would be caught by the Act and that very basic CCTV systems would not be covered.

It is also worth noting that 'sensitive personal data' (to which the Data Protection Act applies more stringent processing guidelines) includes information about the commission or alleged commission of any offence, and about any proceedings relating to an offence committed or which is alleged to have been committed. These more stringent processing guidelines will therefore apply to any CCTV footage showing the possible commission of an offence.

Workplace managers using CCTV systems should also be aware that they must be able to respond to data subject access requests under the Data Protection Act. Requests from data subjects to information held about them must be complied with within a statutory time period (unless one of the limited exemptions in the DPA applies).

Human Rights Act 1998

Public Authorities that use CCTV should be aware that indiscriminate and unjustified use of CCTV surveillance and monitoring could potentially be a breach of the Human Rights Act in relation to the right to respect for privacy.

Facts
- It is believed that Britain has the highest CCTV coverage in the world.
- Some estimate that 4.2 million cameras are in use, one for every 14 people.
- A person may be captured on camera in the UK up to 300 times a day.
- CCTV monitoring technology now incorporates numberplate recognition, and assists with mobile phone triangulation. Digital CCTV systems can be configured to use face-recognition and look for criminal suspects.
- An estimated £500m of public money has been spent on installing CCTV in the last decade.

CCTV monitoring

In the case of *Peck v. United Kingdom* (2003), the European Court of Human Rights held that a man in a public place still had a legitimate expectation of privacy and that the public authority's use of CCTV images breached that right. In the *Peck* case, the Public Authority had broadcast CCTV images of a man brandishing a knife in a public street on TV. This caused him significant embarrassment as he was recognised by neighbours and friends. He had had mental health problems at the time of the incident and had in fact been attempting suicide.

The Human Rights Act also has implications for private organisations using CCTV. In the event that an individual takes a complaint to Court or to the Employment Tribunal, as a 'court or tribunal' falls within the definition of a 'public authority' under the Human Rights Act, it will also have a duty to apply European Human Rights Convention principles when adjudicating a dispute.

If the litigant establishes a statutory or common law cause of action, he or she may apply a human rights argument. For example, an employee of a private company alleging that his Article 8 privacy rights have been infringed by his employer can argue that the Employment Tribunal must (as a Public Authority) ensure that it does not act in a way that is incompatible with that right to privacy in deciding the case.

Code of Practice for users of CCTV

The Information Commissioner published a revised CCTV Code of Practice in January 2008 (which replaces the earlier Code issued in 2000 and the supplementary guidance for small users). It sets out the measures that should be adopted in order to ensure that a CCTV scheme complies with the Data Protection Act and provides guidance on good practice. The Code of Practice does not apply to:

- the covert surveillance activities of the law enforcement community (which are covered by the Regulation of Investigatory Powers Act (RIPA) 2000); or
- the use of conventional cameras (not CCTV) by the news media or for artistic purposes such as for filmmaking.

The Code does apply to the passing on of CCTV images to the media. Appendix 3 of the Code is for employers who may use CCTV to monitor their workers. This supplements the Employment Practices Code guidance on monitoring employees.

Most uses of CCTV by organisations or businesses will be covered by the Data Protection Act (DPA) and the provisions of the 2008 Code, regardless of the size of the system. The Code is available from the Office of the Information Commissioner. The full text should be consulted, but the main practical requirements are summarised in the following paragraphs.

Impact Assessments

Users should conduct an initial impact assessment before installing and using CCTV. The aim of the assessment is to assess whether the objectives of monitoring can be achieved by a less intrusive means. The guidance lists a number of questions that companies should consider before installing CCTV. They must establish the purposes for which they need CCTV and ensure that a notification which covers these purposes has been lodged with the Office of the Information Commissioner.

Camera positioning and signage

Cameras should be positioned in such a way that they are only able to monitor

CCTV monitoring

areas intended to be covered by the CCTV scheme. The operators of the equipment must be aware that they may only use the equipment in order to achieve the purpose notified to the Information Commissioner. If possible, the movement of the cameras should be restricted so that the operators cannot monitor areas that are not intended to be covered. Clearly visible and legible signs of an appropriate size should be used to inform the public that they are entering a zone that is monitored. The signs should contain the following information:

- The identity of the person or organisation responsible for the scheme;
- The purpose of the scheme; and
- Details of whom to contact regarding the scheme.

The contact point should be available to members of the public during office hours, and employees staffing the contact point should be aware of the relevant policies and procedures. Signs may not be appropriate where CCTV is used to obtain evidence of criminal activity. However, the Code sets out tight controls over the use of CCTV in these circumstances.

Image quality

The images captured by CCTV equipment should be as clear as possible, to ensure that they are effective for the purposes intended. Cameras should be properly maintained and serviced, and good-quality tapes should be used. If dates and times are recorded, these should be accurate.

Consideration must also be given to the physical conditions in the camera locations (e.g. infrared equipment may need to be used in poorly lit areas). No sound should accompany the images except in limited circumstances. Images should not be retained for longer than necessary.

While they are retained, access to and security of the images must be controlled in accordance with the seventh Data Protection Principle of the Act, which sets out security requirements. Disclosure of images from the CCTV system must be controlled and the reasons for disclosure must be compatible with the purposes notified to the Information Commissioner. All access to or disclosure of the images should be documented.

If the purpose of the CCTV is solely to prevent and detect crime, then it should not be used for monitoring the amount of work done or compliance with company procedures. In some cases, it may be appropriate to install CCTV specifically for workforce monitoring. This must be justified under the decision-making process outlined in the Code. Workers should normally be aware that they are being monitored, but in exceptional circumstances, covert monitoring may be used as part of a specific investigation.

Cameras and listening devices should not be installed in private areas such as toilets and private offices, except in the most exceptional circumstances where serious crime is suspected. This should only happen where there is an intention to involve the police, not where it is a purely internal disciplinary matter.

Employment Practices Code

Part Three of the Information Commissioner's Employment Practices Code on Monitoring at Work sets out the basic 'dos and don'ts' for employers who monitor the activities of their employees. The Information Commissioner has attempted in the Code to strike a balance between the needs of employers and the needs of employees.

The Code stresses the need for proportionality – any adverse impact of

CCTV monitoring

monitoring must be justified by the benefits to the employer and others. In order to assess whether monitoring is justified, the Code recommends organisations should carry out impact assessments to determine the purpose and likely impact of monitoring, whether there are any alternatives and what obligations will arise.

Where possible, CCTV monitoring should be targeted at areas of particular risk and should not take place in areas where employees have a reasonable expectation of privacy; for example, toilets and private offices. Continuous monitoring of particular employees is only likely to be justified where there are particular safety or security concerns that cannot be adequately dealt with in other, less intrusive, ways.

All employees and visitors should be made aware that CCTV is in operation and of the purposes for which the information will be used. Covert monitoring of employees will only be justified in very limited circumstances; specifically, where openness would prejudice the prevention or detection of crime or the apprehension of offenders. However, before covert monitoring is used, among other things, employers must identify specific criminal activity and establish that there is a need to use covert monitoring to obtain evidence.

Employees and trade unions have resisted the placing of CCTV cameras in the workplace. At Guy's and St Thomas' Hospitals the public sector union UNISON threatened industrial action over the placing of surveillance cameras in locker rooms.

However, where employees or their trade unions perceive a benefit in such surveillance techniques, acceptance of the cameras is likely to follow – e.g. where CCTV surveillance at work is for security purposes or is intended solely to detect, and so protect employees from, intruders. The monitoring of construction sites is now commonplace and in an industrial dispute involving workers on the Jubilee Line, security data was used in reverse of its usual application to prove that union members could not have been in the vicinity of a suspected act of vandalism.

British Standard

The British Standards Institution has issued Code of Practice BS 7958:2005 Closed circuit television (CCTV): management and operation. The Code of Practice assists CCTV operators to comply with the Data Protection Act and to ensure that CCTV evidence can be used by the police to investigate crime. The Code is particularly useful where CCTV systems are used in public places, or have a partial view of a public place, and may therefore be of use to workplace managers.

Conclusion

Workplace managers responsible for CCTV use should familiarise themselves with the Information Commissioner's Code of Practice on CCTV, and the Employment Practices Data Protection Code and the Employment Practices Code Supplementary Guidance. The main points to be aware of are:

- An initial assessment should be carried out before installing the CCTV system.
- Clear guidelines for use should be given to camera operators.
- Warning signs containing the required information should normally be put in place.
- CCTV images should be retained in accordance with the requirements of the Data Protection Act.
- Users should ensure they are able to comply with a data subject access request.

CCTV monitoring

See also: Data protection, p.84; Monitoring employees, p.292.

Sources of further information

Information Commissioner: www.informationcommissioner.gov.uk

CCTV Code of Practice: Revised Edition 2008: www.ico.gov.uk/upload/documents/library/data_protection/detailed_specialist_guides/ico_cctvfinal_2301.pdf

BS 7958:2005 Closed circuit television (CCTV): management and operation.

Security Industry Authority: www.the-sia.org.uk

The law states that you must advise visitors and would-be intruders that you operate CCTV. Workplace Law's new Facilities Store stocks signage for both inside and outside premises as well as complete solutions for managing your CCTV videos or digital recorders. Visit http://facilities-store.workplacelaw.net.

Childcare provisions

Lizzie Mead, Berwin Leighton Paisner

Key points
- According to the Government initiative, Every Child Matters: SureStart (a programme aiming to increase the availability of childcare), an increasing number of employees in UK workplaces have responsibility for the care of children.
- A number of family-friendly rights are granted to such individuals, of which employers must be aware.
- As well as having to comply with the legal and statutory obligations, employers are now increasingly being encouraged, through campaigns such as the Work–Life Balance Campaign, to support Government-driven initiatives that assist employees and workers to meet their childcare needs.

Legislation
- Health and safety legislation.
- Family-friendly legislation.

The so-called family-friendly legislation now encompasses a wide variety of rights (granted to employees but not workers) which employees may exercise in order to assist them with their childcare needs. By way of summary, these rights currently include:

- maternity leave and adoption leave of up to 52 weeks (statutory maternity pay and statutory adoption pay are payable (subject to eligibility) for 39 weeks);
- paternity leave of either one or two consecutive weeks, for which statutory paternity pay is payable;
- unpaid parental leave of up to 13 weeks for each child up to the child's fifth birthday (or 18 weeks' leave in the case of a disabled child up to the child's 18th birthday) or within five years of placement for an adopted child (or the adopted child's 18th birthday, if sooner);
- for employees caring for certain adults the right to request a flexible working arrangement;
- for parents of children up to and including the age of 16 (or 18 if disabled) who have responsibility for the child's upbringing, the right to request a flexible working arrangement; and
- the right to take reasonable unpaid time off work to deal with emergencies involving dependants.

Since 2006, there has been considerable discussion about proposed changes to further extend the family-friendly legislation. In particular:

- extending the period for which statutory maternity pay and statutory adoption pay are payable, from 39 weeks to 52 weeks; and
- giving employed fathers a right to additional paid paternity leave of up to 26 weeks if the mother returns to work without using her full maternity leave entitlement (i.e. fathers taking the second half of the mother's maternity leave).

Childcare provisions

> **Facts**
>
> - All three- and four-year-olds are entitled to 12.5 hours' free early education per week in nurseries, playgroups, pre-schools, children's centres or at their childminders, for 38 weeks a year.
> - In January 2000, 16% of all four-year-olds in England were enrolled in non-school education settings in the private and voluntary sector, such as local playgroups.
> - In spring 2002, 53% of women whose youngest dependent child was under five years of age were working either part-time or full-time (36% and 17% respectively).
>
> *Sources: Government Department for Children, Schools and Families, National Statistics.*

The Government issued a statement in June 2009 that these proposals will not be introduced in April 2010 as previously anticipated, as they are reviewing the appropriateness of all new regulations in light of the economic climate.

Workplace nurseries and employer-supported childcare

Government-driven and trade union-backed initiatives such as the SureStart Strategy are seeking to encourage greater employer-supported childcare through various voluntary schemes. Under these schemes, employees sacrifice a portion of their salary to be paid towards childcare costs. There are tax incentives available to both employer and employee in respect of that portion of the salary sacrificed. The schemes include the following:

- *Workplace nurseries.* This is where the employer is wholly or partly responsible for funding and managing the provision of childcare facilities (either a workplace nursery or an in-house / on-site holiday play scheme) on work premises. For small employers, this can be done jointly with other companies. In respect of this cost, the employer is exempt from employer's National Insurance Contributions (NICs) and the employee is exempt from employee's Class 1 NICs and income tax. In April 2005, this exemption was widened so that if you allow another employer's staff who work on your premises to use your childcare facility, they will benefit from the exemption also.
- *Childcare vouchers.* These are usually paper vouchers issued to employees to pay childcare providers for forms of childcare. There are tax incentives and savings available to both employer and employee, which were extended in April 2005. Currently, the first £55 a week or £243 a month of childcare vouchers paid for by the employer is exempt from NICs for employers, and from income tax and NICs for employees, provided that access to the scheme is available to all employees and that the vouchers are used to pay for registered or approved childcare (for eligible children) only.
- *Enhanced employee rights.* An increasing number of employers are opting to provide enhanced maternity, paternity, adoption and parental leave rights over and above the statutory minimum levels, extra statutory

Childcare provisions

emergency leave to deal with a sick child or problems with childcare, and career breaks or sabbaticals.

Childcare vouchers and maternity leave

Since 2008, women going on maternity leave have been entitled to benefit from the terms and conditions of employment that would have applied to them had they been at work throughout the whole of their maternity leave, except those relating to 'remuneration'. Remuneration is defined within the Maternity and Parental Leave etc. Regulations 1999 as 'sums payable to the employee by way of wages or salary'. It is generally considered that, as they are non-transferrable and cannot be converted into cash, childcare vouchers are benefits rather than remuneration. HMRC has issued guidance to support this view. As a result, an employer has to provide childcare vouchers (together with other benefits) to employees throughout maternity leave even though, unlike other benefits, they are often funded by way of salary sacrifice. This is a potentially significant cost and as such in May 2009 the British Chambers of Commerce warned its members to carefully consider the costs risks before offering childcare vouchers to employees.

The benefit to employers is that if vouchers are funded through a salary sacrifice arrangement, the employer's NIC bill is reduced as it is paying NICs on a lower salary. The cost implications will depend on whether an employer is able to offset any of the cost against maternity pay. If an employer only pays its employees SMP, it cannot offset any of the cost of the vouchers against this and any attempt to do so will be void. If an employer pays contractual maternity pay in excess of SMP, it will be able to deduct the cost of providing the vouchers against this if a policy allows it to be done. It is also theoretically possible to draft a maternity pay policy that allows an employer to further discount any maternity pay at the beginning of leave (if it is at a higher rate) to fund future vouchers during the unpaid or SMP period. However, this has not been tested.

Since the British Chambers of Commerce warning in 2009, there has been considerable debate around whether employers would be better off withdrawing childcare vouchers as a benefit. If employees have a contractual right to receive the benefit this is likely to cause its own problems.

See also: Carers, p.54; Children at work, p.68; Family-friendly rights, p.182; Flexible working, p.190.

Sources of further information

Every Child Matters – SureStart: www.dcsf.gov.uk/everychildmatters

Work and Families Bill: www.publications.parliament.uk/pa/cm200506/cmbills/060/2006060.htm

Right to request flexible working: www.direct.gov.uk

Children at work

Carolyn Haddon, Charles Russell

Key points
A child is a person not over compulsory school age (i.e. up to the last Friday in June in the academic year of his/her 16th birthday). Note that a young person is a person who has ceased to be a child but is under 18.

The employment of children in the UK is subject to limitations regarding the number of hours that they can work. Children also have a number of special rights and protections in the workplace, justified on health and safety grounds. It is important for all employers of children to be aware of the legal framework.

The general principle, subject to exceptions, is that a child under 14 may not work.

Any organisation employing a child of compulsory school age must inform the local education authority in order to obtain an employment permit for that child. Without one, the child may not be covered under the terms of the employer's insurance policy. *Note: This does not apply, however, in respect of children who are carrying out work experience arranged by their school.*

Legislation
- Children and Young Persons Act 1933 and 1963 (as amended).
- Education Act 1996 (as amended).
- Employment Rights Act 1996 (as amended).
- Management of Health and Safety at Work Regulations 1999.
- Children (Protection at Work) Regulations 1998-2000 (implementing the provisions of the EC Directive on the Protection of Young People at Work (94/33/EC)).
- Working Time Regulations 1998.
- Working Time (Amendment) Regulations 2002.

In addition, the United Nations Convention on the Rights of the Child (for these purposes, all persons under 18) provides that Member States have an obligation to protect children at work, set minimum ages for employment and regulate conditions of employment.

Key restrictions on the employment of children
No child may be employed to carry out any work whatsoever (whether paid or unpaid) if s/he is under the age of 14. This is subject to some specific exceptions, e.g. in relation to children working for their parent/guardian, or in sport, television, the theatre or modelling. In the case of a child who is 14 or over, s/he may not:

- do any work other than light work;
- work in any industrial setting, sea-going boat, factory or mine (subject to very specific exceptions);
- work during school hours on a school day;

Children at work

- work before seven a.m. or after seven p.m.;
- work for more than two hours on any school day;
- work for more than 12 hours in any week during term-time;
- work more than two hours on a Sunday;
- work for more than eight hours on any day s/he is not required to attend school (other than a Sunday) (or five hours in the case of a child under the age of 15);
- work for more than 35 hours in any week during school holidays (or 25 hours in the case of a child under the age of 15);
- work for more than four hours in any day without a rest break of at least one hour;
- work without having a two-week break from any work during the school holidays in each calendar year; or
- work without an employment permit, issued by the education department of the local council, and signed by the employer and one of the child's parents.

In addition, each Local Authority has specific, additional by-laws regulating the employment of children in its area.

Work experience

Guidelines were issued by the DTI (now BIS) in 2007 regarding work experience placements in the television industry and these are now regarded as being applicable in various industries. The main points of note in the guidelines are:

- a written document should detail the framework of the work experience placement;
- placements should be for a fixed period of time (ideally between two weeks and a month);
- placements should not entail more than 40 hours work per week;
- before starting the placement, specific learning objectives should be agreed between the child on the placement and the provider of the placement; and
- no unpaid volunteer should be under an obligation to comply with an employer's instructions.

Entitlement to holidays and time off

Under the Working Time Regulations 1998, all adult employees are entitled to at least 5.6 weeks' paid annual leave. In the case of *Addison v. Ashby* (2003), however, the Employment Appeal Tribunal ruled that this entitlement does not apply to a child. The Children and Young Persons Act 1933 provides that a child is entitled to two consecutive weeks without employment during a school holiday; however, this period of time is unpaid.

National minimum wage and sick pay

The national minimum wage for young workers, aged under 18 but above the compulsory school age, but who are not apprentices, is (as of October 2009) £3.57 per hour and is reviewed in October of each year. There is no national minimum wage for children still of the compulsory school age. In England and Wales, a person is no longer of compulsory school age after the last Friday of June of the school year in which their 16th birthday occurs.

The Statutory Sick Pay Regulations specify that workers aged 16 or over are entitled to receive statutory sick pay (SSP). Under 16s are not entitled to SSP.

Age discrimination

As a result of the Employment Equality (Age) Regulations 2006, it is now unlawful to discriminate against any person on the grounds of age. This applies to discrimination against younger individuals

Children at work

as well as older ones. The lower age limit of 18 has also now been removed, meaning that under 18s have the same rights as older workers and can bring unfair dismissal claims.

See also: Childcare provisions, p.65; Minimum wage, p.273; Young persons, p.430.

Sources of further information

Worksmart – children's work rights: www.worksmart.org.uk/rights/viewsubsection.php?sun=75

DirectGov: www.direct.gov.uk/en/Parents/ParentsRights/DG_4002945

Children's Legal Centre – a charity providing advice and information for young people: www.childrenslegalcentre.com/Legal+Advice/Child+law/childemployment/

Contract disputes

Rupert Choat, CMS Cameron McKenna

Key points
As disputes are expensive and time-consuming, it is advisable to manage them by:

- including appropriate dispute resolution provisions in contracts;
- anticipating disputes in record-keeping practices; and
- handling disputes effectively.

Legislation
- Arbitration Act 1996.
- Housing Grants, Construction and Regeneration Act 1996.

Dispute resolution provisions in contracts
Wherever possible, when drafting any pro-forma contracts and when negotiating contracts, it is advisable to consider the various dispute resolution methods available and to include clauses providing for the chosen method(s). Some 'picking and mixing' of methods is possible.

Negotiation
Discussions invariably occur before any dispute goes to formal proceedings. Even if formal proceedings are commenced, negotiation remains one of the most effective ways of resolving disputes.

It may help to discuss disputes on a 'without prejudice' basis, so that what is said cannot be referred to later in any formal proceedings. This can promote a frank exchange of views.

Some contracts provide for a structured approach to discussions. For instance, a dispute may be required to be considered initially by those at project level. If this is unsuccessful within a specified time, the dispute may go to board or principal level. The contract might make compliance with this procedure a precondition to the commencement of any formal proceedings.

Court proceedings
Generally, unless the contract otherwise provides (e.g. by providing for arbitration), the Courts can decide the parties' disputes. Proceedings are started by issuing a claim form.

The Civil Procedure Rules govern court proceedings.

The Courts deal with disputes according to their value and complexity. Directions are given to the parties to prepare their dispute for trial. Directions usually provide for the production of statements of case, disclosure of documents, exchange of witness statements and expert reports (if necessary).

Court proceedings are public.

Arbitration
Parties to a contract can agree that their disputes will be resolved by arbitration rather than by the Courts. This can be done either in the contract or 'ad hoc' once a dispute arises.

The Arbitration Act 1996 governs arbitration.

Contract disputes

> **Facts**
> - About 90% of court cases are settled before trial.
> - Mediation saves UK business over £1bn a year in wasted management time, damaged relationships, lost productivity and legal fees.
> - There are around 1,500 adjudications a year. About 5% of decisions are enforced with the Courts' help. Few are invalid or treated as not finally resolving the dispute.

Generally the parties decide who the arbitrator(s) will be or, failing that, a nominating body decides. The parties can agree the procedure for the arbitration by which the dispute will be decided. They might agree on a procedure similar to court proceedings or they might opt for the dispute being decided on paper without a hearing.

Arbitration is a confidential process.

One disadvantage of arbitration is that third parties cannot be joined in the arbitration without the consent of all concerned. This is not the case with court proceedings.

Adjudication

The Housing Grants, Construction and Regeneration Act 1996 empowers a party to a written 'construction contract' to refer any dispute arising under the contract to adjudication. The option to go to adjudication exists in addition to the right to go to court or arbitration (whichever is applicable).

Adjudication is rough and ready but usually cheaper than court proceedings or arbitration. The appointed adjudicator is required to reach a decision within 28 days of the dispute being referred to him (subject to extensions). The adjudicator's decision is temporarily binding, pending the outcome of any subsequent court proceedings or arbitration.

There is some uncertainty as to the extent to which facilities management contracts are construction contracts. To avoid confusion it is usually sensible to provide expressly for adjudication in such contracts.

Alternative dispute resolution (ADR)

Parties to a contract can agree that their disputes will be resolved by any of a number of forms of ADR. This can be done either in the contract or 'ad hoc' once the dispute arises. The parties may agree that ADR is a precondition to court proceedings or arbitration.

- One method of ADR is mediation. The parties (or an appointing body of the parties' choice) appoint the mediator, whose role is facilitating the resolution of the dispute. The mediator has no decision-making powers, although the parties can empower him to opine on where the merits lie in their dispute. The mediation is held 'without prejudice'. The process is non-binding. Any party can withdraw at any time, and there is no guarantee of a resolution at the end of the mediation.
- Early neutral evaluation involves a third party, who is usually a lawyer, assessing the merits of the dispute and advising the parties of his views in a, usually, non-binding manner. This might help the parties to settle between themselves.

Workplace Law Network
www.workplacelaw.net

Contract disputes

- Another method of ADR is expert determination. It is particularly suited to disputes that turn on technical rather than legal issues. A third-party expert is appointed to reach a decision on the dispute. The parties agree a (usually short) timetable that may allow them to make submissions to the expert. The parties may agree that the expert's decision will be final and binding or that it will be subject to review by the courts or arbitration.

Record keeping

Good documentary records tend to help in resolving disputes and may reduce any legal costs you incur.

Bear in mind that in Court and arbitration proceedings you will invariably be directed to disclose to the other party relevant documents under your control (including documents that are prejudicial to your case). Disclosable documents will include emails and other electronic documents. Documents are generally disclosable even if they contain confidential information.

It is advisable to retain documents for between six and 15 years after the matter to which they relate ends (depending upon the nature of the contract).

Handling disputes

When a dispute arises, try to address it early rather than allowing it to escalate. If it is not possible to resolve the dispute by discussion, check the contract to see which dispute resolution method(s) apply. Consider also whether you want to suggest another method not provided for by the contract (e.g. mediation). In some cases, statute may dictate that a certain dispute resolution method applies even if it is not specified in the contract (e.g. adjudication in construction contracts).

It invariably favours a party during any formal proceedings if they have behaved reasonably in conducting the dispute (especially if the other party has not). For instance, if a party unreasonably refuses a proposal to mediate a dispute, that party may later incur a costs penalty.

Remember, even if you win the dispute, you will not recover all of your legal costs and will find it difficult to recover compensation for management time spent in handling the dispute.

See also: Employment contracts, p.146; Employment disputes, p.150.

Sources of further information

Civil Procedure Rules: www.justice.gov.uk/civil/procrules_fin/index.htm

Arbitration Act 1996: www.hmso.gov.uk/acts/acts1996/1996023.htm

Housing Grants, Construction and Regeneration Act 1996, Part II (at the time of writing due to be amended by the Local Democracy, Economic Development and Construction Bill, Part 8, although it may not come into force before late 2010): www.opsi.gov.uk/acts/acts1996/1996053.htm

Adjudication case summaries: www.law-now.com/law-now/zones/LN_Adjudication.htm

Contractors

Catherine Henney, Kennedys

Key points
Contractors are not normally employees of a business, but have a contract to provide agreed services. This is known as a contract for services, which is in contrast to a contract of service, e.g. a contract of employment. The employment status of contractors has both tax and employment rights implications.

Legislation
- Employment Rights Act 1996 (ERA).

Overview
It is important for anyone hiring a contractor to understand the distinction between employees and contractors so that their legal rights and obligations are clear. Contractors will not normally be considered employees of a business. Instead, they might be self-employed, an agency worker or an employee of another business. Contractors have more control over the type of work they do and how they do it, whereas employees normally have less control over what they do but instead benefit from employment rights that contractors do not. Employees and contractors are also treated differently for tax purposes.

The distinction between employees, workers and contractors is not clear-cut. It is possible that a contractor may actually be considered to have an employment relationship with a business and be categorised as either a worker or (although unlikely) an employee.

In what circumstances could a contractor be an employee or a worker?
Under Section 230(1) of ERA 1996, an employee is 'an individual who has entered into or works under a contract of employment'. A contract of employment is defined in Section 230(2) of ERA 1996 as 'a contract of service or apprenticeship, whether express or implied, and (if it is express) whether oral or in writing'. There is no statutory definition of 'contract of service,' but, generally speaking, under a contract of service a person agrees to serve another.

It is unlikely that a contractor would be found to be an employee of the business that has hired them. However, while the requirements for an 'employee' are hard for a contractor to meet, the bar is set lower for a 'worker' and it is therefore possible that a contractor could be classified as a worker in some situations.

Under Section 230(3) of ERA 1996 a worker is an individual who has entered into or works under a contract of employment, or any other contract of employment, whereby the individual undertakes to do or perform personally any work or service for another party to the contract. The definition of a worker is very wide and will include employees as well as those individuals who provide personal services under a contract, provided the other party to that contract is not a client or customer. Therefore, where an individual is on balance a contractor but there are some factors that point towards an employment

Contractors

relationship, it is possible they could qualify as a worker.

Employment Tribunals look at various factors when determining if an employment relationship exists. The factors to be considered when determining whether an individual is a contractor involve the same factors that arise when deciding if someone is an employee. The following should be considered:

- *Personal Service.* Is there an obligation to perform work personally? If there can be no substitution of the individual and the nature of the duties cannot be delegated then this would indicate worker status.
- *Mutuality of Obligation.* Is there an obligation on the employer to provide work and an obligation on the individual to accept that work? If the employer provides specified work to the individual and the individual has to accept that work, then this would indicate worker status.
- *Control.* Is there overall control over the contractual relationship, such as the power to terminate and to subject the individual to disciplinary procedures? If the contractor is controlled in the manner in which they carry out their tasks, in that they are told what days to perform their work, their working hours, they use equipment provided by the employer and are subject to the employer's rules and policies, this would indicate worker status.

None of these factors on its own is definitive. Consideration should also be made to the surrounding circumstances when determining the nature of the relationship, such as:

- *Economic reality of the situation.* Where the individual is considered to be in business on their own, they are unlikely to be considered to be a worker. Similarly, the tax status of the individual may be considered, i.e. there are no PAYE or National Insurance contributions administration for contractors.
- *Integration.* Where an individual is seen as an integral and involved part of the business, this can help to demonstrate their status as a worker. Long periods working for one business may be more likely to signal an employment relationship, as would inclusion of an individual into any company benefit schemes.

Case law

There have been a number of recent cases where the Courts have grappled with the employment status of contractors. The difficulties lie in the fact that each case turns on its own particular facts and there are a range of factors (as set out above) that may point towards an employment relationship in varying degrees. A few key cases are set out below.

In the case of *Redrow Homes (Yorkshire) Limited v. Wright, Roberts and others* (2004), the Court of Appeal rejected the argument that bricklayers engaged on a sub-contracted basis were not workers because there was no contractual obligation to perform work personally. It held that they were workers because there was a mutuality of obligation and the scheme of payment pointed in the direction of contracts with individual bricklayers to do the work personally.

In reaching this decision, the Court upheld the earlier judgment in *Byrne Bros Ltd v. Baird* (2002), where it was found that while building labourers had been designated as sub-contractors in the contracts, they were in fact workers because they were personally required to perform work and services.

Contractors

With regard to the issue of whether contractors are 'employees,' the EAT stressed in the case of *Autoclenz Ltd v. J Belcher and Ors* (2008) that where the parties clearly intend the relationship to be one of self-employment then, unless this is a sham or intended to mislead, any agreement to this effect would be upheld. In this case, car valeters who signed an agreement stating they were self-employed were found not to be employees; however as they were providing their services in a situation where the contractor was their client, they were held to be workers under the ERA.

In circumstances where self-employed sole traders perform their services personally as part of a business, as in the case of *Bacica v. Muir* (2006), the Court has held that such persons would not qualify as workers.

A further situation where the Court has found that contractors do not qualify as workers came in the recent case of *MPG Contractors Ltd v. (1) A. England (junior) and (2) A. England (senior)* (2009). In this case, the Court held that a contractual term allowing a building contractor to veto substitutes found by its sub-contractors did not impede the sub-contractors' rights of substitution. It was therefore held that there was no contract for personal services, and so the contractors were not 'workers' within the meaning of the Working Time Regulations.

Employment rights

Contractors will generally have no employment rights. However, in some circumstances where a contractor may fall under the definition of a worker, they will have some employment rights and, if in the unlikely event they are found to be an employee, they will have the full range of employment rights.

Workers' rights are becoming more wide-ranging and at present cover the areas set out below:

- Protection against unlawful deduction from wages.
- Working Time Regulations, i.e. the right not to work more than 48 hours per week, the right to rest breaks and the right to paid annual leave.
- Right to minimum wage.
- Protection for making a protected disclosure.
- Protection under the Data Protection Act 1998.
- Right to receive equal pay.
- Right not be discriminated on grounds of sex, race, disability, religion or beliefs, sexual orientation anf not to be victimised for alleging discrimination.
- Right as a part-time worker not to be treated less favourably.

If a business wishes to make sure that a contractor engaged to do a job does not bring an employment claim, it would be helpful to the business if the contractual documentation expressly states that the contractor is not an employee or worker, although the label given to the relationship by the parties will not be decisive. If the relationship has changed over time, it is possible that a Tribunal might find that someone who started work as a contractor has subsequently become a worker or even an employee.

A business hiring a contractor should ensure that the contract is not personalised, that it contains substitution provisions and that it does not contain mutuality of obligation. The business needs to ensure that the contractor is not treated on a day-by-day basis as an employee. This means that, for example, contractors should not be entitled to any employee benefits.

Contractors

If there are any factors that may point to an employment relationship existing, then the business should be careful that the contractor is not denied their worker, or, in some cases, their employee, rights. While determination of employment status remains highly subjective, businesses should err on the side of caution when engaging contractors.

> *See also*: Employment status, p.154; Part-time workers, p.308; Self-employment, p.357.

Sources of further information

See www.inlandrevenue.gov.uk/manuals/esmmanual/index.htm for an employment status manual.

Workplace Law Group's ***Working with contractors 2008: Special Report*** is essential reading for those involved in the appointment of contractors for work activities. It is designed to provide workplace managers with everything they need to know to ensure they, and the contractors they employ, meet their duties under employment law. For more information visit www.workplacelaw.net/Bookshop/SpecialReports.

Criminal records

Howard Lewis-Nunn, Rochman Landau

Key points

Other than in some excepted situations, employees or applicants are not obliged to disclose their past or 'spent' convictions once the appropriate period of time for their conviction has elapsed. The appropriate length of time before the conviction is spent depends on the nature of the sentence.

Sentences of imprisonment for more than 30 months are never spent.

Individuals can be required to disclose spent convictions when applying for jobs in certain sectors, where trust is a particular concern.

Legislation

The principal legislation dealing with the disclosure of spent convictions is the Rehabilitation of Offenders Act 1974. Various amendments have been made by Regulations, chiefly to identify sectors of work where employers are entitled to know about spent convictions.

Criminal records are also classed as 'sensitive personal data' under the Data Protection Act 1998 and so employers will be required to obtain the individual's explicit consent before making use of such information.

Rehabilitation of Offenders Act 1974

The Act provides that, unless there is an express exception, once a conviction has been spent an individual is a 'rehabilitated person'. The Act sets out a tariff for the timescales before various sentences are classed as spent. Sentences exceeding 30 months, for life or at Her Majesty's Pleasure are never spent.

Once a conviction is spent, an individual is not required to give any details and is treated as if he had not been convicted. Any requirement that imposes an obligation (whether legal or contractual) on an individual to disclose information is deemed not to require disclosure of spent convictions or any related matters and he is not required to answer any questions in a way that will reveal his spent convictions. He shall not be prejudiced in law for any failure to disclose his spent convictions. An employer may still ask for disclosure of current (i.e. unspent) convictions.

Consequently, unless an exception applies, an employer has no valid grounds for refusing to employ someone or dismissing him for possessing or failing to disclose a spent conviction. A dismissal on these grounds is likely to be unfair. However, it is not clear what remedy could be pursued for a refusal to employ someone, as an individual must have one year's employment in order to claim unfair dismissal.

Exceptions

A number of occupations have been identified where spent convictions must be disclosed and an individual may therefore be dismissed or excluded from employment because of a spent conviction.

Criminal records

The professions include barristers, solicitors, accountants, teachers, police officers, healthcare professionals, officers of building societies, chartered psychologists, actuaries, registered foreign lawyers, legal executives, and receivers appointed by the Court of Protection. More recently, the exempted occupations have been widened to include anyone who would have access to persons under the age of 18 or vulnerable adults (this includes the elderly and mentally impaired). Organisations employing individuals in any of these occupations are entitled to ask about spent convictions and the potential employee is required to give details.

Criminal Records Bureau

The Government established the Criminal Records Bureau (CRB) as a central point for employers to obtain details of potential employees' or volunteers' criminal convictions. Currently, this system is only available to organisations within the categories of employment that are exempt under the Rehabilitation of Offenders Act 1974, and in particular those working with persons under 18 or vulnerable adults. Two types of disclosure certificates can be obtained at present – Standard and Enhanced Disclosure. Both Standard and Enhanced Disclosure provide details of all convictions including spent convictions as well as cautions, reprimands and warnings held on the police national computer. Where the post involves contact with children the disclosure will also contain any information on lists held by the Department of Health and the Department for Education and Skills. Enhanced disclosure is intended to provide a more thorough check when extensive and unsupervised contact with persons under 18 and particularly vulnerable adults is likely. This is mostly for positions involving social, personal or medical care. It is also available for judicial appointments and for certain positions where licences are required for gaming and lottery. As well as the standard disclosure information, enhanced disclosure includes any information relevant and proportionate to the position applied for held by local police forces that may not necessarily amount to a caution or conviction.

The threshold for what is relevant and proportionate is relatively low. In the case of *R (on the application of John Pinnington) v. Chief Constable of Thames Valley Police* (2008) it was sufficient that the Chief Constable reasonably believed that the allegations disclosed might be true and might be relevant to the post applied for by the applicant. It is therefore up to the employer what it does with the information. Whilst the courts have advised against employers operating a blanket policy of requiring a clean check, employers are likely to be reluctant to take risks if information is disclosed. The results of any check would have to be considered very carefully in the context of the overall application and the post applied for. Details of the disclosure are provided to the registered body making the application and the individual who is the subject of the application. In limited situations the CRB may provide the employer only with additional information which is not to be disclosed to the individual. There is no legal requirement for employers to make CRB checks on employees or volunteers unless the work is in a 'regulated' setting such as a care home or school.

Changes

From October 2009 a new level of checks will be phased in. These will be administered by the Independent Safeguarding Authority (*see below*). Even if they are not legally required it may still be advisable to carry out CRB checks. Where there is no legal requirement to carry out checks it is a matter of risk

Criminal records

management for each organisation whether to do so. In response to criticisms that the CRB regime was discouraging volunteers, the Government's guidance suggests that a risk assessment should be carried out to determine whether checks should be required and they should not be carried out 'just in case'.

CRB checks are free for volunteers although an umbrella body may charge an administration fee for handling an application.

In order to apply for disclosure, employers who are entitled to use the service must either be registered with the CRB or apply through an 'Umbrella body', which is registered. Umbrella bodies can be used by any employer who does not wish to register itself directly with the CRB. Registered bodies are required to abide by the CRB's Code of Practice. Umbrella bodies are required to ensure that their clients abide by the code also. The CRB may audit the user in order to ensure compliance.

Disclosure in Scotland is managed by Disclosure Scotland. Both Disclosure Scotland and CRB provide information relating to convictions in the whole of the UK. The location of the position in question will determine which agency to contact.

The Code's key requirements:

- Registered users should have a written policy on the recruitment of ex-offenders to be given to all job applicants. Umbrella bodies must ensure that their clients have a policy in place and provide a model one to the client if necessary.
- All applicants who will be subject to a CRB request must be informed of the use to which the disclosure information will be put.
- Where a position will require a CRB check the application form should state that a disclosure request will only be made in the event of a successful application and if a conviction is disclosed this will not necessarily mean that the offer of employment is withdrawn.
- The contents of the disclosure should be discussed with the individual before any offer is withdrawn. The existence of the Code should be brought to their attention and the employer's policy on the treatment of ex-offenders made available.
- Only authorised personnel should have access to the disclosure, which includes storing it securely. There should be a written policy on secure storage of disclosure records. It is a criminal offence to pass it on to unauthorised persons.
- Disclosure should not be kept for longer than is necessary and should be securely destroyed.
- Umbrella bodies are required to ensure that their clients observe the Code and that they are in one of the exempt categories under the Rehabilitation of Offenders Act 1974 who can ask about convictions.

Portability

Some individuals may hold more than one position that requires a CRB check and so organisations may be tempted to accept the disclosure results for a previous position if it is sufficiently recent. This is known as portability. The CRB does not support this and so organisations that re-use disclosure results do so at their own risk. However, as part of a risk assessment, unless there is a legal requirement for the employer to carry out its own check, a check carried out by another organisation may be relied on. One risk to relying on previous CRB checks is that they will not reveal whether any additional information was provided to the employer that was not disclosed

Criminal records

to the individual. In deciding whether to make a fresh check the following factors should be considered:

- Is there a legal requirement to obtain a check?
- Is the existing check at the same level required for the new post?
- Is the position for which the check was obtained similar to the new post?
- Have all the checks the organisation needs been carried out?
- Has the identity of the person holding the check been authenticated?
- Is the applicant still living at the same address as the one to which the check relates?
- Has the applicant given consent to contact the organisation that carried out the previous check?
- Is the check more than six months' old?

Where a previous check is being relied on, steps should be taken to confirm the authenticity of the check, such as contacting the person who countersigned the certificate for the applying organisation to confirm the registration number and that the details match. The new employer should ask the previous employer if there is any additional information of which they are aware. While they cannot provide the details they can confirm or deny its existence. If there does appear to be further information, a new check is advisable; however, there may be difficulties in explaining to the applicant why a fresh application is required.

Overseas applicants

Disclosure from the CRB will have limited information on overseas convictions and so records for anyone who has spent a substantial amount of time outside of the UK may not be complete. It is possible to carry out the equivalent of a CRB check in some countries and the CRB can provide guidance on this. The employer can also ask the individual to obtain the equivalent disclosure where he is resident overseas.

Future changes

The CRB has been proposing to introduce a basic disclosure certificate intended for all types of employment for some time, but this has yet to materialise. This will be issued solely to individuals and cover only unspent convictions. Employers may therefore require this as a matter of course from individuals before offering them employment.

Independent Safeguarding Authority

The Government has created the Independent Safeguarding Authority (ISA) to operate a new vetting and barring scheme with the CRB. This is due to start from 12 October 2009. It is intended to be an enhancement of the current disclosure process aimed at preventing individuals who are considered unsuitable from working with children and vulnerable adults from doing so. All employees and volunteers working with these groups will be required to register with the Authority. This will be phased in over a number of years and the ISA registration will be transferable. This scheme will replace the separate lists held by government departments.

Employers, social services and any professional regulators will be under a duty to provide to the ISA any information they have about individuals who may pose a risk. It will also be a criminal offence for an individual to apply for or undertake work with vulnerable groups and for employers who knowingly take them on.

Registration with the ISA will be phased in over several years. Once an individual is registered, their status will be continuously monitored and reassessed should new information come to light.

Criminal records

See also: Data protection, p.84; Interviewing, p.240; Personnel files, p.317; Recruitment and selection, p.335; Unlawfully procuring information, p.403.

Sources of further information

Information Commissioner: www.ico.gov.uk

Criminal Records Bureau: www.crb.gov.uk

Chartered Institute of Personnel and Development: www.cipd.co.uk

Disclosure Scotland: www.disclosurescotland.co.uk

Independent Safeguarding Authority: www.isa-gov.org.uk

National Association for the Care and Resettlement of Offenders (Nacro): www.nacro.org.uk

CIPD accredited training

work place law ♥
hr, health and safety

The Chartered Institute of Personnel and Development (CIPD) has introduced a new course structure which replaces the current certificate level courses. The popular Certificate in Personnel Practice (CPP) will be replaced by the new **Certificate in HR Practice (CHRP)** – Level 3 course in early 2010. The change will be phased in over the next 12 months and Workplace Law will be one of the first training providers in the UK to offer this new course to students.

As a centre of excellence for CIPD courses, Workplace Law will be putting all of the passion and experience developed running the certificate level courses into the new format.

Certificate in HR Practice (CHRP)

The new structure is intended to be more easily accessible to students and will represent the core competencies needed to operate at a particular level in HR practice.

The Certificate in HR Practice (CHRP) provides a firm foundation in all the areas of personnel and is a natural study route towards undertaking the CIPD's Professional Development Scheme (PDS). It will help you develop practical, relevant skills and above all, will give you the confidence to be more effective at work.

Workplace Law's fast-track Certificate in HR Practice (CHRP) courses take between 15 and 20 weeks to complete. A combination of e-learning and intensive classroom study in Cambridge or London leaves you free to study when you want, but with plenty of opportunity to interact with our expert tutors and fellow students during our core residential sessions. What's more, the flexible course programme cuts the cost of travelling and saves your company money by reducing the time you spend away from the workplace.

Certificate in Employment Relations, Law and Practice (CERLAP)

Workplace Law's fast-track course in employment relations, law and practice ideal for all those involved in Human Resource management or embarking on a career in personnel.

The Certificate in Employment Relations, Law and Practice (CERLAP) is designed to give students a comprehensive introduction to the legal framework in employment relations. The course also offers a fast route to associate membership of the Chartered Institute of Personnel and Development (CIPD).

Benefits

- Speed and flexibility of e-learning
- Fast-track courses
- Quality tutor contact time
- Study when you want
- Cut down travelling costs
- Saves your company £££s
- CIPD approved

For more information on our 2010 course dates call 0871 777 8881 or visit cipd.workplacelaw.net

Data protection

Elizabeth Upton, Bird and Bird

Key points

The Data Protection Act 1998 (the Act) came into force on 1 March 2000, replacing the Data Protection Act 1984. The Act offers more protection to individuals than the 1984 Act and imposes more onerous obligations on organisations that process personal data. The Act also gives individuals certain rights in respect of their personal information.

It is important for companies to know about the Act and whether it applies to them, particularly because of certain criminal offences that may be committed as a result of handling personal data incorrectly.

Legislation
- Data Protection Act 1998.
- Freedom of Information Act 2000.
- Criminal Justice and Immigration Act 2008.

Does the Data Protection Act apply to your company?

In short, the Act regulates the processing of personal data which is either held on a computer or intended to be held on a computer, or held in paper form in what the Act describes as a 'relevant filing system'. In order to work out if the Act applies to the activities carried out by your company, it is necessary to look at these and other definitions in the Act in further detail.

Definitions

'Personal data'

This is defined as information that relates to living individuals who can be identified from it (whether from the data on its own or when used in conjunction with other information in the possession of, or likely to come into the possession of, the data controller). This may therefore include details such as postal address or email address as well as facts and opinions held about an individual. The EU Article 29 Working Party, which helps develop European data protection policy, issued guidance in 2007 (WP136, 20 June 2007) on the meaning of personal data, which was followed by guidance on the same topic issued by the Information Commissioner on 21 August 2007. Both sets of guidance look at all the elements of the definition in greater detail and provide useful examples of what is caught by the definition. However, truly anonymous data such as aggregated statistics will not be regulated by the Act. The Act also recognises that some data is to be regarded as sensitive personal data and can be processed only under strict conditions. Such data is information on racial or ethnic origin, political opinions, religious or other beliefs, trade union membership, health, sex life, and criminal proceedings or convictions.

'Processing'

Under the Act this means 'obtaining, recording or holding information or data or carrying out any operation or set of operations on the information or data'. This is a very wide definition, and if your

Data protection

> **Facts**
> - Over 50 nations have personal data protection laws that regulate the handling of consumer information by businesses.
> - The Information Commissioner's Office in the UK received over 25,000 complaints in relation to a breach of the Data Protection Act in 2008/09.
> - Around 25% of complaints to the Information Commissioner's Office relate to Subject Access Requests.
> - In a 2009 survey, 86% of individuals said that they were aware of their right to see information held about them.

company holds personal data then it is likely that any activities carried out by the company in relation to such data will fall within its scope. Processing may only be carried out in accordance with the data protection principles, which are outlined below.

'Data controller'

This is defined as someone who determines how and for what purpose personal data is processed. Obligations in the Act fall mainly on data controllers. This is likely to be the company rather than the individual workplace manager. Lesser obligations fall on data processors who are those people (other than employees of a data controller) who process personal data on behalf of a data controller.

'Relevant filing system'

The key elements of this definition are that there must be a set of information, e.g. a grouping together of things with a common theme or element. It follows that a mere list of names is unlikely to amount to a set of information about individuals. The set must be structured, by reference either to individuals or to criteria relating to individuals, and specific information relating to an individual must be readily accessible. Recent case law has suggested that this definition is to be interpreted narrowly and that (a) files need to indicate clearly at the outset of the search whether personal data is held within the system; and (b) there is a sufficiently sophisticated and detailed means of readily indicating whether and where in an individual file or files specific criteria or information can be readily located. The ICO has published a list of FAQs on relevant filing systems, giving examples of what may constitute such a system.

Data controllers' responsibilities

Having worked out if the Act applies to the information held by your company, you should then consider what responsibilities lie with the data controller.

Anyone processing personal data as a data controller must comply with the eight enforceable principles of good practice. These say that data must:

1. be fairly and lawfully obtained and processed;
2. be processed for limited purposes and not in any manner incompatible with those purposes;
3. be adequate, relevant and not excessive;
4. be accurate and where necessary kept up to date;
5. not be kept for longer than necessary;
6. be processed in line with the data subject's rights;

Data protection

7. be secure; and
8. not be transferred to countries outside the EEA without adequate protection.

Most of these points are self-explanatory, but it is worth mentioning the first principle in further detail. This principle requires that the processing of data must be fair and lawful. The Act states that, in order to ensure fairness, data controllers have to ensure that:

- data is obtained in accordance with the fair processing code. This requires data controllers to make certain information readily available to individuals (e.g. the name of the data controller and the purposes for which the data will be processed);
- certain pre-conditions are met to justify the processing of personal data. At least one condition in Schedule 2 of the Act must be met for any processing of personal data and at least one condition in Schedule 3 must be met if sensitive personal data is being processed; and
- the individuals must not be misled or deceived as to the purposes for which their data will be processed.

Access requests

The data controller also needs to be aware of the data subject's rights when processing personal data. Under the Act, data subjects are granted four key rights:

1. A right of access to personal data held;
2. A right to prevent processing that might cause substantial damage and distress;
3. A right to prevent automated decision-taking; and
4. A right to prevent processing for direct marketing purposes.

Specific rules apply in relation to direct marketing, whether it is carried out by email, telephone, fax, or SMS messaging.

In relation to subject access, data controllers should be aware that generally an individual has a right to be provided with copies of all information held about that individual within 40 days of a request being made. Although there are limited grounds for withholding certain information, systems should be structured so that requests can be satisfied as easily as possible.

Transferring data

It should also be noted, in relation to the eighth principle, that 'adequate protection' is legally defined rather than being a matter of judgement for the company intending to transfer the information. Personal data can only be transferred to a third country outside the EEA if:

- the EU Commission has made a finding of adequacy in respect of the third country;
- an assessment of adequacy has been made by the data controller itself following the guidelines set out in the Act;
- there is no adequacy but the parties have put in place adequate safeguards such as the use of Commission-authorised standard contracts or binding corporate rules; or
- one of the limited derogations to the eighth principle applies (e.g. the individual has consented to the transfer or the transfer is necessary for the performance of a contract between the data controller and the individual).

Notification

Most data controllers will need to notify the Information Commissioner, in broad terms, of the purposes of their processing, the personal data processed, the recipients of the personal data processed and, if relevant, any transfers of data overseas. This information is made publicly available on a register. Under the Act,

Data protection

data controllers must comply with the data protection principles even if they are exempt from the requirement to notify.

Criminal offences

Data controllers can commit criminal offences under the Act. These offences include:

- failing to notify the Information Commissioner either of the processing being undertaken or of any of the changes that have been made to that processing. One of the largest fines that has been seen is a fine of £5,000 (although in this case, the individual had committed a number of breaches of the Act – see '*Consulting Association*' below); and
- failing to respond to an information notice or breaching an enforcement notice issued by the Information Commissioner.

Individuals can also commit criminal offences if they obtain, disclose or sell personal data without the consent of the data controller (known as a Section 55 offence – see '*IT security*,' p.244). The Information Commissioner regards this as the most serious of offences that can be committed under the Act and the Criminal Justice and Immigration Act 2008 recently enhanced penalties for those who disclose information for the illegal buying and selling of data. These penalties will be implemented via secondary legislation, which will introduce custodial sentences for such sentences of up to 12 months (for Magistrates Court convictions) or two years (for conviction on indictment). For more detail on these types of offences, and the practical steps that can be taken to protect against this type of attack, see '*Unlawfully procuring information*,' p.403, and '*IT Security*,' p.244.

The Criminal Justice and Immigration Act also provides the Information Commissioner with a power to impose monetary penalties for certain breaches of the Act. The new power only applies to serious breaches of the Act and will only arise where there have been deliberate breaches of the Act and where the Commissioner thinks that this kind of breach is likely to cause substantial damage or distress. Fines can also be levied for this kind of serious breach if the data controller knew or ought to have known that there was a risk of serious breach which would be likely to cause substantial damage or distress, and failed to take reasonable steps to prevent this.

The Consulting Association

In early 2009, the Information Commissioner's Office announced that it would be taking action against the Consulting Association. This organisation operated a database containing details of 3,213 construction workers, including details of their personal relationships, trade union activity, and employment history It is understood that over 40 construction companies (including high profile companies) used the Consulting Association to obtain information about workers prior to employing them. The Information Commissioner's Office assumed control of the database in order to allow members of the public to ascertain whether they were listed on the database. The ICO's investigation was reported widely in the media.

After an investigation, the Information Commissioner's Office prosecuted the owner of the database. As the Information Commissioner's Office did not, at the time of its investigation, have the power to impose monetary penalties for breaches of the Act, it could only bring action against the database owner for failing to notify the Information Commissioner's Office that it was processing personal data. He was fined £5,000 in the Crown Court for this failure.

Data protection

At the time of writing no action has been brought against the construction companies that used the Consulting Association.

Employment Practices Code

The Information Commissioner has issued a Code of Practice to help companies ensure that they are complying with the data protection legislation with regard to their dealings with their employees. The Code gives employers specific guidance on:

- recruitment and selection processes;
- how best to keep employment records;
- how to monitor their employees at work; and
- issues relating to workers' health.

In addition, the Code provides information about workers' rights under the Act.

Freedom of Information Act 2000

Finally, it should also be noted that the Freedom of Information Act gives individuals the right to request information from a Public Authority. On receipt of the request, the Authority is obliged to:

- tell the individual whether or not it holds the information; and (where applicable)
- provide the individual with the information requested.

See also: Criminal records, p.78; IT security, p.244; Medical records, p.257; Personnel files, p.317; Private life, p.327; Confidential waste, p.410; Unlawfully procuring information, p.433.

Sources of further information

Further information on Freedom of Information may be found on the Ministry of Justice website: www.justice.gov.uk.

ICO guidance on personal information: www.ico.gov.uk/about_us/news_and_views/current_topics/what_is_personal_data.aspx

ICO FAQs on relevant filing systems: www.ico.gov.uk/upload/documents/library/data_protection/detailed_specialist_guides/technical_guidance_note_faqs_relevant_filing_systems.pdf

Employment Practices Code: www.ico.gov.uk/for_organisations/topic_specific_guides/employment.aspx

Workplace Law Group's ***Data Protection Policy and Management Guide v.4.0*** has been published to help employers understand and meet their obligations under data protection legislation and to provide clear guidance for employers on their responsibilities when handling sensitive personal data. For more information go to www.workplacelaw.net/bookshop/policiesAndProcedures.

Directors' responsibilities

Naomi Branston and Andrew Telling, Taylor Wessing

Key points
Company directors are primarily responsible for the management of their companies and generally, their duties are owed to the company. However, they also owe duties to the owners as a whole. In addition, they have responsibilities in respect of the company's employees and its trading partners, and under statute these duties may be supplemented or modified by a company's memorandum and articles of association. Furthermore, many directors will be subject to service agreements (contracts of employment) which may augment these duties.

Directors are responsible for ensuring that the company complies with the various requirements imposed upon it by law.

Although generally the company is liable for any failure to comply with legal requirements, in certain circumstances the directors can be held personally liable where the default was due to their neglect or connivance.

Legislation
- Health and Safety at Work etc. Act 1974.
- Companies Acts 1985, 1989 and 2006.
- Insolvency Act 1986.
- Company Directors Disqualification Act 1986.
- Value Added Tax Act 1994.
- Management of Health and Safety at Work Regulations 1999.
- Corporate Manslaughter and Corporate Homicide Act 2007.

Directors' duties

Companies Act 2006
The Companies Act 2006 (CA 2006) codifies certain key duties of directors. It introduces a statutory statement of seven general duties:

1. A duty to act in accordance with the company's constitution and only to exercise powers for the purposes for which they are conferred.
2. A duty to act in a way which a director considers, in good faith, would be most likely to promote the success of the company for the benefit of its members as a whole.
3. A duty to exercise independent judgement.
4. A duty to exercise reasonable care, skill and diligence.
5. A duty to avoid conflicts of interest.
6. A duty not to accept benefits from third parties.
7. A duty to declare to the other directors an interest in a proposed transaction or arrangement with the company.

The first four of these duties took effect from 1 October 2007. The remaining three, which relate to conflicts of interest, took effect in October 2008.

These duties are (apart from the duty to exercise reasonable care, skill and diligence) all fiduciary duties. They are expressed to replace the existing common law duties but will continue to

Directors' responsibilities

be interpreted by reference to the body of case law in this area.

As before, these duties will be owed to the company and (subject to the new statutory derivative action enabling shareholders to bring a claim on behalf of the company) only the company can enforce these duties.

CA 2006 also extends the common law derivative action, making it easier for shareholders to bring a claim on behalf of the company against directors and others for negligence, default, breach of duty (including the new general duties) or breach of trust, where a prima facie case is disclosed and the court gives permission for the claim to continue.

Duty to act within powers

A director must act in accordance with the company's constitution which, for this purpose, includes resolutions or decisions made by the company in accordance with its articles of association of a company, as well as the articles of association themselves.

Duty to promote the success of the company

In fulfilling this duty, directors must have regard to a statutory non-exhaustive list of factors, namely:

- the likely consequences of any decision in the long term;
- the interests of the company's employees;
- the need to foster the company's business relationships with suppliers, customers and others;
- the impact of the company's operations on the community and the environment;
- the desirability of the company maintaining a reputation for high standards of business conduct; and
- the need to act fairly as between members of the company.

This duty extends and replaces the common law duty on directors to act in good faith and in the best interests of the company.

The decision as to what will promote the success of the company, and what constitutes such success, is one for a director's good faith judgement. For a commercial company, 'success' will usually mean a long-term increase in value.

Duty to exercise independent judgement

This duty is likely to be most relevant where a director wishes to bind himself to a future course of action which might be seen as 'fettering the discretion' of the director to make future decisions. It is not infringed by a director acting in a way authorised by the company's constitution or acting in accordance with an agreement duly entered into by the company that restricts the future exercise of discretion by its directors.

Duty of skill and care

A director of a company must exercise reasonable care, skill and diligence. The standard expected of him is not only the general knowledge, skill and experience he has (for example, a particular expertise in financial matters), but also the general knowledge, skill and experience that may reasonably be expected given his position and responsibilities to the company.

Conflicts of interest

A director must not use information gained by him as a director to further his own interests, nor must he seek to apply company assets for his own gain. For example, a director must not receive commission on a transaction between the company and a third party or offer to take up, on a private basis, work offered to the company.

Directors' responsibilities

A director must disclose any direct or indirect personal interests in a contract and will have to account for any profit made unless he complies with the requirement for disclosure before the contract was entered into.

Since October 2008, new statutory duties relating to conflicts of interests have come into force under CA 2006. These include a statutory duty on a director to avoid a situation in which he has, or can have, a direct or indirect interest that conflicts, or may conflict, with the interests of the company, unless the situation cannot reasonably be regarded as likely to give rise to a conflict of interest.

This applies, in particular, to the exploitation of any property, information or opportunity (and it is immaterial whether the company could take advantage of the property, information or opportunity).

Directors will also have a duty not to accept benefits from third parties, except where the benefit is not likely to give rise to a conflict of interest (in fact, most directors' service agreements will have an express prohibition on accepting benefits or 'kickbacks' from any third party irrespective of whether or not a conflict of interest might arise).

In addition, directors will be subject to a statutory duty to declare the nature and extent of any direct or indirect interest in a proposed transaction or arrangement with the company. No declaration will be needed where:

- the director is not aware of the interest or the transaction in question (unless he ought reasonably to be aware of it);
- it cannot reasonably be regarded as likely to give rise to a conflict of interest;
- the other directors are already aware of it (or ought reasonably to be aware); or
- it concerns terms of his service contract being considered by the board or a board committee.

Directors will also have a statutory obligation (although not a fiduciary duty) to declare any direct or indirect interest in an existing transaction or arrangement with the company.

Duties to employees

While a director owes no common law duty to consider the interests of the workforce, and a director's duties are owed to the company, CA 2006 recognises the principle that the interests of the workforce fall within the wider picture of the interests of the company, as the interests of employees are one of several matters that directors must have regard to when satisfying their duty to act in the way they consider to be most likely to promote the success of the company.

Directors must comply with employment law in dealings with employees. In some circumstances, directors personally can be sued for unfair work practices such as race, sex, disability and other discrimination. Directors must ensure the company complies with any new employment laws.

Financial responsibilities

Accounts

CA 2006 requires directors to maintain accounting records that:

- show the company's transactions and its financial position;
- enable the directors to ensure that accounts required under CA 2006 comply with the CA 2006 requirements;
- contain entries of all receipts and payments, including details of sales

Directors' responsibilities

and purchases of goods, and a record of assets and liabilities; and
- show stock held at the end of each year.

Records must be kept at the company's registered office (unless the directors specify a different location) and retained for a period of six years for a public company or three years for a private company.

Annual audited accounts, consisting of a profit and loss account, must be approved by the members of the company (if it is a public company) at a general meeting (usually the AGM) and then filed with the Registrar of Companies within nine months of the end of the company's financial year (six months for a public company).

These time periods remain ten months and seven months for private and public companies respectively, for financial years beginning before 6 April 2008. CA 2006 has relaxed the requirement for private companies to have their accounts approved by members.

Private companies no longer have a statutory requirement to lay their accounts before the company in general meetings for financial years ending on or after 1 October 2007.

Statutory returns, including the annual report and accounts, the annual return and notice of changes to directors and secretaries, must be filed with the Registrar of Companies on time.

Failure to comply with these requirements renders the company liable to a penalty and directors liable to a fine.

Directors are also responsible for filing tax returns.

Financial management

Directors must exercise prudence in the financial management of the company. In the event of insolvency, directors can find themselves personally liable to creditors where it can be shown that they acted outside of their powers or in breach of their duties or were engaged in wrongful or fraudulent trading.

The latter offences will be committed where a director continues to incur liabilities on behalf of the company where he knows or ought to have known that the company was, or inevitably would become, insolvent or there was no reasonable prospect of repaying debts.

CA 2006 also contains new provisions in respect of annual reporting documents and accounts. Directors have a new obligation, since April 2008, not to approve accounts unless they give a true and fair view of the financial position of the company (or of the companies included in the group accounts, to the extent that this concerns members of the company).

Other duties

Directors must maintain various statutory books at the company's registered office including:

- a register of members;
- a register of mortgages and charges;
- a register of debenture holders; and
- a register of directors.

An annual return must be filed with the Registrar of Companies within 28 days of either the anniversary of its incorporation or made-up date of the company's previous annual return.

Directors must ensure that minutes are taken at board meetings, giving a record of all decisions taken.

Directors' responsibilities

Checklist: practical steps for directors
All directors should:

- ensure that they are fully aware of their new duties under CA 2006 and that their board processes reflect these new duties;
- check the company's memorandum and articles of association to establish the scope of their powers;
- ensure that minutes are maintained;
- be alert to conflicts of interest between the company and themselves as individuals;
- always comply with employment law;
- ensure that the company operates a comprehensive system for assessing and minimising health and safety risks;
- keep informed about the company's financial position – ignorance will not save them from facing personal liability in certain circumstances;
- be very clear about what their service agreements require of them – often their obligations in such agreements are more onerous than their statutory or common law obligations; and
- make sure that the company obtains insurance to protect them in the event of their facing personal liability.

Directors' indemnities
Companies are prohibited from exempting a director from any liability he may incur in connection with any negligence, default, breach of duty or breach of trust by him in relation to the company, unless the provision constitutes a 'qualifying third party indemnity provision' (QTPIP). For the indemnity to be a valid QTPIP the director must not be indemnified against:

- liability the director incurs to the company or a group company;
- fines imposed in criminal proceedings or by regulatory bodies, i.e. the FSA;
- legal costs of criminal proceedings where the director is convicted;
- legal costs of civil proceedings brought by the company or a group company, where judgement is given against the director; or
- liability the director incurs in connection with applications under Sections 144 or 727 CA 1985 (or Sections 661 or 1157 CA 2006) for which the court refuses to grant the director relief.

Companies can therefore indemnify directors against liabilities to third parties, except for legal costs of an unsuccessful defence of criminal proceedings or fines imposed in criminal proceedings or by regulatory bodies.

Companies can pay a director's defence costs as they are incurred, even if the action is brought by the company itself against the director. The director will, however, be liable to repay all amounts advanced if he is convicted in criminal proceedings or if judgement is given against him in civil proceedings brought by the company or an associated company.

Companies can now also provide slightly wider indemnities to directors of corporate trustees of occupational pension schemes against liability incurred in connection with the company's activities as trustee of the scheme. This is known as a 'qualifying pension scheme indemnity provision' (QPSIP).

A QTPIP or QPSIP must be disclosed in the directors' report in each year that the indemnity is in force and a copy (or summary of its terms) must be available for inspection by shareholders. The QTPIP or QPSIP must also be retained by the company for at least one year after its expiry. Departing directors may also ask for such policies to be retained after their termination as part of exit negotiations.

Directors' responsibilities

See also: Criminal records, p.78; Discrimination, p.110; Money laundering, p.279.

Sources of further information

Centre for Corporate Accountability: www.corporateaccountability.org

Institute of Directors: www.iod.uk

Comment...

Complying with the DDA – agreeing to disagree

The issue of 'compliance' with the Disability Discrimination Act has provoked quite a lot of comment in the Workplace Law forum and amongst our more vocal members. Here, Ruth Malkin and Jim Taylor air their views.

Ruth Malkin

Newsflash: you can't comply with the Disability Discrimination Act. It is *not* compliance-based legislation. If a would-be access auditor tells you, "Use my services and you will comply with the DDA," or a salesperson says, "this piece of equipment complies with the DDA," they are misleading you. You should also remember that equipment only assists you to meet your obligations under the Disability Discrimination Act if it a) works and b) is operated by someone who knows how to use it.

If you're thinking, "This woman's from the ministry of the bleeping obvious," you're right – and it's a hard job, but somebody has to do it, because the message simply isn't getting across.

Here's a little anecdote about induction loops for you. I booked a hotel for a conference. I visited the hotel beforehand to check out the access. I made the facilities manager turn the induction loop on so I could test it (I'm a hearing aid user).

Satisfied that it worked, I went away. The day of the conference dawned and I asked the hotel staff to turn the loop on in the conference room. "The facilities manager is the only person who knows how to turn it on," said the duty manager. "Well, go and get him," I said. "He doesn't work today," she said. It turned out that nobody else in the whole hotel knew how to turn the loop system on.

It so happens that I know a thing or two about induction loops. Once I had persuaded the hotel's health and safety officer that I knew how to operate a switch safely, and if he didn't open the cupboard to the induction loop mechanism, there would be merry hell to pay, I switched it on and adjusted the levels myself.

If I hadn't been able to do so, as the conference organiser I would have been liable under the Disability Discrimination Act for the omission – I; not the hotel.

It's hard to tell what is a genuinely necessary adaptation and what is a gimmick when there are loads of firms desperate to sell their products, but a good test is to ask someone who might use the feature for their opinion.

Take tactile signs. There are some environmental features that everyone has to touch – such as keypads on ATMs, and lift buttons. Obviously, raised and Braille numerals means that visually impaired people, who can't see the numerals,

Comment: Complying with the DDA

can find the right button to press on the keypad. Clearly, tactile information is necessary in this case. But tactile / Braille signs on toilet doors? Who wants to grope a toilet door? What happens if someone opens it while you're groping it? You'll get a faceful of door. So not just a waste of money, a dangerous one too. Now, the manufacturers of tactile signs for toilet doors aren't going to tell you that, are they?

The moral of this sorry tale is if you want to know what is going to protect you from claims under the Disability Discrimination Act, ask disabled people what their access requirements are. Don't just guess, because you will probably get it wrong. If you want comprehensive advice about how to meet the access requirements of a range of disabled people then ask an access group that is run by disabled people. After all, we've all had on-the-job training from the University of Life.

Jim Taylor

We are told that the DDA is not compliance-based legislation. However, we have not been told what it is based upon. That's quite important really – the DDA makes it unlawful to discriminate against disabled people, in relation to employment, goods, services and facilities, transport, education and premises.

Actually, it's about simple common sense. Unfortunately, unlike the smoking ban, this belongs to the civil offence category and, therefore, prosecution relies wholly upon the level of tolerance, or not, of an individual, to make a complaint, or start litigation.

So then, no DDA police coming round to inspect your premises or services – no chance of them slapping you round the chops with a hefty fine. Contrast that with the smoking ban? Huge amount of 'compliance' on the one hand, but on the other, well, it's only a few disabled people, aint it?

Which brings me back to what Ruth said about it not being compliance-based. Well, actually … I think it is. Compliance is defined as the act of adhering to, and demonstrating adherence to, a standard or regulation (*Wikipedia*).

OK … semantics? Splitting hairs? Possibly. Is there a point where you can 'reasonably' believe you're complying with the DDA? I look at it like this. The posted speed limit is 70mph – keep to the limit, you're complying with the law. You glance in your mirror and notice a police vehicle coming up fast behind you. I'd guess that most of us will immediately look at the speedo to check we're not breaking the law. All service providers and others should be looking in the figurative mirror for the DDA police – it's the right thing to do.

How do we go about getting DDA compliance? I'm no legal expert, but what I do know is how I would go about it, in four simplified steps. It is a robust procedure, but achievable nonetheless.

Step 1. Carry out audits of your premises, services, policies, practices and procedures.

Step 2. Train the Chairman, executives, management and frontline staff with appropriate levels of Disability Awareness and Disability Equality.

Step 3. Examine the audit results and take steps to address the issues, implement policy to ensure it stays that way. Local Authorities have a duty to conduct Impact Assessments, designed to test the

Comment: Complying with the DDA

effectiveness of any changes, you could do that too.

Step 4. Don't sit back and think, "That's it – we're done," and then file it away; you need to monitor any changes that might affect your service delivery, or recruitment procedure, or whatever – effective policies will stop that.

Now to the point Ruth made about users of Braille and tactile signage, and those people who 'grope' toilet doors with the potential to get a 'faceful' of door, whilst doing so! I couldn't disagree more. Braille and tactile signage is vitally important for people who cannot read print, and who, under the circumstances, are trying to determine the gender of the facility – before they enter.

Current best practice guidance for signage (and the 'bible' for such is the *Sign Design Guide*, published by the Joint Mobility Unit and the Sign Design Society) is that, in brief, signage should ideally be located on the wall, to the latch side of the door. In reality, if signage with Braille is located on the WC door, and someone is touching it to read it, the door will simply open inward, disappearing away from the 'groper's' touch, without them falling headlong into the facility. I personally don't know of any example of mainstream WCs in which the doors open outward.

Finally, if you need advice, certainly, consult with disabled people – consultation can be a key element in achieving outcomes. It can also be a dozen or more people, providing a dozen or more individual opinions.

My advice? Ask a professional – someone qualified, familiar with the issues, Standards and guidance. Having a disability doesn't automatically 'qualify' someone to provide advice in the built environment.

Disability legislation

Dave Allen and Steve Cooper, Butler & Young Group

Key points

The Disability Discrimination Act 1995 (DDA 1995) brought in many rights for disabled people in terms of challenging the discrimination they faced in employment, access to services, transport and education. These rights have subsequently been extended by several measures, including the Special Educational Needs and Disability Act 2001 and the Disability Discrimination Act 2005.

The DDA 1995 imposes separate (but similar) duties on employers, educators, transport providers and organisations that provide services to the public. The overriding duty is not to discriminate against a disabled person. 'Disability' includes any impairment that has a substantial and long-term adverse effect on a person's ability to carry out normal day-to-day activities. Usually, the disability must have lasted for at least 12 months or be likely to last for that period for an individual to be covered by the DDA. However, the definition of disability has been extended by the 2005 Act with respect to the point at which someone with a progressive illness is covered by the DDA 1995, and removal of the need for a mental illness to be clinically well recognised. As such, the provisions of the DDA will cover over ten million people.

To meet the duties imposed by the 1995 Act, employers, educators, transport providers and service providers may be required to make changes to the physical provisions of the buildings they use as well as addressing their organisation's policies, practices and procedures.

Legislation
- Disability Discrimination Act 1995.
- Special Educational Needs and Disability Act 2001.
- Disability Discrimination Act 2005.

Duties and claims

The governing statute is the Disability Discrimination Act 1995, as amended by the Disability Discrimination Act 2005, together with supporting Regulations and Codes of Practice.

The two key duties imposed on employers and service providers by the Act are:

1. Not treating disabled persons less favourably than persons who are not disabled, for a reason that relates to the disability, without justification. There are only limited grounds that constitute justification and they are set out in the Act; and
2. Not breaching certain duties contained in the Act.

Breach of the Act is not a criminal offence. Claims for breach of duty by service providers can be brought by individual disabled people through the civil courts or, for employment issues, through

Disability legislation

Employment Tribunals. Remedies available include unlimited compensation in the case of employment.

Duties on employers

These duties are contained in Part II of the Act. Duties are owed only to employees or job applicants, not to the public at large.

The number of people employed at the premises is not relevant. The normal definition of an employee can extend to self-employed people who provide personal services or contract workers employed by someone else (e.g. an employment business).

The employer's main duty (other than not to discriminate) is to take reasonable steps to ensure that no arrangements or physical features of the employer's premises place a disabled person at a substantial disadvantage compared to a person who is not disabled. This may involve making one or more adjustments, and include, amongst many others:

- making reasonable adjustments to premises (see *'Physical adjustments'* below);
- acquiring or modifying equipment; and
- modifying instructions or reference manuals,

but only where it is reasonable to do so. There is no obligation for an employer to make physical changes to their premises so that they are accessible to disabled people, on the basis that they may at some time in the future employ a disabled person; unlike Part III of the Act, Part II is not anticipatory. However, the employer cannot use the inaccessibility of a building or facility as a reason for not employing a disabled person unless they can demonstrate, if challenged, that it would be unreasonable for them to make any changes necessary. That will depend on the circumstances of each individual situation.

Examples of good practice are contained in a Code of Practice produced by the Disability Rights Commission (as was).

Facts

- It is estimated that disabled people spend around £40bn a year on goods and services.
- There are over two million disabled people in employment in the UK.
- Although 79% state that disabled people still face many barriers to museums, libraries and archives, many (67%) agreed that more disabled people use their services than five years ago.
- Among those establishments that were aware of having employed disabled people, 42% felt that there were advantages to doing so. This compared with only 24% of those who were not aware of having employed disabled people.
- Just over one-third of establishments (36%) report a specific approach to actively encouraging the employment of disabled people.
- 78% of disabled people think that the assumption that disabled people need more support from their colleagues and managers prevents employers from employing disabled people.
- 23% of employees think the fact that their company has never employed a disabled person before might prevent their company employing a disabled person.

Disability legislation

This is not legally binding, although in the case of a dispute, the Tribunal is likely to consider whether the employer has complied with its recommendations.

Many of these possible changes involve management responsibilities, but will have knock-on effects on workplace managers. Meeting these duties will involve a discussion with the disabled 'employee' to ascertain his/her requirements and priorities. This is important because it is not a defence for the employer to simply show that the discrimination took place without its knowledge or approval.

It should be recognised that, in the context of disability discrimination, discrimination against an employee who is disabled and who is dismissed on grounds that have no connection with the disability is not unlawful. However, this demands the keeping of meticulous records to minimise the risk of discrimination claims.

In a landmark ruling, the House of Lords decided that the duty to disabled employees can involve positive discrimination. This can entail transferring, without competitive interviews, a disabled employee from a post, the duties of which he/she can no longer undertake, to a post within their capabilities.

The Disability Discrimination Act 2005 brings (with some exceptions) the functions of Public Authorities and some other organisations not already or appropriately covered by the 1995 Act within its scope, and imposes a duty to ensure or promote equal opportunity.

Duties on service providers

These duties are contained in Part III of the Act. They apply to all organisations, of whatever size, that provide services, goods or facilities to the general public or a section of it, with or without payment. They are described as 'service providers' in this chapter.

Under the 1995 Act, the only exceptions were:

- clubs that are genuinely private; and
- public transport (but infrastructure such as bus stations is subject to the Act).

However, the provisions of the 2005 Act have now, to some extent, included these areas.

The main duties under Part III of the 1995 Act that are owed to disabled visitors are:

- not to discriminate against disabled people (unless the less favourable treatment can be justified);
- to take reasonable steps to change practices, policies and procedures that make it impossible or unreasonably difficult for disabled people to use the service (this is principally a management issue); and
- to provide auxiliary aids where this is reasonable.

One case has demonstrated that the Courts' view of the standard of service that should be offered to disabled people is that it should be one that is as close as is reasonably possible to the standard normally provided to the public at large.

Physical adjustments under Part III

Service providers are required to take reasonable steps to modify physical features of premises that make it impossible or unreasonably difficult for disabled people to use the service. The term 'physical features' includes the fabric of the building or the environment, its facilities, fittings and furnishings. Employers have a similar duty in respect of their employees, as noted above.

Disability legislation

This duty does not override any requirement to obtain any consent that may be necessary, such as planning consent, listed building consent or landlord's consent. Landlords cannot unreasonably withhold consent to make physical adjustments, regardless of what is stated in the lease.

Not all service providers have to make adjustments, or at least on the same scale. The Act only requires them to do what is reasonable in the circumstances of each individual situation. To do this, account will be taken of factors such as the size of the business, the organisation and the financial resources available to it. Other factors that may be relevant include what steps the organisation has already taken to improve accessibility, and factors such as the organisation's involvement or association with the environment (in terms of long-, medium- or short-term responsibility).

Where a building met the requirements of Part M of the Building Regulations at the time of its construction, and continues to meet them, no further adjustments will be necessary for up to ten years after the completion of the property – but this exemption applies only to those elements to which the Part M approval related. Therefore, factors such as, for example, the design of signage, taps, lighting, visual contrast, and decorations, etc., which have not previously been covered by Part M, will not be exempt.

Where this has not been previously undertaken, the Equality and Human Rights Commission (EHRC) recommends the commissioning of an access audit. Practical examples of adjustments, some of which are relatively inexpensive, include:

- management practices;
- staff training;
- employment practices;
- parking;
- approaches to buildings;
- entrances;
- horizontal and vertical circulation (lifts, stairs, handrails, corridors, doors, etc.);
- visual contrast, lighting and acoustics;
- wheelchair-accessible and standard toilet facilities;
- signage; and
- emergency egress.

Examples of reasonable steps to take are contained in the EHRC's Code of Practice, which will be admissible evidence in a civil claim for compensation.

Possible reasons for treating a disabled visitor less favourably

In limited circumstances, the DDA allows for less favourable treatment of disabled people – providing it can be justified. These circumstances may include, for example:

- when the health and safety of the disabled person or any other person is put at significant risk;
- where the disabled person is incapable of giving informed consent or entering into a legally binding agreement;
- if otherwise the service provider would be unable to provide the service;
- when an adjustment would fundamentally alter the nature of a business or service; and
- if, where a disabled customer is charged more for a service, it would cost more in materials or labour to meet his particular needs.

In the event of a claim, a service provider would need to be able to demonstrate that he or she had properly addressed the issues that gave rise to the claim. Therefore, for example, claiming that less favourable treatment towards a disabled person was justifiable on health and safety

Disability legislation

grounds, without having undertaken an appropriate risk assessment to demonstrate the legitimacy of that fact, is unlikely to be seen as appropriate. Any reasons claiming justification will also be tested against the relevant Code of Practice.

The Disability Discrimination Act 2005 (DDA 2005)

The DDA 2005 makes a number of wide-ranging amendments to the DDA 1995 and extends the scope, range, application and duties imposed by that Act. The 2005 Act addresses a number of issues that were omitted from the DDA 1995, or which had proved to be insufficient, unenforceable, or had not been brought fully into effect.

For example, under the DDA 1995, disabled people were not protected by civil rights legislation with regard to bodies exercising what are referred to as 'public functions'. These included, for example, powers of arrest and other activities that are usually only conducted by public sector bodies. As the public sector is a major employer and the provider of key public services, it was seen by Government as having a vital role in creating and promoting equality for disabled people in the way it conducts its activities, and the 2005 Act addressed this.

What does the 2005 Act cover?

The 2005 Act extends civil rights in areas such as the provision of transport services, letting of premises, the responsibilities and duties of Public Authorities, membership of private clubs, and the rights of disabled councillors. It also broadens the definition of disability contained in the DDA 1995 to provide protection for a broader range of people.

Some areas of the Act came into effect in December 2005 and the remainder in December 2006.

Public Authorities and the 2005 Act

Many of the functions carried out by a Public Authority appear as being very similar to the services they provide. However, under the DDA 1995 there were a number of areas of public sector activity where it was unclear as to whether the law would view them as a 'service' or a 'public function'. These included, for example, the provision and management of a public footpath.

The 2005 Act considers the functions carried out by Public Authorities and outlaws discrimination by them in the way they do their work – in the same way that the DDA 1995 does for service providers. Therefore, in essence, a public body will be acting unlawfully if it discriminates against disabled people:

- by treating them less favourably, for a reason related to their disability, in exercising their public function;
- by adopting practices, policies and procedures which, because of the person's disability, lead to a less favourable outcome (and which could have been avoided if the function had been carried out differently); and
- in either case, is not able to justify that treatment by one of the statutory justifications.

In addition, the duties imposed by the 2005 Act require Public Authorities to have regard to the need to:

- eliminate unlawful discrimination against disabled people;
- eliminate unlawful harassment of disabled people; and
- promote equality of opportunity for disabled people.

In doing this, public bodies are subject to a Public Sector Duty (PSD) to eliminate unlawful discrimination against disabled

Disability legislation

people, and to promote and monitor equality of opportunity.

The 2005 Act also requires public bodies to promote a 'cycle of performance improvement', a procedure that should move the public body towards greater equality for disabled people and ensure that the PSD becomes an active, outcome-based development. A specific duty imposed by the 2005 Act is for public bodies to develop a Disability Equality Scheme (DES), which must set out how the body will fulfil its duties to eliminate unlawful discrimination and the harassment of disabled people, and how it will promote equality of opportunity.

They will also be required to produce an action plan to identify how and when the DES will be monitored, reviewed and updated. The DES should be the subject of an annual review, and full revision every three years. The supporting Code of Practice provides a list of those organisations covered by the duty to produce a DES.

Justification for discrimination by public bodies

As with the duties placed on service providers and employers by the DDA 1995, the 2005 Act allows for public sector bodies to provide less favourable treatment, or, in some circumstances, fail to make a reasonable adjustment, if it can be justified. In such cases, justification may be claimed if, for example:

- there are substantiated health and safety reasons;
- the cost of undertaking any alterations is unreasonable given all the circumstances of the particular case;
- complying with the duties imposed on the body adversely affects the rights of others; or

- the Authority believes that the disabled person is incapable of entering into an enforceable agreement, or of giving informed consent.

Private clubs

Under the DDA 1995, private clubs that offer goods, services or facilities to the general public have duties under Part III not to discriminate against disabled people. However, genuine private clubs were (and in some cases, still are) not covered by the Part III duties for goods or services that are available only to their members.

The 2005 Act now places an 'anticipatory' duty on larger private clubs (more than 25 members) not to discriminate against disabled people and brings them into line with the duties already imposed by the DDA 1995 on service providers such as shops, restaurants, theatres, etc.

Definition of disability

Under the DDA 1995, people with progressive conditions such as, for example, multiple sclerosis (MS), HIV infection and cancer were not covered by the definition of disability until the point at which their impairment has an adverse effect on their ability to carry out normal day-to-day activities. Therefore, someone with a progressive condition, such as those described above, would not have been covered by the definition of disability until they also displayed a symptom associated with that condition. In essence, diagnosis without effect would not, in most cases, have triggered the definition.

However, since December 2005, the 2005 Act provides that people with such progressive conditions will be covered from the point of diagnosis, rather than from when there is an effect. This will afford the protection of the DDA 1995 to the period between the diagnosis of a condition and

Disability legislation

an effect being apparent; a time when disabled people were liable to experience discrimination.

The 2005 Act also provides that the requirement in the DDA 1995 for a mental illness to be 'clinically well diagnosed' before if can be considered as a mental impairment is removed. However, a person with a mental illness will still have to show that their impairment has a long-term and substantial adverse effect on their ability to carry out normal day-to-day activities. This also came into effect in December 2005.

Rental and management of premises

The 2005 Act has increased the duties on landlords and managers to make 'reasonable' adjustments when renting a house or flat to a disabled person. However, there is still no duty on them to remove or make changes to physical features that make the property difficult to access, as would be required under Part III of the 1995 Act. Examples of changes that could be made to assist the letting process include, for example, providing forms (paperwork / contracts) in alternative formats, assessing the way the property is managed, and changing, if reasonable to do so, any terms in the letting that might prevent a disabled person renting or using the property.

If requested by a disabled tenant, a landlord or manager will also have to take reasonable steps to provide an auxiliary aid or service if it would assist them in enjoying the premises or any associated benefit or facility. There is no duty on landlords under the 2005 Act to make adjustments to physical features of the tenant's property, or to any other parts of the landlord's building.

Commonhold associations

In 2004, a new system of freehold ownership was introduced in England and Wales. The system, known as 'Commonhold', can be applicable to blocks of flats, shops, offices and other multiple occupation premises. Where commonhold applies in multi-occupied premises, there is no landlord and tenant relationship, the premises instead consisting of interdependent freehold properties (known as 'commonhold units') and common parts.

The 2005 Act now has provisions to make discrimination unlawful against disabled people who are unit-holders.

Advertising

Since October 2004, it has been illegal under the DDA 1995 for a company to place a 'discriminating advert'. Under the 2005 Act, it is now also against the law for publishers – for example, newspapers and magazines – to print discriminatory advertisements.

Councillors

Under the 2005 Act, a Local Authority has a duty not to discriminate against a disabled councillor in the opportunities it affords them. These duties apply to the general work undertaken by the councillor, but do not extend to activities brought about by essentially political decisions, such as appointments to serve on committees or to a position on the Council's executive.

See also: Discrimination, p.110.

Disability legislation

Sources of further information

Disability Discrimination Act 1995: www.opsi.gov.uk/acts/acts1995/ukpga_19950050_en_1

Disability Discrimination Act 2005: www.opsi.gov.uk/acts/acts2005/ukpga_20050013_en_1

Equality and Human Rights Commission: www.equalityhumanrights.com

Workplace Law consultants can advise on your obligations in relation to disabled employees and disabled applicants. Making reasonable adjustments can be a complex area and it is always beneficial to seek advice from an expert. For more information on our equality and diversity training, visit www.workplacelaw.net/training/course/id/24.

Disciplinary and grievance procedures

Pinsent Masons Employment Group

Key points
- Contracts and statements of terms must incorporate disciplinary and grievance procedures.
- Written procedures are helpful in this respect. If there are none, there are certain minimum steps that employers must undertake, as otherwise any decision to dismiss will be automatically unfair. The Advisory, Conciliation and Arbitration Service (ACAS) guidelines form the accepted basis for such procedures.
- The new ACAS Code of Practice is intended to help employers and employees resolve disciplinary and grievance issues in the workplace – it should be applied to all matters arising after 6 April 2009.

Legislation
- Employment Rights Act 1996.
- Employment Act 2002.
- Employment Act 2002 (Dispute Resolution) Regulations 2004.
- Employment Act 2008.

Written procedures
Procedural fairness in the workplace is essential if employers are to avoid falling foul of employment protection laws.

Best practice, therefore, demands the introduction of fair written procedures to deal with disciplinary issues and to resolve grievances.

Statement of terms and conditions
Every employer is obliged to provide to each employee within two months after the beginning of the employee's employment a written statement of terms and conditions of his employment that specifies (among other things):

- any disciplinary rules and any disciplinary or dismissal procedures applicable to the employee (or a reference to a document setting out such rules, which is accessible to the employee);
- a person to whom the employee can apply if dissatisfied with any disciplinary decision;
- a person to whom the employee can apply to seek redress of any grievance; and
- the manner in which any application should be made.

Disciplinary and grievance procedures are generally structured in a tiered system, whereby if the grievance is not resolved or there is a recurrence of misconduct, the next step of the procedure is taken.

Grievance procedure – for grievances arising wholly *after* 6 April 2009
A grievance is a complaint, concern or problem that an employee raises about action which his/her employer has taken or is contemplating taking in relation to him/her.

In a grievance procedure, there will ordinarily be provisions for making several

Disciplinary and grievance procedures

> **Facts**
> - An average total of 10.5 days per year are spent managing disciplinary and grievance cases (4.6 days of management time, 5.6 days of HR staff time and 1.8 days of in-house lawyers' time).
> - Private sector companies are most likely to have to add stages to their disciplinary and grievance procedures (60%), whereas the public services are more likely to be simplifying them (61%).
> - The average UK employer has two disciplinary and grievance cases on bullying/harassment that are mainly settled internally (77%). Fourteen per cent escalate to Employment Tribunals.
> - There has been a dramatic increase in the number of Employment Tribunal claims, from 132,577 in 2007 to 189,303 in 2008.
>
> *Source: CIPD.*

attempts to resolve a grievance. These will start with an informal approach and lead to a requirement for the grievance to be put in writing. A failure to raise the grievance in writing does not prevent an employee bringing a tribunal claim; however, they may recover less compensation.

Each attempt to resolve the grievance typically involves a higher level of management for the employee to approach, usually working directly up the line of management responsibilities. On a practical note, when preparing such a procedure, care should be taken to avoid an open-ended series of hearings coming from the one grievance, which could lead to very senior managers becoming involved. On the other hand, the procedure should make provision for employees to be sure that their grievance is being considered by the employer and not dismissed at a junior manager level. Employees should also be able to bypass a particular manager if that manager is personally involved in the grievance (e.g. where he is alleged to have harassed an employee).

The employer should hold a meeting and investigate the complaint. If the matter requires further investigation, the employer should consider adjourning the meeting and resuming it after the investigation has taken place.

The employee may bring a companion (a fellow worker or trade union representative) to the grievance meeting. The employer should confirm that the employee has a right of appeal when they communicate the decision. The appeal should be in writing. If they bring a Tribunal claim without appealing, any compensation may be reduced.

The new ACAS Code replaces the statutory dispute resolution procedures under the Employment Act 2002. Employers' best practice should not, however, change significantly.

Disciplinary procedure – for dismissals or disciplinary process that start *after* 6 April 2009

The new ACAS Code also applies to disciplinary and dismissal procedures after 6 April 2009. If an employee brings a successful claim for unfair dismissal

Disciplinary and grievance procedures

or another type of claim (i.e. relating to discrimination, breach or contract, working time, detriment and deduction from wages) arising out of dismissal or disciplinary action for misconduct or poor performance, the level of compensation awarded to the employee can be affected if either party failed to follow the Code. It may go up or down by 25%.

Whereas the statutory dismissal and disciplinary procedures (DDPs) applied to dismissal for nearly any reason, the ACAS Code applies only to 'disciplinary situations'. This includes misconduct and poor performance, but excludes dismissals on grounds of redundancy or the non-renewal of a fixed-term contract.

The employer must investigate the issues. If paid suspension is necessary during the investigation, this should be as brief as possible and kept under review. The employer should inform the employee of the issues in writing. Any written evidence, including any witness statements, should be given to the employee. The employee should be informed of the time and place of the disciplinary hearing and informed of their right to bring a companion (either a fellow worker or a trade union representative).

At the hearing:

- the employer should explain the allegations and go through the evidence;
- the employee should be allowed to set out their case and answer the allegations; and
- the employee should have a reasonable opportunity to ask questions, present evidence, call witnesses and raise points about information provided by witnesses.

The employer should inform the employee of the decision in writing without unreasonable delay. If misconduct or poor performance is established, a dismissal would usually only be appropriate if there has been a written warning and a final written warning. Gross misconduct can justify dismissal for a first offence, but not without following the disciplinary procedure.

The employee can appeal (in writing) if they feel that the disciplinary action against them is unjust. If they bring a Tribunal claim without raising an appeal, any compensation may be reduced. The appeal should be heard without delay by a manager who (where possible) has not previously been involved. The employee can bring a companion to the appeal hearing.

The steps

The steps taken by an employer to deal with an issue will be compared by an Employment Tribunal with the ACAS Code when determining whether a fair procedure was followed.

- *Step 1*. Write to the employee notifying him/her of the allegations / issue against him/her and the basis of the allegations / issues and invite him/her to a meeting to discuss the matter.
- *Step 2*. Hold a meeting to discuss the allegations / issue – at which the employee has the right to be accompanied – and notify the employee of the decision.
- *Step 3*. If the employee wishes to appeal, hold an appeal meeting at which he/she has the right to be accompanied – and inform him/her of the final decision.

Best practice suggests that an employer should have a written procedure, carefully drafted to take into account the advice set out in the ACAS Code, and the employer should seek to follow the procedure in each case. Each employer is required to

Disciplinary and grievance procedures

have in place a written procedure, which, if not provided to the employee individually, is reasonably accessible.

The written procedure should be incorporated in such a way so as not to be a part of the employment contract, so that it can more easily be changed from time to time. This can be done by making express provision for the employer to amend it. In the case of a contractual policy, the employee may sue the employer or seek to obtain an injunction or interdict for failure to follow it. Remember that if the procedure does not as a minimum meet the statutory test, following such a procedure will be automatically unfair.

Transitional provisions – pre and post 6 April 2009

Transitional provisions govern whether the old or new regime applies.

In general, for grievances, a grievance concerning facts that occurred wholly before 6 April 2009 will fall under the old regime and any grievance that concerns facts wholly in or after that date will fall under the new ACAS Code regime. For most grievances about a state of affairs spanning that date, the old regime would continue to apply if the grievance or claim is submitted on or before 4 July 2009, although in some cases involving equal pay, redundancy or industrial action, the date is 4 October 2009.

For disciplinary issues, the old regime will continue to apply where the employer has dismissed an employee or taken relevant disciplinary action before 6 April 2009. It will also apply where the employer has sent the employee a 'step 1' letter or held a 'step 2' meeting under the DPPs before that date. However, in other cases, the new regime will apply from 6 April 2009.

See also: Dismissal, p.124; Employment disputes, p.150; Employment Tribunals, p.158.

Sources of further information

ACAS: www.acas.org.uk

Employers should have a clear record of the policy and procedures for disciplinary matters to provide clear guidance to employees on the procedure that will be followed by their employer. Workplace Law Group's ***Non-Contractual Disciplinary and Grievance Policy and Management Guide v.4.0*** helps employers comply with their obligations and can also act as a checklist for managers, in relation to the steps that should be taken, with a view to minimising procedural irregularities and allegations of unfair treatment. For more information visit www.workplacelaw.net/Bookshop/PoliciesAndProcedures.

Workplace Law's experienced consultants are able to assist at all stages of your disciplinary and grievance procedures. We can advise on process and/or act as adviser or an independent chair in hearings or appeals. For more on managing discipline and grievance training visit www.workplacelaw.net/training/course/id/27.

Discrimination

Pinsent Masons Employment Group

Key points
- Employment legislation makes it unlawful to discriminate on the grounds of sex, gender reassignment, marital or civil partner status, pregnancy or maternity leave, race, disability, sexual orientation, religion or belief and age.
- Discrimination will usually be direct or indirect, but can also arise due to harassment and victimisation.
- Workplace managers need to act to avoid discrimination at all stages of employment – job adverts, recruitment, the provision of benefits, terms and conditions of employment, promotion and dismissal – to avoid claims for unlimited compensation being made.

Legislation
- Sex Discrimination Act 1975.
- Race Relations Act 1976.
- Disability Discrimination Act 1995.
- Human Rights Act 1998.
- Part time Workers (Prevention of Less Favourable Treatment) Regulations 2000.
- Disability Discrimination Act 1995 (Amendment) Regulations 2003.
- Race Relations Act 1976 (Amendment) Regulations 2003.
- Employment Equality (Sexual Orientation) Regulations 2003.
- Employment Equality (Religion or Belief) Regulations 2003.
- Disability Discrimination Act 2005.
- Employment Equality (Sex Discrimination) Regulations 2005.
- Employment Equality (Age) Regulations 2006.
- Sex Discrimination Act 1975 (Amendment) Regulations 2008.

What is discrimination?
Discrimination laws preclude employers from treating workers differently for reasons that are based on sex, gender reassignment, marital or civil partner status, pregnancy or maternity leave, race, disability, sexual orientation, religion or belief and age.

The law on racial and sexual discrimination is now quite long established and the legislation on discrimination on grounds of sexual orientation, religion or belief and age follows a similar approach, while that on disability discrimination differs in certain respects. Each area of discrimination will be covered in a separate section in this chapter.

Discrimination can be split into four categories – direct, indirect, harassment and victimisation:

1. *Direct.* This is where a decision or action is taken on the sole grounds of the individual's distinctive characteristics – e.g. preferring a male applicant to a female applicant when the female has the better qualifications.
2. *Indirect.* This occurs where an employer's apparently neutral provision, requirement or practice (PCP) has the effect of putting a particular group at a disadvantage. For example, where an employer

Discrimination

> **Facts**
> - Age discrimination occurs across the age range, although it is most common at the younger and older age ranges, particularly under 25 and over 50.
> - Women who work full-time earn 13% less than men who work full-time, based on median hourly earnings, and 17% less based on mean hourly earnings.
> - 64% of gay men and lesbians reported experience of sexual orientation discrimination in the workplace. Nine per cent said that this resulted from an instruction or encouragement by a boss.
> - 83% of workers claim that the impact of indirect / unintentional discrimination on them was just as damaging as if it had been direct and/or intentional. Consequently, 76% feel that both forms of discrimination should be treated as equally serious.
> - Analysis from the Employment Tribunal Service has revealed an annual increase of between 15 and 25% in the number of race discrimination cases submitted to Employment Tribunals in 2005.

insists on a wide mobility clause in its contract of employment, this could be interpreted as discriminating against women, as they are more likely to be the 'second earner' and therefore less able to relocate. Another example is a requirement for a GCSE in English for a position that does not require any degree of literacy, as this can discriminate against ethnic minorities. Indirect discrimination is often less easy to spot than direct discrimination. Indirect discrimination can be justified if the employer is able to show that its requirement or practice meets a legitimate aim and is a proportionate means of achieving it.

3. *Harassment.* This is now a separate form of discrimination in each potential area of discrimination. It is defined as being a person's unwanted conduct that violates another's dignity or creates an intimidating, hostile, degrading, humiliating or offensive environment.

4. *Victimisation.* This is where an individual is treated less favourably because he has threatened to bring discrimination proceedings, gives evidence or information in connection with such proceedings, or makes some genuinely held allegation of discrimination.

Discrimination laws are couched in terms where those protected are not only employees but also contractors who are engaged personally to carry out work. An employer is responsible for the discriminatory acts carried out by its employees 'in the course of their employment' (a fairly wide definition) unless the employer has taken reasonable steps to prevent the discriminatory conduct. It is therefore important not only that employers have in place policies to prevent discrimination, but also that they take active steps to ensure that staff are aware of their content.

Impact of the Human Rights Act 1998

The Human Rights Act 1998 came into force on 2 October 2000 and requires the Courts and Tribunals to interpret UK law in a way that is compatible with the European Convention on Human Rights.

It includes a right to freedom of conscience, thought or religion, which

Discrimination

could widen the scope of the current laws on discrimination on grounds of racial group / origin or religious group.

Further, other relevant provisions allow the right not to be subjected to inhuman or degrading treatment and the right to respect for private life and freedom of expression (which could include the right to wear certain clothes at work, linked to religion or otherwise).

Moreover, Article 14 of the Convention provides that all of the rights contained within the Convention shall be secured without discrimination on any ground such as sex, race, colour, language, religion, political or other opinion, national or social origin, association with a national minority, property, birth or status. This could potentially widen the concept of discrimination beyond the scope of the discrimination legislation currently in force in the UK. However, the impact of this in the workplace has been fairly limited to date.

One area that may become increasingly contentious is religious observance at work. Article 9 protects freedom of thought, conscience and religion.

Sex discrimination

The Sex Discrimination Act 1975 prevents direct discrimination, indirect discrimination, harassment and victimisation.

Direct sex discrimination, as explained above, is treating a woman less favourably than a man (or vice versa) or a married person less favourably than a non-married person – cases of the latter normally occur where an employer fears that a married woman will want to take time out for a family. The comparison that is used is between the person claiming discrimination and another person with similar skills and qualifications, and the test is generally whether the person would have been treated the same but for his or her sex.

It is also unlawful to discriminate against transsexuals, on grounds of civil partner status, and on grounds of pregnancy or maternity leave.

If a woman is disadvantaged because she is pregnant or on maternity leave, this will be discriminatory. Care should be taken to ensure that during the woman's absence she is kept informed of any new vacancies or promotions that become available and of any other issues that may be of interest that are made available to staff who are not on maternity leave (such as details relating to pay) to avoid any claims that she is being discriminated against.

Provision, criteria or practice

The definition of indirect discrimination changed in October 2005. Indirect discrimination now occurs where an employer applies a provision, criterion or practice (PCP) that puts persons of the claimant's sex at a particular disadvantage when compared to the other sex, and the individual in question suffers that disadvantage, and the employer cannot show that the PCP is a proportionate means of achieving a legitimate aim.

The concept of a 'provision, criterion or practice' is very broad. For example, it may be broad enough to include informal work practices such as a long-hours culture, which would be seen as having a greater impact on women as they tend to have primary childcare responsibilities.

Indirect discrimination has often arisen when fewer or lesser benefits are given to part-time workers than are given to full-time workers, because more women work on a part-time basis (although a part-time worker would also have a claim

Discrimination

under the Part time Workers (Prevention of Less Favourable Treatment) Regulations 2000 in such circumstances. Making decisions on the assumption that women will stay at home and men will go out to work is also liable to lead to claims of discrimination. Indirect discrimination will not be unlawful if the employer is able to show that its PCP meets a legitimate aim and is a proportionate means of achieving that aim. This is the justification test. It requires an objective balance to be struck between the discriminatory effect of the PCP and the reasonable needs of the employer.

So, where female employees are refused requests to return part-time or to job-share after a pregnancy, workplace managers will need to be able to justify why the job has to be done a full-time basis or by one person.

Particular danger arises through discriminatory advertisements and descriptions of jobs suggesting that only men or women should apply, or requiring qualifications or experience that is weighted towards one sex rather than the other.

Harassment related to a person's sex (or that of another person) and harassment of a sexual nature are now prohibited as a matter of statute. Previously, harassment was not expressly covered by the Sex Discrimination Act, although the courts had held that harassment could constitute direct discrimination.

Employers are able to defend a discrimination claim relating to recruitment / promotion where a 'genuine occupational qualification' necessitates the employment of one sex. Examples are where a man or woman is needed for decency or privacy and where there is a need to live at premises provided by the employer and the facilities are only for one sex. Further exceptions exist for institutions such as all-male hospitals and prisons or care services.

Employers should also be aware that, after the employee leaves, any discrimination against that individual will be unlawful if the act of discrimination arises out of and is closely connected to the employment relationship.

Employment Tribunals have unlimited scope to compensate affected individuals not only for pure financial loss but also for injury to feelings.

Race discrimination

The Race Relations Act 1976 prohibits direct discrimination, indirect discrimination, harassment and victimisation. A wide definition of race is provided in the legislation. Discrimination is prohibited on grounds of colour, race, nationality, ethnic or national origins.

As explained at the beginning of this chapter, direct discrimination is where one person is treated less favourably than another. Examples in the context of race discrimination would be not promoting someone because he is Indian or not employing a Sikh because he might not 'fit in' with white workers.

There are two slightly different definitions of indirect race discrimination. The first form of indirect discrimination applies to cases of discrimination on grounds of colour or nationality. It occurs when the employer applies a requirement or condition with which a considerably smaller proportion in a racial group can comply, compared to those who are not in the racial group. Also, the person must have been disadvantaged by the actions. If the employer can justify the requirement for a reason other than the race of the person,

Discrimination

this is a defence to the claim. The second definition of indirect discrimination applies to cases of discrimination on grounds of race, ethnic or national origins. It occurs when the employer applies a provision, criterion or practice which is apparently race-neutral (i.e. it would apply to all races) but puts or would put persons of the employee's race or ethnic or national origins at a particular disadvantage, actually puts the relevant employee at that disadvantage, and cannot be shown to be a proportionate means of achieving a legitimate aim.

If an individual proves a case of indirect discrimination, the burden of proof shifts to the employer to prove that it was not racially discriminatory.

Workplace managers should note that employers can discriminate if they segregate racial groups, even if the facilities given to them are of equal quality.

Genuine occupational qualification defence

A decision to discriminate on racial grounds may be justified in certain cases where being of a particular colour, race, nationality or ethnic or national origin is an essential qualification for the job in question – the 'genuine occupational qualification' defence.

Grounds upon which it may be claimed there is a genuine occupational qualification include:

- being a member of a particular racial group is a requirement for authenticity in a dramatic performance or other entertainment, or for authenticity purposes as an artist's or photographic model;
- the work is in a place where food or drink is consumed by the public and a particular race of person is required for authenticity (e.g. Chinese or Indian restaurants); or
- the job holder provides his or her racial group with personal services promoting their welfare (e.g. an Afro-Caribbean nursery nurse in an Afro-Caribbean area) where those services can be more effectively provided by a person of that racial group.

There is also another defence available but this defence is only available in cases of discrimination on grounds of race, ethnic or national origins (not for discrimination on grounds of colour or nationality). This defence – the 'genuine occupational requirement' defence – applies where being of a particular race, ethnic or national origin is a genuine and determining occupational requirement. Such a requirement must be proportionate in the particular case and the individual who was subject to the discrimination must not be of the race in question. Instructions to or pressure on staff to discriminate is also unlawful (e.g. the owners of a truck rental company instructing staff to tell Asian customers that no trucks are available for hire).

Harassment is now a separate form of discrimination, where a person's unwanted conduct has the purpose or effect of violating another's dignity or creates an intimidating, hostile, degrading, humiliating or offensive environment. The test is an objective one and although the Tribunal must take the complainant's perception into account, it must be conduct that could reasonably be considered as having that effect. Therefore, provided there is no intention, there will not be a claim for harassment if the complainant is hypersensitive. Employment Tribunals have unlimited scope to compensate affected individuals not only for pure financial loss but also for injury to feelings.

Discrimination

Disability discrimination

The Disability Discrimination Act 1995 (DDA) prohibits direct discrimination, disability-related discrimination, victimisation and, since 1 October 2004, harassment has been a separate act, which is regarded as unlawful in its own right. The DDA also provides for a duty to make reasonable adjustments.

The DDA also prohibits discrimination against people with disabilities in terms of services provided to them as members of the public as well as in the field of employment rights. Since 1 October 2004, all employers, regardless of size, can be found guilty of discrimination.

Types of disability discrimination

There are five types of disability discrimination.

The first is where an employer treats a disabled person less favourably on the grounds of his disability than he would a person not having that disability. This is known as direct disability discrimination.

The second applies where an employer treats a person less favourably for a reason related to his disability than he would treat another person to whom that reason does not or would not apply. This is known as disability-related discrimination. Unlike direct disability discrimination, disability-related discrimination can be justified, but there must be substantial reasons for the discrimination. Disability-related discrimination cannot be justified in circumstances where the employer was also under a duty to make reasonable adjustments (*see below*) and he has not complied with that duty.

Direct disability discrimination differs from disability-related discrimination in that it occurs when the reason for the less favourable treatment is the disability itself, whereas disability-related discrimination occurs where the reason relates to the disability but is not the disability itself. For example, direct discrimination will occur where an employer fails to employ a person because he has a facial disfigurement (which amounts to a disability) solely because he will be uncomfortable working with him.

An example of where disability-related discrimination will occur is where an employer dismisses an employee who has been off sick for a long time – in such a case the reason for the treatment is the sickness (which is related to the disability) but is not the disability itself. A recent House of Lords decision (*Mayor and Burgess of the London Borough of Lewisham v. Malcolm*) may have reduced the scope for bringing disability-related discrimination claims as a result of a change to the comparator to be used in such cases. Prior to the decision, it was thought that there were different comparators in cases of direct disability discrimination and disability-related discrimination. For direct discrimination, the comparison is between the way the disabled person is treated and how a non-disabled person would be treated in similar circumstances. For disability-related discrimination purposes, the case of *Clark v. Novacold* held that the correct comparator was someone to whom the reason for the claimant's treatment did not apply.

So, if a person was dismissed for being off sick for too long, the comparison would be with someone to whom that reason (i.e. the sickness absence) did not apply – so it was someone who had not been off work sick at all. Since such a person would not have been dismissed, less favourable treatment would be made out and whether the discrimination was unlawful would depend on whether the employer

Discrimination

could justify its treatment of the disabled employee.

The recent House of Lords decision suggests that the correct comparator in a case of disability-related discrimination is in fact a person without a disability who is otherwise in the same position as the claimant, i.e. the same comparator as for direct disability discrimination. So, in the case of the disabled employee dismissed for being off sick for too long, the comparison would be with a non-disabled employee who has been off work for the same length of time. Since such an employee would presumably also have been dismissed, less favourable treatment is not made out and the disability-related discrimination claim fails.

It remains to be seen how Employment Tribunals will approach disability-related discrimination claims as a result of the *Malcolm* case.

The third type of disability discrimination occurs where an employer fails to make 'reasonable adjustments' to the physical nature of its premises or to any 'provision, criterion or practice' to ensure that disabled people are not placed at a disadvantage. Failure to make a reasonable adjustment will constitute discrimination. It is no longer possible to justify a failure to make a reasonable adjustment – the only defence, therefore, is that the adjustment was not a reasonable one to make. Factors that may be taken into account in assessing the reasonableness of the adjustment include:

- how effective the step will be in ameliorating the disadvantage and the practicability of taking the step;
- the costs to the employer of making the adjustment and the financial and other resources available to the employer; and/or
- the nature of the employer's activities and the size of the undertaking.

Examples of what may be regarded as reasonable adjustments are:

- changing building structure (e.g. by introducing ramps, lowering switches or panels, moving doors and widening entrances) – but remember most people affected by the DDA are not in a wheelchair;
- permitting different working hours (e.g. to deal with tiredness or medical treatments);
- providing specialist or modified equipment (e.g. computer screens or adapted / different chairs); and
- providing training (e.g. for use of specialist equipment or extra training for someone whose disability may make him/her slower).

The fourth type of disability discrimination is victimisation, i.e. less favourable treatment because a person has threatened to bring disability discrimination proceedings, gives evidence or information in connection with such proceedings, or makes some genuinely held allegation of disability discrimination.

Lastly, it is now also unlawful to harass an employee for a reason relating to that person's disability, by engaging in unwanted conduct that has the purpose or effect of violating the person's dignity, or creating an intimidating, hostile, degrading, humiliating or offensive environment for him or her.

A recent decision of the ECJ in the case of *Coleman v. Attridge Law* held that where a person is discriminated against because of their association with a disabled person, rather than because of their own disability, they are protected by the EC Equal Treatment Framework Directive. This means that it may be necessary to interpret the DDA as extending to associative discrimination and, if this is not possible, the DDA will

Discrimination

need amending to ensure it complies with the Directive.

Meaning of 'disability'

There are no duties or liabilities to an individual if there is no 'disability' as defined in the legislation. It is therefore important that there is an understanding that not all medical conditions constitute disability.

For a disability to exist, there needs to be a physical or mental impairment that has a substantial and long-term effect (i.e. lasts or is likely to last, 12 months, or is likely to recur) on the person's ability to carry out 'normal day-to-day activities'.

Certain provisions of the Disability Discrimination Act 2005 came into force in December 2005. This extended the definition of disability to cover people with cancer, multiple sclerosis and HIV from the date of diagnosis. The 2005 Act also removed the previous requirement that people with a mental illness had to show that it was a 'clinically well-recognised' illness before it counted as a mental impairment.

The Disability Rights Commission Code of Practice: Employment and Occupation, provides guidance and there is also guidance, issued by the Secretary of State, on matters to be taken into account in determining questions relating to the definition of disability, to which workplace managers should refer.

The following examples show the type of physical activities that are regarded as being normal or day-to-day:

- Mobility (moving, changing position);
- Manual dexterity (use of hands and fingers with precision – e.g. an inability to use a knife and fork may be a disability, but an inability to pick up a tiny item such as a pin may not);
- Physical coordination (where again it may be a matter of degree);
- Continence;
- Ability to lift, carry or move everyday objects;
- Speech, hearing or eyesight;
- Memory or ability to learn, concentrate or understand; and
- Perception of risk or physical danger.

The Guidance indicates that this does not include 'activities that are normal only for a particular person or small group of people'. However, the Courts have been less restrictive in their approach and said that what is normal cannot sensibly depend on whether the majority of people do it. It is necessary to consider what is 'normal' and what is 'abnormal' or 'unusual' as a regular activity, judged by an objective population standard.

Schizophrenia, claustrophobia, epilepsy, back injuries, depression, blindness, arm pains and dyslexia have all been found to constitute 'disabilities'. However, each of these cases has been decided on the level of disability of an individual, and it cannot be taken to be a rule that because someone suffers from arm pains he is disabled in terms of the law.

The legislation is very specific on the subject of substance abuse, and excludes alcohol, nicotine or substance dependency as a disability. Again, however, caution is warranted as the effects of the abuse could result in physical disabilities (e.g. liver damage), which would be covered by the law.

Workplace managers should take care in avoiding disability discrimination in terms of advertisements, terms and conditions of employment, benefits provided to staff, dismissals and victimisation.

If an employee is ill, particularly where that illness is long-term and a dismissal is

Discrimination

contemplated, the disability discrimination legislation needs to be considered carefully and specialist advice taken as this area is fraught with potential issues.

Discrimination on the grounds of sexual orientation

The EC Equal Treatment Framework Directive sets out an anti-discrimination 'principle of equal treatment' in the context of sexual orientation and this has been implemented through the Employment Equality (Sexual Orientation) Regulations 2003.

The Regulations contain sections dealing with discrimination in employment and vocational training, vicarious liability of employers, exceptions and enforcement.

The law applies to recruitment, terms and conditions, pay, promotion, transfers and dismissals. It applies to all employers regardless of their size.

The Regulations cover:

- direct discrimination (i.e. less favourable treatment on the grounds of sexual orientation);
- indirect discrimination, whereby a provision criterion or practice is applied which disadvantages people of a particular sexual orientation and which is not objectively justified as a proportionate means of achieving a legitimate aim;
- harassment or conduct that violates dignity or creates an intimidating, hostile, degrading, humiliating or offensive environment; and
- victimisation (i.e. less favourable treatment because of something done in connection with the legislation).

'Sexual orientation' covers orientation towards persons of the same sex (gays and lesbians), the opposite sex (heterosexuals), and the same and opposite sex (bisexuals). The law applies to discrimination on the grounds of perceived as well as actual sexual orientation.

The recent case of *English v. Thomas Sanderson Limited* concluded that conduct 'on the grounds of' sexual orientation could amount to harassment, regardless of the victim's true sexual orientation, or his tormentor's perception of it.

Discrimination on the grounds of religion or belief

The EC Equal Treatment Framework Directive sets out an anti-discrimination 'principle of equal treatment' in the context of religion or belief. The Employment Equality (Religion or Belief) Regulations 2003 came into force in December 2003.

The Regulations contain sections dealing with discrimination in employment and vocational training, the vicarious liability of employers, exceptions and enforcement.

The law applies to recruitment, terms and conditions, pay, promotion, transfers and dismissals. It applies to all employers, regardless of their size.

The Regulations prohibit:

- direct discrimination (i.e. less favourable treatment on the grounds of religion or belief);
- indirect discrimination, whereby a provision or practice is applied that disadvantages people of a particular religion or belief and which is not objectively justified as a proportionate means of achieving a legitimate aim;
- harassment or conduct that violates dignity or creates an intimidating, hostile, degrading, humiliating or offensive environment; and
- victimisation (i.e. less favourable treatment because of something done in connection with the legislation).

Discrimination

The Regulations relating to religion or belief define religion or belief as meaning 'any religion, or religious or philosophical belief'. Following a change in the law in April 2007, the requirement that a philosophical belief be similar to a religious belief has been abolished. This clearly widens the scope of the protection, though the extent of this has yet to be tested. See 'Believe it or not,' p.121.

Age discrimination

Age legislation is required to comply with the EC Equal Treatment Framework Directive and, on 1 October 2006, the Employment Equality (Age) Regulations 2006 came into force.

There are four main types of unlawful age discrimination. These are as follows:

1. *Direct discrimination.* This occurs where a person is treated less favourably on grounds of their age without objective justification. For example, setting an upper and lower age limit for a particular job (whether formally or informally) may be direct discrimination against a person outside the age band.
2. *Indirect discrimination.* This occurs where a provision, criterion or practice has a greater impact on workers in one age group compared to those in another and is not objectively justified. These are not always easy to spot because there is no overt less favourable treatment – everyone appears to be treated the same. However, restricting a post to 'recent graduates' is likely to discriminate indirectly against a worker over 30, since most recent graduates are likely to be in their 20s.
3. *Harassment.* This occurs where, on the grounds of age, the person is subjected to unwanted conduct that has the purpose or effect of violating their dignity or creating an intimidating, hostile, degrading, humiliating or offensive environment. Examples of this include intentional bullying, but it can also be unintentional, subtle and insidious, e.g. nicknames, teasing, inappropriate jokes that are not malicious in intent, but which are upsetting. Harassing behaviour may be targeted at an individual or may consist of a general culture that appears to tolerate, for example, the telling of ageist jokes. Harassment is judged from the perception of the victim, although unintentional harassment is subject to the test of reasonableness.
4. *Victimisation.* An employee who complains in good faith of alleged age discrimination or harassment, or who supports another employee in such a complaint, must not be treated less favourably because they have complained / supported a complaint. Employees are protected from acts of victimisation even if the complaint turns out not to be upheld.

It is important to remember that, as with other types of unlawful discrimination at work, age discrimination can arise not just from what managers do, but also from how employees behave towards each other. This may not just be confined to the workplace. For example, if a group of young employees frequently go out for a drink after work, but exclude an older member of their team, this could in some cases amount to discrimination or harassment. Employees should be encouraged to be as inclusive as possible.

Unusually, the new age discrimination law permits employers to justify objectively both direct and indirect discrimination.

However, this is not straightforward. It is difficult to tell what approach the Tribunals will take to the question of objective justification. The new law says that an employer must be pursuing a 'legitimate

Discrimination

aim' (for example, encouraging loyalty, rewarding experience, or maintaining health and safety) and the means of pursuing the same must be 'proportionate'.

In practice, this means that the benefit of a discriminatory practice to an employer must be sufficient to outweigh the discriminatory effect. If there are two ways of achieving a similar aim, the less discriminatory way must be chosen.

Employers also have the option of arguing that there is a genuine occupational requirement for a discriminatory decision, although this will only be relevant in very few cases.

Employers can no longer set their normal retirement ages below the age of 65 unless this can be objectively justified. Although the Regulations allow employers to retire employees at a default retirement age of 65, the question of whether a default retirement age is lawful has been referred to the ECJ. Employers who have a retirement age of 65 may therefore wish to consider whether to rely on it.

Employers have to consider an employee's request to continue beyond normal retirement age and will have to inform employees in writing, in advance, of their intended retirement date and their right to request to work after the intended retirement date.

Employers will therefore need to ensure that their recruitment, retirement, promotion and reward practices do not discriminate directly or indirectly on grounds of age.

See also: Carers, p.54; Disability legislation, p.98; Employment Tribunals, p.158; Equal pay, p.167; HIV and AIDS, p.215; Part-time workers, p.308; Pregnancy, p.324; Recruitment and selection, p.335; Retirement, p.353; Stress, p.381.

Sources of further information

Equality and Human Rights Commission: www.equalityhumanrights.com

Equal Opportunities policies are becoming ever more important in today's increasingly multicultural, multiracial society. The purpose of Workplace Law Group's ***Equal Opportunities Policy and Management Guide v.4.0*** is to set out the obligations on both the employer and the employee to treat all people with equal dignity and respect within the workplace. The aim is to create a pleasant and harmonious working environment for all. For more information visit www.workplacelaw.net/bookshop/policiesAndProcedures.

Workplace Law's experienced consultants can audit your processes and identify any risk areas in your company. They can provide training for managers at all levels in the company to raise their awareness of discrimination issues and such courses can be customised to your particular needs. Workplace Law is anticipating being able to offer a CIPD accredited course on discrimination in 2010. For more information visit http://cipd.workplacelaw.net/.

Comment...

Believe it or not ...

Rebecca Fox is a Solicitor in the employment department at Matthew Arnold & Baldwin LLP and provides advice on all aspects of employment law including advising on employer and employee disputes relating to unfair dismissal, all forms of discrimination and redundancy management. Adam Fuge is a Principal and Head of Employment at Matthew Arnold & Baldwin LLP, specialising in employment issues arising on insolvency, employment aspects of corporate and commercial transactions, directors' duties and liabilities.

Religious and similar beliefs

The Employment Equality (Religion or Belief) Regulations 2003 made it unlawful to discriminate against a worker due to their religion, religious belief or *similar* philosophical belief. Changes to the Regulations under the Equality Act 2006 extended the protection afforded to workers by removing the word 'similar'. Therefore, *any* philosophical belief is now protected under the Regulations (in addition to religion or religious beliefs). An employee's lack of religion, religious belief or philosophical belief is also protected.

'Religion and philosophical belief' are not defined in the Regulations, leaving it open to interpretation. Employers face a difficult balancing act between identifying an individual's right to their religious and philosophical beliefs at work and running an efficient and successful business.

Religion within the Regulations includes all recognised religions such as Islam, Hinduism, Christianity, Judaism and Sikhism, but the extent of the definition of philosophical belief is unclear. Does an employer need to be worried if they have an employee, for example, who has a philosophical belief regarding the environment and climate change? Although some might say that this takes the definition of philosophical belief too far, a Tribunal has decided otherwise in the case of *Nicholson v. Grainger plc and others*. The Tribunal, at a pre-hearing review, held that Mr Nicolson's beliefs about climate change and the environment and climate change amounted to a philosophical belief under the Regulations due to the level of importance of the belief. Is it correct that such modern beliefs should be treated in the same manner as the above listed religions that are thousands of years old with defined practices? An individual passionate about the state of climate change may very well think so.

Even though there is no longer a requirement for philosophical beliefs to be 'similar' to religious beliefs for the Regulations to apply, the Tribunal in this case held that Mr Nicholson's beliefs about climate change and the environment give rise to a 'moral order' similar to most religions. The Tribunal also rejected the argument that beliefs derived from 'empirical' evidence could not be a 'philosophical belief'. It is clear that

Comment: Believe it or not ...

the Employment Tribunal also thought it significant that Mr Nicholson's belief in climate change substantially affected the way he leads his life.

The Tribunal's decision in the *Nicholson* case has provoked some controversy, but does give an indication of the wide interpretation Tribunals may be prepared to apply to the meaning of 'philosophical beliefs'. We can expect more cases to be brought, which will further test the limits of protection in relation to philosophical belief under the Regulations.

It's all political

Interestingly, even though a belief in climate change is now potentially covered by the Regulations, to date there have been no successful cases to show that political beliefs are protected. A few years ago in the case of *Baggs v. Fudge*, a member of the BNP claimed that he was discriminated against due to his membership of the BNP. His claim was dismissed by the Tribunal, and a similar claim by a member of the same party was rejected by the Tribunal in the case of *Finnon v. Asda Stores Ltd*. However, both these cases preceded the amendment to the Regulations mentioned above. It remains to be seen whether any future cases will test this point to decide whether, with the removal of the word 'similar', a political belief (whether in relation to the BNP or otherwise) would now amount to a philosophical belief.

Even though members of the BNP are barred from working in the police force or prison service, employers have taken the Regulations on board and are concerned that members of the BNP may make a claim. The General Teaching Council (GTC) was accused in June 2009 of failing to act to prevent British National Party members from teaching in schools. The GTC have refused to add anything into the teacher's code of practice which would bar BNP workers from working in state schools. This decision was made after receiving legal advice that to do so would 'prejudice' teachers belonging to the far right party. The teaching council states that as a regulatory body, they cannot regulate against the beliefs of professionals, and may only do so in relation to their actions and conduct. Practically, it would be difficult for actions and conduct to be monitored, especially actions and conduct of a BNP member outside the classroom.

Where the dress doesn't impress

Dress codes in the workplace have also been the subject of numerous recent Tribunal claims in the context of religion and religious belief. Where the requirement by an employer for a certain uniform or style of dress conflicts with an individual's belief, then the employer again may find that they are in difficulty. They must be able to justify the uniform or dress code as a legitimate business need, or if it can be justified on health and safety grounds, such as an employer not allowing long beards where food is being prepared. To succeed in a claim, an employee must show that the uniform or dress code has a disproportionate adverse impact upon people of a particular religion. For example, in the case of *Noah v. Desrosiers trading as Wedge*, a Muslim woman who covered her hair was able to show that she had been discriminated against on the basis that the requirement for the hairdresser not to cover her hair was not a proportionate means of achieving the aim of being able to cut hair.

Before employers run scared, in the more recent case of *Azmi v. Kirklees Council*, a Muslim woman who wanted to wear a full veil whilst teaching lost her claim for religious discrimination at both the first instance and on appeal. The Tribunal made it clear that she was not being

Comment: Believe it or not ...

treated less favourably, as any other woman who wanted to cover her face fully whilst teaching would also be prevented from doing so. It seems that, in this instance, the Tribunal took a more practical approach in finding that that she was not being discriminated against.

The Tribunal also adopted a more practical approach in the recent case of *Khoja v. The Commissioner of Police for the Metropolis*, where a Muslim chef claimed that he was stressed and humiliated at the prospect of handling pork products, which Islam prohibits. The chef was provided with gloves so that he did not have to 'touch' the pork but the employee said that this would not protect him from 'the risk of splashes'. The employer, the Metropolitan Police Force, was cleared of all claims of discrimination.

Genuine occupational requirement

As mentioned above, employers should also bear in mind that the Regulations also now expressly apply to those employees who feel they have been discriminated against due to a *lack of* religion, religious belief or philosophical belief. This could mean that if an employee does not share a religious or philosophical belief held by colleagues (or required by their employer) and is treated less favourably as a consequence, they may be able to bring a successful claim under the Regulations. Employers may be able to rely on a defence that it is a genuine occupational requirement (GOR) for a belief to be held in relation to matters such as recruitment, promotion or dismissal (though not in relation to the terms on which individuals are employed or in relation to any other detriment such as demotion). However, the Regulations set out very strict standards to be met for a GOR to be relied upon. The case of *Glasgow City Council v. McNab* made clear that a GOR must arise out of the nature of the job in question, and not simply the organisation.

Numerous cases since the Regulations came into force have shown that this area is a minefield for employers and how important it is to ensure that potential difficulties with employees are avoided. If an employee is successful in making a claim, damages in a Tribunal are uncapped and can include a substantial 'injury to feelings' award. Even if the employee is not successful, employers will normally bear the costs of defending a claim, although if the employer can show that the employee has bought a 'frivolous, vexatious, unreasonable or misconceived' claim, they may be able to request that an order for costs is made against the claimant. It is essential that through effective equal opportunities monitoring and by carrying out an audit of all policies and procedures relevant to the employment process, from recruitment to termination, employers are aware of their individual employees' religious and/or philosophical beliefs and that they identify any practical areas of concern. This knowledge can then allow the employer to consider whether all its actions, policies and procedures in relation to its business are potentially discriminatory, and if so, whether they can be justified as being proportionate and necessary.

With such a diverse workforce with both men and women of all faiths and wide-ranging beliefs (as well as non-believers) in employment it is important to get the balancing act right. Employers need to be aware of the key aspects of the Regulations, the way they have been interpreted by Employment Tribunals to date, and also of the potential for the boundaries of protection under the Regulations to be extended further as new claims are brought.

Dismissal

Pinsent Masons Employment Group

Key points
Employers must dismiss employees in accordance with contract terms in order not to breach the contract and become liable for wrongful dismissal. Regardless of whether there is a breach of contract, dismissals will be unfair unless:

- the dismissal is for one of a list of potentially fair reasons;
- the employer acts reasonably in dismissing the employee;
- the employer has followed a fair procedure; and
- pre-April 2009, the employer has followed the statutory dismissal and disciplinary procedure.

Legislation
- Disability Discrimination Act 1995.
- Employment Rights Act 1996.
- National Minimum Wage Act 1998.
- Working Time Regulations 1998.
- Employment Act 2002.
- Employment Act 2002 (Dispute Resolution) Regulations 2004.
- The Employment Equality (Age) Regulations 2006.

What is dismissal?
A number of key employment law rights arise when a 'dismissal' takes place. Dismissal is an act of the employer which occasions a termination of the employment relationship. A resignation – although an act of the employee, not the employer – can also constitute a 'constructive dismissal' where it is in response to a breach of contract by the employer.

Dismissal can also include the expiry and non-renewal of a fixed-term contract.

Notice
Dismissal by an employer can be with or without notice. The amount of notice required will usually be set out in the employment contract. If that is silent, 'reasonable' notice must be given, the length of which will vary depending on the employee's circumstances.

In any event, the following statutory minimum notice must be given by an employer:

- An employee who has been continuously employed for one month or more but less than two years is entitled to not less than one week's notice.
- An employee who has been continuously employed for two years or more but less than 12 years is entitled to one week's notice for each year of continuous employment.
- An employee who has been employed for 12 years or more is entitled to not less than 12 weeks' notice.

Generally, once notice has been given it cannot be withdrawn, save by mutual consent.

Failure by an employer to give notice in accordance with the terms of the contract will leave the employer liable to pay damages to the employee in respect of salary and other benefits that would have fallen due in the notice period. If there is

Dismissal

a 'pay in lieu of notice' (PILON) clause in the employee's contract, there will be no breach of contract if notice money is paid instead of the employee working out his notice.

The tax treatments of these two types of payment are different. As the latter payment is contractual, the employee will be liable for income tax, whereas the former is treated as damages and may generally be free of tax up to £30,000. An act of gross misconduct or gross negligence on the part of an employee may be expected to justify dismissal without notice, sometimes referred to as 'summary dismissal'.

Unfair dismissal

Save for certain special cases (*see below*), employees must have one year's continuous service (at the date the dismissal takes effect) in order to have the right to claim that they have been unfairly dismissed. A fair dismissal has two elements:

1. The employer's reason to dismiss must be one of a list of potentially fair reasons (Section 98(1), Employment Rights Act 1996 (ERA)).
2. Even if a fair reason exists, it must have been reasonable in all the circumstances for the employer to dismiss the employee (Section 94(4), ERA). In other words, the employer must follow a fair procedure.

Potentially fair reasons for dismissal
- *Lack of capability or qualifications*. Capability is skill and ability to do the job. This is most often relevant for poor performance or physical incapability such as injury or sickness. Lack of qualifications could involve a practical qualification necessary to do the job, which may be lost during employment (e.g. a driver losing a driving licence).
- *Conduct*. In other words, misconduct on the part of the employee.
- *Redundancy*. For the purposes of the ERA, an employee who is dismissed shall be taken to be dismissed by reason of redundancy if the dismissal is wholly or mainly attributable to the fact that his employer has ceased or intends to cease to carry on the business for the purposes of which the employee was employed by him, or to carry on that business in the place where the employee was so employed, or where the requirements of that business for employees to carry out work of a particular kind, or for employees to carry out work of a particular kind in the place where the employee was employed by the employer, have ceased or diminished or are expected to cease or diminish.
- *Retirement*. The Employment Equality (Age) Regulations 2006 introduced retirement as a potentially fair reason for dismissal.
- *Continued employment would breach legislation*. For example where, if the employment continued, either the employer or the employee would be in breach of health and safety laws.
- *'Some other substantial reason'*. In some ways this is a catch-all to allow Tribunals to respond to the circumstances of individual cases. It can cover a multitude of cases including dismissals by reason of a reorganisation, and dismissals in order to effect changes in terms and conditions of employment.

Fairness of the dismissal

Having determined that a potentially fair reason exists, one must then ask the question whether the employer has acted reasonably in all the circumstances in dismissing the employee as a consequence of the reason. Has the employer followed a fair and proper procedure?

Dismissal

Tribunals will take account of the size and administrative resources of the employer. The question of fairness is closely linked to disciplinary procedures and the need to follow a fair procedure in disciplining and dismissing the employee and meeting the minimum statutory standards.

What is appropriate in terms of procedure will vary depending on the reason for the dismissal. The employer must follow a fair and reasonable procedure and the Tribunal will look at whether the decision to dismiss the employee and the procedures followed measure up to the standards expected of employers.

Some key procedural points that workplace managers should follow for the most common dismissals are as follows.

Capability
- Tell the employee precisely why his performance is poor and what is needed to improve it.
- Explain the next stage of disciplinary action if there is still no improvement (leading up to eventual dismissal).
- Give the employee an opportunity to explain his case at each stage.
- Consider whether training is needed or if an alternative job can be offered.

Sickness
- Investigate the true medical position and prognosis for recovery (usually through a medical report).
- Consult with the employee.
- Can the employer be expected to wait any longer for recovery?
- The employer should also consider the Disability Discrimination Act 1995 before taking further action.

Conduct
- The question is whether the employer has reasonable grounds to believe the employee is guilty of misconduct.
- Carry out a full investigation.
- Inform the employee of all the allegations in advance of disciplinary meetings.
- Put all the evidence of misconduct to the employee.
- The employee must have an opportunity to put his case on the evidence.
- Dismiss only on the evidence put to the employee.

Redundancy
Although a potentially fair reason for dismissal, redundancy can give rise to unfair dismissals where there is a failure to follow a fair procedure. Fair and proper procedures are based on:

- giving the employee advance warning of the potential redundancy situation;
- consulting with the employee as to the selection criteria to be used;
- considering alternative employment;
- the employer taking a decision to dismiss for reasons of redundancy only after proper consultation has taken place;
- allowing the employee time off to look for alternative jobs; and
- continuing to look for alternative jobs for the employee within the organisation.

Retirement
An employer may, although is not obliged to, retire employees at the employer's normal retirement age, or the default retirement age of 65. However, although retirement is a potentially fair reason for dismissal, employers must follow a 'planned retirement' procedure that includes:

- giving employees at least six months' notice of their retirement date; and
- ensuring employees have the right to request to work past their retirement date and complying with the duty to consider such a request.

Dismissal

If an employer retires an employee before their normal retirement age, or the age of 65, this may amount to unfair dismissal and age discrimination.

Dismissals before 6 April 2009

The statutory dispute resolution procedures apply to dismissals before 6 April 2009. The statutory dismissal and disciplinary procedures (DDPs) apply where the employer is contemplating dismissing an employee or taking relevant disciplinary action against them. The statutory grievance procedures apply where an employee has a grievance against the employer. Failure to follow the correct procedure will mean that the dismissal will be unfair. Where an employer has followed the correct procedure but there has been some other procedural failing, it may be possible to argue that the dismissal was fair on the basis that, even if the correct procedure had been followed, the dismissal could still have occurred.

Dismissals after 6 April 2009

The statutory dispute resolution procedures do not apply to dismissals after 6 April 2009. For dismissals after this date, employers should follow the new ACAS Code. The ACAS Code applies to 'disciplinary situations' and this includes misconduct or poor performance dismissals. The ACAS Code does not apply to dismissals for reason of redundancy or non-renewal of a fixed-term contract.

Unfair dismissal remedies

Employees have three months after the date of dismissal in which to bring a claim before an Employment Tribunal or, alternatively, employers and employees can decide to place the dispute before an ACAS-appointed arbitrator under the ACAS Arbitration Scheme. The scheme is devised to provide a quicker, cheaper and, where possible, more amicable resolution to this type of dispute. However, very few people have elected to follow this route to date. Remedies available to both the Tribunal and an ACAS arbitrator include re-engagement or reinstatement, both of which are imposed only rarely. More usually, compensation is awarded.

This falls under two heads:

1. The first is the basic award, calculated by reference to salary, age and length of service, subject to a maximum, which was increased on 1 February 2009 to £10,500.
2. The second is the compensatory award, which is designed to reimburse the employee for actual losses and is at the discretion of the Tribunal, subject to a maximum, also increased on 1 February 2009, and now set at £66,200. The overall cap has been increased significantly in recent years and is likely to keep rising in the future.

Automatically unfair reasons

Detailed provisions exist for claims that do not require one year's continuous service and where dismissal for that reason will be automatically unfair.

The most important of these are dismissals for:

- membership of a trade union or for participating in trade union activities;
- taking part in protected industrial action;
- taking action on specified health and safety grounds (including leaving premises due to danger);
- asserting statutory rights against the employer;
- pregnancy or related reasons;
- holding the status of a part-time worker or a fixed-term employee;

Dismissal

- reasons connected with rights under the Working Time Regulations 1998 or National Minimum Wage Act 1998;
- exercising a right to be accompanied by a union representative or fellow worker at a disciplinary or grievance hearing;
- asserting rights under the 'whistleblowers' legislation;
- taking leave for family reasons;
- making a flexible working application;
- refusal of Sunday working by shop and betting employees;
- performing certain functions as a trustee of an occupational pension scheme;
- performing certain functions as an employee representative under TUPE or collective redundancy legislation; and
- selection for redundancy for any of the above reasons.

Dismissal for the following reasons will be automatically unfair but the employee will still need one year's service to bring the claim:

- dismissal because of a spent conviction;
- certain dismissals in connection with a TUPE transfer; and
- where the employer has not completed the statutory dismissal procedure.

See also: Disciplinary and grievance procedures, p.106; Discrimination, p.110; Employment contracts, p.146; Notice periods, p.xx; Redundancy, p.339; Retirement, p.353.

Sources of further information

ACAS: www.acas.org.uk

Employers should have a clear record of the policy and procedures for disciplinary matters to provide clear guidance to employees on the procedure that will be followed by their employer. Workplace Law Group's ***Non-Contractual Disciplinary and Dismissal Policy and Management Guide, v.4.0*** can also act as a checklist for managers, in relation to the steps that should be taken, with a view to minimising procedural irregularities and allegations of unfair treatment.

The draft policy also comes with a nine-page Management Guide containing helpful notes on the policy and alternative provisions for employers. For more information visit www.workplacelaw.net/Bookshop/PoliciesAndProcedures.

Dismissals can be a complex area as every individual case is different. Workplace Law's consultants can explain the procedures in easy-to-understand language and guide your managers as required, including writing letters and any other relevant documentation. Our consultants can also attend any meetings with the employee so that your managers feel supported at every step. In-house training courses are available that can be customised to your particular environment and we are anticipating being able to offer an accredited CIPD course on discipline and dismissal in 2010. For more information visit http://cipd.workplacelaw.net/.

Dress codes

Jackie Thomas, Berwin Leighton Paisner

Key points

Employers seek to apply dress codes to their employees for many reasons. In doing so, however, it is important that employers consider any potentially discriminatory implications as dress codes have historically been challenged under both the Sex Discrimination Act 1975 (SDA), the Race Relations Act 1976 (RRA) and, more recently, the Employment Equality (Religion or Belief) Regulations 2003.

Furthermore, since the European Convention on Human Rights has been incorporated into UK law by way of the Human Rights Act 1998 (HRA), it may also be possible to challenge the application of a dress code on the basis that it infringes the employee's human rights.

To avoid potential liability, employers should ensure that the policy applies evenly to both men and women, and that any requirements imposed are reasonable when balancing the rights of the employee and the requirements of the employer's business.

Factors that may be relevant include:

- whether the employee has contact with the public;
- whether the dress code is necessary for performance;
- health and safety; and
- illegality.

Legislation

- Sex Discrimination Act 1975 (SDA).
- Race Relations Act 1976 (RRA).
- Human Rights Act 1998.
- The Employment Equality (Religion or Belief) Regulations 2003.

In what situations will an employer seek to enforce a dress code?

Dress codes are used in the workplace for a number of reasons. Firstly, dress codes may be applied for reasons of food hygiene or other safety related reasons. Secondly, employers may require employees to wear a uniform in order to signify their status (for example a ticket inspector). Finally, they are also used by many employers merely as a way of ensuring that their employees are dressed appropriately (where the employees concerned come into contact with the employer's clients or customers).

The impact of the SDA on dress codes

The SDA provides that it is discriminatory for an employer to treat an employee less favourably than it would treat an employee of the opposite sex. This amounts to direct discrimination and the employer cannot defend such a claim on the grounds that the treatment is justified.

Dress codes

> **Facts**
> - 64% of those employers operating a dress code policy relax their dress codes rules at times, while just under a third (31%) do not.
> - 66% of UK companies and public sector bodies found that while standards of dress are becoming less formal, the policing of what is and is not acceptable clothing for the office is being tightened up.
> - A significant minority of employers (27%) say that while their dress code policy is observed, it still has to be policed.
> - More than two-thirds (67%) of dress code policies now have the force of the employment contract behind them.
> - Most employers (73%) say enhancing the external image of the company is the most common reason for having a dress code.
> - Fewer than one in ten employers involve their staff in devising the organisation's dress code.
> - Employees have to wear a uniform or overalls at less than half of organisations (46%).
> - Two-thirds of companies support people in meeting the dress codes of their religion.
> - Only around one in ten employers with a policy impose restrictions on religious dress or jewellery.

There are numerous cases of employees claiming that their employer's dress code is directly discriminatory. Examples include provisions of policies that prevented female employees from wearing trousers or that prevented male employees from having long hair. Interestingly, two Tribunals simultaneously considered whether it was discriminatory for a policy to require a male employee to wear a tie; each Tribunal reached conflicting conclusions –
in one case finding that such a policy was discriminatory and in the other concluding that the employer's policy was acceptable.

The reasoning for this conflict is that Tribunals will not directly compare the treatment of men and women in respect of each requirement of the dress code. The crucial issue will be whether, when viewed as a whole, the policy treats men and women in a generally equivalent manner in order to enforce a 'common principle of smartness'. In fact, this principle was expressly reaffirmed by the EAT in relation to the appeal of the case in which the Tribunal had found the dress code to be discriminatory. The EAT held that the policy did require women to dress to an equivalent level of smartness (despite the fact that they did not do so in practice) and so the Tribunal should properly have considered whether the requirement for a man to wear a collar and tie with no specific requirements for what a woman should wear was in itself discriminatory. The Tribunal had not considered this point and so the matter was remitted to a fresh Tribunal.

Potential claims under the RRA

It is also possible for claims to arise under the RRA if an employer's policy has a disparate impact on a particular racial group. This type of claim is an 'indirect discrimination' claim and is

Dress codes

therefore capable of being justified by the employer. Broadly, justification involves demonstrating that the policy is a proportionate means of achieving a legitimate aim (although the test varies slightly under the two different pieces of legislation).

An example that resulted in a claim was a policy that required a Sikh to shave his beard for health and safety reasons. The employee claimed that this amounted to indirect discrimination (in that it was more difficult for Sikhs as a racial group to comply). However, the Tribunals held that the employer's actions were justifiable as the policy was in place for reasons of food hygiene. To the extent that such a requirement could not be justified it would be discriminatory. Historically, such claims were limited by the fact that the RRA did not prevent discrimination on the grounds of religious belief unless the individual could also be said to fall within a particular racial group; however this loophole has now been closed by the introduction of the Employment Equality (Religion or Belief) Regulations 2003.

This issue also arose in the *Azmi v. Kirklees Metropolitan Council* case, which held that the refusal by a school to permit a Muslim teaching assistant to wear a veil did not amount to either direct or indirect race discrimination. The Tribunal and the EAT both found that this treatment did not amount to direct discrimination (on the basis of the correct comparator being a person who wore a face covering but was not Muslim). They went on to find that it was not indirect discrimination because the treatment could be justified.

Another recent case, *Eweida v. British Airways plc*, saw a female member of BA's check-in staff challenge BA's policy that prevented the wearing of non-uniform items. The policy excluded 'mandatory' religious items; for example, turbans. However, Miss Eweida wished to wear a cross on the grounds that she was a devout Christian. BA refused on the basis that this was not mandatory for Christians. Miss Eweida lost her case at both the Tribunal and the EAT on the basis that the policy did not result in group disadvantage, merely subjective disadvantage for the employee. Interestingly, however, the Tribunal and EAT both held that the policy would not have been objectively justifiable had the group disadvantage been established. This case is due to be considered by the Court of Appeal in 2010. Further, despite succeeding, BA still changed its policy, potentially as a result of significant unfavourable press generated by the case. This demonstrates that, particularly for large, public organisations, the interaction between dress codes and religious beliefs is problematic if an employer misjudges its position and does not correctly balance business needs and employee rights.

Human rights issues

As well as being potentially discriminatory, it is also possible for a dress code to infringe an employee's human rights. The European Convention on Human Rights has now been incorporated into UK law by the HRA. Of the rights it enshrines, Article 10 (the right to freedom of expression), Article 9 (freedom of thought, conscience and religion) and Article 14 (prohibition on discrimination) are all relevant when considering dress codes. In the case of most private sector employers, employees will not be able to bring a claim directly under the HRA but the employees of Public Authorities may be able to do so. Further, since the Tribunals are required to construe existing laws in a way that is

Dress codes

compatible with these rights, future claims based on discrimination legislation may also need to take into account these rights when balancing the needs of the employer with the rights of the employee.

See also: Discrimination, p.110; Human rights, p.226.

Sources of further information

Equality and Human Rights Commission: www.equalityhumanrights.com

Driving at work

Kathryn Gilbertson, Greenwoods Solicitors LLP

Key points
Employers need to manage the use of both the company car driver and the person using his own vehicle for business using risk assessments and a driving for work policy.

Legislation
- Road Traffic Act 1988.
- The Road Transport (Working Time) Regulations 2005.
- The Health Act 2006.
- Road Safety Act 2006.
- The Smoke-Free (Vehicle Operators and Penalty Notices) Regulations 2007.
- The Highway Code.

Road traffic law and the Highway Code
These lay down certain rules and restrictions (e.g. speed limits) and are normally enforced by the police and the courts. While the driver of the vehicle will primarily be held responsible for any offence, employers may also be liable, for instance in setting schedules that are so tight that the driver would consistently be breaking the speed limits if he attempted to meet them. The Magistrates Act 1980 may also be relevant to employers in England and Wales who aid, abet, counsel or procure an offence. Employers are responsible for ensuring their company vehicles are properly taxed and insured.

Working time

The Road Transport (Working Time) Regulations 2005
The Regulations cover mobile workers who will, in the main, be drivers and accompanying crew involved in road transport activities in a vehicle that is required by EU laws to have a tachograph (Council Regulation 3821/85 on recording equipment in road transport). The Regulations include the following provisions:

- A mobile worker's working time shall not exceed an average 48-hour working week, typically calculated over a four-month reference period;
- A maximum of 60 hours may be worked in a single week (provided that the average working week does not exceed 48 hours);
- There is a ten-hour limit for night workers over a 24-hour period;
- Workers cannot work more than six consecutive hours without taking a break. If working between six and nine hours, a break of at least 30 minutes is required. If working over nine hours, breaks totalling 45 minutes are required. Each break may be made up of separate periods of not less than 15 minutes each.
- The Regulations now affect self-employed drivers. Other drivers who fall outside the scope of the new Regulations, such as drivers of smaller vehicles or drivers exempt from the EU Drivers Hours Rules, are covered by the WTR; for example, the 48-hour average working week and the need for adequate rest. However, unlike the WTR, employees covered by the new Regulations cannot 'opt out'.

Driving at work

> **Facts**
> - Company drivers who drive more than 80% of their annual mileage on work-related journeys have 50% more accidents than similar drivers who do no work-related mileage.
> - Every week around 200 road deaths and serious injuries involve someone at work.
> - About 300 people are killed each year as a result of drivers falling asleep at the wheel.
> - Around four in ten tiredness-related crashes involve someone driving a commercial vehicle.

- Employers must monitor working time and should do what they can to ensure the limits are not breached. Records need to be kept for two years. Generally speaking, annual leave / sick leave cannot be used to reduce the average working time of a mobile worker. For each week of leave that is taken, 48 hours working time must be added to their working time; for each day's leave, eight hours must be added to working time.
- If no employer exists, the agency, employment business or even the worker themselves should monitor working time.

For further guidance on working time issues: www.dft.gov.uk/162259/165226/roadtransportworkingtimeguid3241

Mobile phones

Motorists can be prosecuted for driving while using a handheld mobile phone. Drivers committing this offence will be liable to pay a fixed penalty or a fine on conviction in court. The offence also attracts three penalty points.

The Regulations apply in all circumstances other than when the vehicle is parked, with the engine off. This means that the prohibition applies even if a vehicle has paused at traffic lights, stopped in a temporary traffic jam, or is in very slow-moving traffic.

The definition of 'handheld' means a mobile phone or other device that is held at some point during the course of making or receiving a call or fulfilling some other interactive communication function. An interactive communication function includes sending or receiving oral or written messages; facsimile documents; still or moving images; or accessing the internet.

Hands-free products, which do not require drivers to significantly alter their position in relation to the steering wheel in order to use them, have not fallen foul of the change in the law.

Employers' liability for mobile phone use whilst driving

The Regulations also created an offence of 'causing or permitting' another person to drive while using a handheld phone or other similar device. Employers may, therefore, be prosecuted if they require their employees to use their phones when driving.

The DfT has stated that employers cannot expect their employees to make or receive mobile phone calls while driving. This must be reflected in the company's health and

Driving at work

safety policy and risk management policy. Employers will not be liable simply for supplying a telephone or for telephoning an employee who was driving. However, employers must send a clear message to employees that they are forbidden to use their handheld mobile phones while driving and their employer will not require them to make or receive calls when driving.

Employers should inform their staff that, when driving, handheld mobile phones should be switched off, or, if switched on, the calls should be left to go through to voicemail, and that a safe place to stop should be found to check messages and return calls. Company policy should specify that using a handheld phone or similar device while driving is a criminal offence and will be treated as a disciplinary matter.

If no policy is implemented and employers are shown to have permitted the use of a handheld mobile phone while driving, they may be:

- liable under the Road Vehicles (Construction and Use) Regulations 2003;
- vicariously liable if an employee causes an accident while driving on business;
- liable under the Health and Safety at Work etc. Act 1974 as employers are obliged to provide a safe system of work and to do what they reasonably can to ensure the safety of staff and others; and
- liable if there is a fatal accident involving the use of a handheld mobile phone while driving. Where this practice was well known and encouraged throughout the company, there could be the possibility of a corporate manslaughter prosecution against directors, as has been the case with reference to the Working Time Regulations. The Corporate Manslaughter and Corporate Homicide Act 2007 will undoubtedly affect such prosecutions.

Hands-free mobile phones

Hands-free kits are widely available and the use of these kits is still legal. However, employers should be aware that this does not mean that drivers will be exempt from prosecution altogether if they use hands-free kits. Dangerous and careless driving can still be committed as separate offences under the Road Traffic Act 1988.

Research shows that using a hands-free phone while driving distracts the driver and increases the risk of an accident. Therefore, many businesses have banned them outright.

Employers who install hands-free kits should balance the commercial advantage of this with the potential risk of future liability, were an employee to cause an accident while speaking on the phone and driving.

General guidance
- Switch off the phone while driving and let it take messages.
- Alternatively, leave the phone switched on and let the calls go into voicemail.
- Alternatively, ask a passenger to deal with the call.
- Find a safe place to stop before turning off the engine and picking up the messages and returning calls.

Smoking

The Health Act 2006 provided that all enclosed public places and workplaces are smoke-free. These include company cars and hire vehicles. If a work vehicle is used as a workplace by more than one person it must be smoke-free at all times. The legislation does not extend to private vehicles.

Driving at work

If a private vehicle is used for work and the employee doesn't ever use it with others, it is permissible to smoke in that vehicle. There is no guidance available at present with regard to vehicles when used for primarily private journeys but sometimes used for business together with others.

Owners or managers of smoke-free premises will be guilty of an offence if they fail to prevent people from smoking. 'No smoking' signs must be displayed in all work vehicles. Managers should as a matter of good practice require that vehicles be smoke-free.

Workplace transport cases

A case that illustrates the combination of working time and dangerous driving and which resulted in a manslaughter conviction for the company director is that of *R v. Melvyn Spree* (2004).

Melvyn Spree, a road haulage director, was jailed for seven years after one of his lorry drivers fell asleep at the wheel and killed three motorists. It was held that Melvyn Spree, a director of Keymark Services, encouraged and enabled his drivers to work dangerously long hours, through fraudulent record-keeping and tachograph tampering. Melvyn Spree's fellow director, Lorraine March, was also jailed for conspiracy offences and Keymark Services was fined £50,000 for manslaughter.

Police investigations had found that the driver, Stephen Law, was part-way through an 18-hour shift when the accident occurred. The police also discovered systematic abuse of working hours' restrictions. Drivers were rewarded with a profit-share scheme. Melvyn Spree showed drivers how to jam tachographs and to keep false records of working times that demonstrated legal compliance.

In December 2005, Raymond Knapman, Partner at R&D Drivers, was prosecuted for manslaughter but acquitted after it could not be established that a fatal accident involving the deaths of two lorry drivers was caused by excessive hours or a heart attack by one of the drivers. However, Knapman was subsequently charged with eight counts of obtaining property by deception due to consistently requiring drivers to work excessive hours. Knapman pleaded guilty to the offences and to a breach of Section 3(2) of the HSWA for failing to ensure the health and safety of persons not in his employment and was sentenced to two-and-a-half-years' imprisonment in January 2006.

Conclusion

It is essential that there is a driving at work policy and risk assessment in place so that compliance with health and safety and working time legislation can be seen to be actively implemented and ongoing. This will not only assist in any HSE investigations but will also help to protect against any civil claims.

See also: Smoking, p.369.

Driving at work

Sources of further information

INDG382 *Driving at work: managing work-related road safety* can be downloaded from www.hse.gov.uk/pubns/indg382.pdf

Managing Occupational Road Risk: The RoSPA Guide is available from RoSPA. Call 0870 777 2090, or visit www.rospa.org.uk

The Work-related Road Safety Task Group's Report is accessible at www.hse.gov.uk/roadsafety/traffic1.pdf

Think! Road Safety website: www.thinkroadsafety.gov.uk

Workplace Law Group's ***Driving at Work Policy and Management Guide v.5.0*** helps you cover yourself and your staff and ensure that your employees keep to the highest standards of safe driving at work. This comprehensive new edition of the policy and management guide updates several elements of the original including the implications of recent legislation such as the Health Act 2006, the Road Safety Act 2007 and the Corporate Manslaughter and Corporate Homicide Act 2007. If your business hasn't already got a driving at work policy in place, or your current policy is not up-to-date, this is an essential publication. The policy highlights the issue of liability should prosecution occur following a driving at work accident, and who might face prosecution as a result. Visit www.workplacelaw.net/bookshop/policiesAndProcedures.

Workplace Law Group has also published the new and revised ***Driving at Work 2008: Special Report***, updated from the bestselling first edition. As well as corporate manslaughter legislation the report considers changes to the Road Safety Act 2006, the smoking ban, mobile phones and the increasing number of environmental schemes affecting vehicles. Written by experts in the field, this new Special Report is packed with extensive, up-to-date, high-level research and provides a unique insight into practical measures required to comply with the law. Visit www.workplacelaw.net/bookshop/specialReports.

Employee benefits

Roger Byard, Cripps Harries Hall

Key points

Employers use benefits to attract, retain and provide incentives for employees. Commonly they are provided as part of an overall strategy designed to achieve defined business objectives. Such benefits take many forms, offering both financial and non-financial rewards, and go to make up an employee's total reward. The benefits employers make available to employees have seen considerable enlargement in recent years. These now range from traditional occupational pensions and sick pay, to flexible working and voluntary arrangements. Many employers offer flexible benefit schemes under which employees are given a sum of money to buy those benefits that reflect their circumstances at the time. However, by offering employees cash to buy their own benefits, employers shift the burden of responsibility to make an informed choice to employees, which may not always be appropriate.

Some benefits have tax advantages, the most obvious being a pension, although for higher earners there are now restrictions that make pension provision less attractive. Voluntary benefits, which use an employer's bargaining power to negotiate discounts on products and services for employees, promote the employer's reputation for providing a good place to work.

The value of employee benefits can be difficult to assess. In a recent study, less than half of the employees surveyed had evaluated what the benefits package was worth to them. However the cost to the employer to provide and administer the benefits should not be underestimated.

The impact of the age discrimination legislation (introduced on 1 October 2006) on employee benefits appears to be minimal, although there is evidence that benefits providers have modified their products to make the level of benefits less age-related.

Legislation

- Equal Pay Act 1970.
- Social Security Contributions and Benefits Act 1992.
- Employment Rights Act 1996.
- Data Protection Act 1998.
- National Minimum Wage Act 1998.
- Finance Act 2003.
- Income Tax (Earnings and Pensions) Act 2003.
- Civil Partnerships Act 2004.
- Pensions Act 2004.
- Employment Equality (Age) Regulations 2006.
- Work and Families Act 2006.
- Pensions Act 2008.

Types of benefit

Financial benefits

These benefits include sick pay, pensions, company cars, bonuses, share option

Employee benefits

schemes, income protection insurance, medical insurance, life assurance and sports benefits.

Non-financial benefits
Flexitime, home working and discount schemes.

Tax-advantaged benefits
Salary sacrifice, pensions, childcare vouchers, bicycle loans, and season ticket loans up to £5,000.

Particular benefits

Pensions
Income tax relief is available at an employee's highest marginal rate on their own contributions to a pension scheme (although new restrictions on high earners will limit the relief on their contributions to 20%). Employers are able to offset the contributions they make against corporation tax. There is also a saving of both employers' and employees' National Insurance contributions. As an encouragement to employees to contribute to their personal pension provision, employers often offer to match what their employees pay in, up to certain limits. In 2012, Personal Accounts are to be introduced, which require automatic enrolment of employees over 22 and compulsory contributions of 4% of wages by the employee, 3% by the employer and 1% by the Government (as tax relief). See 'Pensions,' p.312 for more.

Salary sacrifice
The employer agrees to provide a benefit in exchange for the employee giving up part of their gross annual salary to optimise tax efficiencies. Where, for example, an employee makes a sacrifice of part of their pay, and the employer makes an equivalent contribution to their pension, the employee saves on income tax at their marginal rate. Both employer and employee save on National Insurance contributions. A salary sacrifice is a change to terms of employment and should be put in writing. There are pitfalls. For lower-paid employees, care needs to be exercised as it might impact on the minimum wage.

Facts

- 64% of employers offer a core benefits package, 19% provide a flexible benefits scheme, 64% a voluntary benefits plan and 71% perks through a salary sacrifice arrangement to all staff.
- In response to the recession, 43% plan to motivate employees to maintain morale and 33% intend to review benefits providers in order to get a cheaper or better deal.
- Just 39% of employers evaluate the effectiveness of their benefits strategy.
- 79% of employers believe their benefits package provides value for money and 70% say it reflects their employer brand.
- The most popular method of communicating benefits is at induction meetings for new joiners, which is offered by 78%, while leaflets, brochures or booklets are the most common way of communicating pension schemes (76%).
- Just under half (45%) of employers have made changes to their benefits package in the past year.

Source: www.employeebenefits.co.uk. Survey carried out in January 2009.

Employee benefits

In October 2008, amendments made to the Sex Discrimination Act mean that employers must continue to provide non-cash contractual benefits to employees throughout statutory maternity leave. HMRC guidance states that statutory maternity pay cannot be sacrificed and that benefits will continue even if an employee is not in receipt of any salary that could be sacrificed (see 'Childcare provisions,' p.65).

Healthcare and other risk benefits

These benefits include occupational sick pay (where employers pay more than is provided under the statutory sick pay scheme), and are typically insurance-based, such as private medical insurance (including counselling services), critical illness insurance, permanent health insurance and life assurance. The attraction of these benefits is the lower cost to employees of securing the protection that is achieved through economies of scale. Benefits such as insurance cover for death in service and income protection retain a moral or paternalistic element to them. Recent years have seen the insurance market harden in relation to these particular benefits, and premiums increase substantially. This is set to continue and prompts questions about the business rationale for continuing to provide them.

An increasing number of employers are offering other health benefits, such as reduced cost dental care, an in-house GP service, physiotherapy and health awareness and fitness programmes.

Company cars or cash allowance and travel loans

Company cars are commonly provided to enable an employee to do their job (e.g. a sales representative) or as a recognition of status. HMRC has always taxed the provision of this benefit. The basis for taxation is now referable not only to the make and engine size but also its environmental impact. The shift to environmental taxation has reduced the value of this benefit and as a result there is a trend for employers to offer as an alternative a cash sum by way of an annual allowance to employees who supply their own vehicle for business use.

Loans to employees to purchase season tickets to use public transport is a benefit employers based in city centres have offered for many years but which is seeing increased take-up as towns become more congested.

Introducing or changing employee benefits

- Identify the business goals that the introduction or modification of benefits are intended to support.
- Consult with employees, to learn what benefits would be most valued.
- When these have been identified, thoroughly research the market for the best products.
- Promote the introduction of the benefits by raising employees' awareness of the benefits on offer and their value to them, according to their own circumstances, by good and effective communication.
- Secure the employee's agreement to the introduction of, or changes to, the benefits, and record them in writing as a variation to the terms of employment.

Age discrimination

On 1 October 2006 it became unlawful to discriminate against employees on the ground of their age. Decisions made or policies applied that are based on age-related factors could give rise to discrimination. Employee benefits are most likely to be affected by indirect discrimination since they may constitute a 'policy, practice or criterion' that

Employee benefits

disadvantages a group of people who are defined by their age. This means that employee benefits that are provided by reference to length of employment would be discriminatory as younger workers are likely to have shorter periods of employment. For example, it is common for employers to reward employees with an additional day's holiday after a number of years of employment. This would be unlawful unless it could be justified. However, the legislation provides an important exemption for service-related benefits and allows an employer to use a service-related criterion when determining eligibility to benefits of up to five years.

While an employer may defer providing employee-related benefits to an employee for the first five years of their employment, the legislation does not permit an employer to stop providing benefits to an employee reaching a particular age. For example, if an employee works on beyond a retirement age of, say, 65, it will not be possible for an employer to refuse to continue to provide healthcare benefits, simply on the ground of cost.

To justify discrimination, an employer would need to show on an objective basis that they are pursuing a legitimate business aim in a proportionate way. The few cases on the point have shown that for employers to satisfy this test, the offending policy is the least discriminatory option and that there has been proper consultation with employees before it was introduced.

Conclusion

- Employee benefits offer a wide range of financial and non-financial rewards by which employers may attract, retain and incentivise employees.
- It is important that an employer looking to introduce or change benefits has identified clear business goals and analysed how the benefits will affect their employees.
- For the value of benefits offered to be fully appreciated it is essential that there is effective communication with employees.
- Employers need to be sensitive to anti-discrimination legislation, particularly with regard to age.

See also: Expenses, p.177; Flexible working, p.190; Pensions, p.312.

Sources of further information

HM Revenue & Customs: www.hmrc.gov.uk

BIS (formerly BERR): www.berr.gov.uk

Employee Benefits Research Institute: www.ebri.org

Pension Guide: www.thepensionservice.gov.uk

Employee Benefits: www.employeebenefits.co.uk

CIPD: www.cipd.co.uk

Employee consultation

Mark McCanney, Taylor Wessing LLP

Key points
- The Information and Consultation of Employees Regulations 2004 (ICER or 'the Regulations') came into force in April 2005. Depending on the number of employees employed in the undertaking, the Regulations applied at different stages:
  - undertakings with 150 or more employees from 6 April 2005;
  - undertakings with 100 or more employees from 6 April 2007; and
  - undertakings with 50 or more employees from 6 April 2008.
- Therefore, all undertakings with 50 or more employees are now subject to the Regulations.
- The Regulations provide a statutory basis for reaching agreement on the process of keeping employees informed and consulted about matters affecting their employment.
- The request to negotiate an agreement is triggered where either the employer starts the process and wishes to negotiate an existing agreement or introduce a new one, or there is a valid employee request. Therefore, there is no automatic obligation on any employer to do anything under the Regulations.
- Where there is a valid pre-existing agreement in place, the employer may ballot the workforce to determine whether they endorse the employee request or whether they are happy with the existing agreement.
- If the workforce does not endorse the request, the pre-existing arrangement continues.
- If negotiations fail to lead to agreement, the 'default provisions' will apply.
- If there is no employee request or the employer does not commence negotiations, there is no obligation to establish an information and consultation (I and C) agreement.

Legislation
- Information and Consultation Directive (2002/14/EC).
- Information and Consultation of Employees Regulations 2004.

Introduction
ICER came into force in April 2005 and implemented the EU Information and Consultation Directive. These Regulations are aimed at providing a statutory basis for keeping employees informed and consulted about employment issues that affect them in the workplace. This is a significant piece of legislation, which will affect the management of industrial relations in the UK, particularly for employers who are not used to dealing with issues on a collective basis.

The Regulations have been implemented on a phased basis depending on the number of employees in the particular undertaking and the last phase was introduced on 6 April 2008. Now all undertakings in the UK with 50 or more employees are potentially affected by the Regulations.

ICER applies to both public and private undertakings carrying out an economic

Employee consultation

> **Facts**
> - 37% of organisations have modified their information and consultation arrangements in response to the ICE Regulations.
> - A total of 41% of organisations report they have an information and consultation body or employee forum. 50% inform and consult via recognised trade unions.
> - Direct information and consultation takes place in 64% of unionised organisations and 46% have information and consultation bodies.
> - Amongst non-union organisations, direct information and consultation is the most popular practice (50%), while one-third (33%) have information and consultation bodies.

activity, whether or not operating for gain. It is the number of employees employed by an individual undertaking that is relevant, not those employed by a subsidiary or parent company.

Pre-existing agreements

If there is a valid pre-existing agreement and fewer than 40% of employees in an undertaking make a request for an I and C body, an employer may (but is not obliged to) ballot its workforce to see whether it endorses the request for a new body.

Where a ballot is held, and 40% of the workforce and a majority of those who vote endorse the employee request for a new I and C body, the employer is obliged to negotiate a new agreement (as set out below).

Where fewer than 40% of the workforce or a minority of those voting endorse the employee request for a new agreement, the employer will not be under an obligation to negotiate a new I and C agreement.

ICER sets out the conditions that need to be satisfied to be a valid pre-existing agreement. These include that it must be in writing; cover all the employees of the undertaking; have been approved by them; set out how information is given; and how the employees' views on this information will be sought.

The agreement must have been in place before an employee request under ICER was made.

Negotiating an I and C agreement under ICER

There are two ways to trigger negotiations for an I and C agreement:

1. If a valid request under ICER has been made by at least 10% of the employees in an undertaking (subject to a minimum of 15 and a maximum of 2,500 employees); or
2. If the employer initiates the process itself.

Any disputes about the validity of employee requests will be dealt with by the Central Arbitration Committee (CAC).

An employer must initiate negotiations for an agreement as soon as reasonably practicable and within three months at the latest. During this three-month period, the employer must:

- make arrangements for its employees to appoint or elect negotiating representatives; and

Employee consultation

- inform employees in writing of the identity of the representatives who have been elected and then invite those representatives to enter into negotiations to reach an ICER agreement.

Negotiations for reaching an agreement may last for up to six months, which is extendable by agreement. If a negotiated agreement is not reached, the 'default model' will apply (*see below*). There is a further six-month period for an employer to set up the necessary consultation body or reach a negotiated agreement.

Criteria for a negotiated ICER agreement

A negotiated agreement must comply with certain criteria. It must:

- be in writing and dated;
- cover all employees in the undertaking or group of undertakings;
- be signed by or on behalf of the employer;
- set out the circumstances in which employers will inform and consult – ICER gives employers and employees the freedom to agree on the subject matter, method, frequency and timing of information and consultation best suited to the employer's particular circumstances;
- provide either for the appointment or election of I and C representatives or for information and consultation directly with employees; and
- be approved by the employees.

Duration of agreement
Once a negotiated agreement is in place, there is a three-year moratorium on making further requests.

The 'default model'
If negotiations to reach an agreement fail, the 'default model' will apply. Employers have a further six months to facilitate the election of representatives. This must be via a ballot with one employee representative per 50 employees, subject to a minimum of two and a maximum of 25. If an employer fails to arrange this, it may be subject to a penalty fine of up to £75,000.

Information must be provided to I and C representatives at an appropriate time on:

- the recent and probable development of the undertaking's activities and economic situation;
- the situation, structure and probable development of employment within the undertaking and on any anticipatory measures envisaged, in particular where there is a threat to employment; and
- decisions likely to lead to substantial changes in work organisation or in contractual relations (including those covered by existing legislation in the area of collective consultation on collective redundancies and business transfers).

In respect of the second and third issues, the representatives must be consulted as well as informed.

Other factors

Protection of confidential information
There is a statutory duty of confidentiality on all I and C representatives in respect of information the employer discloses to them. However, they can challenge this duty before the CAC. Employers need not disclose information where to do so would 'seriously harm the functioning of the undertaking or be prejudicial to it'.

Compliance and enforcement
A complaint may be made to the CAC that an employer has failed to establish a negotiated agreement or has failed to inform and consult with employees in accordance with a negotiated agreement or the default model. This must be done within three months of the failure.

Employee consultation

These compliance mechanisms do not apply to pre-existing agreements. The CAC may make a declaration and an order requiring the defaulting party to take such specified steps as are necessary to comply with the I and C agreement within a specific period of time.

There is a maximum penalty of £75,000 for the employer's failure.

Overlapping issues

Where an employer is under information and consultation obligations arising from TUPE or collective redundancy legislation, it is excused from the obligations to consult under ICER, provided it notifies I and C representatives of this.

Protection for I and C representatives

I and C representatives are entitled to reasonable paid time off work during normal working hours and have the right not to be dismissed or suffer any detriment.

Practical steps for employers

Now that the Regulations have come into force for all undertakings with 50 or more employees, employers essentially have the option to either:

- negotiate a voluntary I and C agreement;
- negotiate an I and C agreement with employee representatives once a request has been made; or
- do nothing and allow the default provisions in ICER to apply.

The advantages to an employer of negotiating a voluntary agreement are that it is seen to be proactive, it can seize control of the process and a more flexible agreement may result. The default model is much less flexible with set categories of information and consultation and a predetermined number of representatives.

In preparation and in order to determine which option to follow, employers should:

- carry out an audit of any existing information and consultation processes;
- assess the likelihood of employees making an ICER request or other improvements to existing information and consultation structures;
- develop a strategy for dealing with any request – e.g. how to run internal elections, what the organisation is willing to 'consult' with employee representatives about;
- educate and train management in dealing with employees collectively, particularly where trade unions are likely to be represented on the consultation body;
- consider improving on existing consultation bodies / procedures; and
- consider what competitors are doing.

See also: Employment disputes, p.150; Trade unions, p.391; TUPE, p.399.

Sources of further information

BIS – Information and consultation: www.berr.gov.uk/employment/employment-legislation/ice/index.html

ACAS – Information and consultation: www.acas.org.uk/index.aspx?articleid=1017

Employment contracts

Chris McDowall, Anderson Strathern

Key points

A contract of employment can be created very simply. It does not require to be in writing. However, statutory requirements impose minimum obligations on employers to issue a written statement confirming the main particulars of employment. Employers can seek to regulate the employment relationship and comply with legal obligations by providing a more extensive written contract. Once contractual terms have been created, they cannot be changed unilaterally. Whether they are in writing or not, any proposed changes require to be handled appropriately to avoid claims of breach of contract and constructive unfair dismissal.

Legislation

- Equal Pay Act 1970 (Section 1).
- Copyright, Designs and Patents Act 1988.
- Data Protection Act 1988.
- Employment Rights Act 1996.
- Working Time Regulations 1998.
- Employment Act 2002.
- Employment Equality (Age) Regulations 2006.

Introduction

A contract of employment is created when one party accepts an offer of employment from another. Although a written contract is not required in order to create an employer–employee relationship, it is a statutory requirement and good practice to record the terms of the employment in writing. This can often be done by issuing the proposed contract or a statement of the main contractual terms that will apply, with the offer of employment. The employee should be asked to sign a copy of the written contract to clearly signify acceptance of its terms.

It should be noted, however, that a written term in a contract of employment could be rendered void if it seeks to avoid or restrict certain statutory rights or is deemed to be contrary to public policy.

Certain terms are implied into every contract by law, such as the implied duty of trust and confidence or the duty to take care of health and safety. Other terms are also incorporated into the contract, such as the obligation of equal pay or as a result of a collective agreement.

Providing written terms: the compulsory elements

Section 1 of the Employment Rights Act 1996 (ERA) places a statutory duty on employers to provide employees with particulars in writing of certain fundamental contractual terms. Since 1 October 2004 employers have been able to provide these in the form of a written contract, although they can still be provided in a simple statement of employment particulars.

The main requirements are as follows:

- Where an employee begins employment, the employer must give the employee a written statement of particulars of employment (Section 1(1), ERA).

Employment contracts

- The written statement may be given in instalments but shall not be given later than two months after commencement of employment (Section 1(2), ERA).
- The written statement shall contain names of the employer and employee, the date when the employment commenced and the date when the period of continuous employment commenced (Section 1(3), ERA).
- The written statement requires to contain details of all of the following particulars as at a date not more than seven days before the date of the statement (Section 1(4), ERA):
    - scale or rate of remuneration, or method of calculating remuneration;
    - the intervals at which remuneration is paid;
    - any terms and conditions relating to normal hours of work;
    - any terms and conditions relating to entitlement to holidays, including public holidays and holiday pay (the latter sufficient to calculate the precise amount payable), incapacity for work due to sickness or injury, and the provision of sick pay;
    - length of notice required to terminate employment;
    - title of the job the employee is employed to do or a brief description of it;
    - the duration of the employment if it is not permanent;
    - the place or places the employee is required to work at;
    - any collective agreements that affect the terms of employment;
    - where the employee is required to work outside the UK, the length of that period and the currency he will be paid in and any additional remuneration or benefits payable to him as a result; and
    - whether there is a contracting-out certificate in force for the purposes of the Pensions Schemes Act 1993, stating that the employment is contracted out.

The written statement must also contain a note specifying any disciplinary rules applicable to the employee or referring the employee to an easily accessible document containing that information (Section 3, ERA). The note must contain details of to whom the employee can apply if dissatisfied with a disciplinary decision or for the purposes of seeking redress of any grievance. These requirements apply to all employers. Employers who fail to comply with these requirements now risk financial penalties of between two and four weeks' pay if relevant Employment Tribunal claims are made.

Any changes to the compulsory elements of the statement of terms and conditions should be notified to the employee in writing within one month of the change.

Providing written terms: other important issues

Many employers will employ written contractual terms to exercise control over other important issues. Which issues will be appropriate will always depend on the individual circumstances of the particular contract. Some examples of these additional terms are as follows:

- Probationary period permitting the employer to terminate the contract, normally within the first few months of employment, on minimal notice.
- Data protection terms, designed to give fair notice of the purposes for which data processing will be carried out, for compliance with the Data Protection Act 1988.

Employment contracts

> **Facts**
> - In 2007/08, 4,955 claims were lodged with the Employment Tribunal Service for failure to provide written statement of terms and conditions. This was an increase from 3,429 in 2006/07, and 3,078 in 2005/06.
> - In 2007/08, 25,054 claims were lodged with the Employment Tribunal Service for breach of contract. This was down from 27,298 claims in 2006/07, and 26,230 in 2005/06.
>
> Source: www.employmenttribunals.gov.uk

- Restrictions on acceptance of other work during employment.
- Flexibility clause (e.g. requirements to work overtime, undertake other duties, mobility clauses).
- The ability to put employees on lay-off or short-term working.
- Confidentiality terms, which give the employee notice of the types of information to be regarded as confidential during and after employment.
- Authority for deductions from wages (e.g. overpayments of holiday pay or expenses).
- Garden leave terms, designed to allow the employer to require the employee to stay away from work, often used to protect business interests during notice periods.
- Intellectual property terms, which set out ownership of copyright of work created during employment and assign rights to it.
- Restrictive covenants, which impose restraints post-employment on competition, solicitation of customers and significant employees and the use of trade secrets of the employer.
- Payment in lieu of notice clause, to allow the employer to dismiss an employee immediately without adhering to the notice period provided for in the contract. If this term is not expressly written into the contract, the employer will be unable to make a payment to the employee in lieu of notice, without being in breach of contract.
- Opt-out arrangements under the Working Time Regulations 1998. While this is often included in the contract and therefore signed before the contract begins or during the probationary period, there is an argument that such consent is not freely given. If an employee's working time will or could exceed the working time limits, considerations should be given to asking the employee to sign a separate opt-out agreement after the end of the probationary period
- Normal retirement age clause, if an employer's normal retirement age is below the default age of 65, provided by the Employment Equality (Age) Regulations 2006. Only where a retirement age below 65 can be objectively justified, which in practice will be very rare, will such a retirement age comply with the Employment Equality (Age) Regulations 2006.
- Many of these clauses will be subject to legal restrictions in relation to enforceability and it is essential that they are drafted in a manner that will be legally compliant.

Altering terms and conditions of employment

Once established, contractual terms can be varied but only if the consent of *both* parties to the proposed variation is achieved. This can sometimes

Employment contracts

involve 'buying out' existing terms with a compensatory financial payment.

If consent is not forthcoming, the only potentially valid alternative is to serve appropriate notice that the contract is being terminated and at the same time, offer a new contract, containing the new terms, to take effect immediately upon termination. However, such an approach can give rise to claims of unfair dismissal, so before taking such action, careful analysis is advised. If the original contract is not brought to an end effectively, breach of contract claims may ensue following any change. If the breach is fundamental, this can lead to a claim that the employee has been constructively unfairly dismissed.

See also: Data protection, p.84; Flexible working, p.190; Holiday, p.219; Leave, p.252; Notice periods, p.301; Personnel files, p.317; Probationary periods, p.332; Restrictive covenants and garden leave, p.350; Retirement, p.353; Staff handbooks, p.375.

Sources of further information

ACAS: www.acas.org.uk

UK Department for Business Innovation and Skills: www.bis.gov.uk

Office of Public Sector Information: www.opsi.gov.uk

All employers are required to issue employees with a written statement of certain terms of employment. Workplace Law Group's **Employment Contract and Management Guide, v.5.0** has been published to help employers ensure that they comply with their requirements under law and to provide a clear record of the agreement between employer and employee. The policy also comes with a 20-page Management Guide containing helpful notes on the policy and alternative provisions for employers. Visit www.workplacelaw.net/Bookshop/PoliciesAndProcedures for more details.

Employment disputes

Tania Revell, Taylor Wessing

Key points

Most claims brought against a company by job applicants, employees, workers and ex-employees (and also contractors and agency workers) are brought in an Employment Tribunal. Sometimes claims may be brought in the County Court or High Court.

The Employment Tribunal has jurisdiction to hear most employment-related litigation (dismissal, discrimination, working time, TUPE). It is a relatively less expensive forum than other civil courts and is less formal. Historically, each party has met its own legal costs although Tribunals are more frequently making costs awards in particular circumstances.

Breach of contract claims arising or outstanding on termination of employment can be brought in the Employment Tribunal if they are for £25,000 or less. Breach of contract claims where the possible damages are above £25,000 should be brought in the County or High Courts.

The County and High Courts are more formal and expensive. It is possible to get costs awards against the losing party.

Mediation is an increasingly popular option for employers and employees as a means of avoiding having to go to Court or to an Employment Tribunal. It is likely that mediation will become even more widespread since the introduction of the Acas Code of Practice in April 2009, as the Code encourages employers to consider using independent third parties to resolve workplace disciplinary or grievance issues such as external mediators.

ACAS is the Government's conciliation service and is responsible for conciliating between the parties in cases brought in the Employment Tribunal.

It is now also possible to use ACAS as an arbitrator in a dispute if it is an unfair dismissal case.

Legislation
- Employment Tribunal: Employment Tribunals (Constitution and Rules of Procedure) Regulations 2004.
- County / High Court: Civil Procedural Rules.
- Employment Act 2008.

Proceedings brought in the Employment Tribunal
The Tribunal's procedural regulations are governed by the 'overriding objective,' which is to enable Tribunals to deal with cases justly, such as ensuring the parties are on an equal footing, saving expense,

Employment disputes

dealing with the case in ways that are proportionate to the complexity of the issues, and ensuring the case is dealt with expeditiously and fairly.

A case is started when the employee, known as the 'claimant,' presents the Secretary of the Tribunals with a written application in the appropriate form known as the claim form (or ET1).

There are distinctive time limits for lodging claims in the Employment Tribunal – these are normally three months from the date of the termination of the employee's employment, or the act being complained of. The time limits are strictly enforced. However, in certain circumstances, a claimant may apply for an extension of time to submit a claim.

The employer is 'the respondent' and submits a defence known as a 'response form' (or ET3) within the 28-day limit, as advised by the Tribunal.

After the response form is received by the Employment Tribunal, the case will be prepared for a hearing. To do so, a number of tasks must be undertaken by both parties – disclosure of documents, requests for additional information, exchanging witness statements. Sometimes these matters will be ordered by the Employment Tribunal in correspondence or following a case management discussion.

Sometimes there may be issues that would be dealt with at a pre-hearing review (e.g. in complex discrimination cases). After the full hearing, usually presided over by an employment judge and two lay wing members, judgment is made either orally or in writing or both. A judgment might deal with both liability and remedy, or it might only deal with the question of liability, in which case if the claimant is successful the remedy is decided by the Employment Tribunal at a remedies hearing. Either party may appeal the decision to the Employment Appeal Tribunal. Again, strict time limits apply.

The Employment Tribunal does not normally order that the unsuccessful party pay the costs of the winner. However, there is an increasing trend towards the Tribunal making costs orders. The Employment Tribunal and EAT statistics for 1 April 2007 to 31 March 2008 demonstrated that in 134 cases the Tribunals awarded costs in favour of the claimant, and in 327 cases the Tribunal awarded costs in favour of the respondent. The maximum award was £17,775 and the average award was £2,095.

The Tribunal can order costs in certain circumstances such as where:

- a party or his representative has acted vexatiously, abusively, disruptively, or otherwise unreasonably in bringing or conducting the proceedings, or the bringing or conducting of proceedings has been misconceived;
- the hearing was adjourned at the request of one party; or
- a party has not complied with a Tribunal's directions order (e.g. to supply documents or particulars).

The Employment Tribunal can also make wasted costs orders and preparation time orders.

The Tribunal only has the power to award up to £10,000 in costs without ordering a detailed assessment. If the costs are above £10,000, the bill of costs claimed will then be subject to a detailed assessment by the county court.

Employment disputes

Settlement via the Advisory, Conciliation and Arbitration Service (ACAS)

An ACAS officer is attached to every claim for unfair dismissal or unlawful discrimination and until recently had a duty to conciliate during certain 'conciliation periods,' depending on the type of claim. While these conciliation periods still apply for employment disputes that arose before 6 April 2009, following the enactment of the Employment Act 2008 these fixed periods have now been removed and an Acas officer can conciliate between the parties at any point from the ET1 being submitted to the hearing taking place. The ACAS officer has no duty to advise on the merits of the claim and will not enter into lengthy discussion on legal points.

The ACAS officer will contact each party (by letter or telephone) at the start of proceedings in the Employment Tribunal. He can negotiate between the parties towards a settlement. A settlement agreement reached through ACAS is binding and effective. It is normally recorded on a 'COT3 form'.

ACAS has also set up an arbitration scheme for unfair dismissal cases as a form of alternative dispute resolution (see below). This is different from conciliation in that ACAS provides an independent arbitrator who hears the evidence and decides the case for the employer and employee. As an arbitrator, ACAS can award the same level of payments as a Tribunal against employers.

County Court and High Court

Employment disputes can also give rise to a civil action that is heard in either a County Court (if it is a small claim or if it is not a complex matter) or the High Court. The High Court will not hear a claim whose value is £15,000 or less (or less than £50,000 where personal injury damages are involved). There are three tracks – small claims (under £5,000); fast track, which is for claims between £5,000 and £15,000; and multi-track for claims above £15,000. The main types of civil actions relating to employment are wrongful dismissal/breach of contract or injunctions to stop employees joining a competitor, setting up in competition, or disclosing confidential information.

The High Court sits at the Royal Courts of Justice in London as well as at some major court centres around the country. Most employment-related civil actions are heard in the Queen's Bench Division of the High Court.

The parties can appeal a decision of the High Court to the Court of Appeal and in certain rare circumstances on to the House of Lords or European Court of Justice.

Alternative dispute resolution

Alternative dispute resolution encompasses many methods for parties avoiding going to Court and settling legal disputes through other means. Mediation is one of those means; arbitration is another.

Mediation is used in employment-related claims very successfully because:

- it can be a cost saving for both parties;
- it is less intimidating than a Court or Tribunal;
- it does not involve lengthy trials or hearings; and
- it focuses less on the legal issues and so can be a lot less complex.

Arbitration is used in more complex commercial cases and international cases and is not generally used in domestic employment disputes apart from the new ACAS arbitration scheme mentioned above.

Employment disputes

There are a number of bodies that provide alternative dispute resolution, such as the Centre for Effective Dispute Resolution (CEDR), the ADR Group and In Place of Strife. Also, many barristers' chambers provide mediation services.

The Employment Act 2008

The Employment Act 2008 repealed the statutory dispute resolution procedure with a new Code of Practice on handling discipline and grievance. The Code only applies to misconduct issues, poor performance and grievances. It does not apply to individual redundancies or the non-renewal of fixed-term contracts, but in either of these circumstances employers should still follow a fair procedure, in accordance with other legislation or case law as appropriate. Employment Tribunals can take the Code into account and increase awards by up to 25% for unreasonable failure of an employer to comply with any part of it. Similarly, an employee's unreasonable failure to comply may result in a decrease of their award by 25%. ACAS has also published a guide to complement the Code, which provides detailed advice to employers on practical aspects of disciplinary and grievance issues in the workplace.

The ACAS Code has reverted to the pre-2004 position whereby a Tribunal may reduce a compensatory award for a procedurally unfair dismissal to reflect the likelihood that the dismissal would have occurred anyway even if the correct procedure had been followed.

See also: Disciplinary and grievance procedures, p.106; Dismissal, p.124; Employment Tribunals, p.158.

Sources of further information

Centre for Effective Dispute Resolution: www.cedr.co.uk/

ADR Group: www.adrgroup.co.uk

Employment Tribunals Service: www.employmenttribunals.gov.uk

ACAS: www.acas.org.uk/index.aspx?articleid=1461

ACAS – Code of Practice on discipline and grievance: www.acas.org.uk/CHttpHandler.ashx?id=1041

Employment status

Sarah Lee and Lisa Norman, BPE Solicitors

Key points

Given that quite distinct rules exist for those who are employees and those who are sub-contractors or workers, it is of great importance to be aware of the factors that go towards determining whether an individual is likely to be an employee or a sub-contractor. The main issue is to distinguish between a 'Contract of Service' on the one hand, and a 'Contract for Services' on the other.

Under a Contract of Service, a person essentially agrees to serve another, whereas under a Contract for Services, a person agrees to provide services to another.

However, it is important to note that what the parties call themselves and how they enable or define the agreement in question is not the decisive factor. If there is a dispute, Employment Tribunals have generally sought to ascertain the true nature of the relationship between the parties. The key element seems to be whether the 'employer' is obliged to provide work for the 'employee' and, in turn, whether the employee is then obliged to personally perform that work. These mutual obligations are a strong indicator that the worker is an employer. Secondly, the worker has to expressly or impliedly agree to be subject to the control of the employer.

Legislation

Although there is a limited amount of legislation in respect of determining 'status' itself, there is a vast amount of legislation that becomes relevant as a knock-on effect of the determination of whether an individual is an employee or a worker or, indeed, a sub-contractor. The relevant legislation is listed below:

- Sex Discrimination Act 1975.
- Race Relations Act 1976.
- Transfer of Employment (Protection of Employment) Regulations 1981.
- Social Security Contributions and Benefits Act 1992.
- Disability Discrimination Act 1995.
- Employment Rights Act 1996.
- National Minimum Wage Act 1998.
- Public Interest Disclosure Act 1998.
- Working Time Regulations 1998.
- Employment Relations Act 1999.
- Part-Time Workers (Prevention of Less Favourable Treatment) Regulations 2000.
- Employment Act 2002.
- Fixed Term Employees (Prevention of Less Favourable Treatment) Regulations 2002.
- Conduct of Employment Agencies Employment Businesses Regulations 2003.
- Employment Equality (Religion or Belief) Regulations 2003.
- Employment Equality (Sexual Orientation) Regulations 2003.

Basic categories

Essentially, the basic types of status in employment law are:

Employment status

- Employee; or
- Worker / independent contractor – self-employed (note that an independent contractor could mean a separate entity, namely, a company).

Employees

There are three essential elements to a contract of employment, without which such a contract could not be deemed to be a contract of employment:

1. The contract must impose an obligation on a person to provide work personally;
2. There must be a mutuality of obligation between employer and employee; and
3. The worker must expressly and impliedly agree to be subject to the control of the person for whom he works to a sufficient degree, to make that person master.

Similarly, where the terms of the contract express negative mutuality of obligations, there cannot be a contract of employment. Further, if the contract does not require the services in question to be carried out personally by the individual in question, or those in their control, then again, the contract in question cannot be a contract of employment. In saying that, often the Employment Tribunals are required to look at the reality of the situation and go beyond the written contract themselves. Often, individuals are engaged as 'sub-contractors' when in fact an Employment Tribunal may deem them to be an employee.

By way of an example, the more personal responsibility that an individual has in relation to his own investment and manager, financial risk and opportunity for profiting, the more likely that person is considered to be an independent contractor, rather than an employee. In contrast, some factors that sometimes go towards demonstrating the existence of a contract of employment are listed below:

- Remuneration by way of payment of wages or salary;
- Payment during absence through illness;
- Paid holiday;
- Membership of the company pension scheme;
- Control by a disciplinary code laid down by the employer; and
- A prohibition on working for other companies or individuals.

By way of a summary in relation to 'employees', if one can say yes to all of the following questions then an individual is likely to be an employee:

- Do you have to do the work yourself?
- Can someone tell you at any time, what to do, where to carry out the work, or when and how to do it?
- Do you work a set amount of hours?
- Can someone move you from task to task?
- Are you paid by the hour, week or month?
- Can you get overtime or bonus payment?

Worker / sub-contractor

As mentioned at the start of the chapter, a worker / sub-contractor is someone who operates under a 'Contract for Services' as opposed to a 'Contract of Service'.

If one can answer yes to all of the following questions, it will usually mean an individual is self-employed:

- Can you hire someone to do the work for you or engage help at your own expense?
- Do you risk your own money?
- Do you provide the main items of equipment that you need to do your job, not just the small tools that many employees provide themselves?

Employment status

- Do you agree to do a job for a fixed price, regardless of how long the job may take?
- Can you decide what work to do, how and when to do work, and where to provide the services?
- Do you regularly work for a number of different people?
- Do you have to correct unsatisfactory work at your own time and at your own expense?

Legal consequences of the distinction

An 'employee' enjoys (subject to the satisfaction of relevant qualifying conditions) the following rights (*note: this list is not exhaustive*):

- Unfair dismissal protection;
- Redundancy payment entitlement;
- Written Particulars of Terms of Employment;
- Statutory minimum period of notice;
- Guaranteed payment;
- Medical suspension payment;
- Protection from discrimination on grounds of race, sex, disability, religious belief and sexual orientation;
- Equal pay;
- Maternity rights;
- Time off for trade union activities;
- The option to be employed for the agreed period or be given the agreed length of notice;
- A safe place of work;
- Statutory sick pay;
- Wages free of any deductions not properly authorised;
- Rights under the Working Time Regulations 1998; and
- In the case of those employed as shop workers or betting workers, the right to object to working on Sundays.

With regard to the self-employed, the following rights are applicable:

- To benefit from all contractual entitlements;
- Protection against discrimination on the grounds of race, sex, disability, sexual orientation or religious belief and equal pay;
- Where applicable, to be provided with a safe place and a safe system of work;
- Wages free of any deductions not properly authorised; and
- Rights under the Working Time Regulations 1998.

Status and the Construction Industry Scheme 2006

As an aside, HM Revenue and Customs has introduced a new scheme in order to tighten up on the status of employees and sub-contractors, given the differences in tax and National Insurance contributions. Under the changes, which came into force in April 2007, sub-contractors will no longer supply certificates and registration cards but, rather, will be registered centrally.

There will be an obligation on the 'contractors' to enquire as to whether the individual in question is likely to be an employee or a sub-contractor and, once a month, produce a report to the Revenue declaring that 'status' has been properly considered.

HMRC is also considering how to formalise the employment relationship in the construction industry so as only genuinely self-employed contractors retain self-employed status. This means that a larger number of 'contractors' may have worker status and entitlements

Shareholders

Whilst it has been traditionally thought that shareholders are not employees, the case of *Secretary of State for Business, Enterprise and Regulatory Reform v. Neufeld & Anor* (2009) altered this. Mr Neufeld held 90% of the issued shares in the company, and had two co-directors who each had 5% shareholdings.

Employment status

He worked long hours for the company, did not take all his holiday entitlement, and gave personal guarantees in respect of the company's liabilities, but when the business went into receivership, he was denied a payment from the National Insurance Fund on the basis that his 90% shareholding was not compatible with employee status.

Mr Neufeld took his claim to the Employment Tribunal (where he lost), to the Employment Appeal Tribunal (where he won), following which the Secretary of State for Business, Enterprise and Regulatory Reform took the matter to the Court of Appeal. In their judgment, the Court of Appeal made it clear there is no reason in principle why someone who is a shareholder and director of a company cannot also be an employee of that same company under a contract of employment. Their Lordships endorsed the point that a person as one legal entity can be willing to work for and make a contract (of employment) with a company which is another legal entity, and they clarified the guiding principles to be taken into account by tribunals and courts in determining the question of fact as to whether or not a shareholder / director is an employee of a company.

Neufeld is set to become the leading case on this issue, and will bring some degree of comfort, particularly in the current economic climate, to those shareholder/employees who in the past not only had to face the heartache of losing the business in which they worked incredibly hard, but also the denial of their claim for any payment from the National Insurance Fund.

> *See also*: Employment contracts, p.146; Fixed-term workers, p.187; Part-time workers, p.308; Self-employment, p.357; Work experience, internships and apprenticeships, p.417.

Sources of further information

Inland Revenue: www.inlandrevenue.co.uk

HM Revenue and Customs – Construction Industry Scheme: www.hmrc.gov.uk/cis

Employment Tribunals

Anna Youngs, Mills & Reeve

Key points
- Parties do not have to be legally represented, but representation is of assistance in more complex cases, particularly discrimination issues.
- Use only the prescribed forms to issue or respond to a claim.
- Follow the Tribunal's Orders.
- Consider settlement via compromise agreement / ACAS conciliation.

Legislation
- Employment Tribunals Rules of Procedure 2004 (which are set out at Schedule 1 of the Employment Tribunals (Constitution and Rules of Procedure) Regulations 2004 as amended by The Employment Tribunals (Constitution and Rules of Procedure) (Amendment) Regulations 2008.

Introduction to proceedings in the Employment Tribunals
The Employment Tribunals are less formal than the other Courts of England and Wales. The idea is that anybody can bring or defend a claim, without necessarily seeking legal advice. That said, employment issues are notoriously complex, particularly where discrimination is alleged and in such cases legal advice is likely to be needed.

The Employment Tribunals Rules of Procedure 2004 (the Rules) set out the way in which proceedings must be lodged and conducted. This chapter will highlight some general practice points for conducting proceedings.

The Overriding Objective
The Overriding Objective is a principle that runs throughout our litigation system. The Objective is to enable the Courts and Tribunal to deal with cases justly. This must be considered when making applications to the Tribunal and when conducting Tribunal proceedings in general, because the Tribunal will make its decisions in accordance with the Overriding Objective.

The Overriding Objective is set out at Regulation 3 of the Employment Tribunals (Constitution and Rules of Procedure) Regulations 2004, which states that dealing with a case justly includes, so far as practicable:

- ensuring that the parties are on an equal footing;
- dealing with the case in ways that are proportionate to the complexity or importance of the issues;
- ensuring that it is dealt with expeditiously and fairly; and
- saving expense.

Using the prescribed form
There are set forms that must be used when bringing (form ET1) and responding (form ET3) to a claim in the Employment Tribunal. If the correct form is not used, the claim or response will not be accepted. The current forms can be downloaded from the Employment Tribunals' website (www.employmenttribunals.gov.uk). There are some sections on the form that are marked with a star (*). These sections must be answered, or the claim or the response can be rejected.

Employment Tribunals

Time limits
Strict time limits apply in the Employment Tribunals. When a claim is sent to the employer, the Tribunal will state on the accompanying letter the date by which they must respond. Failure to respond by that deadline is likely to result in a default judgment being entered in favour of the claimant, unless the employer has applied for and received an extension of time (which should not be relied upon as a given).

The claimant also has to comply with time limits. Generally claims must be lodged within three months of either the date of dismissal, or the last act complained of, although there are some exceptions and variations. Due to the various discretions that can be exercised by the Tribunal, it is worth seeking legal advice.

Management of the case
Once the claim has been received and the response has been accepted, the next step is for the Tribunal to set down directions for the future conduct of the case. This is usually done at a Case Management Discussion. These directions will set dates by which the following must have been done:

- *Exchange of documents*. All relevant documents within your possession or control, whether or not they help your case, help your opponent's case, or damage either case.
- *Agree a 'bundle' of documents*. The bundle should contain all documents relevant to the matters in issue. The claimant is responsible for preparing the bundle, but many respondents take on this responsibility as they have more resources and generally have more documents in their possession.
- *Exchange of witness statements*. This is usually done by way of mutual or simultaneous exchange, but may be done by sequential exchange if the claimant's case is not clear from their claim form or any further particulars of claim.
- Date and length of the hearing.

Parties may also be required to agree a chronology, statement of agreed facts and statement of issues that the Tribunal must determine, although even if the Tribunal does not order a statement of issues, it is important that you know what the issues are so that you can focus your case effectively.

Facts
- In 2007/08, Employment Tribunals accepted over 189,000 claims, more than 50,000 more than the previous year. The increase is likely to be due to the mass equal pay litigation, and provisional figures indicate that Tribunals accepted approximately 131,000 claims in 2008/09.
- In 2007/08, approximately 31,000 claimants represented themselves.
- The average award for unfair dismissal was £8,058 in 2007/08.
- The average award for race discrimination was £14,566 in 2007/08, and the highest award was £68,991.
- The average award for sex discrimination was £11,263 in 2007/08, and the highest award was £13,1466.
- The average award for disability discrimination was £19,523 in 2007/08, and the highest award was £227,208.

Employment Tribunals

An important document is the schedule of loss. The Tribunal will require the claimant to serve a schedule setting out what financial losses they have suffered. This is usually ordered at the earliest stage in the hope of promoting settlement. If this is not ordered by the Tribunal, employers should certainly ask for one. This will help you assess the cost effectiveness of resisting the claim.

Documents that do not have to be disclosed or included in the Bundle
'Without prejudice' documents, which generally take the form of negotiations between the parties, should not be included in the Bundle.

Documents that attract legal advice or litigation 'privilege' (which is the right not to disclose) do not have to be disclosed:

- Legal advice privilege protects communications passing between lawyer and client created for the purpose of giving or receiving advice. This type of privilege is not confined to advice about legal rights and obligations but it will not arise unless the advice is given in a relevant legal context.
- Litigation privilege protects documents created for the dominant purpose of gathering evidence for use in proceedings if they are made:
  - confidentially;
  - between a lawyer and a client, a lawyer and his agent or a lawyer and a third party; and
  - for the dominant purpose of conducting or aiding the conduct of actual litigation or litigation which is reasonably in prospect.

The Tribunal has powers to award costs or even to strike out a claim for failure to comply with an Order.

The hearing
In full hearings, where the merits of a claim are to be decided, the Tribunal panel will be made up of three people:

- A legally qualified Employment Judge (who sits in the middle of the panel and is addressed as 'Sir' or 'Madam').
- Two lay members – one who has an employee background, such as someone from a Union, and one who has an employer background.

The idea is that there is a balanced panel, who will make a balanced decision. As the Tribunal is a civil court, liability will be determined on the 'balance of probabilities', which means, for example, whether it is more likely than not that the dismissal was unfair.

There are differing rules as to which side goes first, depending on the type of claim. The Tribunal will assist unrepresented parties with procedure as far as possible, but as a rule of thumb, where discrimination is alleged, the claimant's case will be heard first (as the claimant must prove facts out of which discrimination could be inferred), and in unfair dismissal cases, the respondent will go first.

Whichever side goes first, the procedure is the same for the witnesses. Using the claimant's witness as an example:

- the witness may have to read their statement aloud (bear this in mind when drafting statements);
- the claimant's representative may be able to ask some questions;
- the other side will then cross-examine the witness;
- the Employment Judge or the panel members may ask some questions; and
- the claimant's representative will have the opportunity to ask further questions to clarify points made by the other side.

After all the evidence from both sides is heard, each side will make 'submissions' about their case. This is an opportunity for each side to put forward their best

Employment Tribunals

points, address any damage done to their case by the other side, and highlight the weaknesses in the other side's case.

Top tips for witnesses
- Don't avoid answering a question.
- If you don't know or don't remember, say so (but don't use this as a get out!).
- Don't fill silences by talking (this is where the most damage is commonly done!).
- Familiarise yourself with your witness statement and read documents relevant to your evidence.

The judgment
The Employment Judge may give an oral judgment on the day. If s/he does this, s/he will only provide a full written judgment if you ask for one. A party must have a written judgment if you think you have grounds for appeal.

If you win, you may be able to get costs from the other side. Costs are not given automatically in the Tribunal. Refer to the rules for the circumstances in which you can apply for costs and the time limits for doing so.

The Tribunal has a booklet on Tribunal Judgments that they send out with the written judgment, which should be of use.

Costs or expenses orders may be made if:

- a hearing or pre-hearing review is postponed;
- in bringing or conducting the proceedings, a party has been misconceived or if the party or his representative has acted vexatiously, abusively, disruptively or otherwise unreasonably; and/or
- a party has not complied with an order or practice direction.

The Tribunal may also make preparation time orders and wasted costs orders as appropriate.

Withdrawal by the claimant
Please note that if the claimant withdraws their claim at any stage, this ends the proceedings. However, it does not necessarily prevent them from re-issuing fresh proceedings. Therefore, upon receipt of a notice of withdrawal it is advisable for respondents to apply to the Tribunal for the claim to be 'dismissed' pursuant to Rule 25(4) of the Rules. This prevents the claimant from being able to re-issue the proceedings. An application should be made within 28 days from the date that the notice of withdrawal is sent to the parties by the Tribunal. The practice is that the claimant (or their representative) should be copied in to the application and given time to object (some Tribunals currently say that the claimant should be given 14 days to object). This is not now necessary if conciliation is agreed through ACAS.

ACAS and conciliation
An ACAS officer is assigned to each case in order to try to assist the parties to conciliate or settle the case. ACAS' services are free and confidential, and therefore settling a claim through ACAS can avoid unwanted costs and publicity.

Litigation risk is avoided if a case settles, and an ACAS settlement can include things that a Tribunal would not be able to consider; for example, an agreed reference can be consideration for a settlement, but the Tribunal cannot order an employer to provide a reference. This is a key negotiation point (but when providing references employers must consider their duty of care to both the employee and to future employers).

Fixed conciliation periods were introduced in October 2004 but have since been abolished.

Judicial mediation
Certain Employment Tribunals (Birmingham, London Central and

Employment Tribunals

Newcastle) are currently running a Judicial Mediation pilot scheme. The pilot commenced in July 2006 and is still ongoing.

The aim is to encourage resolution of disputes without having a full Employment Tribunal hearing (and therefore will normally be appropriate for cases where there is an ongoing relationship between the parties). The intention is that this will save time and costs.

The pilot scheme is running in relation to cases that include an element of sex, race or disability discrimination.

If the parties agree to Judicial Mediation, the Tribunal proceedings will be stayed and the case will be referred to a full-time Employment Judge who is trained in mediation. The Employment Judge will not make a decision in the case or give what is effectively a judgment in the case.

The mediation will be in private, and will be confidential. The Employment Judge who mediated the case will not be involved further in the case if the mediation is not successful and it proceeds to a hearing. The mediation files and Tribunal hearing files will be kept completely separate so that the parties can speak freely in mediation.

See also: Contract disputes, p.71; Disciplinary and grievance procedures, p.106; Discrimination, p.110; Dismissal, p.124; Employment disputes, p.150; Crunching the numbers, p.164.

Sources of further information

Tribunals Service: www.employmenttribunals.gov.uk

Tribunals Service – Employment Appeal Tribunal: www.employmentappeals.gov.uk

ACAS: www.acas.org.uk

Mock Employment Tribunal

About this event

This highly interactive event involves role play as well as observation and will give you first-hand experience of an Employment Tribunal in a safe environment: the only way you can take part in proceedings at an Employment Tribunal without actually being at the real thing.

Benefits of taking part

- Gain the confidence to know when to resist a claim and how to win.
- Highly interactive sessions using group work and role play to give you first-hand experience in a safe environment.
- Understand how to avoid making mistakes that could cost your organisation thousands of pounds.
- CPD log – a certificate of attendance will be provided upon completion of the course.
- Choose to volunteer for the roles such as witness, claimant, respondent and representative.
- Learn from expert Employment Lawyers with practical experience and a current Lay member of an Employment Tribunal Panel.

Who should attend?

The Mock Employment Tribunal is a must-attend event for anyone in HR, company directors and owners, senior managers or anyone whose role may be affected by an Employment Tribunal.

Call us today on **0871 777 8881** to find out more about our in-house training events in 2010

Comment...

Crunching the numbers

Philippa Skrein is a Solicitor in the Employment Group at Kennedys. She has experience of a variety of claims including unfair dismissal, discrimination, breach of contract, unlawful deductions, flexible working and equal pay. Philippa advises HR Managers and in-house legal departments on employment issues, negotiates compensation packages representing both employers and employees, and drafts and advises on compromise agreements.

Statistics released by the Employment Tribunal Service over the past two years make for interesting reading. For the year April 2007 to March 2008 the number of claims accepted by Employment Tribunals rose from 132,577 to a record high of 189,303; an increase of 43%.

For the first time in nine years, unfair dismissal was knocked off the top spot. The highest number of claims in 2007/08 were equal pay claims, which rose 42% from 44,013 in 2006/07 to 62,706 in 2007/08. The second highest number of claims were made under the Working Time Directive, and rose 163% from 21,123 in 2006/07 to 55,712 in 2007/08. Unfair dismissal claims came in third with the 2007/08 figures down 9% from 44,491 to 40,941.

The reason for such significant rises in the areas of equal pay and the Working Time Directive appears to be the fact that the majority of cases under these headings involve multiple claims. In the case of equal pay, large-scale multiple claims are currently being run by trade unions against Local Authorities and NHS Trusts. Similarly, the Employment Tribunal Service has identified one reason for the rise in the number of claims brought under the Working Time Directive as the fact that the figures include approximately 10,000 airline workers' cases relating to annual leave entitlements, which have been resubmitted every few months to ensure that the Claimants' annual leave entitlements are up-to-date when the cases are eventually heard.

The number of age discrimination claims submitted in 2007/08 rose from 972 to 2,942, a rise of some 203%. This is perhaps unsurprising given that this was only the second year that age discrimination has featured in these statistics. One reason for the number of claims in the system may be a backlog which has built up while the Heyday challenge made its way to the European Court of Justice.

In addition to age discrimination, with the exception of sex, the number of claims relating to all other forms of discrimination rose.

One other substantial increase materialised under the heading 'others,' which was up from 5,072 to 13,873, an increase of 173%. The Employment Tribunal Service suggests this increase was due to a rise in claims relating to trade union membership.

Comment: Crunching the numbers

Of the 8,312 unfair dismissal cases proceeding to a hearing, 45.6% were upheld while of the remaining 54.4%, 14.2% were dismissed at a preliminary hearing and 40.2% were unsuccessful at hearing.

The figures for awards made by the Tribunal show that the average award made for unfair dismissal was £8,058.

The figures for 2008/09 show a different pattern emerging. Most notable is the fact that the total number of claims brought is down from 189,303 in 2007/08 to 151,028, which is more in line with the number of claims brought in similar years. Tentatively, it appears therefore that last year's rise in figures was attributable to temporary factors such as those outlined above. Certainly the number of claims brought under the headings Equal Pay, Working Time Directive and 'Others' have fallen substantially and reverted back to their previous levels.

During difficult economic times there tends to be a rise in the number of unfair dismissal claims and that is reflected in the statistics for 2008/09, which show the figure rose from 40,941 in 2007/08 to 52,711 in 2008/09. This pattern has also been noted in ACAS' annual report for 2008/09, which reveals that the economic downturn led to a 'rapid and sustained increase' in the number of cases passed to it for conciliation in the latter half of 2008/09.

As one might expect, the number of claims for redundancy pay and failure to inform and consult as part of the redundancy process also rose significantly, from 7,313 to 10,839, and from 4,480 to 11,371 respectively, this latter a huge increase of 154%.

Given the continuing recession, it is likely that this pattern will continue for perhaps the next couple of years. Employees who have been made redundant may be more willing to issue claims as a way of bolstering their redundancy pay and, in turn, employers looking to save costs and make redundancies quickly may cut corners and expose themselves to a greater number of claims. Potentially, the number of discrimination claims may also rise during the recession as claimants issuing claims arising out of redundancy situations look to receive larger, uncapped, awards. Such claims could arise in situations where more experienced, and therefore more expensive, members of staff are made redundant.

Comment: Crunching the numbers

	2005/06	2006/07	2007/08	2008/09
Total number of claims accepted	115,039	132,577	189,303	151,028

Jurisdiction mix of claims accepted	2005/06	2006/07	2007/08	2008/09
Unfair dismissal	41,832	44,491	40,941	52,711
Unauthorised deductions	32,330	34,857	34,583	33,839
Breach of contract	26,230	21,298	25,054	32,829
Sex discrimination	14,250	28,153	26,907	18,637
Working Time Directive	35.474	21,127	55,712	23,976
Redundancy pay	7,214	7,692	7,313	10,839
Disability discrimination	4,585	5,533	5,833	6,578
Redundancy – failure to inform and consult	4,056	4,802	4,480	11,371
Equal pay	17,268	44,013	62,706	45,748
Race discrimination	4,103	3,780	4,130	4,983
Written statement of terms and conditions	3,078	3,429	4,955	3,919
Written statement of reasons for dismissal	955	1,064	1,098	1,105
Written pay statement	794	990	1,086	1,144
Transfer of an undertaking – failure to inform and consult	899	1,108	1,308	1,262
Suffer a detriment / unfair dismissal – pregnancy	1,504	1,465	1,646	1,835
Part-time workers Regulations	402	776	595	664
National Minimum Wage	440	806	431	595
Discrimination on grounds of religion or belief	486	648	709	832
Discrimination on grounds of sexual orientation	395	770	582	600
Age discrimination	N/A	972	2,949	3,801
Others	5,219	5,072	13,873	9,274

Workplace Law Network
www.workplacelaw.net

Equal pay

Derick MacLean, MacRoberts

Key points
- The principle of equal pay originates from Article 141 of the Treaty of Rome (previously Article 119). Article 141 and, later, the Equal Pay Directive, underpinned the rights in Europe to equal pay between men and women. The UK implemented these EU provisions by the Equal Pay Act 1970 (EPA).
- The EPA gives the right to equal pay to men and women, although for ease of reference the presumption in this chapter is that a woman is the affected employee.
- The EPA implies an equality clause into any employment contract that does not already include one. This provision applies to all terms and conditions of employment and not only to pay but, for example, sick pay provisions. Any term in a contract that purports to limit or exclude any provision of the EPA is unenforceable (with the exception of a COT3 Agreement or a Compromise Agreement).
- The implied equality clause modifies the contract of employment in any situation where a woman is engaged in like work to a man, on work rated as equivalent to work done by a man, or on work of equal value to that done by a man, unless her employer can justify the difference in pay due to a material factor that is not sex.
- Equal pay questionnaires can be served before a claim is issued at the Employment Tribunal to establish facts that are material to a potential claim. If the employer fails to respond to the questionnaire, or the employer's response is evasive, the Tribunal is entitled to draw adverse inferences from the employer's failure.

Legislation
- Treaty of Rome, Article 141.
- Equal Pay Directive (75/117/EEC).
- Equal Pay Act 1970.
- Sex Discrimination Act 1975.
- Data Protection Act 1998.
- Equal Pay Act 1970 (Amendment) Regulations 2003.
- Equal Pay (Questions and Replies) Order 2003.
- Employment Tribunals (Constitution and Rules of Procedure) Regulations 2004.
- Employment Equality (Sex Discrimination) Regulations 2005.
- Occupational Pension Schemes (Equal Treatment) (Amendment) Regulations 2005.

Like work, work rated as equivalent and work of equal value

Like work
A woman is employed on like work with a man if the woman's and man's work is of the same or a broadly similar nature. Employers need to consider the nature and extent of the differences between the work and the frequency with which such differences occur. For example, a cook in a director's dining room was held to be engaged on like work with the assistant chefs of the company's factory canteen.

Work rated as equivalent
An objective job evaluation study can be carried out in respect of a woman's and

Equal pay

man's work, and the woman's job is rated for equivalence on the basis of the demand made in terms of matters such as skill or effort required, or level of responsibility. A woman can compare herself to a man who is rated at the same level or lower than her in the job evaluation study. Where a woman raises a rated as equivalent claim, any back pay awarded (see '*Remedies*,' below) should reflect only the period when the job evaluation scheme was in place (although the employee could also raise an equal value claim in respect of the period prior to the job evaluation study).

Work of equal value

A woman's work may be of equal value to a man's in terms of the demands made on her, even if it is not like work or rated as equivalent. A woman may therefore potentially still claim equal pay with a man even if he is doing a different job. For example, a female cook employed as a canteen assistant succeeded in a claim for equal pay with a male skilled tradesman. Where work is claimed to be of equal value, an independent expert is often appointed to determine the issue.

Appropriate comparator

A person making a claim under the EPA must select a comparator, that is, a person of the opposite sex whose terms and conditions can be compared for the purpose of determining equality. There is one limited exception to the requirement to

---

Facts

- Women who work full-time earn, on average, 17% less per hour than men working full-time. For women who work part-time, the gap in pay relative to full-time men is a huge 38% per hour.
- An Equal Opportunities Commission (EOC) survey showed that 95% of people agree that women should have their own individual pension rights and should not rely on a husband or partner.
- According to the EOC's reports, under the current pension system, just 25% of women are entitled to a full basic state pension, compared to 95% of men.
- According to the EOC's reports, the gender pay gap was narrower in Wales for hourly, weekly and annual earnings than in England and Scotland. The main reason for this was the low average male earnings in Wales; 18% of male full-time employees in Wales earned less than £250 per week, compared with 12% in Britain overall.
- In the 35 years since the Equal Pay Act came into force, major changes in the UK's economy and society have increased the opportunities available to women. It has become more socially acceptable for women to work. At December 2008, 70% of women of working age were in employment, compared to 56% in 1971.
- According to the EOC's reports, women who were single had lower average hourly earnings than those who were either married, cohabiting or separated, divorced or widowed; the pattern for men was the same. However, the gender gap for all employees was widest in the married / cohabiting group (27%).

Sources: Equal Opportunities Commission and National Statistics.

Equal pay

cite a comparator and that is in pregnancy-related cases where:

- a pay rise that the woman would have been entitled to had she not been on maternity leave is not taken into account in calculating her maternity pay; and
- contractual bonuses are missed during a period of time before or after her maternity leave.

The comparator cannot be hypothetical. In the case of *Walton Centre for Neurology v. Bewley,* the EAT held, overturning previous case law, that a Claimant cannot compare herself to her successor. The choice of comparator under the EPA is limited by the requirement for the comparator to be employed by the same employer or associated employers. However, under Article 141, the scope for comparison is wider and the ECJ has established that it may not be limited to the same employer. The important factor is whether the relationship between the two employers is sufficiently close and, in particular, whether the disparity in terms and conditions can be attributed to a 'single source'. In the case of *Robertson v. Defra* (2005), the Court of Appeal held that the Crown was not the 'single source' responsible for determining pay and conditions with the effect that the Claimants could not compare themselves with employees in different departments within the Civil Service.

In the recent case of *Dumfries and Galloway Council v. North and Others* (2009), the EAT overturned a Tribunal that had held that a group of claimants who worked as Classroom Assistants, Support for Learning Assistants and Nursery Nurses were in the same employment for the purposes of the EPA as their comparators who were Groundsmen, Refuse Collectors, Refuse Drivers and Leisure Attendants.

This was despite the fact the Claimants were each based at particular schools and the comparators (with the exception of leisure attendants) were based at depots but worked at a variety of locations across the geographical area covered by the Council. The Tribunal had relied on the case of *British Coal Corporation v. Smith and Others* (1996), in which the House of Lords held that a claimant can satisfy the 'same employment' test by showing that male comparators at her establishment share common terms and conditions with male comparators at other establishments.

The EAT held that the Tribunal had misapplied *British Coal* and that to be 'in the same employment' must have a basis in reality; there must be a real possibility that the male comparator could be employed at the same establishment as the woman, carrying out the same, or broadly similar, job to the one he does at his current establishment. However, even having demonstrated that there was such a possibility, there was a further need to provide evidence that the male comparator's employment at the woman's establishment would have broadly similar terms and conditions.

A comparison can be made, using the principles of indirect discrimination, between groups of employees where one group is predominantly female and the other group is predominantly male and there is a disparity in the terms and conditions between the groups of employees.

Meaning of 'pay'

The scope of the EPA is not limited to 'pay' in the usual sense of the word. In this context, the word 'pay' can generally be regarded as meaning 'terms and conditions'. For example, the EPA covers ex-gratia perks, redundancy pay and pension contributions.

Equal pay

In one case, the Court of Appeal took the unusual approach of aggregating the employees' basic pay, fixed bonuses and attendance allowances in order to work out an overall hourly rate for the purposes of comparison. The Court of Appeal clarified that an employee cannot pick and choose terms from the comparator's contract for comparison.

Genuine material factor (GMF) defence

An employer can defend an equal pay claim by establishing that the variation between the woman's contract and the man's contract is genuinely due to a material factor that is not the difference of sex; for example, qualifications or performance. The courts, both at a European and national level, have accepted that economic reasons can constitute 'material factors'. An example would be where an employer recruits a new female employee and offers her more advantageous terms and conditions than an existing male employee carrying out a similar role, on the basis that the job market is such that competitive terms and conditions are essential to recruit quality employees.

In the case of *Cadman v. Health and Safety Executive* (2006), the ECJ confirmed that where the difference in pay can be attributed to length of service, it will usually be justifiable unless "the worker provides evidence capable of raising serious doubts in that regard".

There has been confusion surrounding whether it is sufficient for an employer to demonstrate that there is a reason for the disparity in terms and conditions that are not related to gender or whether the employer has to go one step further and objectively justify the difference. Domestic case law has held that the employer will not be required to justify objectively any difference in pay unless the claimant has shown there to be a potentially indirectly discriminatory reason for the difference. The European Court of Justice, however, has held that an employer must objectively justify any difference in pay, even where the claimant has failed to establish that the difference in pay is potentially indirectly discriminatory.

In the case of *Sharp v. Caledonia Group Services* (2006), the EAT preferred the ECJ's approach. This decision was appealed to the Court of Appeal, but the case settled before the appeal was heard. However, *Middlesbrough Borough Council v. Surtees and Others* (2007) adds significant weight to the argument that objective justification is only required where the explanation being put forward for the difference in pay is tainted by sex.

The case of *West Midlands Police v. Blackburn* (2009) is an interesting example of a Tribunal misunderstanding the purpose of the GMF defence. The Claimants were police officers who received less than their male comparator who was employed on like work. The reason for the disparity in pay was that the comparator worked shifts involving night work and received a special payment (effectively a bonus) for this, but the Claimants did receive similar special payments because they did not work at night due to childcare responsibilities. The Tribunal held that it was a legitimate objective to reward night work, but that the Chief Constable could have paid the claimants as though they had done night work even though they had not. It would not have been a significant expenditure and would have eliminated the discrimination. The EAT upheld the Chief Constable's appeal and held that the Tribunal had misunderstood the nature of the justification defence and had erred in concluding that the differential was not reasonably justified.

Equal pay

Elias P stated that:

"The payment of money to compensate for the economic disadvantages suffered by those who have childcare responsibilities is not what the Equal Pay Act requires. Nor is the assessment of the employer's ability to pay sums of this kind a task which Parliament could conceivably have expected Tribunals to do." (Paragraph 46.)

The Court of Appeal subsequently held that the analysis of objective justification, aims and means in the judgment of the EAT was correct.

Implied equality clause

If the employer cannot justify the difference in pay, the implied equality clause operates so that:

- any contractual term that is less favourable to a woman is modified to become as favourable as the corresponding term in the man's contract; and
- any beneficial term in a man's contract that is not included in the woman's contract is included into the woman's contract.

To give a simple example, if a man is paid £500 more per month than a woman for like work, the equality clause will entitle the woman to that extra £500 per month.

Remedies

These are:

- back pay (limited to six years, or five in Scotland from claim date), representing the difference in pay between the woman and the 'equal' or 'equivalent' employee, with interest; and
- the same level of pay or benefits as her comparator for the future (if the complainant remains in the same job).

The EAT has confirmed that a claim under the EPA cannot include an element for non-pecuniary losses (e.g. injury to feelings).

Procedure

As with discrimination claims, cases can be brought while the employee is still employed. In the standard case, claims must be brought at any time during employment or within six months of leaving employment.

An individual may submit equal pay questionnaires to the employer, either before a claim is made to the Tribunal or within 21 days of such a claim being lodged. Employers are not obliged to answer these questionnaires, but the Tribunal may draw an adverse inference if a questionnaire is not answered deliberately and without reasonable cause in an eight-week window from it being served, or where the reply is evasive or equivocal. This includes an inference that the equality clause has been breached. An employer may be reluctant to disclose certain information when responding to the questionnaire on the basis that it may result in a breach of the Data Protection Act 1998 (DPA). That may be appropriate in some cases; however, if the Tribunal subsequently issues an Order compelling the employer to disclose the information, and the processing can be deemed 'fair,' it will have no liability under the DPA.

Pay protection

Consideration was given to the justification of pay protection arrangements, introduced by Local Authorities in order to preserve the position of disadvantaged (predominantly male) workers, following the introduction of job evaluation schemes in the case of *Redcar and Cleveland Borough Council v. Bainbridge and Ors, and Surtees and Ors v. Middlesbrough Borough Council* (2008).

Equal pay

The Court of Appeal held that, on the facts of these cases, the Councils' pay protection schemes were prima facie discriminatory and therefore could not be justified. The Court did go on to say, however, that even though such arrangements may be found to be discriminatory, they might nevertheless be justified in some circumstances.

Those circumstances will depend on the facts of each case and consideration may be given to whether the employer had an awareness that the introduction of a particular pay protection scheme would directly or indirectly discriminate against certain groups of workers, usually women. The Court further stated that the employer's motivation in introducing the scheme can be taken into account when the Employment Tribunal is considering whether or not the scheme can be justified.

Recent legislation

The Equal Pay Act 1970 (Amendment) Regulations 2004 came into force on 1 October 2004, amending the EPA and the tribunal procedural rules. Under the amended EPA, a Tribunal can choose to determine the question of equal value itself rather than appoint an independent expert. Where a job evaluation study ascribes different values to the work of the claimant and the comparator, the Tribunal will be bound to conclude that the work is not of equal value unless it has reasonable grounds for suspecting that the study discriminated on the ground of sex, or that there are other reasons why it cannot be relied upon.

Schedule 6 of the Employment Tribunals (Constitution and Rules of Procedure) Regulations 2004, which came into force on 1 October 2004, contains procedural rules that apply exclusively to equal pay claims.

The Occupational Pension Schemes (Equal Treatment) (Amendment) Regulations 2005 came into force on 10 October 2005. The Regulations updated the Occupational Pension Schemes (Equal Treatment) Regulations 1995, which were enacted for the purpose of importing an equal treatment rule into the rules of all occupational pensions schemes.

The Employment Equality (Sex Discrimination) Regulations 2005 introduced new definitions of indirect discrimination and harassment, and explicitly prohibit discrimination on the grounds of pregnancy or maternity leave, setting out the extent to which it is discriminatory to pay a woman less than she would otherwise have been paid due to pregnancy or maternity issues.

The Equality Bill was published at the end of April 2009. If and when it becomes law, it will replace the Equal Pay Act 1970 and all the various discrimination statutes and regulations. The Bill is currently some 205 sections and 28 schedules and the Government has stated that the Bill has two main purposes:

- to harmonise discrimination law; and
- to strengthen the law to support progress on equality.

See also: Discrimination, p.110; Equality doesn't happen overnight, p.174.

Equal pay

Sources of further information

Equality and Human Rights Commission: www.equalityhumanrights.com

Equal Opportunities policies are becoming ever more important in today's increasingly multicultural, multiracial society. The purpose of this type of policy is to set out the obligations on both the employer and the employee to treat all people with equal dignity and respect within the workplace. The aim is to create a pleasant and harmonious working environment for all.

Workplace Law Group's *Equal Opportunities Policy and Management Guide v.4.0* sets out and explains the rights of each employee. A well-drafted Equal Opportunities policy, combined with good management, will ensure your organisation meets its legal obligation to provide a non-discriminatory work environment and persuade employees that an equal opportunities policy at work is for the benefit of the whole workforce. For more information visit www.workplacelaw.net/bookshop/policiesAndProcedures.

Comment...

Equality doesn't happen overnight

Daniel Cotton is an Employment Law Specialist at Davies Arnold Cooper, and advises clients on the full range of employment issues, including both contentious and non-contentious matters. Daniel acts for clients from a wide range of sectors including charities, finance and the medical profession.

The Equality Bill 2008/09 is the culmination of years of work, which began in February 2005 with the Discrimination Law Review and the Equalities Review. A Green Paper followed in June 2007, setting out the Government's proposals and seeking consultation over the course of the summer. The proposals had three principal objectives, namely:

1. Harmonising and simplifying the law;
2. A more effective law; and
3. Modernising the law.

Despite publishing a White Paper in June 2008, it was not until the following month that a much fuller response to the consultation was published with detailed proposals, rather than the summary proposals set out in the White Paper. This finally resulted in the draft Equality Bill being published on 27 April 2009.

Progress through Parliament

Needless to say, given the wide aims of the Bill, it is a substantial document that covers a significant amount of ground. At the time of writing, the Equality Bill has passed the Committee Stage in the House of Commons. This has involved 20 sittings of the committee, who have run through the Bill, clause by clause, and discussed proposed amendments. The revised Bill has now been published, including the changes made at Committee Stage, and this will be debated in the House of Commons at the Report Stage. No date has yet been set for this. Presuming it passes through the Commons, the Bill will then be sent to the House of Lords for its consideration. Currently, the expectation is that the Equality Bill will not receive Royal Assent before Spring 2010 and it is unlikely that any of the Bill will come into force prior to some time in Autumn 2010. In view of this time frame, many people are understandably asking whether the Bill will come into force at all. Given that a general election will undoubtedly have happened before this time, we may have a new government and the Bill could be abandoned.

Debates

In the course of bills going through Parliament, there is inevitably often political motivation for opposing certain proposed legislation, and this Bill has not been an exception. In March 2009, prior to the publication of the Equality Bill, Theresa May, Shadow Secretary of State for Work and Pensions, stated in a speech to Parliament that the Conservative Party proposed to "engage constructively with the Bill," and she went on to say that she welcomed the opportunity that it would

Comment: Equality doesn't happen overnight

present to consolidate equality legislation. She continued by talking about her commitment to reducing the gender pay gap and to flexible working. These aspects of the Equality Bill form a significant part of the content, and the consolidation and simplification of an enormous numbers of Acts, Regulations and Codes of Practice is a major aim of the Bill.

However, two months after making this speech, Theresa May introduced the motion in the second reading in the House of Commons to reject the Bill in its entirety, although she did note that she welcomed many of the Bill's aims. The Conservatives' position was that the Bill should be re-drafted before being re-introduced, rather than simply amended. This clearly demonstrates that there is deep-felt opposition to certain elements of the Bill. Indeed, John Penrose MP, who is a Conservative Member of the Committee that dealt with the proposed amendments in detail, stated on 1 July 2009 that most of the Bill was fine but he was very concerned over potential 'red tape' that could strangle the economy. He raised concerns about the equal pay reporting requirements and age discrimination in the provision of services, particularly on behalf of many businesses who currently have age specific products, e.g. Saga and Club 18-30. It was acknowledged in the Discrimination Law Review prior to publication of the Bill that there will always be a need for age-specific services, although this is not specifically addressed in the Bill other than provision for ministers to issue regulations dealing with this point.

In contrast to this, the Government appears to be presenting the Equality Bill as a panacea for equality issues and in particular in respect of equal pay. Whilst there may not be many people who would deny that equal pay remains a serious problem within most sectors of the economy, it is by no means certain that greater transparency and an obligation to report gender pay levels will resolve this issue. It is a complex issue with a number of root causes. Indeed, the Conservatives have stated that they do not believe the proposed obligations for gender pay reporting would have any positive impact on equality and would simply result in reams of bureaucracy. They also criticised the absence of compulsory pay audits for employers found to have discriminated against employees in terms of pay. This was a proposed Conservative amendment, which was not adopted. This part of the Bill seems destined for a turbulent future and a difficult passage through Parliament, despite the consensus that the gender pay gap remains stubbornly large and needs addressing.

Positive action is one aspect of the Bill that has gained a lot of publicity. This would, in theory, allow employers to take into account under-representation amongst protected groups when selecting between equally qualified candidates. The Government has stated that it does not intend to allow positive discrimination (where a less well qualified candidate could be selected) by the back door but, as drafted, it is not entirely clear how 'qualified' is meant to be interpreted. The Conservatives have raised concerns about this aspect and fear that the lack of clarity means that this provision will either never be used or will in fact allow positive discrimination. The Solicitor General has confirmed that the Equality and Human Rights Commission would produce clear guidance but this remains a contentious point and some of her comments have suggested that the question of 'qualification' could be interpreted very broadly.

The Conservatives have also raised concerns about the extended powers for

Comment: Equality doesn't happen overnight

Tribunals to make recommendations, the lack of focus on the disability pay gap, and the fact that they believe that "it fails to address the root causes of the reduction in social mobility in recent years". Clearly, there remain serious reservations about the Bill and its effectiveness in its current form.

Committee Stage

The Committee Stage has made a number of significant amendments to the Bill and it is important to remember that this is a cross-party committee. As a result, the Government has committed to look again at the provisions it has proposed for disability discrimination as it was not felt that these went far enough to fully mitigate the impact of the House of Lords' decision in *London Borough of Lewisham v. Malcolm*, which restricted the ability of disabled people to bring disability-related discrimination claims. There is a new offence of indirect disability discrimination contained in the Bill and a recent development in the EAT means that a dismissal can be discriminatory if it amounts to a failure to make reasonable adjustments (*Fareham College v. Walters*), both of which assist in partially reversing the effects of *Malcolm*.

Unsurprisingly, the committee also approved the insertion of a combined discrimination offence. This would arise when an individual suffers discrimination because of a combination of any two of the protected characteristics. This appears destined to become law.

Conclusion

Despite the progress that the Bill has made through Parliament thus far, there remains a gulf between the Government and the Opposition on some significant aspects of the Equality Bill. It appears likely that the Bill will be implemented in some form, whoever is in power. However, it would not be surprising if, in the event of there being a Conservative Government in 2010, the measures to reduce inequality in pay and positive action, in particular, are in a very different form. The general harmonisation and consolidation exercise is likely to proceed without too much dispute, but several of the new measures remain very much in the balance.

Expenses

Pam Loch, Loch Associates

Key points
- Under general tax law, some expenses payments are taxable remuneration.
- Expenses payments include:
  - advance payments and reimbursements, including all kinds of travelling and entertaining;
  - allowances related to specific expenses, for example based on mileage or calculated by referring to a fixed scale;
  - round sum allowances for entertaining and other expenses;
  - amounts made available to the employee in respect of expenses and paid away by the employee; and
  - expenses paid by the employee by means of a credit card in the employer's name.
- Employers should have a clear expenses policy in place and enforce its provisions consistently.
- The majority of expenses are taxable and an effective policy can help to ensure compliance with HMRC.
- Employees who breach the expenses policy may risk disciplinary action, including dismissal.
- Employers who do dismiss for breach of the expenses policy should ensure this is the main (or preferably only) reason for dismissal.

Legislation
- Income Tax (Earnings and Pensions) Act 2003 (ITEPA).

Background
Reclaiming the cost of horse manure, moat cleaning and repairing a portico on expenses by MPs became the hot topic of conversation in 2009 by drawing attention to the potential opportunities for employees to abuse expenses. The public horror that 'our' money had been abused by MPs to purchase these goods and services fuelled the fire of anger.

It also led to many more general conversations about expenses; what you can and can't claim and what employers can do to protect their business from illegitimate expense claims. Employers also need to be aware of the tax implications of expenses and what is and isn't taxable can often be a confusing area.

In most organisations, expenses are monitored very closely, with rigid policies and numerous controls in place to ensure compliance with procedures to avoid abuse taking place. The employee's contract of employment will usually set out that expenses are payable but only if the expense is incurred in accordance with the expenses policy.

Expenses policies
The expense policy should clearly set out what is regarded as an expense by the organisation. It can be difficult to set out specific examples and usually there will be a generic reference to what is covered and then it is over to accounts, HR, or whoever is given the responsibility to approve expenses.

Expenses

The person who approves expenses plays an important role. Not only must they interpret how the policy applies but they must resist the pressure that can be placed on them to agree that something is a legitimate expense.

In some sectors there is far less rigidity and expenses policies may have limited application. One could take the view that this is not really an issue to be concerned about, as it only impacts on the organisation itself. However, that is not the case. Expenses are generally a tax-deductible business expense as long as it is not for entertaining clients or customers. Therefore, HMRC also has certain rules that apply to ensure there is no abuse of the tax system.

An abuse of an organisation's expenses policy usually results in disciplinary action being taken and ultimately could lead to an employee being dismissed. Despite the potential risks, however, some employees will stretch the boundaries of expenses for the sake of securing extra funds that are not taxable.

For example, some employees will arrange a meeting in a city they would like to spend the weekend in to be able to reclaim the cost of the travel. In other instances, personal and business expenses become closely entwined – visits to lap dancing clubs being one example.

Preventative measures

So what can an employer do when its employee is caught cheating the expenses policy?

Employers who discover an employee abusing their expenses policy will want to take action against that employee. Depending on the degree of dishonesty and abuse involved, the employer may often feel that an unacceptable breach of trust has taken place and dismissal is the only option.

Employers should always investigate fully before taking any disciplinary action – it may be the case that an employee has simply misunderstood the policy and the employer discovers that a review of the policy wording is required to make it clearer.

Where there is a clear expenses policy in place and an obvious case of dishonesty or fraud involved in obtaining funds as expenses has taken place, summary dismissal following an investigation

---

Facts

- Employers may provide employees with an annual party tax-free, provided the cost is no more than £150 per head and the invitation is open to all employees.
- The Global Expense Employee Expenses Benchmark Report 2009 estimates that British businesses are losing around £2bn each year for wrongly-approved employee expense payments.
- According to the same report, around 11% of all employee expense claims should not be paid as the items are not covered by company policy, but managers approve the payments anyway.
- The expenses of employees earning less than £8,500 p.a. generally will not be taxable.

Expenses

for gross misconduct may well be a reasonable response.

Employers should be aware, however, of cases highlighting the approach the Employment Tribunals may take in assessing whether an unfair dismissal has taken place. Early 2009 saw the case of *Thompson v. Brick Services Limited* in which an employee was dismissed for submitting a false expenses claim. The employee argued he had asked a hotel receptionist to add £27 to a receipt to cover drinks he had bought personally, which he considered to be a legitimate business expense. The Tribunal heard evidence that Brick Services Ltd had been putting pressure on Mr Thompson for some time to agree less favourable terms and conditions of employment, which he refused to do. The Tribunal found that the employer had used the expenses claim as an excuse to dismiss the employee without conducting a full and impartial investigation, and the dismissal was found to be unfair.

In the case of *East Lancashire Coachbuilders v. Hilton*, Mr Hilton was dismissed on the grounds of gross misconduct after taking his wife on a business trip to Mexico and claiming her fare as well as his own. The Tribunal found that whilst the employer could reasonably have treated Mr Hilton's conduct as justifying immediate dismissal, the real reason for his dismissal was for other reasons. Because the employer's main reason for dismissal was for matters other than the expenses issue (which was essentially used as a smokescreen), the conclusion was that there was an unfair dismissal.

See also: Disciplinary and grievance procedures, p.106; Dismissal, p.124.

Sources of further information

In its Money, Tax and Benefits section, Directgov online has some useful guidance on tax on company benefits, such as what employees may have to pay tax on and which benefits are tax-free: www.directgov.uk

Businesslink.gov.uk and the HMRC website provide useful practical advice for businesses in relation to a wide range of topics, including business expenses.

Facilities management contracts

Marc Hanson, Ashurst

Key points
Like all other forms of contract, a facilities management contract is essentially a legally binding and enforceable bargain between two parties. Each party contributes something to the bargain; the facilities management contractor – the provision of certain services; and the client – payment for those services.

Negotiation
For a contract to be legally binding, there must be an offer from one party, an unconditional acceptance of that offer by the other party, and consideration provided by each party for the promise made by the other party. A client's invitation to tender is not usually an 'offer' – it is usually no more than an offer to negotiate.

A facilities management contractor's tender to carry out the services will, usually, amount to the initial 'offer'.

When the client accepts the facilities management contractor's tender and each party gives consideration, then, provided both parties have an intention to be legally bound, a legally enforceable contract will come into place. Offers and acceptance can be made in writing, orally or by conduct.

It is of course unusual for facilities management contractors' tenders to be accepted without qualification by a client. There may be areas of extensive negotiation, e.g. in relation to scope of services and fees. Every time each party provides any revised proposals, then each revised proposal will take effect as a 'counter-offer'.

When eventually all outstanding points have been agreed, one party will invariably 'accept' the other party's final 'offer'.

When does the contract start?
The process of negotiating a facilities management contract can be protracted. In many cases, services may be provided to the client and payment may be made without any form of contract having been signed. Where relationships subsequently deteriorate, it can be extremely difficult to establish whether there was ever a binding contract in place and, if there was, on what terms it was made.

Whether a binding contract exists in such circumstances will depend on whether the parties managed to agree all the key terms of the contract and whether the terms of the alleged contract included all terms that would be essential for a contract to exist. It would be unlikely that there was a contract agreed if key elements of the contract were still outstanding; for example, if the exact scope of the services was undecided or if a price had not been agreed. However, a contract can still come into effect where certain points in the contract terms are still to be agreed, provided that the key elements have been finalised and agreed.

Facilities management contracts

Scope of contracts
When drafting facilities management contracts, it is important to ensure that they cover the complete understanding and agreement between the parties. As such, it is necessary to include not only a list of the services to be provided by the supplier but also a mechanism for dealing with changes to the services and also any details as to what equipment or facilities are to be provided to the supplier by the client in relation to the services.

Payment
Careful thought needs to be given as to how payment to the facilities management contractor will be structured. Will it be on the basis of a lump-sum price, by prime cost or by reference to a schedule of rates? If the price is to adjust, then a mechanism needs to be set out allowing for this, detailing the circumstances in which adjustments will be made. Careful consideration also needs to be given to any mechanism to be included in the contract that would allow the contract price to be adjusted to reflect performance or non-performance by the supplier of the services.

Service levels
Service levels should be included in the contract against which the performance by the supplier can be assessed. Consideration needs to be given as to how poor performance is dealt with and whether the liability of the supplier under the contract is to be limited in any way.

Duration
The duration of a facilities management contract is of critical importance, and this should be clearly stated in the contract, together with the circumstances in which it can be extended or terminated by either party.

Facilities management contracts should also address other key areas such as compliance with statutory requirements, transfer of undertakings provisions, insurance requirements and provisions dealing with dispute resolution.

See also: Contract disputes, p.71; Contractors, p.74; TUPE, p.399.

Sources of further information

Workplace Law Group's **Facilities Management Contracts 2008** follows the success of two editions of the *Guide to Facilities Management Contracts*. Now fully updated, it provides an introduction to contract law as it relates to FM contracts, and a guide to common contractual law provisions. This extended publication looks at new areas of law including amendments to the Construction Act, amendments to CDM Regulations, revised TUPE Regulations, revised EU Procurement law, dispute resolution procedures, and European standards for facilities management. For more information visit www.workplacelaw.net/Bookshop/Handbooks.

Family-friendly rights

Pinsent Masons Employment Group

Key points
- Pregnant employees, regardless of their length of service, are entitled to 26 weeks' ordinary maternity leave and 26 weeks' additional maternity leave. Additional maternity leave will follow straight on from ordinary maternity leave.
- An employee who is the father of the child or the mother's husband or partner is entitled to take up to two weeks' paid paternity leave on the birth or adoption of a child.
- Eligible employees are now entitled to take 26 weeks' ordinary adoption leave and 26 weeks' additional adoption leave.
- Employees with sufficient continuous service will be entitled to statutory maternity pay or statutory adoption pay for 39 weeks.
- Employees (both male and female) with one year's continuous service are entitled to take up to 13 weeks' unpaid parental leave, or 18 weeks in the case of a disabled child, to care for each of their children.
- Employees who have responsibility for looking after a child can request a variation in their contractual hours.

Legislation
- Social Security Contributions and Benefits Act 1992.
- Employment Rights Act 1996.
- Employment Relations Act 1999.
- Maternity and Parental Leave etc. Regulations 1999.
- Employment Act 2002.
- Flexible Working (Eligibility, Complaints and Remedies) Regulations 2002.
- Flexible Working (Procedural Requirements) Regulations 2002.
- Maternity and Parental Leave (Amendment) Regulations 2002.
- Paternity and Adoption Leave Regulations 2002.
- Maternity and Parental Leave etc. and the Paternity and Adoption Leave (Amendment) Regulations 2006.
- Statutory Paternity Pay and Statutory Adoption Pay (General) and the Statutory Paternity Pay and Statutory Adoption Pay (Weekly Rates) (Amendment) Regulations 2006.
- Work and Families Act 2006.

Employment Act 2002 and Work and Families Act 2006

The Employment Act 2002 contains a number of family-friendly provisions relating to maternity rights, paternity leave and adoption leave. Four new sets of Regulations implemented changes to the previous law and created new rights for pregnant women and parents. The Work and Families Act 2006 extended a number of these rights. Many of these changes have been implemented by the Maternity and Parental Leave etc. and the Paternity and Adoption Leave (Amendment) Regulations 2006 (the 2006 Regulations), which came into force on 1 October 2006.

Family-friendly rights

Maternity rights

The 2006 Regulations amend the Maternity and Parental Leave etc. Regulations 1999 for women whose expected week of childbirth is on or after 1 April 2007. The 2006 Regulations remove the length of service requirement for entitlement to additional maternity leave (AML) and provide that a woman will be entitled to 26 weeks' ordinary maternity leave (OML) and 26 weeks' AML regardless of her length of service.

The employee is required to inform her employer before the end of the 15th week before EWC of the date on which she intends to start her OML.

Employees are entitled not to be unreasonably refused time off with pay to attend antenatal care appointments, subject to providing their employer with details about the appointment. Thereafter, women are protected from suffering treatment to their detriment by employers (including dismissal) because they are pregnant.

Pregnancy-related dismissals are automatically unfair, and one year's continuous service is not needed to claim unfair dismissal. Amendments to the Sex Discrimination Act in October 2005 make it clear as a matter of statute that less favourable treatment on grounds of pregnancy or maternity leave will constitute sex discrimination. Previously, this was established as a matter of case law, but the change will make the position clear as a matter of statute.

Employers must not allow women who qualify for maternity leave to work at all in the two weeks immediately following childbirth.

Women entitled to OML have a statutory right to return to their job without giving notice. During OML, employment terms continue to apply to the employee, except for the right to pay.

Women whose babies are due on or after 5 October 2008 are also entitled to the same rights during AML as during OML (although an exception exists for pension rights). Care should be taken to ensure that during the woman's absence she is kept informed of any new vacancies or promoted positions or of any other relevant matters (such as details regarding pay rises made available to other employees) which become available to avoid any claims that she is being discriminated against.

Women on maternity leave will now be able to go into work for up to ten mutually agreed 'Keeping in Touch' days, without losing entitlement to statutory maternity pay.

The notice required from women on maternity leave to return earlier or later than planned has been increased from 28 days to eight weeks.

Maternity pay is often covered in the contract of employment, but must be no less than the statutory maternity pay (SMP) equivalent. Employees will only be entitled to SMP if they have 26 weeks' continuous service at the 15th week before the week their baby is due. The SMP pay period is currently 39 weeks. The first six weeks of the maternity pay period are paid at 90% of the employee's average weekly earnings, calculated on the basis of earnings during the eight weeks that end with the 15th week before the expected week of childbirth. The remaining 33 weeks are paid at the flat rate, which is currently £123.06 per week.

The Work and Families Act 2006 extends the maximum maternity pay period that

Family-friendly rights

may be prescribed by Regulations to 52 weeks, and the Government intends to extend the period to the full 52 weeks by 2009 or 2010.

Paternity leave

The Paternity and Adoption Leave Regulations 2002 came into force on 8 December 2002 and provide rights for employees who qualify to take paternity leave.

An employee is entitled to take paternity leave when the purpose of the absence is to care for a newborn child or to support the child's mother.

To qualify for paid paternity leave, employees must:

- be the father of the child or the mother's husband or partner (partner is a person of the same or different sex who lives with the mother and the child and is in an enduring family relationship but who is not a relative of the mother);
- have or expect to have responsibilities for the upbringing of the child; and
- have 26 weeks' service.

Statutory paternity pay is paid for two weeks and is £123.06 per week (or 90% of the employee's average weekly earnings if less).

Employees cannot lawfully be subjected to any detriment or dismissed due to taking or requesting paternity leave. Any such dismissal will be automatically unfair.

The Work and Families Act 2006 introduced a new statutory right to additional paternity leave (APL) up to a maximum of 26 weeks, and additional paternity pay (APP) for employees during the second six months of the 12-month maternity leave or adoption leave period. The Regulations that will introduce APL and APP have not yet been published. It is expected that they will be introduced at the same time as Regulations to extend maternity and adoption pay to 52 weeks.

Adoption leave

The 2006 Regulations amend the Paternity and Adoption Leave Regulations 2002 to provide that eligible employees now have the statutory right to 26 weeks' ordinary adoption leave and 26 weeks' unpaid additional adoption leave.

To be eligible for adoption leave, an employee needs to be an individual who has been newly matched with a child for adoption by an adoption agency, or be one member of a couple where the couple has jointly been newly matched with a child for adoption by an adoption agency (the couple must choose which partner takes adoption leave) and have completed at least 26 weeks' continuous service with the employer ending with the week (beginning with the Sunday and ending with the Saturday) in which the employee is notified of being matched with the child for adoption.

The partner of an individual who adopts or the other member of a couple who are adopting jointly may be entitled to paternity leave pay (*see above*).

Adoption leave will not be available in circumstances where a child is not newly matched for adoption (e.g. when a step-parent is adopting a partner's child).

Other changes have also been made that reflect the statutory changes to maternity leave and pay. These include the:

- increase to the statutory adoption pay (SAP) period to 39 weeks (employees entitled to SAP are those with 26 weeks' continuous service leading into the week of notification of an adoption match);

Family-friendly rights

- introduction of ten 'Keeping in Touch' days; and
- increase to the notice period required to return to work earlier or later than planned, from 28 days to eight weeks.

The Work and Families Act 2006 also extends the maximum adoption pay period that may be prescribed by Regulations to 52 weeks, and the Government currently intends to extend the adoption pay period to the full 52 weeks by 2009 or 2010.

Parental leave

Employees, both mothers and fathers, who have completed one year's service with their current employer are entitled to take 13 weeks' (18 weeks where the child is disabled) unpaid parental leave to care for their child.

The right applies per child; so an employee with one child may take 13 weeks' leave, an employee with two children may take 26 weeks' leave.

Parental leave can usually be taken up to five years from the date of birth or, in the case of adoption, five years from the date of placement (or up to the child's 18th birthday if that is sooner). In the case of a child entitled to a disability living allowance, parental leave can be taken at any time before the child's 18th birthday. In the case of children born or adopted between 15 December 1994 and 14 December 1999, the employee's right lasts until 31 March 2005 (or in the case of adoption until the child's 18th birthday if that is sooner) and in this case one year's service with a previous employer between 15 December 1998 and 9 January 2002 gives entitlement.

At the end of parental leave an employee is guaranteed the right to return to the same job as before, or, if that is not practicable, a similar job that has the same or better status, terms and conditions as the old job. If, however, the period of parental leave is for a period of four weeks or less, the employee is entitled to go back to the same job.

Wherever possible, employers and employees should make their own arrangements about how parental leave will work, how much notice should be given, arrangements for postponing the leave when the business cannot cope and how it should be taken.

Where employers and employees have not entered into an agreement about these matters, or until they have done so, the fallback scheme set out in the Regulations applies. The fallback scheme provides for employees to take parental leave in blocks or multiples of one week, after giving 21 days' notice, up to a maximum of four weeks' leave in a year and subject to postponement by the employer for up to six months where the business cannot cope. Leave cannot be postponed when the employee gives notice to take it immediately after the time the child is born or is placed with the family for adoption.

Flexible working

Parents and others (as listed in the Flexible Working Regulations) who have responsibility for looking after a child who is under six (or under 18 in the case of a disabled child) can request a variation in their contract of employment to have a more flexible working pattern. However, there is no right to work flexibly. If an employee makes such a request, the employer must follow a set procedure for meeting the employee to discuss the request, making a decision and issuing a decision with reasons. If the employer fails to follow the procedure, the employee may make an application to the Employment Tribunal.

Family-friendly rights

Since 6 April 2007, under the Work and Families Act 2006, employees caring for adults have also had the right to request flexible working. After consultation with various carers groups and business organisations, a carer has been defined as an employee who is or expects to be caring for an adult who:

- is married to, or the partner or civil partner of the employee; or
- is a near relative of the employee; or
- falls into neither category but lives at the same address as the employee.

The 'near relative' definition includes parents, parents-in-law, adult child, adopted adult child, siblings (including those who are in-laws), uncles, aunts or grandparents and step-relatives.

See also: Carers, p.54; Discrimination, p.110; Flexible working, p.190; Pregnancy, p.324.

Sources of further information

Template adoption, maternity and paternity policies are available as electronic downloads from Workplace Law Group. Visit www.workplacelaw.net/Bookshop/PoliciesAndProcedures or call 0871 777 8881 for further details.

BIS: Work and Families: www.berr.gov.uk/employment/workandfamilies/work-families-history/index.html.

Fixed-term workers

Pinsent Masons Employment Group

Key points
- Legislation introduced in 2002 provides statutory protection for fixed-term employees.
- The Regulations state that fixed-term employees have the right not to be treated less favourably than comparable permanent employees because they are employed on a fixed-term basis, unless the different treatment can be objectively justified.
- Employees cannot agree to waive their right to bring a claim for unfair dismissal as part of a fixed-term contract.
- After four years on successive fixed-term contracts, employees will be regarded as permanent.
- Workplace managers should take care in using fixed-term contracts, and should not now assume that they provide employers with any greater protection than they would have in relation to employees on other forms of contracts.

Legislation
- Employment Rights Act 1999.
- Fixed-term Employees (Prevention of Less Favourable Treatment) Regulations 2002.

Who has fixed-term contracts?
In 2002 it was estimated that between 1.1 and 1.3 million workers in the UK were employed on fixed-term contracts, approximately half of whom were public sector employees mainly working in education, healthcare and public administration, while the remainder were employed predominantly by larger businesses.

The Regulations apply only to 'employees' rather than a wider category of workers.

What is a fixed-term contract?
The Regulations define a fixed-term contract as a contract of employment that will terminate:

- on the expiry of a specific term;
- on the completion of a particular task; or
- on the occurrence or non-occurrence of any other specific event other than the attainment by the employee of any normal and bona-fide retiring age in the establishment for an employee holding the position held by him.

Scope of the Regulations
The Regulations came into force on 1 October 2002. They transposed the EC Directive on Fixed-term Work into UK law.

There are a number of categories of employees that are specifically excluded from the scope of the Regulations, namely:

- employees working under contracts of apprenticeship;
- agency workers;
- people employed on training schemes supported by the Government or an EU institution;

Fixed-term workers

- people employed on work experience placements of one year or less that they are required to attend as part of a higher-education course; and
- serving members of the armed forces.

The main provisions of the Regulations can be summarised as follows:

- Fixed-term employees have the right not to be treated less favourably than comparable permanent employees, unless the different treatment can be objectively justified.
- Fixed-term employees are not to be treated less favourably than similar permanent employees as regards the terms of their contract, or by being subjected to any other detriment by an act, or deliberate failure to act, of the employer.
- It is open to an employer to objectively justify any less favourable treatment and where the less favourable treatment concerns the terms of the contract, it can be justified if, overall, the terms of the fixed-term employee's contract, taken as a whole, are at least as favourable as those of the permanent employee.
- The right not to be treated less favourably includes a right not to be treated less favourably in relation to the opportunity to secure any permanent position in an organisation. An employer will be required to objectively justify any difference in the availability of internal permanent vacancies between fixed-term and permanent employees.
- An employee who considers that he has been treated by an employer in a manner that infringes a right conferred by the Regulations may submit a request in writing to the employer for a written statement of the reasons for the treatment. Under the Regulations the employer must provide a written statement within 21 days of the request.

- After four years on successive fixed-term contracts (discounting any period before 10 July 2002) an employee shall be regarded as a permanent employee, unless a further fixed-term contract can be objectively justified.
- A waiver of redundancy and unfair dismissal rights in fixed-term contracts is unlawful.
- An employee shall not be subjected to a detriment for relying upon his rights under the Regulations.

Termination of employment

Failure to renew a fixed-term contract on its expiry constitutes a dismissal for the purposes of employment legislation. In such circumstances, workplace managers should take care to avoid the possibility of a claim for unfair dismissal being brought by a fixed-term employee (see *'Dismissal,'* p.124), remembering the statutory process and steps required to be taken for compliance.

Whether the dismissal was fair or unfair will be determined by whether or not the employer can show that it acted reasonably in not renewing the contract.

Previously, employers have tried to get around this problem by including clauses in the fixed-term contract under which the employee in question agreed to waive his right to bring a claim for unfair dismissal due to the expiry and non-renewal of the contract if it was for one year or longer. Further, employers often engaged in the practice of renewing a fixed-term contract for a further fixed-term period, and still including such an unfair dismissal waiver relating to the end of that further term. However, Section 18(1) of the Employment Rights Act 1999 provided that these waivers of unfair dismissal rights would no longer be effective. The waiver of redundancy rights in fixed-term contracts was made unlawful as from 1 October 2002.

Workplace Law Network
www.workplacelaw.net

Fixed-term workers

By virtue of the Regulations, a dismissal will be automatically unfair if the reason for the dismissal is that the employee has brought proceedings against the employer under the Regulations, or requested from the employer a written statement of reasons for less favourable treatment or otherwise done anything under the Regulations in relation to the employer or any other person. No qualifying period of employment is required for such a claim.

Enforcement

Under the Regulations, a fixed-term employee may bring a complaint to an Employment Tribunal that he has suffered less favourable treatment, not been informed of available vacancies or suffered a detriment. The complaint will require to be brought within three months of the date of the act complained of.

> *See also*: Employee benefits, p.138; Employment contracts, p.146; Flexible working, p.190; Part-time workers, p.308.

Sources of further information

BIS – Fixed-term workers: www.berr.gov.uk/employment/employment-legislation/fixed-term-employees/index.html

Flexible working

Mark Kaye, Berwin Leighton Paisner

Key points
From 6 April 2003 employers have been under a legal obligation to consider applications for flexible working. Parents of young children have the right to submit a request to their employer to allow them to work 'flexibly', by changing hours, changing days or working from home. The change, if agreed, will be a permanent change to the employee's terms and conditions. The right applies to parents of children under six (or under the age of 18 if disabled) with more than 26 weeks' service who have responsibility for the child's upbringing and make the request to enable them to care for the child and where the employee is the 'carer' of an adult relative or someone living at the same address.

Legislation
- Employment Act 2002.

The law
The procedure for making a flexible working request is as follows:

- The employee makes a written, signed and dated request, specifying the change requested and proposed date from which it should apply. The request should also state what effect (if any) the employee thinks the change will have on the employer and how any such effect may be dealt with.
- The employer must either agree to the request in writing or hold a meeting to discuss the application with the employee within 28 days of the application being made.
- The employer must notify the employee in writing of its decision within 14 days of the meeting (which may include detailing any compromise agreed in the meeting).
- Any refusal must specify the grounds (*see below*) with a sufficient explanation for the refusal.
- The employee has the right of appeal against any refusal within 14 days of receiving the employer's notification.
- The employer must hold a meeting with the employee within 14 days of receiving the notice of appeal in order to discuss the appeal.
- The employer must give the employee notice of its decision in writing within 14 days of the appeal meeting. If the appeal is dismissed, grounds of the dismissal must be provided by the employer.

The following are permitted reasons for refusing a request:

- Burden of additional costs.
- Detrimental effect on ability to meet customer demand.
- Inability to reorganise work among existing staff.
- Inability to recruit additional staff.
- Detrimental impact on quality.
- Detrimental impact on performance.
- Insufficiency of work during the period the employee proposes to work.
- Planned structural changes.

Flexible working

> **Facts**
> - The majority of families (68%) with dependent children have two working parents.
> - In addition, there are over 1.9 million families with dependent children that are headed by a single parent, and 53% of those parents are working.
> - The 2001 Census, carried out by the Office for National Statistics, estimates that there are 5.2 million carers in England and Wales.
> - Of the 15.2 million employees in full-time work, 1.6 million of them are providing some unpaid care.

These allow an employer to refuse a request, for example, where the employee wishes to change his days or hours from peak periods to quiet times or where the operational needs of the business require staff at a particular time. For example, a bartender who asked to change his hours to work from 11 a.m. to five p.m. could have his request turned down on the grounds that customer demand is highest in the evening.

An employee can complain to a Tribunal that the ground given did not fall within one of the permitted reasons, or that the employer's decision was based on incorrect facts. However, the Tribunal cannot question the commercial validity of the employer's decision or substitute its own view on the employer's business reason. The Tribunal's role is to determine whether the employer has given serious consideration to a request to work flexibly and whether the employer has complied with the statutory procedure.

If the employee's complaint is successful, the Tribunal can either order that the employee's request is reconsidered or award up to eight weeks' pay, subject to the statutory cap, currently £330, making the maximum award £2,640. It is worth noting, however, that these rights exist independently of other employment rights and therefore an employee can bring a sex discrimination claim, for example, arising out of the same facts as a claim under the flexible working provisions, and could potentially be successful in one claim and fail in the other.

Practical guidance for employers
- Treat requests for flexible working seriously.
- Follow the statutory procedure.
- If the request cannot be accommodated, identify the reason and provide an explanation.
- Allow the employee to appeal.
- Consider if a refusal to allow the employer's request for flexible working could give rise to a claim such as indirect sex discrimination.

See also: Carers, p.54; Employment contracts, p.146; Family-friendly rights, p.182; Homeworking, p.222; Pregnancy, p.324.

Flexible working

Sources of further information

BIS – Flexible working: www.dti.gov.uk/employment/workandfamilies/flexible-working/index.html

Workplace Law's *Flexible Working Policy and Management Guide, v.4.0*, has been fully revised and updated to take into account the changes in the law. For more details visit: www.workplacelaw.net/bookshop/policiesAndProcedures.

Workplace Law Group's *Guide to Flexible Working 2008* provides information on the formal legislative right to request to work flexibly, but also considers working patterns in a wider sense. It covers the reasons why some employers are looking to introduce flexible working into their workplace, explores different flexible working patters, including their benefits and disadvantages, and provides detail on the formal legislative right to request. It also looks at the employment and non-employment legal issues that surround flexible working and the necessary amendments that need to be made to an employee's contractual terms and conditions if a flexible working pattern is agreed. Finally, it gives practical advice in relation to drafting and implementing a flexible working policy. For more information visit www.workplacelaw.net/bookshop/GuidesTo.

Join us

Join our 50,000+ membership base. It couldn't be easier

Join the Network for free

Just go to **www.workplacelaw.net** and register to join as a free member.

Alternatively, call our membership services team and we'll complete your registration for you.

Why not try a seven-day premium membership free trial while you're at it?

Join the Network as a premium member

Join the Network today as premium member and get:

- Full access to all areas of the Workplace Law Network
- A free copy of the Workplace Law Handbook
- Exclusive invitations to premium member online seminars
- And much more...

I'm already a member: I want to renew!

Renew online at **www.workplacelaw.net** or call our membership services team.

Save even more ... By renewing for two or three years, you can fix your current membership rate and save £££s.

Contact us

Chat to us online at **www.workplacelaw.net**

Need help? Chat to a representative who'll be pleased to provide assistance.
Click to chat

t 0871 777 8881
f 0871 777 8882
e membership@workplacelaw.net

Workplace Law Group
Second floor
Daedalus House
Station Road
Cambridge CB1 2RE

Workplace Law Network
Join the UK's fastest growing legal network
www.workplacelaw.net

Foreign nationals

Aliya Khan, Tyndallwoods Solicitors

Key points
- It is a criminal offence to employ someone who does not have permission to live and work in the UK.
- A statutory defence is available if employers inspect, take copies of, and keep a record of certain documents.
- Employers must apply for a work permit for employees, if one is needed.
- Employers must not discriminate when recruiting foreign nationals.
- Employers must ensure the health and safety of foreign nationals.

Legislation
- Immigration Act 1971.
- Asylum and Immigration Act 1996.
- Nationality and Immigration Asylum Act 2002.
- Immigration (Restrictions on Employment) Order 2004.
- Immigration and Nationality Act 2006.

General principles

Employers may offer employment to Commonwealth Citizens and Foreign Nationals without a permanent right of residence ('indefinite leave to enter or remain') as if they were a British Citizen if they are:

- a Commonwealth Citizen in the UK as a working holiday-maker (a two-year visa given for Commonwealth Citizens between the ages of 17 and 30);
- a Commonwealth Citizen or Foreign National (excluding EEA Nationals) who have been granted permission to enter or remain in the UK on the basis of marriage (two-year visa or extension);
- an EEA National (except 'A8' Nationals within the first 12 months);
- an A8 National within the first 12 months of entry in possession of a registration document and, for each particular employment, a certificate;
- a student who can take employment up to 20 hours a week in term-time or full time during holidays;
- those granted 12 months' leave under the International Graduates Scheme;
- those in possession of an Immigration Employment document (IED) from Work Permits (UK), a specialist division of the Immigration and Nationality Directorate (part of the Home Office) which may be given to the individual under Tier 1 or to the company for a specific employee; or
- Asylum Seekers (those waiting for a decision on their claim to refugee status) with Application Registration Card endorsed 'Employment Permitted'.

Passports are not generally endorsed with 'Permission to Work'. It is the absence of a 'prohibition on employment' that demonstrates that a person has permission to work. Students have a 'restriction' on employment endorsed on their passports; in other words limited to 20 hours a week term-time, but they are not required to obtain any form of permit or Immigration Employment Document. Permission to work is not the same as permission to live in the UK. An employer who obtains a

Foreign nationals

> **Facts**
> - In total, around 3.6 million people of working age were born outside the UK.
> - Regionally, London and the South East are host to the largest numbers of migrant workers. In 2000, London was home to 47% of migrant workers (520,000), and the rest of the South East had a further 20% of all migrant workers in the UK. More than two-thirds of foreign national workers were in this corner of England (compared with only 42% of British workers).
> - There were 1.5 million foreign migrants working in the UK in 2005; 5.4% of the UK employed population.
> - The annual number of work permits approved in 2005 was 129,660. The three main occupations were nurses and carers (19.9%), software professionals (19.5%) and manager and proprietors in other services sectors (12.8%).
> - A CIPD labour market outlook report showed that few employers hire migrants mainly due to lower wage costs, but that this objective was more important for employers hiring less skilled (9%) than skilled (2%) migrants.
> - Overall, the work permit system and the Worker Registration Scheme (WRS) are currently bringing in at least 300,000 workers per annum, covering the full range of the occupational spectrum.

Work Permit (*see below*) for an employee must also ensure that the individual obtains permission to enter (by obtaining a visa) or remain in the UK (by an application for variation of leave). This is a process of application that the individual must go through before their employment commences.

Someone who has permission to work can continue in their employment (or take alternative employment) whilst waiting for a decision on their application for an extension of stay, providing they applied to extend their leave before their last extension expired. Home Office acknowledgement letters sent in response to extension applications contain the standard wording:

"Provided an Applicant has permission to be in the UK when an application is made, he or she is legally entitled to remain here on the same conditions previously granted until the application has been decided."

Responsibilities under the Asylum and Immigration Act 1996

The offence

Section 8 of the Asylum and Immigration Act 1996 (the Act) makes it a criminal offence to employ someone who is not entitled to live and work in the UK. Employers and individual managers can face fines of up to £5,000 per employee.

The Act provides a defence if, before the employment commences, the employer checks (Step one), copies (Step two) and retains (Step three) copies of specified documents.

Step one – requesting documents
- Before the employment commences, employers must require prospective employees to produce originals of documents from lists drawn up by the Home Office, full details of which can be found on the Home Office Website at: www.employingmigrantworkers.org.uk.

Foreign nationals

- To avoid committing the criminal offence, employers should refuse to employ an applicant if the relevant document or combination of documents cannot be produced.

Step two – checking documents
- Check all details and photos are consistent with the applicant's details and appearance (for example age, gender, race) and that the documents are in date.
- The Immigration and Nationality Directorate (IND) advises that if there are any inconsistencies between the documents, the reason for the difference must be proved by documents showing a valid reason for a change of name.

Step three – record keeping
- Copy the front page and all pages showing any of the employee's details, including photos and signatures.
- Copy pages with an immigration endorsement or stamp.
- The employer must retain the copies.
- If the copies cannot be produced, the defence will not be available.

The defence is not available if the employer knows that the employee is not entitled to live and/or work in the UK – even if they have checked the documents.

Note: These changes apply to employees taken on after 30 April 2004, not for those already in employment at that date. An employer who curtails the employment of Commonwealth Citizens or Foreign Nationals after 1 May 2004 for failure to produce documents specified in the Home Office lists may be liable to a claim for unfair dismissal. Other requirements were in force for employees who were taken on before 1 May 2004.

Immigration issues in employment

Compliance issues for employers
In their employment practices and procedures, employers must avoid discrimination on prohibited grounds, but must also avoid offering or continuing employment to people who are not, for immigration reasons, permitted to take it. The primary Government tools for prevention of illegal working are the imposition of civil penalties, up to £10,000 per illegal worker, and prosecution of the employer, with fines, forfeiture of cash found, and on indictment up to two years' imprisonment.

In general terms, citizens of the EU have unrestricted access to the labour market; migrants sponsored within the UKBA's Points Based System (PBS) work only for the licensed sponsor; highly skilled migrants within Tier 1 (Post-Study Work) or (General) may work for any employer, as may foreign nationals with indefinite leave to remain, or whose limited duration residence permits do not prohibit employment.

Determining whether a foreign national is entitled to take the particular employment may not be straightforward, even when the passport is carefully examined. It is essential to make the assessment of entitlement to take the employment *before* employment commences.

Where the employment is permitted, it may, for example with students, be limited to 20 hours per week in term-time, or limited to the unexpired duration of a visa or certificate of sponsorship.

The UKBA consequently provide an employers telephone helpline on 0845 010 677 and assistance with online document verification at www.bia.homeoffice.gov.uk/employingmigrants.

Foreign nationals

Key documents to establish the right to work must be originals; copies should be retained throughout the employment and for at least two years after it ends. The employment should be monitored to ensure that its terms, conditions and duration coincide with the right to work.

Key documents:

- Passport or EEA Identity Card.
- UKBA Residence Card.
- UK Birth, Adoption, Naturalisation or Registration Certificate.
- UKBA Immigration Status Document or Application Registration Card.
- P45, P60 or National Insurance Card.
- Letter issued by UKBA permitting the employment.

It is essential to consider the comprehensive UKBA guidance on prevention of initial working, which can be downloaded from its website.

Particular categories

Visitors

Visitors to the UK are prohibited from taking employment. Business visitors, including academics, religious workers, sports people and consultants, can undertake only types of activity that are specifically permitted by the Immigration Rules and UKBA Guidance.

Students

The 20 hours per term-time week limitation on student employment applies to PhD students until any application to vary leave (for example into Tier 1 (Post-Study Work)) into a category permitting full-time work is determined by UKBA.

A8 nationals

Although EEA citizens and any non-EEA dependants are generally entitled to work, A8 nationals (Czech Republic, Estonia, Latvia, Lithuania, Hungary, Poland, Slovenia and Slovakia) are required (with exceptions) to register within their first 12 months in the UK. Once the Certificate of Registration is received, the employer must retain a copy but, in the meantime, must retain a copy of the application.

A2 nationals

A2 nationals (Bulgaria and Romania) are freely entitled to undertake self-employment but their access to the labour market continues to be limited so that they require explicit permission to work within the residual Work Permit Scheme, unless the terms of their Visa / Residence Permit (for example as a dependant of a person settled in the UK) implicitly allow them to take employment.

Migrants with 'temporary admission'

Migrants with 'temporary admission,' which, confusingly, is not a form of leave to enter or a Residence Permit, will generally have a pending immigration or asylum application. They are usually not permitted to work. In some cases they are permitted, and should have documentation to prove it.

Although the online Employer Check-In Service may be helpful, their advice cannot be regarded as authoritative. Such migrants and other foreign nationals with pending immigration applications may be unable to produce original documents, as those documents will be in the Home Office with the applications. In such cases, originals may be unavailable for very extensive periods. Original correspondence from UKBA may then be required to authorise the employment. This may be very slow to arrive.

Foreign nationals

Extending permission to remain in the UK other than via the Points Based System (PBS)

Nationals of EEA countries

Nationals of EEA countries (except in A2 and Switzerland), may, but are not required to, obtain Residence Cards. Such cards are initially valid for five years. Any non-EEA dependants should be admitted to the UK with family permits endorsed in their passports. Applications for removal of time limits must be supported by original documents. In the case of EEA nationals, applications may well take over six months to resolve. In the case of non-EEA dependants, the delay may be much greater. Their right to remain in the UK at the date of their in-time application continue by operation of law, until the UKBA decision is received.

It is the *employer's duty* to ensure that they prevent illegal working, but it is the *migrant's obligation* to ensure that their permission to remain in the UK is valid and that they do not conduct themselves so as to breach the terms of such permission. Any such breach could be enforced by curtailment to their leave and/or administrative removal from the UK. Such removal could lead to a mandatory refusal of subsequent application for visa.

Where a migrant has time-limited permission to remain in the UK and/or where their permission is for a purpose now superseded, they must ensure that their application to vary the terms of the permission or to remove conditions, is received by the Secretary of State before expiry of their valid permission. An application must be on the currently applicable form, with the appropriate fee, and supported by all relevant documents. Great care must be taken to meet all of these requirements. All the pre-existing terms and conditions of the most recent permission will continue until the application is finally determined. If the application should fail, whether only because an out-of-date form was inadvertently used, or fee payment fails through a dishonoured cheque or refused credit card payment, then the migrant with dependants who lack independent rights to remain, may well have to leave the UK.

Expiry of work permits

If an employee's work permit or visa is due to expire, the employer should apply under the new Points Based System for a Sponsorship Licence before the expiry of the old work permit, and the employee should apply for further leave to remain before their current leave expires. This enables an employee to live and work in the UK until a decision is reached by the Home Office – even if in the meantime their permit and/or visa expires.

Health and safety

Employers have health and safety obligations towards all employees. For foreign nationals, one additional consideration may be whether they can speak English sufficiently for the role and to recognise any safety notices. Employers should consider whether training or assistance can be provided.

Avoiding race discrimination

All checks must be performed in a non-discriminatory way. The Government has issued a Code of Practice on 'Avoidance of race discrimination in recruitment practice while seeking to prevent illegal working'. The main points are:

- Failure to follow the Code may be considered by an Employment Tribunal.
- All job selections should be based on suitability for the post.

Foreign nationals

- Make no assumptions based on colour, race, nationality, ethnic or national origins or the length of time someone has been in the UK.
- Identical checks should be performed for all applicants, although employers may decide to only perform checks on candidates who reach a certain stage.
- If someone cannot produce the necessary documents, ask them to seek advice.

Changes to the system

Significant changes have taken place in Managed Migration. Employers are now required to register as sponsors, prove qualifications, and take active responsibility for employees.

The Points Based System

The UK Border Agency has rolled out the new Points Based System (PBS). The System is based on an 'Australian style' points system where an applicant wishing to work and reside in the UK will be required to obtain the necessary points before being granted permission to do so. The Points System is broken down into the following Tiers:

- *Tier 1* – Highly Skilled Migrants (previously HSMP) – leads to settlement.
- *Tier 2* – Skilled Workers requiring a Sponsorship Licence (previously work permits) – leads to settlement.
- *Tier 3* – Low Skilled Workers – currently suspended until further notice.
- *Tier 4* – Students.
- *Tier 5* – Sponsorship Licence required – temporary leave.

The Scheme combines more than 80 previous work and study routes to the UK into five tiers. Points are awarded according to workers' skills, experience and age and also the demand for those skills in the UK. This allows the UK to respond flexibly to changes in the labour market.

Tier 1 – Highly Skilled Individuals

Applicants in the Highly Skilled tier will *not* be required to have sponsors. This will make it easy for employers to take on such migrants, without having to issue certificates of sponsorship. The Highly Skilled tier embraces the following categories.

General

For migrants who qualify for highly skilled employment in the UK.

Entrepreneurs

For those investing in the UK by setting up or taking over, and being actively involved, in the running of a business. They must have £200,000 held in a regulated financial institution, disposable in the UK.

Investors

For high net worth individuals making a substantial financial investment in the UK. They must have £1m held in a regulated financial institution and disposable in the UK. Investors can take paid employment. These individuals are the only people who *do not* have to gain points for the English Language Requirement.

Post-study work

This category aims to retain the most able international graduates who have studied in the UK. Post-study workers are granted a three-year visa if applying from abroad and two years' leave to remain if applying from inside the UK.

Note: Time spent under this category will not count towards settlement. Therefore, post-study workers must switch category either into Tier 1 (General) or under Tier 2 (Sponsorship).

Foreign nationals

Who should apply?
An applicant does not have to apply under the Points Based System if:

- they are an EEA or Swiss national;
- they are a British overseas territories citizen, unless they are from one of the sovereign base areas in Cyprus;
- they are a Commonwealth citizen with permission to enter or stay in the UK because at least one of their grandparents was born here;
- their spouse or civil partner, unmarried or same-sex partner, or (if the applicant is under 18) one of their parents has permission to stay in the UK under Tier 1 (General) – highly skilled worker of the PBS; or
- they have no conditions or time limit attached to their stay.

Ways of applying
- Entering the UK in a Highly Skilled sub-category.
- Extending a stay in the UK in a Highly skilled sub-category.
- Switching while in the UK into or out of a Highly Skilled sub-category.

Points
Highly Skilled applicants will need to show that they have enough points to qualify to enter or remain in the UK.

An applicant must score at least:

- 75 points for his/her attributes (age, qualifications, previous earnings, and experience in the UK; and
- ten points for English language; and
- ten points for available maintenance (funds).

If the applicant does not score a minimum of 75 points for his/her attributes and ten points for English language and ten points for available maintenance (funds), the application will be refused.

The requirements that an applicant must meet in order to be awarded points differ depending on whether the applicant is:

- applying to enter Tier 1 (General) – Highly Skilled Worker for the first time (initial applications); or
- applying to extend existing permission to stay granted under the Highly Skilled Migrant Programme (HSMP).

Points will be earned against three seats of objective criteria:

1. Criteria specific to each sub-category (pass mark 75).
2. Competence in English language.
3. Maintenance. Migrants are to be able to support themselves and their dependants. The test will be based upon the latest cost of living figures provided in the annual British Council publication, 'Studying and Living in the United Kingdom'.

Maintenance
As with the whole of the Points Based System, the main applicant requires £800 in their bank account for three months, if they are applying from the UK. If the main applicant is applying from abroad then they will require £2,800. If the main applicant is applying from abroad or has been in the UK for fewer than 12 months, they require £1,600 per dependant for three months. However, if the main applicant has been in the UK for 12 months or more, each dependant will require £533 for three months.

Previous earnings
This will be measured over a single consecutive 12-month period from 15 months immediately prior to the date of application *unless* the applicant has been either:

- in full-time study at some point during the previous 12 months; or

Foreign nationals

- absent due to maternity or adoption related leave.

Earnings can include both salaried employment and self-employed activities. The earnings can be from several sources and so can be from different employers and from full-time, part-time, temporary and short-term work. The earnings can also be from dividends, property rental income when it constitutes a part of the applicant's business, maternity pay and allowances that form part of a remuneration package.

Dependants

Successful applicants will be able to bring dependants (children aged under 18, spouses, civil partners, same-sex partners and unmarried partners) into the UK if they can prove that they maintain them.

Grant of leave

The grant of leave will initially be for three years. A further two years will be given on extension. Settlement can be applied for after five years.

For post-study work, there is a two-year maximum and then there should be an application to switch into another Tier 1 or Tier 2 category.

Challenges to decision

There are full appeal rights for in-country refusals, though this will be limited with regard to the points-based element. An Appellant cannot submit new evidence. Therefore it is essential to ensure the application is correct first time. Documentary evidence will be rigorously checked. No points will be awarded if there are reasonable grounds to doubt that the evidence is genuine.

There is no substantive right of appeal against refusal of a visa under the PBS.

Tier 2 – Skilled Workers

The main aim of Tier 2 is to enable the UK employer to recruit from outside the European Economic Area (EEA) in jobs that cannot be filled by EEA workers. There must be a genuine vacancy.

The applicant will require 70 points made up of ten points for English Language proficiency, ten points for sufficient maintenance and 50 points for the Sponsorship Licence.

All Tier 2 applicants will require entry clearance or be able to switch into this category. Entry clearance applicants will need to obtain a biometric identity card so the UK Border Agency (UKBA) knows exactly who they are and what they are entitled to do.

As with other PBS Tiers, the employee will need to obtain enough points to qualify.

The sponsor / employer

The Sponsorship Licence itself is worth 50 points. To be granted a licence the employer should apply online, demonstrating that the job is in the Shortage Occupation List, or the job satisfies the Resident Labour Market Test (RLMT) (that no qualified person can be found from inside the EEA to fill the position), or that the employee would be an intra-company transfer (i.e. is already working with the company in a sister company abroad).

The prospective employer must submit the application form themselves electronically and get the support documentation to the UKBA within ten days of submitting the application. This is to verify that the vacancy is a genuine vacancy that cannot be filled by an EEA national and that the sponsor, the employer, will accept responsibilities of sponsorship in respect of the employee.

Foreign nationals

Qualifications		Previous earnings (£s per annum)		Age		Other	
Bachelor's (only for extension applications). Applicants making their first application will gain no points in this category.	30	16,000-17,999 (extensions only)	5	Under 28	20	If previous earnings or qualifications have been gained in the UK	5
Master's	35	18,000-19,999 (extensions only)	10	28 or 29	10		
PhD	50	20,000-22,999	15	30 or 31	5		
		23,000-25,999	20				
		26,000-28,999	25				
		29,000-31,999	30				
		32,000-34,999	35				
		35,000-39,999	40				
		40,000+	45				
Criteria specific to the sub-category. Pass mark = 75 points							

English Language	10 points
Maintenance	10 points

Table 1: Tier 1 (General). Total: 95 points

The Shortage Occupation List is drawn up by the Migration Advisory Committee (MAC). If a job title is listed on the Shortage Occupation List then the full 50 points are awarded for the Sponsorship Licence. If a job is not listed on the Shortage Occupation List then the employer must advertise the position and satisfy the Resident Labour Market Test.

To satisfy the RLMT the employer must have advertised the vacancy either for at least two weeks at Job Centre Plus; or for one week if the salary offered for the position is £40,000 per annum and over; or advertised as agreed in a sector-specific Code of Practice (these can be found on the UK Border Agency website (www.ukba.homeoffice.gov.uk). The RLMT does not need to be carried out if the employee is a post-study worker, working for six months or more, as a post-study worker is already considered part of the Resident Labour Market.

The vacancy must be at NVQ 3 level or above to ensure it is a skilled job. The UKBA has published a list of occupations

Foreign nationals

that fall below the NVQ 3 skill level. With regard to the skill level required, employers must ensure they are offering the appropriate rate of pay for the job so as to ensure there is no undercutting of the domestic labour market and the vacancy is genuine. The appropriate rate may be checked from the Annual Survey of Hours and Earnings (ASHE), published by the Office for National Statistics. If an occupation is not listed in ASHE, checks may be made on 'Jobs4U,' a Government-maintained website.

The Sponsor Management System (SMS) is a system set up by UKBA, which allows an employer to access the system for the purposes of applying for a licence and assigning certificates. Before applying electronically an employer should identify key personnel in the company to play important roles such as accessing the SMS. These key personnel must be based in the UK and must be people of good character. The key personnel are listed below.

Authorising Officer

This person is responsible for the activities of anyone acting on the company's behalf with regard to the sponsorship licence. They ensure the employer meets their duties. They must be an honest, reliable and competent member of staff. Legal representatives cannot act as an Authorising Officer. An un-discharged bankrupt cannot act as an Authorising Officer. The Authorising Officer can have more than one role.

Key contact

This person is the main point of UKBA contact and acts as a liaison between the employer and the UKBA. This person is called upon by the UKBA if there is a problem with the application process. The Authorising Officer can act in this role.

Level 1 User

This person operates the employer's activities on a day-to-day basis via the sponsor Management System. They will be able to:

- create and remove other users;
- assign certificates;
- request an increase in certificates;
- complete the change of circumstances screen;
- report migrant activity; and
- appoint Level 2 Users.

A legal representative can be appointed to act as a Level 1 User. Only one person can be appointed as a Level 1 User. The Level 1 User will be held responsible for the actions of the Level 2 Users.

Level 2 User

These can be more than one person appointed by the Level 1 User. Legal representatives can act as a Level 2 User. A Level 2 User's duties may include assigning Certificates of Sponsorship to migrants, and reporting migrant activity to the UK Border Agency.

As the Authorising Officer is responsible for *all* users, it is sensible to keep Level 2 users to a minimum and only appoint when absolutely necessary.

The UKBA will do checks on the individuals against the Police National Computer and will as a minimum carry out checks against the Authorising Officer and Level 1 Users.

The UKBA has set out what they call their overriding principles. The questions they will ask are:

- Is the employer a bona fide organisation operating lawfully in the UK? In order to prove this, the employer is required to provide certain documents from a list.

Foreign nationals

- Is the employer trustworthy? In order to judge this the UKBA will look at the company's previous history and background and that of the key personnel. Any negative findings of previous immigration crimes or dishonesty will be considered and may lead to the refusal of the licence.
- Is the employer capable of carrying out its duties as sponsor? The UKBA proposes to check a prospective employer's Human Resources practices to ensure that there is a system in place to enable the employer to carry out his duties.

As a condition of keeping the licence an employer will need to alert the UKBA if their employee does not comply with their immigration conditions.

Human resources practices
The UK Border Agency will check the human resources records of a sponsor. Sponsors must be aware of how many foreign nationals it employs. They must have a system in place to monitor absences from work and inform the UK Border Agency of any absences of more than ten days.

The UK Border Agency may arrange for a site visit to the sponsor's premises to carry out inspections.

Rating A or B
The sponsor will be given an A or B rating. If the sponsor meets all the requirements they will be given an A rating. If the sponsor fails to meet either the compliance check or the human resources check they will receive a B rating. If the sponsor does not meet either compliance or human resources checks, the UK Border Agency will refuse to grant a Certificate of Sponsorship.

Transitional ratings
B rated organisations may be given a short period of time (possibly three months) to improve their performance and obtain an A rating. An action plan will be drawn up that will include steps the sponsor should take to improve. This is a joint project; however, the UK Border Agency will have the final say. After three months the UK Border Agency will check to see if genuine attempts have been made to meet the requirements. If the sponsor does not improve they will lose their licence. However, if there are circumstances outside of the sponsor's control then the sponsor may be put on probation for 12 months.

The UKBA will then review the B rating and possibly grant an A rating. There are certain circumstances where the Sponsorship Licence *will* be refused (or B rating granted) or will *normally* be refused (or B rating granted) or *may* be refused (or B rating granted).

A refusal or B rating will depend on the breach or failure to comply such as:

- not supplying compulsory documents;
- providing forged or false documents;
- when the sponsor / employer does not meet the criteria for a specific tier;
- where one of the key personnel is legally prohibited from becoming a company director;
- any previous convictions for an immigration-related offence or being issued with civil penalty; and/or
- a civil penalty being unpaid with regards to an immigration offence.

The UK Border Agency has the power to cancel a Certificate of Sponsorship and in certain circumstances they will refuse a Certificate. In other situations they may or normally will refuse a licence or award a B rating.

Foreign nationals

Franchises
If an organisation has a number of franchises that are under its control, each branch may apply for a separate licence or they may apply for one licence covering all the other franchises. If the franchises are separate business not under the control of the parent company, each branch will be required to apply separately.

The applicant / employee
Up to 15 points are awarded to the employee for their qualifications. All jobs must be at or above NVQ3 skill level and salary must be at the appropriate rate.

A maximum of 20 points is granted to an employee for his prospective earnings in the UK.

Ten points will be granted to the employee (the main applicant), if they can prove they have at least £800 in their bank account for the past three months and a further £600 for each dependant for those applicants in the UK.

The final ten points will be granted to the applicant if they can prove they satisfy the English language requirement.

Once a Certificate of Approval and the above documentation is to hand, the applicant / employee must then apply for entry clearance or for leave to remain.

At least 70 points are required from Table 2 (including ten for maintenance and ten for English). All jobs must be at or above NVQ 3 skill level and salary must be at or above the appropriate rate.

Grant of leave to remain / visa
The grant of leave will initially be for three years. A further two years will be given on extension. Settlement can be applied for after five years.

Section	Certificate of Sponsorship		Qualifications (or NARIC equivalents)		Prospective earnings (£)	
A	Offer of job in shortage occupation	50	No qualifications	0	17,000-19,999	5
(50 points needed)	Offer of job that passes Resident Labour Market Test (RLMT)	30	NVQ 3	5	20,000-21,999	10
			Bachelors or Masters	10	22,000-23,999	15
	Intra-company transfer	30	PhD	15	24,000+	20
B	Maintenance requirement					10
C	Competence in English					10

Table 2: Tier 2 (Skilled Workers). Total: 70 points

Foreign nationals

Tier 5 – Sponsorship Licence required

Employers applying under this category are required to have a Sponsorship Licence. The applicant must have sufficient maintenance. This category is designed for temporary workers, each category requires a sponsor and the applicant will be required to satisfy the maintenance requirement.

Creative and sporting

Before an employer can assign a certificate, they must have an endorsement from the particular sporting governing body confirming the applicant meets the governing body's requirements. The governing body must be a recognised body. A list of recognised bodies are found on the UK Border Agency website. Points are granted for sponsorship and maintenance. An applicant may apply from abroad or, if they have already been granted permission to come to the UK as a creative *and* sporting worker, they may extend their leave up to 12 months. If the applicant is already in the UK and wishes to extend their visa as a creative worker *only,* permission may be granted up to 24 months in total. This category is not for people who wish to come or who are already in the UK as sports visitors or entertainers, including for special festivals, which come under Business and Special Visitors.

Charity workers

Charity workers do voluntary unpaid work. The work must be directly related to the work of the sponsoring organisation. The applicant can apply to enter as a charity worker and get a visa for 12 months or if the applicant is already in the UK as a charity worker but was granted fewer than 12 months, they may extend their visa up to 12 months in total.

Religious worker

The applicant may carry out work preaching, pastoral work and non-pastoral work. This work must be done during a break from the applicant's job overseas. The period of leave granted is 24 months. Dependants of the main applicant are allowed to take up employment. Those who are already in the UK as religious workers but have not been granted the full 24 months may apply for an extension up to the full 24 months.

Government-authorised exchanges

The Government-authorised exchange category is for people coming to the UK through approved schemes that aim to share knowledge, experience and best practice and experience the social and cultural life of the UK. This category must not be used to fill job vacancies or to bring unskilled labour to the UK.

The sponsor for this category will be the overarching body who manages the scheme with the UK. Sponsored researchers are sponsored by the Higher Education Institution they have been sponsored by. All other employers will not be allowed to sponsor an applicant in this category, even if they are licensed as sponsors under other tiers or other categories of Tier 5.

Any work done must be skilled, which means it must be equivalent to NVQ Level 3 or above, unless the work is part of the European Union's lifelong learning programme, where permission is granted to do vocational education and training at a lower skill level.

Applicants are allowed to stay in the UK for up to 24 months under this category.

International Agreement

The types of work that are covered by this agreement are:

- the General Agreement on Trade in Services (GATS);

Foreign nationals

- similar agreements between the UK and another country;
- employees of overseas governments and international organisations; and
- private servants in diplomatic households.

An applicant can live and work in the UK for a maximum of 24 months.

A private servant in a diplomatic household, or as an employee of an overseas government or international organisation, may apply to extend their visas for a maximum of 12 months at a time, up to a total of six years.

Youth Mobility Scheme

The Youth Mobility Scheme is for young people from the age of 18 to 30 from participating countries who would like to experience life in the UK. This is based on a quota system. Once the quota has been reached, no more applicants from that particular country will be accepted until the next year. Under this scheme national government is the sponsor.

The countries in the scheme are:

- Australia;
- Canada;
- Japan; and
- New Zealand.

The applicants must have £1,600 maintenance to qualify under this scheme.

See also: Discrimination, p.110; Migrant workers, p.269; Recruitment and selection, p.335.

Sources of further information

Home Office: www.employingmigrantworkers.org.uk

Immigration and Nationality Directorate: www.ind.homeoffice.gov.uk/applying/eeaeunationals

UK Border Agency: www.bia.homeoffice.gov.uk/

Code of Practice on 'Avoidance of race discrimination in recruitment practice while seeking to prevent illegal working': www.ukba.homeoffice.gov.uk/sitecontent/documents/employersandsponsors/preventingillegalworking/currentguidanceandcodes/antidiscriminationcode2008.pdf

Annual Survey of Hours and Earnings (ASHE), published by the Office for National Statistics: www.statistics.gov.uk/ashe

Employers' Telephone Helpline: 0845 010 677.

Freedom of information

Louise Townsend, Pinsent Masons Employment Group

Key points

The Freedom of Information Act 2000 (FOIA) came into full force on 1 January 2005, giving individuals a statutory right for the first time to see a huge amount of information held by government departments and public bodies. The Data Protection Act has traditionally provided individuals with a right of access to information held about themselves. FOIA extends this right to cover information about third parties as well as any other information that may be held by the Public Authority or private companies that have public sector contracts.

Under FOIA, anyone of any nationality, and living anywhere in the world, can make a written request for information, and expect a response within 20 working days. The Public Authority will be obliged to meet that request, subject to a number of specified exemptions and certain practical and financial constraints.

FOIA has imposed a substantial burden on those responsible for administering freedom of information (FOI) requests in Public Authorities. However, it is not only Public Authorities that have been affected by the Act. Whilst the primary impact of the Act will be on Public Authorities, it will have a knock-on effect on private companies dealing with Public Authorities.

Legislation
- Data Protection Act 1998.
- Freedom of Information Act 2000 (FOIA).

Some FOI examples

The following are all examples of requests that could be made to a Public Authority in the HR context – whether you disclose the information depends on the circumstances of each case; each request has to be treated individually. In some cases, an exemption may apply, in particular the exemption that protects personal data about individuals that requires a balancing act between freedom of information and protection of privacy.

- Aggregated information about salary and overtime levels of senior employees.
- Summary information about the number of grievances and disciplinaries dealt with by an organisation.
- Witness statements relating to a grievance.
- CCTV footage of an incident in the workplace.
- A copy of HR policies, for example on sickness, discrimination, IT use etc.

Remember that if an individual asks for information about themselves, this is treated as a request under the Data Protection Act 1998, but if a request is for information about someone other than the requestor then FOIA applies, subject to privacy considerations.

Other relevant exemptions include information provided in confidence by

Freedom of information

a third party and information whose disclosure would prejudice the commercial interests of any party. Some exemptions are subject to an additional public interest test.

What does this mean for public sector employers?

The public sector employer is to a large extent caught between a rock and a hard place. Whilst the aim of FOIA is to increase openness in the public sector, and disclosing information about decisions and activities of employees may promote this, it is recognised that employees also have legitimate concerns over privacy and rights to have those concerns respected.

With this delicate balancing act, how should the public sector employer deal with requests made by third parties about their employees? They could consider the following factors.

Consider your publication scheme

The Information Commissioner has issued a model publication scheme for all Public Authorities to follow. This includes organisational information and contacts, policies and procedures etc. There should already, therefore, be some HR-related information in the public domain and the Authority should ensure that its employees are aware of what this is and that it is regularly reviewed and maintained. Because Authorities are encouraged to be open and transparent, it may be helpful to include standard policies in the scheme and information about key individuals in the organisation.

Implement policies

The public sector employer should draw up a policy setting out how it intends to deal with requests for employee information to provide a clear view of how information will be dealt with under the Act. This policy should be made available to all employees and ideally be published on the publication scheme for all to see. Policies could cover what types of information and in what circumstances information will or will not generally be disclosed, and also what issues will be considered in determining whether to disclose employee information. Issuing this policy will help the Authority meet its Data Protection Act obligations to employees. Remember, it is not just personal data that may be requested but any information including HR policies and procedures.

Know your information

Records management is important. Try to know what personal data you have and have clear filing and records management practices so that information is easy to find. This will also be useful in dealing with subject access requests under the Data Protection Act. Consider separating or flagging information at the point of collection or creation to information which is not exempt from third party requests and other information.

Raise awareness

One potential factor to consider when determining whether information should be disclosed is what the employee was told when the information was collected. With this in mind, the Authority could consider alerting new employees to the potential for disclosure of employee information under the Act by including a notice on induction. Including FOIA as part of new employees' training would provide them with a greater understanding of the Authority's obligations under the Act, and also the relevant exemptions, and they could be given a basic information sheet to use as a checklist for FOIA compliance.

Give notice of, or consult the employee about, any proposed disclosure and certainly where there is any doubt as to whether the information should be disclosed.

Freedom of information

> **Facts**
> - Individuals or organisations have the right to request information from any Public Authority, for any reason.
> - Requests must generally be responded to within 20 working days.
> - Public Authorities could receive requests from employees or former employees or for information about employees or former employees – some of this will overlap with the Data Protection Act.
> - Public Authorities must also provide information proactively through a Publication Scheme.
> - Private companies contracted by Public Authorities should be aware that their information may be caught too, and should know about the Freedom of Information Act (FOIA).

Impact on private sector employers

Although it may seem that FOIA will only be relevant to Public Authorities, in practice it will also have an effect on the private sector. While there are limited circumstances where a private company may be deemed a Public Authority for the purposes of the Act (and therefore required to disclose information that it holds), the more concerning effect of the Act relates to information that private sector businesses hand over to the public sector.

Most Public Authorities contract on a regular basis with private sector companies for the provision of goods and services. Many of these contracts contain sensitive information (about HR, commercial or financial issues), which the private sector company would rather not be disclosed. However, all of this information is held by Public Authorities and, in theory, is accessible by anyone requesting it.

In the future it is possible that some private sector companies will be caught directly by FOIA. The Government issued a response to consultation in 2009 that only suggested limited additions to the FOIA, but it has reserved the position for the future so that it may extend, for example, to fostering organisations, private prisons, utility companies, and so on.

What can private sector businesses do to protect their interests? They may consider the following factors.

Put in place clear internal policies

Make it clear which individuals are authorised to release information to Public Authorities and identify individuals to liaise with Public Authorities with regard to monitoring the information once the Authority has it.

Raise awareness within the organisation of the risk that any information disclosed to a Public Authority may potentially end up being disclosed to a member of the public or a competitor.

Manage information that is provided to Public Authorities

Identify which customers may be Public Authorities and review what information is provided to them. Record what information is provided to aid monitoring of this.

If information is particularly sensitive, consider whether it is really necessary to disclose it or whether it can be redacted or anonymised.

Freedom of information

Confidential information
Amend standard terms and conditions used for dealing with Public Authorities to include drafting to minimise the impact of the Act. Blanket confidentiality clauses are no longer likely to be accepted by Public Authorities or by the Information Commissioner. Consider segregating confidential and non-confidential material to reduce the risk of inadvertent disclosure, and to increase the likelihood of the confidentiality exemption applying.

Consider negotiating a clause in the contract that provides a right to be notified about, and make submissions in relation to, an information request that may contain employee / commercially sensitive information. This is important as it is the Authority's decision whether to disclose and, similarly, if a decision made by the Information Commissioner is unfavourable to you, it will be the decision of the Authority, not you, as to whether to appeal. There is no obligation on the Authority to consult any interested third parties.

Be aware that information that is passed to Public Authorities may contain employee information such as CVs, experience etc.

Thought should be given to consulting any affected third parties prior to releasing the information. Consider providing induction training on FOIA, amending your data protection notices and alerting employees when their information may be disclosed.

Use the Act to your advantage
Consider what types of information might be available from the public sector to assist your business and make use of your own rights to access that information. Training employees about the Act will increase your effectiveness in this area.

Conclusion
Both the public and private sectors are increasingly being affected by obligations imposed by the Act, albeit in different ways. What is clear is that it is essential for both sectors to implement policies, training and raise awareness within their organisations as to how the Act should be dealt with within their individual business.

See also: Data protection, p.84; Internet and email policies, p.236.

Sources of further information

Freedom of Information Act: www.foi.gov.uk

Information Commissioner's Office: www.ico.gov.uk

Guidance on access to information about public sector employees: www.ico.gov.uk/upload/documents/library/data_protection/detailed_specialist_guides/public_authority_staff_info_v2.0_final.pdf

When should salaries be disclosed: www.ico.gov.uk/upload/documents/library/freedom_of_information/practical_application/salaries_v1.pdf

When should names be disclosed: www.ico.gov.uk/upload/documents/library/freedom_of_information/practical_application/whenshouldnamesbedisclosed.pdf

Health surveillance

David Sinclair, Hempsons

Key points

Employers who expose their employees to certain chemicals, physical agents, materials or ergonomic risks may be required to undertake systematic, regular and appropriate health surveillance on those employees.

Health surveillance may be either specified in Regulations or covered by the umbrella provisions of health and safety legislation.

Where health surveillance is required, it should be undertaken only by competent people, who in many cases must be medically qualified.

Employers are required to provide adequate information to employees on health surveillance provisions, results and the records they keep. Records may have to be kept for up to 50 years.

Legislation
- Health and Safety at Work etc. Act 1974.
- Opticians Act 1989.
- Sight Testing (Examination and Prescription) (No. 2) Regulations 1989.
- Health and Safety (Display Screen Equipment) Regulations 1992.
- Manual Handling Operations Regulations 1992.
- Disability Discrimination Acts 1995 and 2005.
- Data Protection Act 1998.
- Management of Health and Safety at Work Regulations 1999.
- Control of Substances Hazardous to Health Regulations 2002.
- Control of Vibration at Work Regulations 2005.
- Noise at Work Regulations 2005.
- Control of Asbestos Regulations 2006.

Specific and non-specific duties

Health and safety Regulations can specify mandatory health surveillance – e.g. Regulation 22(2) of the Control of Asbestos Regulations 2006 and the Noise at Work Regulations 2005 – where employers expose their employees to certain biological hazards, chemicals or physical agents (e.g. asbestos, lead, noise, radiation, or vibration).

In such circumstances, the relevant Regulations will specify the type, level and frequency of the surveillance to be undertaken, along with details on what records are to be kept by the employer and for how long.

In circumstances where there is no specific duty on the employer to carry out health surveillance, the employer has general duties under Section 2 of the Health and Safety at Work etc. Act 1974 and Regulation 6 of the Management of Health and Safety at Work Regulations 1999 to carry out appropriate health surveillance.

Health surveillance

This general duty applies where the employer's risk assessments identify that:

- there is an identifiable disease or adverse health condition related to the work;
- there is a valid technique available to detect indications of the disease or condition;
- there is a reasonable likelihood that the disease or condition may occur under the particular conditions of the work; and
- health surveillance is likely to further the protection of the health and safety of the employees concerned.

Health surveillance can only be carried out in the above circumstances where the techniques used to undertake the surveillance pose a low risk to the employee.

Employers may need to carry out health surveillance in the following situations:

- Post-accident (or during long-term illness);
- On forklift truck and other machinery operators; and
- On drivers to test for colour blindness.

Employers should be extremely careful in undertaking pre-employment health surveillance, so that if, for example, they require candidates to complete pre-employment health questionnaires, they do not discriminate against disabled candidates in breach of the Disability Discrimination Acts 1995 and 2005. Employers should seek expert assistance in deciding what surveillance is needed and who is competent to provide that surveillance.

Objectives
The objectives of health surveillance are to:

- protect the health of individual employees by detecting, as early as possible, adverse changes that might be caused by exposure to hazardous substances;
- help to evaluate the measures taken to control exposure to health hazards; and
- collect, keep, update and use data and information for determining and evaluating hazards to health.

Procedures
There are a number of health surveillance procedures that employers can use, including:

- biological monitoring, i.e. taking samples of blood, urine, breath, etc. to detect the presence of hazardous substances;
- biological effect monitoring, i.e. assessing the early biological effects in exposed workers;
- clinical examinations by occupational doctors or nurses to measure physiological changes in the body of exposed people, e.g. reduced lung function; and
- medical enquiries (often accompanied by a medical examination) by a suitably qualified occupational health practitioner to detect symptoms in people.

Competent people acting within the limits of their training and experience should determine the appropriate level, frequency and procedure to be followed.

For most types of health surveillance the appropriate competent person will be a suitably qualified occupational medical practitioner, occupational health nurse or occupational hygienist.

Once health surveillance has been started, it must be maintained throughout the remainder of the employee's period of employment, unless the risks to which the employee is exposed and the associated health effects are rare and short-term.

Health surveillance

Display screen equipment

Regulation 5 of the Health and Safety (Display Screen Equipment) Regulations 1992 (DSE Regulations) places a duty on employers to provide, when requested to do so, an eye or eyesight test to employees who are about to become (or who are already) display screen users.

Eye and eyesight tests are defined in Section 36(2) of the Opticians Act 1989 and the Sight Testing Examination and Prescription (No. 2) Regulations 1989, which specify what examinations the doctor or optician should perform as part of the test.

Although the employer only needs to provide the eye or eyesight test when requested to do so, he is under a duty by Regulation 7(3) of the DSE Regulations to provide employees with adequate information about the risks to their health and their entitlement under Regulation 5.

Records

Where health surveillance is undertaken in compliance with particular Regulations, those Regulations will state what data is to be collected and the minimum period for which information is to be stored. Other health surveillance records should be kept for:

- the period specified in the Regulations; or

- three years after the end of the last date of the individual's employment (the date after which the employee cannot normally bring a claim against the employer); whichever is the longer.

Employers will need to provide employees with access to their personal health records and copies of such records may have to be provided to the Enforcing Authorities.

To comply with the employer's duty to provide information to employees (and others who might be affected), employers should provide the appropriate people with the general results of health surveillance, but keep confidential individuals' surveillance data.

Data gathered during health surveillance is regarded as 'sensitive data' within the meaning of Section 2 of the Data Protection Act 1998. As such, all health surveillance data must be processed in accordance with the requirements of that Act. Detailed advice should be sought as to these requirements.

See also: Discrimination, p.110; Medical records, p.257; Occupational health, p.304.

Sources of further information

HSE: Understanding health surveillance at work: www.hse.gov.uk/pubns/indg304.pdf

Workplace Law Group's *Occupational Health 2008: Making the business case – Special Report* addresses the issues of health at work, discusses the influence of work on health and highlights the business case for occupational health services at work. For more information visit www.workplacelaw.net/Bookshop/SpecialReports.

HIV and AIDS

Lisa Jinks and John Macaulay, Greenwoods Solicitors LLP

Key points
- Employers and employees need to understand what HIV and AIDS are.
- Employers need to be aware of their liability under various employment-related laws as well as health and safety legislation.
- Specific employment issues include discrimination on grounds of disability and/or sexual orientation, unfair / constructive dismissal and aspects of data protection law.
- Key areas of the employment relationship that need addressing include recruitment, disclosure, medical testing and reasonable adjustments to working conditions.
- Employers should implement an HIV and AIDS policy.

Legislation
- Health and Safety at Work etc. Act 1974.
- Employment Rights Act 1996.
- Data Protection Act 1998.
- Management of Health and Safety at Work Regulations 1999.
- Employment Equality (Sexual Orientation) Regulations 2003.
- Disability Discrimination Act 1995 (DDA), as amended by the Disability Discrimination Act 2005.

What are HIV and AIDS and what are the real risks for the workplace?

It is important for employers and employees to understand what HIV and AIDS are as there are many common misconceptions.

AIDS stands for Acquired Immune Deficiency Syndrome. It is caused by the human immunodeficiency virus (HIV), which attacks the body's natural defence system and leaves it open to various infections and cancers.

HIV is mainly contained in blood. There is a minimal risk of it being contained in other bodily fluids such as urine, saliva and sweat unless these are contaminated with infected blood.

HIV is not spread through normal social interaction such as sharing cutlery or toilets – it is transmitted through sexual intercourse or direct exposure to infected blood through accidental contamination.

The risk of infection at work is very low for the majority of workplaces. The types of occupation where the risk is higher include healthcare, custodial (e.g. prisons), education, emergency services, hair and beauty and plumbing.

Note: The strict requirements on such specialist occupations are beyond the scope of this chapter.

There is no reason to treat workers with HIV differently from other workers. People who have the virus but have not developed AIDS will not usually be ill and their ability to work will normally be unaffected. There is often a time lag of many years before their ability to do their job will be affected.

HIV and AIDS

In many instances this time lag would be longer than people stay in their job on average in ordinary circumstances.

Those who develop AIDS will have severe illnesses inevitably affecting performance and should be treated in the same way as anyone with any other life threatening illness.

Discrimination

Protection from discrimination covers the whole of the working relationship – from recruitment, benefits, promotion and training, dismissal and harassment through to post-termination discrimination, such as the giving of references. Unlike unfair dismissal claims, there is no financial cap on awards made for discrimination claims and additional awards can be made for injury to feelings.

Disability discrimination

From December 2005, HIV-infected employees have been deemed to have a disability from the point of diagnosis – irrespective of whether they exhibit any symptoms – and are therefore protected from disability discrimination. This contrasts with the previous legal position where an employee was only held to be disabled when he was in the symptomatic stages of HIV or had AIDS.

Reasonable adjustments

One key area of disability discrimination is the duty on employers to make reasonable adjustments to working conditions once they are aware that an employee is HIV-infected. In such circumstances, an employer is under a positive duty to take whatever steps are reasonably necessary to prevent the employee from being disadvantaged. For instance, this may require an employer to provide time off for treatment, allocate duties to others and so on.

If an employee requires time off work for an HIV-related reason, the reason for the time off should, as far as possible, be treated in strictest confidence. Managers should not need to know the precise reason for the time off.

Discrimination on grounds of sexual orientation

Dismissal or other detrimental treatment of a worker on the grounds that they are, or are perceived to be, gay is unlawful. This may extend to discrimination or harassment on the basis that a worker is, or is assumed to be, HIV positive. Note that a claim could also be brought on the basis of discriminatory acts against the worker on the basis of association (if, for example, they have gay or HIV positive friends).

Recruitment, disclosure and medical testing

Medical information is protected under the Data Protection Act 1998 and is classified as 'sensitive personal data'. There are various stringent requirements on the 'processing' of medical information, which include obtaining, holding and disclosing such data.

Recruitment

Generally, employers would not be able to justify asking applicants about their HIV status. In addition to a potential claim for disability or sexual orientation discrimination, a claim for indirect sex discrimination might be brought on the basis that more men than women are HIV positive.

However, employers are entitled to ask applicants about any disabilities that may impact upon the job in question so long as they ask all applicants in a consistent way and do not use this information to discriminate. It is also good practice to ask whether the applicant considers that any reasonable adjustments are required to be made to their working conditions, such as

HIV and AIDS

> **Facts**
> - There are approximately 80,000 adults in the UK living with HIV.
> - It is not known what proportion of those will progress to AIDS and the incubation period between infection and onset of AIDS can be very long.
> - During this time, the individual is unlikely to be ill or even aware of the infection.
> - Although there is no known cure for AIDS, HIV symptoms, such as swollen lymph glands, weight loss and minor infections, can be treated with anti-retroviral drugs and enable HIV positive people to lead healthy lives.

time off for treatment. Ideally, employers should have a detachable medical questionnaire which can be given to their HR department.

In the USA and a significant number of EU member states, pre-interview disclosure of disability is against the law, offering significant protection to people with disabilities and long-term medical conditions (such as HIV). The National AIDS Trust is currently calling for the Equality Bill, which is due to come into force in 2010, to ban pre-employment health questionnaires in Great Britain.

Disclosure
Applicants do not have to disclose their HIV status, although it may be a condition of employment in certain higher risk occupations. However, if the applicant fails to disclose such information, the employer cannot be expected to make reasonable adjustments.

Medical testing
Again, generally, there will be no justification for requiring applicants or employees to take an HIV/AIDS test unless the occupation is high risk or the job requires travel to countries asking for evidence of HIV status.

Employers may ask applicants to undertake a medical test but this is subject to various conditions under data protection principles. Employers must have a legitimate reason as to why they need this information which outweighs any intrusion to the worker, such as a genuine health and safety reason and applicants should not be tested unless there is a real likelihood that they will be employed. The worker must be assured that the results will be treated in strictest confidence. Employers should also respect the right to privacy and should always obtain the worker's consent, particularly before seeking a medical report from the employee's own medical practitioner under the Access to Medical Reports Act 1988.

Employers cannot insist that an applicant undertakes a medical test, but if they refuse, the employer can refuse to employ them. It is preferable, wherever possible, to use health questionnaires rather than medical tests, as these are less intrusive.

Note: If the penalty for an existing employee's refusal to consent to testing is dismissal, then the consent is highly unlikely to be considered by an Employment Tribunal to be freely given and will be invalid.

Unfair / constructive dismissal
In extreme cases, workers have been dismissed because of their HIV status.

HIV and AIDS

More likely, however, is that an employee with HIV is treated detrimentally, whether by way of harassment, being denied equal benefits and so on. In addition to any claim for discrimination, such treatment could lead an employee to resign, resulting in a claim for constructive dismissal.

Colleagues may refuse to work alongside an employee with HIV or pressurise an employer into dismissing that employee. Employers are also responsible for the actions of their staff and should take steps to deal with such issues, preferably by consulting with and educating such workers but where necessary, by taking disciplinary action. The 'best practice' approach would be to have an effective HIV/AIDS policy already in place.

Checklist: policy document and implementation

Employers are advised to draw up a policy on HIV and AIDS so that, if a problem arises, this can be dealt with in accordance with the policy. The policy should be developed in consultation with employee representatives. Once finalised, managers should be provided with appropriate training and an employee awareness programme implemented.

The policy will vary depending upon the type of organisation but could include:

- a brief description of HIV and AIDS and how HIV is transmitted;
- the organisation's position on HIV testing;
- an assurance of confidentiality;
- a guarantee that absenteeism or other AIDS-related work issues are to be treated like any other serious illness;
- assurances that colleagues are expected to work normally with such workers and that any refusal to work normally will be dealt with and if appropriate under the disciplinary procedure;
- identifying help available;
- first-aid procedures; and
- provisions for overseas travel – the risks of infection through inadequate medical practices as well as sexual encounters.

It is also advisable to make express reference to HIV / AIDS in anti-discrimination and harassment policies.

See also: Discrimination, p.110; Medical records, p.257; Occupational health, p.304; Recruitment and selection, p.335.

Sources of further information

Blood-borne viruses in the workplace – guidance for employers and employees: www.hse.gov.uk/pubns/indg342.pdf

Protection against blood-borne infections in the workplace: HIV and hepatitis available from the Stationary Office (ISBN: 9780113219537) www.tsoshop.co.uk

Equality and Human Rights Commission (EHRC): www.equalityhumanrights.com

National AIDS helpline: 0800 567 123

Holiday

Sarah Lee and Lisa Norman, BPE Solicitors

Key points

The Working Time Regulations 1998 were introduced by Tony Blair's 1997 Government. One of the main parts of the 1998 Regulations sets out a worker's entitlement to four weeks' (20 days') paid leave each holiday year. However, employers quickly noticed that the minimum paid holiday they had to provide was 12 days' paid leave in addition to the eight public holidays. In January 2007 it was reported that 22% of the British workforce received 12 paid days' holidays in addition to the eight bank holidays.

The Government held a two-stage consultation process in June 2006 and then again in January 2007, during which it received the views of trade unions and employers' representatives with regard to a proposed increase in the holiday entitlement for full-time workers from four weeks to 5.6 weeks (28 days).

Legislation

The Work and Families Act was introduced in 2006, in which the Government extended workers' annual statutory holiday entitlement from four weeks to 4.8 weeks and then to 5.6 weeks by 1 April 2009 (subject to a maximum of 28 days). The increase was enacted by the Working Time (Amendment) Regulations 2007, which took effect on 1 October 2007.

Public holidays

The 2007 Regulations satisfy the political intention to provide an additional eight days' holiday per year for a full-time worker. However, on closer inspection, the 2007 Regulations are careful not to introduce a right to have public holidays as paid leave. If a worker wishes to take paid annual leave on a public holiday, then the worker must make a request to his/her employer in the normal way and the employer is entitled to refuse any such request as long as it is done in accordance with the procedures set out in the 1998 Regulations.

Problems for employers

Following the introduction of the 2007 Regulations, employers should review their contracts of employment. Existing contracts may contain holiday clauses along the lines of 'Statutory Entitlement plus Bank / Public Holidays'. At first glance this would appear to provide for 28 days' annual leave for full-time workers (20 days' statutory leave plus eight public holidays).

An employer whose contracts have the above wording might be confronted by an employee who claims that his paid annual leave increased to 32 days in October 2007 and will increase again to 36 days from 1 April 2009.

The 2007 Regulations cater for this potential problem. The new Regulation 26a enables an employer to avoid raising the holiday entitlement of such workers beyond 28 days as long as the following provisions are in place:

Holiday

- A relevant agreement between the employer and the workforce providing that each worker will receive paid annual leave entitlement of 1.6 weeks / eight days in addition to each worker's current four-week statutory entitlement;
- No provision for payment in lieu of that leave except on termination of employment; and
- Statutory leave cannot be carried over beyond the next leave year.

Carrying over leave entitlement

Employers are often unsure whether or not they are obliged to carry over the remaining annual leave into the next holiday year of a worker who has not exhausted their annual leave.

The 2007 Regulations do allow that the additional entitlement of 1.6 weeks (eight days) can be carried over into the subsequent leave year. This was expressly prohibited by the 1997 Regulations.

The new Regulation 13a(7) provides that the carry-over of 1.6 weeks (eight days) can be done by means of a 'relevant agreement'. This is a document by which an employer agrees with its workers to modify particular aspects of the Working Time Regulations.

Therefore for Regulation 13a(7) to have effect, an employer should ensure that it has specific wording in the relevant agreement to carry over of 1.6 weeks' (eight days') statutory leave.

Small employers will be dismayed by the new Regulation 13a(7) as it will increase their administrative burden. Employers will need to keep track of workers' holiday entitlement, past and present, and distinguish between holidays taken in the previous holiday year and those taken in the current holiday year. However, this carry forward entitlement is not a right for the employees. It only comes into effect if it is agreed between a worker and its employer by means of a relevant agreement. An employer can refuse to agree to a request to carry forward annual leave and an employer can insist that the full 28 days' leave is taken in one holiday leave year.

Holiday pay for the long-term sick

The issue of whether or not an employee, on long-term sick, is entitled to receive paid annual leave has vexed the UK courts in recent years. The Advocate General handed down his 'Opinion' on 24 January 2008. His Opinion is often followed by the subsequent European Court of Justice ruling so attention should be paid to the Opinion. The Advocate General stated that:

- entitlement to paid holiday does accrue whilst a worker is absent on sick leave; but
- to take the paid holiday, the worker must return to work to do so; and
- workers should be paid in lieu of their accrued but untaken paid holiday when they are dismissed.

If followed, the Opinion produces a number of issues. Employees on long-term sickness might never be able to take their statutory paid holiday, which reduces the cost of holiday for the employer. Equally an employer might be faced with a health and safety dilemma where long-term sick employees return to work, insisting they are fit, in order to take accrued paid holiday. Finally, employers might attempt to time the dismissal of any long-term sick employee for the beginning of the holiday year in order that the accrued holiday payment to the employee is minimised.

The House of Lords considered a limit aspect of this case in 2009. The current position remains unclear save that workers will accrue holidays whilst off sick.

Holiday

The new Regulations are silent. However, in the Government's January 2007 consultation document, the wording from the Government hinted that it could foresee a situation in which the 2007 Regulations were interpreted so that a worker on long-term sickness absence does receive the benefit of paid holiday entitlement.

New contracts of employment

The Working Time Regulations apply to workers. However, under the Employment Rights Act 1996 employers are under a duty to give 'employees' a written statement with particulars of employment detailing such things as rates of pay, hours of work and holiday entitlement. The law states that whenever there is a change in detail, the employer is under a duty to provide a written statement containing particulars of that change.

Employers should ensure that they have already provided amended particulars of employment to their employees to update them regarding the increase to 28 days' paid annual leave from 1 April 2009 and if they have not done so, then they should do so as soon as possible.

> *See also*: Agency and temporary workers, p.35; Employee benefits, p.138; Flexible working, p.190; Leave, p.252; Sickness benefits, p.361.

Sources of further information

Business Link has an interactive holiday pay calculator that allows you to work out your employees' annual holiday entitlement: www.businesslink.gov.uk

BIS – holiday entitlement: www.berr.gov.uk/employment/holidays/index.html

Homeworking

Dale Collins, Bond Pearce

Key points
Employers have a duty to protect the health, safety and welfare of their employees and other staff members working at an employer's workplace. This duty extends to all employees who work either at, or from, their home. As a general guide, therefore, employers should treat both the work area and the equipment used in an employee's own home as though they were in the main office. This approach should be reflected in the employer's employment policies and guidelines, as well as in the Home Working Agreement made and signed between the employer and the employee before homeworking is approved.

Legislation
- Health and Safety (Display Screen Equipment) Regulations 1992.
- Data Protection Act 1998.
- Health and Safety (Miscellaneous Amendments) Regulations 2002.

Computer (display) screens
The main legislation relevant to homeworkers (or teleworkers) here is the Display Screen Equipment Directive (90/270/EEC). This is implemented in the UK by the Health and Safety (Display Screen Equipment) Regulations 1992 – as amended by the Health and Safety (Miscellaneous Amendments) Regulations 2002.

This requires that there should be:

- a clear and stable screen, bright and free from glare, which should swivel and tilt easily;
- adequate arrangement of keyboard characters, adjustable keyboard with sufficient space to support the hands and arms of the user;
- sufficient user space to change positions and vary movements, a sufficiently large work desk, a document holder that is adjustable and stable;
- satisfactory lighting conditions;
- minimised glare and reflection at the workstation, and minimisation of radiation levels;
- a work chair that is adjustable in height, including the backrest;
- a footrest available if required; and
- provision to reduce environmental factors to a minimum, including the effects of reflection or glare, noise, heat and humidity.

Computer users can request an eye examination and an eye test from their employer.

The working environment
Employers should put in place a system for their homeworkers to report accidents or hazards, as there would be in a conventional workplace. Practical experience within the Telework Association suggests that the following areas also often need attention:

- There should be a sufficient number of power sockets, avoiding overuse of extension leads, trailing cables

Homeworking

- and adaptors. Home offices may need rewiring for more sockets – have the homeworker's installation checked by an electrician.
- The use of IT equipment usually requires an additional two power outlets, and one or two telecoms sockets. Safely stowing cabling is important.
- Electrical equipment needs to be checked for safety (e.g. all cable grips in place, no burn marks on plugs or cracked sockets).
- Shelves should be conveniently situated so that when heavy files are placed and replaced there is no risk of stress on the spine or overbalancing.
- Office chairs and tables should all be of the appropriate height and adjustability for long periods of work.
- If the homeworker wears reading glasses, the prescription should be correct for close work. Anyone working with computers should have their eyes tested, and the optician should be informed of the computer work.
- Spotlights and anglepoise-type lamps are generally less tiring than fluorescents in small spaces. Light levels should be about 350 lux.
- Computer screens should be positioned at right angles to windows. Blinds to prevent sunlight making screens hard to read should be installed where needed.
- Temperatures should be as near as possible to 18.5°C. Small home offices can easily overheat because IT equipment generates heat. Temperatures may become uncomfortably hot in summer unless adequate ventilation can be provided.
- Adequate ventilation is also important where equipment such as laser printers may give off ozone or other fumes.
- Psychologically, most homeworkers prefer to be situated so that they can see out of a window if possible, although, as noted above, it is important to avoid problems with glare and reflection on computer screens.
- Rest breaks are vital. There are now a number of software packages that can be set up to remind homeworkers to take frequent breaks and so interrupt their more concentrated work environment.

Tax implications for homeworkers

If you set aside part of the house for the sole use of the business, that part of the house is potentially liable for capital gains tax. The precise implications of this will vary from year to year, and so, particularly if the homeworker is self-employed, it is advisable for him to discuss these with an accountant who will also advise on the proportions of household expenses attributable to home-office use that can be legitimately claimed.

'Business' charges by public utilities

There have been rare instances of power utility companies charging a non-domestic rate. The practical situation is that they would have to know that someone is working from home before any change could be made, and that the exact conditions vary from company to company.

For telephone service, BT does not compel people to use the business rate, but points out that the business service has the advantage of Yellow Pages and Business Pages entries. BT also puts business users on a higher priority for fault correction than residential users. In both cases, compensation is paid if the fault is not repaired within 24 hours.

Insurance

The insurance market has pretty much caught up with the shift to homeworking. It is still the case that a standard home contents policy is unlikely to cover home office equipment, but specific policies targeted at home offices have

Homeworking

been produced to replace the plethora of computer, office and home policies previously designed to confuse the homeworker. These new policies also cover important business issues that can affect homeworkers, such as public liability, employee liability and loss of earnings.

Areas particularly to consider include the following:

- Insurance against loss of data (e.g. through virus or malicious attack). Employers should clarify the position on home-stored data with their insurers.
- Public liability or employer's liability insurance if other people work at or visit the homeworker's home office (this is mandatory in the Republic of Ireland). It is also important for employers to ensure that employees other than the homeworker visiting the home office are covered (e.g. managers or those involved in health and safety checks).
- Business interruption insurance, which, in the case of the self-employed or small home-based businesses, would provide compensation for the costs of putting a business back together and other expenditure incurred after an incident.
- Computer breakdown insurance. In some situations this can be cheaper than holding a maintenance contract and ensures that expensive part replacements are covered. Employers need to check rather than assume that this insurance applies to computers off site.
- Cover off the premises (e.g. for portable computers at the homeworker's home or in transit).

Employment issues

The degree of employment protection available to a homeworker depends on whether they are self-employed or an employee or a worker. However, there are issues that will be relevant to all categories.

Data protection issues and confidentiality

The importance of this depends on the nature of the work but it is likely that the majority of homeworkers will have at home some confidential information belonging to the employer, either on a computer or in another format.

Whilst all employees are subject to an implied duty of confidentiality, most employers will want an express clause on the issue setting out what amounts to confidential information and ensuring that the duty of confidentiality continues post-termination of employment. As ensuring compliance with confidentiality is more difficult for those employees who are not habitually in the office, employers need to address their minds to this issue more closely.

In addition, the Data Protection Act 1998 places additional responsibilities on data controllers, in this instance the employer, to ensure that all personal data is kept in compliance with the data protection principles. Consequently, employers should ensure that homeworkers are trained on the provisions of the Data Protection Act 1998 and what their responsibilities are under the Act. Compliance with any data protection policy should also be stated in the contract.

Competency, supervision and monitoring

As with all employees, it is important to ensure that homeworkers are appraised and meet their objectives. Whilst working remotely or at separate times to a supervisor may cause some difficulties, nevertheless a suitable system for appraising such employees is important. It is important, not just for employers, but also for the employees, who may feel more

Homeworking

vulnerable than their colleagues whose output is more obvious.

Supervision of employees who do not necessarily work either at the same location or the same time as their supervisor is clearly more complicated. However, there are ways of monitoring employees remotely and supervisors should also be encouraged to spend time working with the homeworker, for example by arranging a regular time to meet with the homeworker to discuss issues. Monitoring of employees should only be done for specific reasons, and employees should be made aware of the amount of monitoring that will take place, the methods for monitoring, and how the information obtained from monitoring will be used and stored. Any monitoring must be proportionate to the objectives to be met (which in themselves must be reasonable) and must be the least intrusive method of achieving those reasonable objectives.

Disabled homeworkers

Employers should look at each individual homeworker to ensure that any duties they may have towards that individual are complied with, such as duties that relate to disabled homeworkers in respect of making reasonable adjustments and regularly monitoring and reviewing such adjustments going forward.

Flexible working

Since April 2009, all employees with children under the age of 17 or disabled children under 18 have been able to request homeworking, and employers are under an obligation to consider the request in accordance with the relevant statutory provisions relating to requests for flexible working.

See also: Carers, p.54; Flexible working, p.190; IT security, p.244.

Sources of further information

The Telework Association: www.telework.org.uk

The datasheet 'Teleworking' can be downloaded free from the Institute of Occupational Health and Safety's website: www.iosh.co.uk. The datasheet includes a homework premises assessment form and stresses the importance of adequate training and regular reassessment of the risks.

Workplace Law Group's **Guide to Flexible Working 2008** provides information on the formal legislative right to request to work flexibly, but also considers working patterns in a wider sense. It covers the reasons why some employers are looking to introduce flexible working into their workplace, explores different flexible working patterns, including their benefits and disadvantages, and provides detail on the formal legislative right to request. It also looks at the employment and non-employment legal issues that surround flexible working and the necessary amendments that need to be made to an employee's contractual terms and conditions if a flexible working pattern is agreed. Finally, it gives practical advice in relation to drafting and implementing a flexible working policy. For more information visit www.workplacelaw.net/bookshop/GuidesTo.

Human rights

Susan Thomas, Charles Russell

Key points
- An employee of a Public Authority can bring a freestanding claim against their employer directly for a breach of any right provided by the Human Rights Act.
- An employee of a semi-Public Authority or private employer can *only* bring a claim under the Human Rights Act that is attached to an existing employment claim.
- All employee policies should be reviewed to ensure any interference with human rights is justifiable.

Legislation
- Human Rights Act 1998.
- European Convention on Human Rights and Fundamental Freedoms.

Application of the Human Rights Act
The Human Rights Act 1998 (the HRA) adopted the European Convention for the Protection of Human Rights and Fundamental Freedoms into UK law on 2 October 2000. Some of the rights and freedoms set out in the Convention relevant to the workplace are:

- Prohibition of slavery and forced labour (Article 4);
- Right to a fair trial (Article 6);
- Right to respect for private and family life (Article 8) (see '*Private Life,*' p.327);
- Freedom of expression (Article 10); and
- Freedom of assembly and association (Article 11).

The HRA requires Public Authorities to act in compliance with the Convention. Public Authorities include all courts and tribunals, and any person exercising functions of a public nature. UK courts must interpret legislation in a way that is compatible with the Convention.

This means that the HRA affects different types of employers differently.

Public Authorities
Employees can bring a claim against a public authority employer *directly* for a breach of a right set out in the HRA.

Public Authority employers include the police, the Government, Local Authorities, the NHS, and so on.

Semi-Public Authorities
Private bodies that carry out public functions are also defined as Public Authorities, but only insofar as they are carrying out their *public function*. The relationship between employer and employee would normally be considered to be within the scope of their private function as employer, and any related acts to be outside the scope of their public function. This means that semi-Public Authority employers are affected by the HRA in the same way as private employers.

Semi-Public Authorities include privatised utility companies, or a private security company exercising public functions in relation to the management of a prison.

Private employers

Human rights

These are organisations that carry out no public function. The HRA is only *indirectly* enforceable against such employers, in that an Employment Tribunal's decision about workplace conduct and workplace decisions must be compatible with the HRA. An employee cannot directly bring a claim for breach of the HRA, but may 'attach' a claim that the employer has breached the HRA to an existing employment claim, such as unfair dismissal. Therefore, if an employer were to have unjustifiably breached an employee's human rights in its treatment of the employee in a dismissal situation, a Tribunal might find that the employer's actions made the dismissal unfair.

The Act sets out 'justifications' that an employer may be able to rely on, such as the prevention of crime, or the prevention of infringement of rights of others. Whenever a Convention right is breached by an employer, the breach must not only be justified but must also not go beyond what is strictly necessary.

Example
P was employed by the Probation Service, and worked mainly with sex offenders. His employer discovered that he sold bondage and sado-masochism products on the Internet, and dismissed him. P brought a claim for unfair dismissal and breach of his rights under Articles 8 and 10 of the Convention (the right to respect for private life, and the right to freedom of expression). The Employment Appeal Tribunal decided that a probation officer, as a professional, had a reputation to maintain; that P's activities were publicised on a website and in the public domain, and were therefore not part of his private life. This meant that Article 8 was not engaged. There was an interference with P's right to freedom of expression, but this was justified due to the potential damage to the Service's reputation.

Two recent decisions indicate the potential rise of a right to legal representation at disciplinary hearings as a result of Article 6 (right to a fair trial). In one case, the Court of Appeal decision considered whether a doctor was contractually entitled to be represented by a lawyer at a disciplinary hearing. In doing so, the Court of Appeal held that (although the case didn't turn on this point), Article 6 may be engaged in disciplinary proceedings where the employee risked losing his or her ability to practice their profession, resulting in an implied right to legal representation at disciplinary hearings. The Court of Appeal acknowledged that its conclusions on when such a right might apply were not definitive and suggested that it would be sensible for the Secretary of State to give further thought to the question of legal representation in the light of this decision. The case is due to be appealed to the Supreme Court, but the case has potentially significant implications for the public sector and possibly even private sector employers.

Equality and Human Rights Commission (EHRC)
The EHRC came into existence on 1 October 2007 and has taken over the functions of the previous equality bodies (such as the Equal Opportunities Commission and the Commission for Racial Equality) and is also responsible for promoting the awareness, understanding and protection of human rights.

Issues for employers

Disciplinary procedures
Disciplinary procedures must now satisfy ACAS's statutory Code of Practice requirements and are therefore likely to respect the employee's right to a fair trial, incorporating an opportunity to hear and consider the employee's case and a mechanism for appeal. However, given

Human rights

recent decisions upholding a right to legal representation at disciplinary hearings in certain situations, both public and private sector employers should take advice before refusing legal representation where an adverse finding may affect an employee's ability to practise a profession.

Dismissal

Any dismissal procedure must also be fair, and any reason given for dismissal must not represent an unreasonable breach of a Convention right. For example, dismissing an employee on the grounds of membership of a political party may lead a Tribunal to find that the dismissal was not fair, since for a Tribunal to uphold such a reason for dismissal would represent an unreasonable breach of the employee's freedom of expression.

Investigating a complaint

The investigation of an employee's complaint or conduct should not involve breach of a Convention right. For example, one individual was awarded £10,000 compensation when her employer tapped her phone without warning during its investigation of her sex discrimination complaint.

However, it was also recently held that the actions of a public sector employer who undertook covert surveillance to track an employee's movements were justified as the employer was investigating the suspected submission of fraudulent timesheets, which is a criminal activity.

Codes of Conduct

Codes of Conduct should be reviewed to ensure that they do not unnecessarily restrict an employee's Convention rights. For example, provisions on how an employee wears their hair, or whether they wear a nose ring, could raise issues about the way an individual expresses his or her personality in the workplace. See 'Dress codes,' p.129.

Employee checks

The right to respect for private life may include matters such as moral or physical integrity, so that 'private' in this context means 'personal'. This means that a security check that collects wide-ranging information about a person's personal affairs may go too far.

Also potentially unlawful is the practice of carrying out random drug or alcohol tests, as such testing is likely to entail an invasion of Article 8 – personal privacy. However, such testing could be justified if it was in the interests of public safety, for example where workers are in high risk situations such as pilots or train drivers.

Employers should also ensure that any procedures such as security checks comply with the requirements of

> See also: Data protection, p.84; Discrimination, p.110; Private life, p.327; Unlawfully procuring information, p.403.

Sources of further information

Information commissioner's Office: www.informationcommissioner.gov.uk

ACAS: www.acas.org.uk

Intellectual property

Ian de Freitas and Toby Headdon, Berwin Leighton Paisner

Key points
- Intellectual property can be a valuable asset. Every business will own intellectual property rights of one sort or another. Intellectual property rights should, therefore, be protected and enforced in order to ensure that they retain their value.
- Use of a third party's intellectual property rights (whether knowingly or otherwise) without their permission can be disastrous: infringement is usually very expensive.
- Copyright, unregistered design rights and database rights arise automatically.
- UK patents, registered trademarks and registered designs are granted by the UK Intellectual Property Office based in Newport, Wales.
- Protection is now provided in all 27 Member States of the European Community (EC) for trademarks by the Community Trade Mark and for designs by the Community design right. Applications for these registered rights are made to the Office of Harmonisation for the Internal Market (OHIM) in Alicante, Spain.
- Internet domain names are administered by a network of private non-governmental registries.
- Intellectual property is territorial in scope and an international protection strategy should be considered.

Legislation
- Registered Designs Act 1949.
- Patents Act 1977.
- Copyright, Designs and Patents Act 1988.
- Trade Marks Act 1994.
- Data Protection Act 1998.
- Human Rights Act 1998.
- Council Regulation (EC) No. 6/2002 on Community Designs.

Copyright
Copyright arises automatically in any:

- original artistic, literary (which includes computer programs), musical or dramatic works;
- sound recordings, films or broadcasts; and
- typographical arrangements in published works,

which have been recorded in some tangible form. Ideas and concepts are not protected by copyright. It is the way that they are expressed or recorded that is protected. For a work to be original, it must not have been copied from another work and it must involve some skill or judgement (however small). Independent copyrights may therefore subsist in two identical works so long as their respective creators did not copy each other or a third party. In this sense, copyright protection does not confer a monopoly.

Broadly speaking, copyright will last for:

- 70 years from the death of the author in the case of literary, dramatic, musical, or artistic works (but only 25 years in the case of

Intellectual property

industrially-exploited artistic works), and films; and
- 50 years in the case of sound recordings and broadcasts.

As copyright arises automatically, there is no need in this country for the owner to register it. A UK national's copyright will also be recognised in all countries that are signatories to the Berne Convention 1886, the WIPO Copyright Treaty 1996, and the WTO Agreement. The copyright owner will usually be the person who created the work, unless that person was an employee acting in the course of his/her employment, in which case the employer will own the copyright. An independent contractor is not an employee, so the independent contractor will, generally speaking, own any copyright in the work created for the commissioning party. Copyright can be assigned (transferred) or licensed (a permission is given to use it) to a third party.

When engaging an independent contractor to create a copyright work it is important that they assign (or at least licence) the copyright in the work to the commissioning party so that the commissioning party owns the copyright in the work that they have paid for (or, in the case of a licence, they have express permission to use it).

Copyright is infringed by someone copying the whole or a substantial part of a copyright work without the permission of the copyright owner. A substantial part can be quite a small part of the work provided that is significant qualitatively. So far as proving that copying has occurred, the Court may assume copying has taken place if the similarities are significant and it can be shown that there was an opportunity to copy.

Design rights
Design rights fall into two main categories: unregistered and registered rights. These rights can either be UK-only rights or EC-wide rights.

Unregistered UK design right
Design right protects aspects of the shape and configuration of a design, with certain exclusions for features that are designed to create an interface with or match the appearance of other articles. To qualify for protection, a design must be:

- original (it must be the result of the independent skill and labour of the designer); and
- not commonplace in the relevant design field at the time it was designed.

Unregistered design right protection lasts for ten years, unless the design has not been commercially exploited. In addition, anyone can ask for a licence to copy a design protected by unregistered design right after the first five years of its being put into the marketplace. Owing to the limitations of the UK unregistered design right, designers are strongly advised to consider registering their designs in order to benefit from the greater protection that a registration offers.

UK and Community registered designs
The owner of a registered design can prevent a third party from using a design that is the same as or that creates the same overall impression as the registered design, even if the third party can show that they did not copy the registered design. A registered design can protect aspects of:

- shape and configuration of a design;
- contours and lines;
- texture or materials;
- ornamentation;
- colours; and
- packaging, logos, motifs and typefaces.

Intellectual property

> **Facts**
>
> Get a free IP check on the UK Intellectual Property website. If you go to www.ipo.gov.uk you can find guidance on:
>
> - whether you have any IP to protect;
> - whether you own the IP and, if you don't, who does;
> - how to protect the IP, and whether you should; and
> - how you can exploit the IP commercially.
>
> The site also provides information on upcoming IP events and workshops around the country where you can learn about the benefits of IP in the workplace.

Designs can be registered if they:

- are 'new' (that is, they differ from existing designs in the marketplace to a material extent); and
- create a different overall impression from other designs.

A design can be marketed for up to 12 months in order to test the market before making an application for registration without prejudicing the registrability of the design. Since it is the design itself that is protected, once registered, it can be applied to any number of different products. The duration of a registered design is 25 years, renewable every five years on payment of a fee. The Community registered design allows one registration to be filed for all 27 Member States of the EC. The protection given is the same as for the UK.

Unregistered Community design right

This is based on the Community registered design system. Therefore, the same criteria for protection apply. The period of protection is only three years, however, from the date that the design is first made available to the public. Although the term of protection is less favourable than under UK unregistered design right, the sort of designs covered by the Community unregistered right are the same as under the Community registered design. The unregistered Community right may therefore be of use where UK design right fails to protect a design, such as where the shape of a design is commonplace but what makes it new and of individual character is its texture or ornamentation.

Trademarks

A trademark is any sign capable of being represented graphically and which distinguishes goods or services of one business from those of another business. In theory, sounds and smells are registrable as trademarks, although trademarks usually consist of:

- words, designs, letters, numerals (or a combination of these); or
- the shape of goods or their packaging.

Trademarks are territorial in nature and therefore there is a need to seek registration in all countries that may be of interest to the business. Trademarks may be registered through national trademark applications. An international trademark application can cover those countries that are signatories to the Madrid Protocol. A Community Trade Mark application (CTM) will automatically cover the countries of the EC. It is advisable to

Intellectual property

search the relevant trademarks registers prior to filing an application. The searches should reveal the existence of any prior, identical or similar marks in respect of identical or similar goods or services that may be potential obstacles to the use and registration of the proposed mark. Applications are usually examined for 'distinctiveness' of the mark applied for and in some countries there is an examination for conflicts with existing trademarks (no longer the case in the UK). Once the application has been examined, the application is published and, depending upon where the application has been made, third parties may have the opportunity to file an opposition against the registration of the mark. Once registered, trademarks can be renewed indefinitely. However, a trademark that is not used for a continuous period of five years will be vulnerable to cancellation. A registered trademark is infringed by someone:

- using an identical sign in respect of identical goods or services; or
- using an identical sign in respect of similar goods or services, where there is a likelihood of confusion by the public; or
- using a similar sign in respect of identical or similar goods or services, where there is a likelihood of confusion by the public; or
- using an identical or similar sign in respect of any goods or services where the trademark is well known and the use of the sign takes unfair advantage of, or is detrimental to, the distinctive character or the reputation of the trademark.

Passing off

The identity of a business – its reputation, as well as its name – is generally embodied in its branding. Registering that brand identity as a trademark (or portfolio of trademarks) will make it easier to protect and enforce its rights in that identity. However, it may be possible for a business to enforce its rights in its unregistered trademarks and associated goodwill by bringing a claim under the law of passing off.

Such actions can be costly as substantial evidence needs to be provided to show:

- the extent of the reputation and goodwill that the business has in the unregistered trademark/branding;
- confusion (or the likelihood of confusion) on the part of the public; and
- the damage suffered by the business as a result of the passing off.

Patents

Patents protect inventions. To be patentable, a patent must:

- be novel;
- involve an inventive step; and
- be capable of industrial application.

A patent will not be granted if the invention is obvious to persons skilled in the field in question or if it has been disclosed to the public prior to the patent application. It is therefore important not to discuss an invention with third parties prior to making an application, unless the discussions are confidential. It is advisable in those circumstances to put a confidentiality agreement in place before such discussions take place. Some things cannot be patented, including some inventions relating to software, business methods, discoveries, and games. To obtain a patent, applications are made to the UK Intellectual Property Office (for a UK patent) with a description of the invention and payment of an application fee.

Intellectual property

A separate patent is required for each country where protection is needed, although there is a centralised procedure for making multiple applications within Europe (a European patent application under the European Patent Convention). In the UK, patents last for up to 20 years (sometimes 25 years for pharmaceuticals), with annual renewal fees payable on a rising scale.

- As part of the application process, full details of it are published, meaning that some businesses decide not to patent their inventions but instead keep the nature of their invention secret.
- A patent does not give its owner an absolute right to use the invention, if its use infringes someone else's patent, confidential information or design right. Also, it is possible for a patent to be declared invalid following an attack by a third party.
- Like registered design rights, a patent is infringed even if the alleged infringer can prove that their invention was independently developed without copying. In this sense the patent grants a monopoly to the patent holder.
- In most cases, it is the inventor who has the right to apply for the patent, unless he/she was an employee acting within the course of their employment, in which case it is generally the employer who has the right. In such cases, the employer may have to make a compensatory payment to the employee if the patent is particularly valuable.

Database rights

A database is a collection of independent works, data or other materials that are arranged in a systematic or methodical way and are individually accessible by electronic or other means. A database may be protected by copyright and/or a database right. To benefit from copyright protection, a database must be original. A database will be original where, by reason of the selection or arrangement of its contents, it constitutes the author's own intellectual creation. The copyright expires after 70 years from the end of the year in which the author dies. Where there is a substantial investment in obtaining, verifying or presenting the contents of a database, the maker will own a separate database right. A database right entitles its owner to take action against a person who extracts or reutilises all or a substantial part of the contents of the database. The database right expires after the later of 15 years from the end of the year in which the database was completed or when the database is made available to the public.

There are exceptions to both rights enabling others to make limited use of the contents of a database, although unauthorised use of a database may also give rise to issues under the Data Protection Act 1998.

Domain names

Domain names are available for registration through a number of registries as a 'private' contractual arrangement. Businesses need to think about not just registering domain names for their trading names and brands, but misspellings as well. They should also ensure that domain names are registered in the company's name, not in the name of an employee (as often happens). Following the inception of the Internet, businesses developed significant internet brands which became a target for third parties to infringe. Cybersquatting (the registration of infringing domain names as a blocking tactic or to sell on to brand owners for

Intellectual property

inflated prices) became a particular problem. However, more importantly, infringing domain names were registered and used to point to third parties' websites, which often sold goods or offered services similar to those provided by the brand owner. Therefore, right holders were forced to protect their brands by taking legal action (usually registered trademark infringement or passing off proceedings) against anyone registering domain names similar to their own.

As a result of the increasing number of court actions involving domain names, the bodies that regulate domain names introduced alternative dispute resolution processes solely for domain name disputes. Nominet, the body that regulates co.uk domains, EURid (the regulator of the .eu domain names) and the World Intellectual Property Organisation (WIPO), which regulates other top-level domains, have put in place separate dispute resolution policies and procedures, enabling internet brand owners to bring quick and cheap actions to prevent third parties from using infringing domain names, without having to resort to formal court proceedings.

Confidence

The law of confidence has been developed by the courts to protect confidential or secret information, such as trade secrets or inventions before a patent is granted. To bring a claim for breach of confidence, a person must demonstrate that:

- the information has the necessary quality of confidence;
- the information has been imparted in circumstances importing an obligation of confidence or be obviously confidential; and
- there must have been an unauthorised use of the information.

A claim for breach of confidence can be defeated if the information has already entered the public domain. The law of confidence will not protect immoral information or where there is a public interest in the disclosure of the information. The Human Rights Act 1998 has had a significant impact on the traditional model of breach of confidence, having to strike a balance between the right to respect for private and family life and the contrasting right to freedom of expression. This has been seen in several high-profile cases involving celebrities who have argued that a publication has infringed their right to privacy. The current position is that there is no law of privacy in this country, but instead the law of confidence has been adapted by the courts to cover situations where an individual is aggrieved by an invasion of their privacy. This has led to the development of two distinct new limbs of confidentiality: the right of a celebrity to control the use of their image where they trade on such image; and the right of a person to prevent disclosure or further disclosure of private information, even where they may be public figures.

Remedies for infringement of intellectual property rights

The penalties for infringement of intellectual property rights vary depending upon the right infringed, but typically include:

- court orders to stop infringement, including urgent interim injunctions before a full trial takes place;
- damages (such as loss of sales or a payment equivalent to a licence fee to use the intellectual property right) or an account of the profits made from the infringement (whichever is the greater); and
- delivery up or destruction of infringing goods.

Intellectual property

For some intellectual property rights, criminal sanctions apply, including fines and custodial sentences.

Groundless threats

Owners of patents, trademarks and registered and unregistered UK and Community design rights must be wary of making anything amounting to a 'groundless threat' to an alleged infringer. An accusation of particular types of infringement that cannot later be substantiated may result in the accuser being sued.

See also: Data protection, p.84; Private life, p.327.

Sources of further information

Workplace Law Network provides premium members with unrestricted access to a comprehensive range of online information – factsheets, case reports and daily news items – on employment, health and safety and premises management. Members also benefit from an online advice service and a free subscription to the *Workplace Law Magazine*. For more information email membership@workplacelaw.net or call our membership services team on 0871 777 8881.

Internet and email policies

David Browne, Martineau Solicitors

Key points
- Where relevant, employers should have in place a written internet and email policy making employees aware of what, if any, personal usage of the internet and email systems is reasonable.
- This policy needs to be effectively and transparently communicated to employees at the earliest opportunity.
- Employers must take into account the rights of employees (particularly their right to privacy under Article 8 of the European Convention on Human Rights) in assessing how to monitor employees' usage of the internet and email systems and should make employees aware of what monitoring will take place.

Legislation
- Copyright, Designs and Patents Act 1988.
- Defamation Act 1996.
- Protection from Harassment Act 1997.
- Data Protection Act 1998.
- Human Rights Act 1998.
- Regulation of Investigatory Powers Act 2000.
- All discrimination legislation.

The need for a suitable internet and email policy

A survey conducted in 2008 by the then Department for Business, Enterprise and Regulatory Reform (BERR) showed that the proportion of UK companies with a broadband connection to the internet stands at 97%, with 16% of UK companies suffering from staff misuse of information systems (which rises to 47% of large businesses suffering from staff misuse).

It is clear that the advantages to businesses of the internet and email systems are undermined by the greater potential for staff to abuse these facilities. The legal issues that an employer may face as a consequence of staff misusing either the internet or email are also surprisingly broad. For example, these may include email harassment or unauthorised use of computer systems, issues surrounding agency law where employees inadvertently form contracts through email correspondence, intellectual property law in disputes over the downloading or dissemination of material subject to copyright, the law of defamation for libel following comments made about individuals or businesses in emails, and criminal law where employees download obscene material or are involved in hacking.

In light of these potential pitfalls for employers, setting out employees' rights, responsibilities and limitations on the use of the internet and email systems will help employers prevent any unauthorised or careless use, which may result in one of the legal risks detailed above. Any such policy should also make clear any monitoring or interception that the employer may lawfully undertake and the reasons for this.

Content of the policy

The content of an internet and email policy will largely depend on issues such as the

Internet and email policies

> **Facts**
> - Nearly 50% of large businesses suffer from staff misuse of the internet or email facilities.
> - The term applied to staff who use their work internet access for personal reasons while maintaining the appearance of working is 'goldbricking'.
>
> *Source: BERR 2008 Information Breaches Survey.*

size and nature of the business, and there is no one policy that would be appropriate for all businesses. Whilst model policies are useful, they must be tailored to suit the needs of the organisation and its employees.

However, a typical internet and email policy should make provision for the following:

- An indication of the extent to which personal use of the internet and the email is acceptable, if at all. Employers should be conscious of the fact that employees have a reasonable expectation of some privacy in the workplace and if personal use of email is prohibited (or monitored), employers are recommended to provide workers with some means of making personal communications that are not subject to monitoring (by telephone, for example).
- An instruction not to share passwords with other employees and to make appropriate arrangements for relevant staff to access work emails when absent.
- A statement that both internet and email use are intended predominantly for business use.
- Advice on email etiquette, including guidance on when staff should add signatures / disclaimers to emails.
- Guidance on what is deemed 'acceptable use', in particular an outline of the types of websites that are considered inappropriate to access from work, particularly those that contain obscene, offensive or pornographic content. This should include a warning to employees not to access, download or disseminate any material that could be construed as offensive in nature.
- A clear statement informing employees that their email and internet usage may be subject to monitoring.
- Details of what may happen if employees breach the policy.

In addition, employers should cross reference any internet and email policy with other relevant policies it has in place. Examples include policies relating to the handling of confidential information, use and storage of personal data, consultation and communications at work, training, equal opportunities and harassment, and the employer's disciplinary and grievance policies and procedures, which should state what types of misuse would be considered misconduct and/or gross misconduct.

Monitoring

It is essential that any internet and email policy contains a clear statement about how employees' use of the internet and email systems is to be monitored. A failure to do so may lead to claims from employees that the employer is in breach

Internet and email policies

of Article 8 of the European Convention on Human Rights (right to respect for private and family life). If, however, the employer's policy makes clear that monitoring will take place (and what form this monitoring will take), employees cannot have a reasonable expectation of privacy and this should be sufficient for employers to escape such liability.

It should be noted that, by its very nature, monitoring of employees' internet and email usage is intrusive. Careful consideration should therefore be given to the impact of such monitoring on workplace relations, as it may be interpreted by employees as a lack of trust in staff. Providing employees with clear reasons as to why the monitoring is taking place, together with assurances that it will only be done within the strict limits set out in the policy, should help to allay any concerns employees have in relation to the monitoring of their internet and email activity.

Employers should be aware that monitoring should be proportionate to the legitimate business needs of the organisation. Covert monitoring is likely to be unlawful and should be restricted to circumstances where it is used for the prevention or detection of crime.

The Information Commissioner has provided specific advice on monitoring in relation to data protection issues which can be found at www.ico.gov.uk.

Communicating and enforcing the policy

It is not only essential for employers to have an adequate internet and email policy in place, but also to ensure that the policy's existence is adequately communicated to employees. Tribunals have found employees to be unfairly dismissed in circumstances where the employer did not make them properly aware of its policy, even when employees had clearly carried out acts of misconduct serious enough to be dismissed, such as accessing and distributing pornographic images.

There is no one particular way in which such employees should be made familiar with the contents of the policy, but communication methods may include:

- via email (although employers may require a read receipt to know that employees have opened and read the email);
- a circular sent to all staff, or to incorporate the policy into a staff handbook (which could then be made available to staff either electronically or in hard copy);
- incorporating the policy into the employee's contract of employment;
- a presentation to staff explaining the system and its use; and/or
- holding training sessions on the new policy.

Additionally, employers may wish to get employees to 'sign off' that they have read and understood the policy.

> *See also*: Data protection, p.84; Intellectual property, p.229; IT security, p.244; Monitoring employees, p.292; Private life, p.327.

Internet and email policies

Sources of further information

Information Commissioner's guidance on how to comply with obligations under the Data Protection Act 1998, available at www.ico.gov.uk.

2008 Information Breaches Survey, commissioned by BERR, available at www.berr.gov.uk.

Technological advances in the field of information technology have resulted in many positive benefits for employers. However, the increase in technological advances has also brought with it many employment-related issues. These include harassment, discrimination, and breach of contract issues. Workplace Law's *IT and Email Policy and Management Guide v.3.0* has been designed to alert employers of the potential problems associated with using computer systems, the internet, and email systems within the workplace and to provide certain safeguards. For more information visit www.workplacelaw.net/Bookshop/PoliciesAndProcedures.

Interviewing

Jo Bradbury, Martineau Solicitors

Key points
- Planning and preparation are essential.
- Bear in mind equality and diversity legislation.
- Avoid stereotypical assumptions to minimise the risk of a discrimination claim.
- Be objective: avoid whims or gut instincts.
- Be fair, consistent and transparent.
- Where possible have a mixed interview panel.
- Be organised: plan out questions in advance.
- Focus on the job description and person specification, as the basis for questioning.
- Ask open questions.
- Avoid questions that are not job-related.
- Be able to justify your decisions and record this justification.
- Choose the best person for the job.

Legislation
The recruitment and selection process can be a minefield from a legal perspective, particularly in the context of equal opportunities legislation. It is therefore important for the interviewers to understand how employment law can impact on the interview process, what potential liabilities can be incurred and the consequences for getting it wrong.

Overview
Staff are an employer's most important asset and largest investment, but recruitment is a two-way process and is as much about an individual deciding whether he/she wants to work for the employer as it is about the employer deciding which candidate to appoint. The interview is often the first and a very powerful impression for both the candidate and the employer.

In order to recruit and retain the best candidates, an interview selection panel needs to gather all the information it needs during the interview process.

Time spent at the beginning of the process, identifying precisely what the role is and what skills and experience are needed to fill it, will aid the decision-making process.

Diversity in recruitment
Diversity should be seen as a positive thing, and something to aspire to. There is often a tendency for employers to look for people who are similar to the person already employed in a particular role, but cloning existing staff is unlikely to add value. Interviewers should therefore bear this in mind from the outset.

Legal perspective
Equality is not a new concept in employment relationships. The UK is used to the raft of legislation from Europe, including discrimination on the grounds of sex, race, disability, sexual orientation, religion, belief and age. In addition, employers are encouraged to offer flexible working and to address work–life balance issues.

Interviewing

Interview panels should ensure they do not ask questions that expose the employer to potential claims. For example, a panel should not put too much emphasis on the desirability of having qualifications from a UK educational institution, or work experience within the UK, as non-British nationals will find this more difficult to comply with than British nationals.

A panel should use the interview to establish the quality of the qualifications and experience. Similarly, if in an interview situation a non-British candidate's spoken English is not as fluent as that of a British national, an employer may not be justified in using this as a criterion for turning down the non-British candidate from all posts; it will depend on whether fluency in spoken English is an essential requirement for the post.

As a further example, if an interview panel knows in advance that a candidate who is coming for interview is disabled, the panel should consider whether any adjustments need to be made to the physical arrangements for the interview or the interview process itself. From a practical point of view, the panel may want to ask, during the interview, whether the disabled candidate has any particular requirements to help him/her fulfil the role, but should not make any decisions about whether or not to employ him/her based on his/her disability, or the effects, without very good reasons for doing so.

It is imperative to avoid making stereotypical assumptions. If an interview panel gets this wrong, an unsuccessful candidate can bring an Employment Tribunal claim within three months of the act of discrimination (or within such further period as the Employment Tribunal considers just and equitable). The remedies are a declaration of rights, a recommendation and/or potentially unlimited compensation.

The process

As selection is, by its very nature, a subjective process, it is important to consider the process in as objective a way as possible.

The key focuses for the panel during the interview process are:

- To gain all the information needed to decide who is most suitable for the role;
- To ensure that selection is carried out in a fair, objective, consistent and open manner;
- To avoid falling foul of the employment legislation; and
- To appoint the right person.

At the outset, a panel needs to decide how to assess the shortlist of candidates in person. The most common method is interviewing (although alternatives include assessment centres, written testing and psychometric testing).

For interviewing, the following issues need to be considered early on:

- Will there be one stage or two?
- The make-up of the panel. Where possible, the panel should not be potentially gender- or racially-biased. Instead, there should be a mixed panel if this is feasible.
- Is there going to be a Chair? If so, will he/she have a deciding vote?
- What will the structure of the interview be? Be organised and decide beforehand who will ask what.
- How long will the interview last? This is important for both planning and consistency.
- Ensure that the interview takes place in an appropriate setting, without interruptions.

Interviewing

- Be prepared and know what you are asking for. The panel should meet to discuss the interview beforehand and should be familiar with the job description and person specification.

The form
Interviews can take a variety of forms. One suggested format would be to welcome the candidate, introduce the panel and explain the interview format; acquire information by asking relevant questions; supply information by giving the candidate an opportunity to ask questions; make the candidate aware of the next stage, including when he/she will find out the outcome; and thank him/her for attending.

The purpose
The key purpose of the interview is to assess the candidate's suitability for the post. As an interviewer, you should ask yourself if the candidate can do the job; and what he/she would bring to the job. The job description and person specification should be used as the basis for areas of questioning and the questions should draw out information about the candidate's knowledge, experience and skills. The interviewer needs to be satisfied with the candidate's evidence, whilst considering the relative importance of each of the selection criteria.

It is usually best to ask all candidates the same basic questions, in order to ascertain whether they are right for the role. However, the panel should feel confident about deviating from basic questions and to probe further to obtain the evidence needed.

Where possible, interviewers should ask open questions that are experience-based, rather than questions that just require a 'yes' or 'no' answer. Follow-up questions could also include hypothetical situations, to measure thought processes.

As a general rule, questions that are not job-related should not be asked (e.g. questions related to family, marital status, childcare commitments, age and ethnic origin). Also, assumptions about these issues should not be made. These questions or assumptions could cause a panel to inadvertently discriminate against a candidate, which would then be compounded if the decision is based upon the answer to the question.

Subjective judgement
Although gut instincts should be avoided, interview panels will inevitably also take into account the more subjective aspects of a person's character, attitude and confidence. These are likely to be relevant and so, in many cases, the best thing to do is to include these criteria in the scoring grid, together with a space for writing down any comment that an interviewer feels helps to justify the score given. Care should be taken to ensure that any written comments cannot be construed as discriminatory in any form. Where a number of candidates meet the essential criteria for the job, the likelihood is that the successful candidate will be chosen on the basis of how the panel rated his/her more subjective criteria.

In terms of scoring subjective criteria, it is probably prudent to attach less weight to subjective scores than to objective scores. In reality though, where candidates are otherwise equal, the subjective score is likely to tip the balance in any event.

Considerations with internal candidates
Interviewing an internal candidate, or someone you know, presents its own set of challenges. Interviewers should not make assumptions, but should gather evidence of whether he/she satisfies the selection criteria in the same way as with any other candidate. Interview questions should (still) be objective and probing. Interviewers

Interviewing

should steer clear of irrelevant points and keep the interview formal, rather than being tempted to adopt a more informal approach.

Written notes

It is a good idea to take brief notes or use an interview form, as this will act as a reminder when the interviewer comes to make a decision. It is also good evidence of why a particular candidate was or was not selected. However, interviewers should avoid making copious notes, as this could make it difficult to establish a rapport with candidates. Also, bear in mind that any notes taken, even on scraps of paper, will be discoverable documents in any subsequent legal proceedings. Therefore, it is important to avoid discriminatory comments or comments that could be interpreted as such. Where notes are not made during the interview, they should be written up as soon after the interview as is reasonably practicable, in order to ensure that the details are recalled accurately. All notes should be returned to Personnel for storage with the job file and should be kept for at least six months.

Selection

It is crucial to go back to the job description and person specification when deciding which candidate to select for the position. Ideally, each panel member should assess each of the candidates him/herself, where possible immediately after the interview, formulating his/her own view and scoring the candidate before any discussion takes place. It is helpful to have a standard evaluation form to complete, to ensure consistency in ratings. (In practice, the panel will also take into account information from the application process, any references and so on.) These records should be kept for six months.

Each candidate should then be discussed by the panel in turn. Candidates who do not meet the essential criteria can be eliminated. In terms of the remaining candidates, the panel should not come to a premature decision based on personality / who they like best, but should focus on the (essential and preferred) selection criteria.

The panel should then rank the candidates as unappointable and appointable, in order of preference. Again, a record should be kept of this process. The first choice candidate can then be offered the job, ideally with a time limit for acceptance.

Those deemed unappointable can also be informed at this stage. However, it may be prudent to delay informing any reserves of the final decision, in case the first choice declines the offer. It is best practice to keep reserves informed of the situation.

In the long run, it is always better to appoint the right person for the job, even if this means waiting or extending the recruitment process (including any associated costs), so as to avoid ending up with someone who is not suitable for the post.

See also: Criminal records, p.78; Discrimination, p.110; Personnel files, p.317; Probationary periods, p.332; Recruitment and selection, p.335; References, p.347; Staff handbooks, p.375.

Sources of further information

ACAS – Advisory booklet – Recruitment and selection: www.acas.org.uk

IT security

Rhian Hill, Bird and Bird

Key points
Serious breaches of IT security and major losses of customer or employee data regularly feature in the news. Clearly, such breaches of security have a major impact on the organisation affected, not least in terms of negative PR. Workplace managers can take a number of steps to protect their organisation against security breaches:

- Put security breach action plans in place;
- Put security policies in place, implement them and ensure that they are regularly reviewed;
- Update security software regularly; and
- Put effective systems administration procedures in place.

Legislation
- Computer Misuse Act 1990.
- Data Protection Act 1998.

Security breaches in the news
Serious breaches of security have been hitting the headlines with alarming regularity, with both public and private sector organisations reporting security breaches to the Information Commissioner regularly. This is not simply an UK issue, but companies globally are suffering the effects of security breaches. In March 2007, TJX, the parent company of TK Maxx (a US and UK retailer), paid just under $10m to 41 American states in settlement over a growing dispute regarding the financial losses incurred by banks as a result of a security breach that made customers' credit card details available (see 'Confidential waste,' p.410).

In late 2008, micro-blogging site Twitter admitted that some of its most high profile bloggers had been targeted by hackers. It announced that 33 accounts had been hacked, including those belonging to president elect, Barack Obama, and singer, Britney Spears.

A recent study has shown that 70% of IT businesses have been affected by at least one data breach security incident during the last year, a figure up from the 60% seen in the previous corresponding period, according to the British Computer Society (BCS).

As more of these types of cases are reported in the media, most workplace managers do not need to be convinced of the devastating effect on business of such incidents. A common initial reaction might be to ask how this could happen. No doubt the board / stakeholders / financiers of the business would be asking themselves the same question. If managing a business is seen to be all about managing risk while achieving the highest return on investment, recent cases have shown that the risk of security breaches is really very serious.

IT security

> **Facts**
> - In the UK, 45% of small companies (with fewer than 50 staff) had a security incident in 2007/08.
> - 96% of very large companies (with more than 500 staff) reported a security incident in 2007/08.
> - For a small company, the average cost of the worst security incidents was £10,000 to £20,000.
> - For very large companies, the average cost of the worst security incidents was between £1m and £2m.
> - Over 711,000 new viruses were identified between April 2007 and April 2008 – an increase of 468% on the number identified in the previous year.
>
> *Source: BERR Information Security Breaches Survey 2008.*

The threats

Companies face a number of security threats. These could involve threats to system availability, integrity or general data losses. In the first part of this chapter we look at the key threats that companies may face.

Breach of IT security through human error and organisational failures

Many high-profile incidents of data loss are blamed either on human error or on communication and system failures. Security breaches are increasingly occurring as a result of human error or ineffective procedures. Breaches commonly occur as a result of non-encrypted laptops, mislaid disks and a failure to dispose of customer details in a secure way. As many such breaches are not publicised, it is difficult to estimate how many businesses are affected by a physical breach of IT security.

As the use of social engineering increases, i.e. individuals using confidence tricks to obtain access to a company's premises and/or obtaining information from employees or their passwords, companies should ensure that they provide training on IT security to all staff. Companies should ensure that their staff are aware of the possibility of social engineering, and should promote an organisational culture that seeks to reduce the risk of such activities. For example, companies should seek to develop a culture where unidentified individuals within buildings are challenged, where sensitive information is not provided over the phone, and where there are clear policies on the use and protection of passwords. Many companies now develop IT use policies that put in place clear rules about use and sharing of passwords. Although these steps cannot guarantee protection against a social engineering attack, especially as these attacks become more sophisticated, greater awareness may reduce the risk of such attacks.

In addition to the risk of adverse publicity in the event of security breaches, businesses may in some circumstances face sanctions from regulators. The ICO in the UK can issue enforcement notices against companies as well as ask senior directors to sign undertakings. The ICO

IT security

may also have the power to impose fines on organisations that deliberately or recklessly break the Data Protection Act (DPA), although these powers are not yet in force.

Malicious software

It is very likely that malicious software will attempt to attack your network. Popular malicious installations include key loggers that spring to life if particular websites are visited or programs, such as online games, are started up. However, it is also believed that malicious software authors are moving away from the mass mailing of viruses and instead are launching targeted attacks. It is believed that malicious software authors will increasingly target social networking sites, where individuals may be less wary of clicking on links. New viruses, worms and Trojan horses are being created all the time. In fact, the vast majority of malicious software is made possible by vulnerabilities in a small number of common operating system services. An increasing amount of malicious code is infecting computers via vulnerabilities in web browsers. They count on organisations not fixing the problems, or not uploading patches as they become available. It is therefore important to ensure your system is always updated with the latest 'patches' released by the software developer. Unfortunately, no firewall or scanning of viruses, worms and Trojan horses is capable of eliminating all risk from intrusion by malicious software.

Hacking

Again, no system is foolproof. Any network that has an external connectivity is open to the risk of hacking. Hacking may involve a variety of unacceptable activities, e.g. malicious file destruction, theft of money or intellectual property or a catastrophic denial of service attack.

Additionally, there is an increased use of Phishing. This can take a number of guises but it is often used as a means of obtaining personal details from individuals, by impersonating a reputable company. For example, this can be done where an email is sent to a user claiming to be from the user's bank, requesting personal details.

Hacking is definitely on the increase, but it is difficult to find accurate figures because, like corporate fraud, most activity is not reported due to the embarrassment and damage to business reputation. For example, the Computer Misuse Act 1990 has been in force for 19 years, but, as there have only ever been a handful of successful prosecutions under this Act, it is clearly not providing a deterrent. However, if these laws are to be a true deterrent, more organisations will have to report incidents, and the police must be more willing to investigate and take on more cases. The biggest threat of hacking, however, is from inside a large organisation, and businesses should be particularly wary in times of economic slowdown. Unfortunately, staff that are laid off may become disgruntled and present a real security risk. Difficulties may also arise where an ex-supplier has control of the source code, passwords and so on.

Risk management

Businesses take on financial risk with a view to making a return on their investment. However, investing in IT security, and in creating internal controls, does not in itself provide a direct return on investment – it is more about loss avoidance. Reducing the risk of a disastrous system failure will, however, contribute to the bottom line, because in the current climate, doing nothing or nothing much may ensure that the risk of a systems attack is realised.

IT security

It would be naïve to suggest that the risk of system intrusion or failure could be eliminated, but it can be properly managed. Indeed, it is worth bearing in mind that every director has a duty to manage serious corporate risk. As with most business risks, a judgement has to be made on:

- which risks can be reduced by using security products or services?
- which risks can be covered by insurance?
- which risks are to be borne by the organisation?

The proportion of risk in the first and last categories is to a large extent determined by the steps an organisation takes to protect its systems and equipment. In any event, it will need to keep its house in order if it is to avoid invalidating its insurance.

What do you need to do to protect your data systems and equipment?

In the second half of this chapter, we consider some of the practical steps that can be taken to protect data systems and equipment. Whilst security technology is extremely important, IT security workplace managers should also ensure that they have other security measures in place to prevent or minimise the risk resulting from security breaches through human error, complacency or malice. There are many measures that are common sense, and that should form part of your general security policy. Costs range from the minimal, where it is simply a case of more vigorously applying existing procedures, to the highly expensive, where the latest technology is implemented.

Physical security

Physical security measures are important to reduce the risk of intruders and theft of equipment. Some physical measures that should be adopted are as follows:

- Control and monitor access to your building properly, using a record of visitors and badging. Also consider installing CCTV systems. Note, however, that CCTV must be used in a proportionate way (see '*CCTV monitoring*,' p.59).
- Require all staff to take responsibility for security by, for example, challenging 'strangers' out of hours and/or who appear in restricted or non-public areas.
- Make sure that the most important servers are situated in a secure and non-visible part of the premises, or perhaps even at another site.
- If appropriate, consider using biometrics (e.g. retina / iris scans, finger / handprint or facial feature scans, voice pattern scans, keystroke analysis) to identify those authorised to access the most sensitive equipment. However, note that there are data protection issues to consider with this type of monitoring (see '*Monitoring employees*,' p.292).
- Keep an inventory of computer equipment, especially equipment that can be taken from the building, and carry out periodical stock checks.
- Staff using laptops and other portable computer equipment should be reminded to ensure that they keep the equipment secure at all times.
- Sensitive information and customer data held on laptops (and other removable media) should be encrypted. The ICO expects computers containing personal data to be encrypted.
- Draft and circulate a policy to staff on what to do if their IT equipment is lost or stolen.

IT security

Basic system administration

Basic system administration measures include the following:

- Write a system security policy, and require staff to apply it and police it. This policy should oblige staff to avoid opening emails and attachments when they do not know their origin. Restrict staff use of Hotmail and similar web-based email services, as these could increase the risk of virus attacks. Some organisations limit or ban their staff's use of social networking sites such as Facebook and MySpace due to the risk that malicious software may be inadvertently downloaded with video and other files.
- Oblige staff to follow instructions from their IT managers, such as warnings about current virus attacks.
- Segment the network with appropriate authorisation procedures to limit the number of IT support staff that have entire system access.
- Limit system privileges as much as possible and develop a hierarchy of access.
- Implement an effective password policy and require regular password changes.
- Keep the system 'patched' (updated) regularly.
- Warn staff to look out for scams.

Protective software and audit activity

Some of the software protection and audit measures that can be employed are as follows:

- Ensure that virus-sweeping software is regularly updated across the network.
- Carry out regular monitoring of the firewall and general network integrity.
- Use code review software and consider penetration testing (although workplace managers should note that there may be data protection implications if customer or staff data may be accessed during testing).

Staff issues

Whilst difficult to counter, there are a number of measures that businesses can take in order to protect themselves from fraud or malicious acts by staff members. As noted above, good systems administration plays a major part. Passwords should be protected and changed regularly, and access to sensitive systems carefully controlled. It has been found that staff committing fraudulent acts often fail to take time off (presumably for fear that they may be found out in their absence), so it is worth considering checking the leave records of key staff from time to time. Staff access to systems should be carefully controlled from the date of resignation until the person leaves, when access should be immediately terminated. Access should be terminated immediately on dismissal.

What can you do to limit the damage if an incident does occur?

The following procedures and precautions are recommended:

- Ensure that your staff know who to contact in the event of a security breach and that the matter is escalated quickly.
- Have a contingency plan in place for restoring / recovering / recreating important data in the event of a disaster, as well as malicious or negligent damage. This could mean regularly backing up data or having a Secure Disaster Recovery Site.
- Ensure that forensic evidence is not destroyed in the course of the disaster response as this may deny recourse against the perpetrators or, more importantly, prevent discovery of what went wrong.

IT security

- Document IP rights and, where relevant, secure software source code (both sensible business practice) to assist fast remedies in preventing unauthorised use by hackers.
- Ensure that system security obligations are written into staff employment contracts to avoid arguments over what staff were required to do or not do.

Importance of security

Security is not just 'flavour of the month' in the IT world but has been regarded as a serious issue for a number of years. As regulators' powers in this area are increased by the Information Commissioner, the stability and security of data is likely to be a business priority and an important part of workplace management.

> *See also*: CCTV monitoring, p.59; Data protection, p.84; Internet and email policies, p.236; Monitoring employees, p.292; Confidential waste, p.410; Unlawfully procuring information, p.403.

Sources of further information

ICO – Guidance on data security breach management: www.ico.gov.uk/upload/documents/library/data_protection/practical_application/guidance_on_data_security_breach_management.pdf

Workplace Law Group's *IT and Email Policy and Management Guide, v.3.0*, has been designed to alert employers of the potential problems associated with using computer systems, the internet, and email systems within the workplace, and to provide certain safeguards. For more information visit www.workplacelaw.net/bookshop/policiesAndProcedures.

Jury service

Robert Dillarstone and Lisa Jinks, Greenwoods Solicitors LLP

Key points
- Ensure that you cover jury service and related salary payments in your staff handbook or contract of employment.
- Instruct your employees to claim compensation for loss of earnings from the Court.
- Deduct compensation for loss of earnings from salary payments.
- Plan ahead to cover absences caused by jury service.
- Consider requesting your employee to ask for a deferment if jury service would cause hardship.

Legislation
- Juries Act 1974.

Jury selection
All jurors are selected at random by computer from the electoral register. Everyone on the electoral register between the ages of 18 and 70 may be selected even if they are not eligible to serve on a jury. Some people never get called; others get called more than once. Jurors usually try the more serious criminal cases such as murder, rape and assault and are asked to decide on guilt or innocence.

Eligibility
Jury service is a public duty and four weeks' notice is usually given. Unless someone is ineligible, has the right to be excused or has a valid reason for discretionary excusal, then they must serve. Individuals who are ineligible to serve as a juror are those who:

- are under 18, or 70 plus, on the date they are due to start their jury service;
- are currently on bail in criminal proceedings;
- have ever been sentenced to imprisonment for five years or more, or those who have been sentenced to imprisonment or a community order within the last ten years;
- have, or have had in the past, a mental illness, psychotic disorder, or mental handicap;
- have not lived in the UK, the Channel Islands or the Isle of Man for one period of at least five years since the age of 13; and/or
- are not eligible to vote in parliamentary or Local Authority elections.

Jury service is an average of ten working days but may be longer or shorter than this, depending on the case.

Deferral and excusal
Anyone may apply for discretionary deferment or excusal. Jury service can only be deferred once up to a maximum of 12 months from the original date. The normal expectation is that everyone summoned for jury service will serve at the time for which they are summoned. Only in extreme circumstances will a person be excused. The normal procedure is to defer the individual to a more appropriate time, e.g. if a holiday is booked or to avoid a shift worker attending on a rest day.

Application for excusal could be given on the following grounds:

- Insufficient understanding of English;

Jury service

- Membership of religious orders whose ideology or beliefs are incompatible with jury service;
- Valid business reason (e.g. if a small business would suffer unusual hardship) – application for deferral or excusal cannot be accepted from third parties such as employers;
- Conflict with other important public duties; and/or
- Illness or a physical disability.

Application for excusal can also be given to an individual who has completed jury service during the two years prior to the current summons.

Loss of earnings and other expenses

With regard to loss of earnings, courts can pay for these together with travel costs and a subsistence rate. Currently, losses of earnings are paid up to a maximum of £61.28 per day for the first ten days and a maximum of £122.57 for subsequent days. Should the juror be required to serve for over 200 days, loss of earnings will then be paid up to a maximum of £215.17 for subsequent days.

Public transport costs will be paid, although jurors must obtain permission before using taxis. A standard mileage rate will be paid to jurors to travel by car but permission should be sought before incurring parking fees. Payment is made directly to the juror and courts cannot pay third parties such as employers.

As soon as a summons has been received, the employee should forward the juror's loss of earnings certificate provided by the court (Form 5223) to their employer. Employers should note the dates and organise a deduction from salary of the amount representing the value of the allowance for days attended at court. However, unless specified in the contract of employment or staff handbook, there is no legal right to receive regular salary payments while undertaking jury service. In circumstances where deduction of the jury service allowance results in a nil salary payment, any additional superannuation contributions can be deducted from the next available salary payment to provide continuity of pensionable service.

Employment rights

Jury service will count as part of an employee's continuous employment. This means that an employee will continue to accumulate or keep existing employment rights gained through length of service.

It is not advisable to refuse permission to release your employee for jury service. This could result in contempt of court issues with penalties such as a fine or even imprisonment for the employer. Dismissing your employee may result in a claim against your business for compensation for the loss of employment.

Planning ahead will help to minimise the impact on the business. Encourage employees to inform you immediately when summoned because this will give you approximately four weeks to make the necessary plans. If you work in a small business, you may consider requesting your employee to apply for a deferment.

See also: Absence management, p.30; Criminal records, p.78.

Sources of further information

Criminal Justice Service website: http://juror.cjsonline.gov.uk

Leave

Michelle Billingsley, Martineau Solicitors

Key points
- Adopting carefully defined policies that formalise practices on compassionate leave, time off for dependants, and sabbatical leave can help employers promote fair and consistent treatment of their employees.
- Preparing a written policy is also a good opportunity for employers to clarify their attitudes and approach to sensitive issues, which, in turn, should help to increase staff morale and wellbeing.
- Employers should avoid the implication of a contractual right to compassionate leave, sabbatical leave and time off for dependants, unless this is clearly intended.
- The right to time off for dependants is not applicable in all circumstances. A burst boiler or problems with a pet do not count.
- The right to time off under the Employment Rights Act 1996 for unexpected disruptions or the termination of care arrangements for dependants is not limited to last minute unavailability or emergencies.
- Sabbatical leave can be an effective alternative to making an employee redundant.

Legislation
- Employment Rights Act 1996 (section 57A).
- Employment Equality (Religion or Belief) Regulations 2003.

Case law
- *Forster v. Cartwright Black* (2004).
- *Royal Bank of Scotland plc v. Harrison* (2009).

Types of leave
- Annual leave (see '*Holiday,*' p.219).
- Compassionate leave.
- Maternity, paternity and adoption leave (see '*Family-friendly rights,*' p.182).
- Sabbatical.
- Time off for dependants.

What is compassionate leave?
Compassionate leave is a term used to describe a period of time off work (either paid or unpaid) that an employer allows an employee who is faced with difficult personal circumstances, such as the death of a family member.

Whilst employees are not legally entitled to compassionate leave as a result of a bereavement, employers should take a serious and sympathetic view of requests for time off following the death of a dependant or family member. However, there is a statutory right to take time off for the death of a dependant (section 57A (1)(c) ERA 1996) (*see below*).

Practical tips
- Ensure that policies are applied consistently and fairly to all employees.
- Set out a clear reporting structure in the event that compassionate leave is needed (i.e. supervisor / Head of HR).
- Ensure that bad news affecting an employee is communicated promptly

Leave

- but sensitively to the rest of the team or department and that workloads are delegated effectively.
- Recognise that employees affected by bereavement may not be able to comply rigidly with a policy (i.e. often death and emergencies will be unexpected the and employee will not be able to report his/her absence straightaway or may not feel emotionally able to make the call to HR personally).
- Arrange a 'return to work interview' with the affected employee.
- Employees who develop psychological illness following a bereavement may find themselves needing to extend their periods of compassionate leave with sickness absence. Employers may therefore wish to offer return to work interviews to affected employees to assess their ability to cope with the stresses and strains of the workplace. They may also wish to offer employees a period of free bereavement counselling via Occupational Health.

Time off for dependants

Compassionate leave should be distinguished from an employee's statutory right to take a reasonable amount of unpaid time off during the employee's working hours to deal with certain unexpected or sudden emergencies, such as the death of a dependant (see section 57A(1)(c) ERA 1996). The right is to 'take action which is necessary,' such as to organise or to attend a funeral.

In *Forster v. Cartwright Black*, the Employment Appeals Tribunal (EAT) considered the scope of qualifying actions for time off work taken in consequence of the death of a dependant. Following the death of her mother, Forster had taken five days' bereavement leave followed by two consecutive periods of sick leave (each lasting two weeks), which her doctor had certified as 'bereavement reaction'. Following receipt of the second sick note, she was dismissed due to her period of absence following her mother's death and her general absence record. The EAT held that the right to time off in consequence of the death of a dependant covered time off to make funeral arrangements, to attend a dependant's funeral and to make necessary practical arrangements, such as registering a death and applying for probate. However, it stated that section 57A(1)(c) did not cover time off as a result of the emotional consequences and grief associated with the death of a dependant. To avoid any doubt arising, employers should therefore refer to time taken off to grieve the psychological effects of a bereavement in a separate compassionate leave policy.

As well as having the right to time off to deal with the death of a dependant, an employee is entitled to take unpaid time off in the following circumstances, which are set out in section 57A ERA 1996:

- Where a dependant falls ill, or has been injured or assaulted;
- When a dependant is having a baby (please note that this does not include taking time off after the birth to care for the child, but an employee may be entitled to take maternity, paternity or parental leave for this purpose);
- To make long-term care arrangements for a dependant who is ill or injured;
- To deal with a death of a dependant – this enables an employee to take time off to make funeral arrangements and attend the funeral;
- To deal with an unexpected disruption or breakdown of care arrangements for a dependant; and/or
- To deal with an incident involving the employee's child and which occurs during school hours.

Leave

When can this right be exercised?
The right to take time off because of the unexpected disruption or termination of arrangements for the care of a dependent is not limited to emergencies. In the case of *Royal Bank of Scotland v. Harrison*, the Employment Appeal Tribunal held that the entitlement to dependant leave under the Employment Rights Act 1996 is not limited to last minute unavailability or emergencies. Ms Harrison had two young children. Her childminder told her on 8 December that she would no longer be available on 22 December as previously arranged. Ms Harrison asked her employer for time off and this was refused. Having failed to make alternative childcare arrangements, Ms Harrison did not go to work on 22 December so that she could look after her children and, as a consequence, was issued with a verbal warning that would remain on her record for six months. Ms Harrison was successful in bringing a claim against RBS on the grounds that she had suffered a detriment as a result of staying off work to look after her children.

The EAT upheld the decision of the Tribunal and concluded that the word 'unexpected' in section 57A(1)(d) ERA 1996 does not involve a time element and that it is not appropriate to seek to incorporate into statute words which are simply not there, such as 'sudden' or 'in an emergency'. The right to time off applies to all employees, namely any individual (male or female, full-time or part-time) who has entered into or works under a contract of employment (whether that is express or implied, written or oral). There is no minimum period of qualifying service required. The case serves as a useful example of the flexibility employers must show when dealing with employees with dependants and requests for time off work in relation to those dependants.

Who counts as a dependant?
A dependant is defined as the employee's spouse, civil partner, child or parent; or a person living in the same household other than by reason of being a tenant, lodger, boarder or employee. This could include a partner or an elderly aunt or grandparent.

Additional issues to be considered by the employer
Although the statutory right to time off work is unpaid, an employer may want to consider offering its employees paid leave to organise or to attend a funeral. This could improve staff loyalty and retention and help achieve a better work–life balance. Depending on the composition of an employer's workforce, it may wish to consider extending the application of its policy beyond employees to include other types of worker or to include other emergency situations; such as house fire or flood etc. The right to time off for dependants is intended to cover genuine unexpected situations, so the employer should not set a limit on the number of times that an employee can be absent from work under this right. However, employers who are concerned that abuse of the right to time off to care for dependants may become an issue, should consider stating that abuse of the right is a specific disciplinary offence that could lead to disciplinary action under its disciplinary procedures.

If a funeral is taking place overseas, an employer should agree a length of absence that is reasonable and fair in all the circumstances. This may mean the employer striking a balance between its own business needs and the needs of the individual employee.

The right to time off does not apply unless the employee tells the employer the reason for his/her absence 'as soon as

Leave

reasonably practicable' (unless it is not reasonable for the employee to tell the employer the reason for his/her absence until after his/her return to work). Any policy should therefore set out expected timescales for receipt of this information.

An employee who exercises the right to time off for dependants is protected against dismissal or victimisation. This means that it would be unfair to dismiss an employee or to select him/her for redundancy for taking, or seeking to take, time off to exercise this right. Similarly, an employee who is not offered a promotion or an appraisal because he/she has exercised this right would be able to complain that he/she has suffered a detriment. If the dismissed employee is also female, the employer may also be at risk of a claim of indirect sex discrimination.

In order to comply with the requirements of the Employment Equality (Religion or Belief) Regulations 2003, employers should, where reasonably practicable, accommodate the requirements of their employees' religions or beliefs when a death occurs. This may mean creating less rigid compassionate leave policies to cater for specific bereavement customs. For example, Hindus believe that cremation must take place as soon as possible following death and it is usual for close relatives of the deceased to remain at home and observe a 13-day mourning period.

Sabbatical leave

Sabbatical leave is a period of leave (usually unpaid), typically lasting between three and six months, which employers allow employees to take in order to spend more time with family, to work on a specific project or to merely recharge their batteries. In the current economic climate, sabbaticals can be an effective way for employers to cut costs and be an alternative to making redundancies if demand picks up.

Sabbatical breaks are not officially recognised by law. However, more and more employers are recognising that it is in their best interests to implement well thought out sabbatical schemes.

What are the advantages to employers of offering sabbatical schemes?

- Adopting a flexible 'can do' approach to sabbatical leave can be an effective way of recruiting and retaining the best talent.
- In demonstrating a sensitivity to the work–life balance, employees often return to their former roles feeling more refreshed, motivated and productive.
- They allow employers to streamline the workforce on a short-term basis with the option of re-integrating the employee back into the organisation at the end of the leave period, without excessive training costs.
- Staff can acquire new skills during their sabbatical, and bring valuable knowledge to the workplace.
- Encouraging a culture of flexibility amongst employees can have a positive effect on staff retention and turnover.
- Sabbaticals can be used by employers to prevent burnout of employees and to assert a progressive approach towards work.

To formalise requests for sabbatical leave, employers are advised to have a formal policy in place. This should help to reduce any potential disputes and give the employer and the employee an agreed procedure to follow. In the absence of any agreement, sabbatical leave can be viewed as a resignation in the hope of later re-engagement. If this is the case, the employer has no certainty as to whether

Leave

the employee will return to the organisation at the end of his/her break and the employee has no certainty that there will be a job for him/her upon his/her return. This will rarely be the case and sabbatical leave terms and conditions should be agreed in advance. Any terms regarding the leave should be clearly documented in an agreement. Depending on what is negotiated, employees can return to work at the end of their period of sabbatical leave on the same terms and conditions as before, without having had their continuity of employment broken. However, in the current downturn, the most employers will want to do is offer to conduct a reasonable search for opportunities on the employee's return in what could be a substantially different business a year down the line.

Additional concerns for the employer

Employers should word policies carefully to ensure that the employee has no automatic right to return to the same job or on the same terms and conditions at the end of the sabbatical leave period.

A sabbatical leave package requires careful planning and good communication, so that each party fully understands the implications of any commitments made. It may be useful for individuals to have an obligation to inform employers, by a particular date, of whether they intend to return to the organisation.

The needs of the business should determine the length of any period of sabbatical leave granted. However, a limit of three months may be reasonable, on the basis that it is not long enough for the employee to forget know-how or technical skills, but long enough to have a meaningful break.

> *See also*: Absence management, p.30; Holiday, p.219; Family-friendly rights, p.182; Jury service, p.250; Pregnancy, p.324; Restrictive covenants and garden leave, p.350; Sickness benefits, p.361.

Sources of further information

Workplace Law Network provides premium members with unrestricted access to a comprehensive range of online information – factsheets, case reports and daily news items – on employment, health and safety and premises management. Members also benefit from an online advice service and a free subscription to the *Workplace Law Magazine*. For more information email membership@workplacelaw.net or call our membership services team on 0871 777 8881.

Medical records

Lisa Jinks and John Macaulay, Greenwoods Solicitors LLP

Key points
- 'Medical records' encompass any records that may contain information about workers' medical conditions.
- Employers need to be aware of the legal procedure under the Access to Medical Reports Act 1988.
- Employers should be aware of data protection principles as they apply to medical records and establish who in the organisation is responsible for ensuring compliance.
- Employment contracts should contain a provision allowing employers access to medical information.
- Employers should always bear in mind the principles of the Disability Discrimination Act 1995 as amended by the Disability Discrimination Act 2005.
- Employers also need to be aware of the right to privacy.

Legislation
- Access to Medical Reports Act 1988.
- Disability Discrimination Act 1995 as amended by the Disability Discrimination Act 2005.
- Data Protection Act 1998.
- Human Rights Act 1998.

Background
A major issue for employers is how they can access and use information on workers' medical conditions. This may arise in a variety of situations, for example, where an employee is off on long-term sickness absence, where employers wish to use pre-employment medical questionnaires or carry out drugs and alcohol testing etc. They may also need to collate information for insurance schemes such as private medical insurance or permanent health insurance. Employers need to understand what information they may have access to, and how they may process such information once received.

In addition, employers always need to be careful not to discriminate against employees on grounds of disability.

Access to medical reports
Employers may obtain access to employees' medical records, subject to certain conditions. If they wish to obtain a report from a medical practitioner who has been responsible for the employee's clinical care, they need to comply with the Access to Medical Reports Act 1988 (the Act). Such practitioners include the employee's GP but also others who have such responsibility such as the employee's physiotherapist, psychiatrist or other specialist.

The Act requires that the employer must:

- obtain the employee's express consent in writing before applying to the medical practitioner for a report; and
- notify the employee of their rights under the Act. These include the

Medical records

right to withhold permission from the employer obtaining the report, the right to have access to the report either before it is sent to the employer or afterwards and, on seeing the report, the right to withdraw consent or request amendment of the report.

The medical practitioner will normally have to provide the report within 21 days. One frustration for an employer is that an employee who has stated that they do not want to see the report may subsequently write to their doctor and request to see the report, without informing the employer. If this happens within 21 days of the employer's request, the doctor may not release the report until the patient gives consent. In this situation it may be sensible for the employer to contact the employee directly to discuss the issue.

The requirements of the Act do not apply if an employer wishes to refer the employee to a medical practitioner who has not been responsible for the employee's clinical care. This means that employers can, subject to having the contractual right to do so, request an employee to be examined by a company-appointed doctor whether from within the organisation or externally without complying with the above procedure (provided that the doctor concerned has not previously treated the employee). In these circumstances, the employee does not have the same rights to see or challenge the report before the employer sees it. Hence the importance of an express provision in the contract of employment stating that the employee consents to be referred to a medical practitioner of the employer's choice at any time.

However, even if such a provision exists, it is always advisable to obtain an employee's *written* consent before carrying out any medical assessment. The issue of consent and the right to privacy are considered below. It is also recommended that any in-house medical adviser should inform the employee of any advice that will be passed to management following a health assessment.

Data protection

Medical records amount to 'sensitive personal data' under the Data Protection Act 1998 (DPA). If sickness records are to be 'processed' under the DPA (e.g. obtained, retained, disclosed, disposed of etc.), then employers must comply with the sensitive personal data rules. It is worth noting that the DPA only comes into play when such information is held on a computer system or in a 'relevant filing system' (which may include certain structured personnel files).

Under the Data Protection Employment Practices Code, some core principles are set out regarding the processing of information about workers' health. These include:

- the intrusiveness to workers of obtaining information about their health;
- a worker's right to privacy;
- the need for employers to be clear about the purpose of processing such information and whether this is justified by real benefits; and
- the requirement for one of the sensitive data conditions to be satisfied (*see below*).

Workers should be made aware of the extent information about their health is held and the reasons for this. Decisions on workers' suitability for particular jobs are management decisions but the interpretation of medical information should be left to qualified health professionals.

Medical records

With regard to the sensitive personal data rules that must be satisfied to process medical information, the following are likely to be the most relevant:

- *Processing is necessary by law*. This condition has quite a wide application in the employment context. Typical examples would be maintaining records of statutory sick pay, maternity pay, ensuring health and safety and preventing disability discrimination.
- *The processing is necessary to protect the vital interests of the worker / some other person*. This would occur when it is vital to access medical records where consent cannot be given. An example would be if an employee was involved in a medical emergency and the employee or another person was at risk of harm.
- *The processing is necessary in connection with actual or prospective legal proceedings*. This is most likely to occur when an employer is trying to rely upon medical information to defend a claim for unfair dismissal or unlawful discrimination.
- *Worker's 'explicit' consent*. There are limitations on how far consent can be relied upon. To be valid, consent must be explicit and freely given. 'Explicit' means the worker must have been clearly told what personal data is involved and informed about the use of this information. The worker must give a positive indication of their agreement, e.g. a signature. 'Freely given' means the worker must have a real choice whether to consent or not and there must be no penalty imposed for refusing to give consent.

'Processing' of medical records

The processing of medical records (e.g. obtaining, holding, disclosing, disposing of etc.) must comply with data protection principles. Before processing medical information, employers should carry out an impact assessment, i.e. identifying the purpose for which the medical information is required and the likely benefits of this, identifying any adverse impact on the worker, considering alternative options and judging whether the processing of such information is justified.

It is also advisable that employers identify who within their organisation is authorised to process workers' medical information. In addition, access to medical information by managers / colleagues should be undertaken no more than is necessary. For example, managers should not access information about a worker's medical condition when information is only needed about length of absence. It is also recommended that medical records (giving details of the medical condition) are separated from absence records (which do not have such details) and that medical records are subject to enhanced security, perhaps being password-protected.

Workers' access to records

Workers have a right to access information held about them. This is known as subject access and covers, amongst other information, sickness or absence records held about an individual, whether on computerised files or as part of a 'relevant filing system'.

An employer can charge a fee of £10 to provide this information and must respond to a request within 40 days of receipt. The employer must provide the information in a hard copy or other readily readable, permanent electronic form, making clear any codes used and the sources of information. Note, however, that access does not have to be granted where it is likely to cause serious harm to the

Medical records

health / condition of the worker or any other person. In this situation, the employer should consult with an appropriate health professional.

Refusal to consent / right to privacy

Although an employee may refuse to give consent for their employer to access their medical records, the Courts will balance the right to privacy against the rights of the employer. For example, it is possible that a sick employee who claims a right to privacy by consistently refusing access to medical information could still be fairly dismissed on grounds of incapability where it is considered that the employer has followed the appropriate procedures and otherwise done all it could to resolve the matter.

> *See also*: Data protection, p.84; Health surveillance, p.212; Occupational health, p.304; Personnel files, p.317; Private life, p.327.

Sources of further information

The Employment Practices Code can be downloaded from www.ico.gov.uk

Mental health

Elizabeth Stevens, Steeles Law

Key points

Employers are subject to a variety of legal obligations in respect of their employees' health and wellbeing. These obligations arise from health and safety legislation, the breach of which is a criminal offence, and also from the law of negligence, contract and discrimination. Injury to an employee's mental health is treated by the law in the same way as injury to physical health. The Health and Safety Executive (HSE) defines 'workplace stress' as 'the adverse reaction people have to excessive pressure or other types of demand placed on them'. According to the HSE, stress is not an illness but a 'state'; it is only if stress becomes too excessive and prolonged that mental and physical illness may develop.

Employers are not under a duty to eliminate all stress in the workplace, but once an employee has raised the issue of stress, an employer is under a duty to take steps to minimise the risk to the individual. A failure to do so could render the employer liable for a future personal injury claim and/or constructive unfair dismissal claim.

Employers are also under certain duties in respect of those individuals whose mental health (whether or not impacted by work) amounts to a disability under the provisions of the Disability Discrimination Act 1995.

Legislation
- Health and Safety at Work etc. Act 1974.
- Disability Discrimination Act 1995.
- Protection from Harassment Act 1997.
- Working Time Regulations 1998.
- Management of Health and Safety at Work Regulations 1999.

Main cases
- *Sutherland (Chairman of the Governors of St Thomas Beckett RC High School) v. Hatton and others* (2002).
- *Barber v. Somerset County Council* (2004).
- *Essa v. Laing Ltd* (2004).
- *Nottinghamshire County Council v. Meikle* (2004).
- *Hartman v. South Essex Mental Health and Community Care NHS Trust and other cases* (2005).
- *Green v. DB Group Services Limited* (2006).
- *Hone v. Six Continents Retail Ltd* (2006).
- *Majrowski v. Guy's and St Thomas' NHS Trust* (2006).
- *Sayers v. Cambridgeshire County Council* (2006).
- *Intel Corporation (UK) Ltd v. Daw* (2007).
- *McAdie v. Royal Bank of Scotland plc* (2007).
- *Sunderland City Council v. Conn* (2007).
- *Dickens v. O2 PLC* (2008).
- *Cheltenham Borough Council v. Laird* (2009).

Mental health

Health and safety legislation

The Health and Safety at Work etc. Act 1974 (HSWA 1974) places a duty on employers to ensure the health, safety and welfare of their employees as far as is reasonably practicable. This includes taking steps to minimise the risk of stress-related illness or injury to employees. Under the Management of Health and Safety at Work Regulations 1999 employers are obliged to carry out an assessment of the risks to employees' health, including a suitable and sufficient risk assessment for stress. If, after completing an assessment, an employer believes there is a potential risk to employees' health, they should take all reasonable steps to limit this risk and to monitor the situation.

An employer's breach of the statutory duties imposed by the HSWA 1974 is a criminal offence, enforceable by the HSE but not directly actionable by individual employees. However, a breach of health and safety regulations may give rise to a civil liability for damages, where an employee can show that the employer's breach caused illness or injury to the employee. In addition, a failure by an employer to have due regard for the health and safety of its employees may amount to a fundamental breach of contract, entitling an employee to resign and bring a claim for constructive unfair dismissal.

HSE Management Standards

To assist employers in fulfilling their duties in respect of carrying out risk assessments, and to measure performance in managing work-related stress, the HSE has devised its 'Management Standards'. These are a set of best practice statements of management competencies, to provide a framework for dealing with workplace stress and to help employers meet their legal obligations. It is widely recognised that managers, through their management style and their role as 'gatekeepers' of working conditions, have a significant

---

Facts

- Around three in every ten employees will experience stress, depression or some other form of mental health issue in any one year.
- Stress is cited as the biggest cause of long-term sickness absence among non-manual employees, with mental ill health such as clinical depression and anxiety the third biggest cause.
- The top three causes of work-related stress are workload, management style and relationships at work.
- 21 days is the average length of time an employee takes off for stress; for depression it is nearer to 30 days.
- Estimates from the Labour Force Survey indicate that self-reported work-related stress, depression or anxiety accounted for 13.5 million lost working days in Britain in 2007/08.
- Two-thirds of employers (66%) are taking steps to identify and reduce stress, including staff surveys, stress risk assessments and training in stress management.
- The cost of sickness absence resulting from mental health problems that are directly work-related is estimated at £1.26bn a year.

Sources: HSE, CIPD, MIND 2005, Sainsbury Centre for Mental Health.

Mental health

impact on levels of employee stress and therefore play a crucial role in identifying and resolving any problems, and preventing unacceptable levels of stress occurring.

The Management Standards are voluntary, but may be used as evidence by the HSE of an employer's failure to comply with their duty to manage stress under the HSWA. The HSE, in conjunction with the CIPD and Investors in People, has also developed a 'Stress Management Competency Indicator Tool,' to allow managers to assess whether they currently have the behaviours identified as effective for preventing and reducing stress at work. The aim is to help managers reflect on their behaviour and management style. Further tools designed to assist managers and those who train and support them in that role are also being developed. The HSE website has further details.

Working Time Regulations

The Working Time Regulations 1998 implement the European Working Time Directive (93/104/EC), which was adopted by the EC as a health and safety measure and is consistently interpreted as such by the Courts and Employment Tribunals. Long working hours are a recognised contributory factor to the incidence of work-related stress and an employer's breach of its obligations under the Regulations is actionable by the HSE and in some cases (in relation to rest and leave entitlements) directly enforceable by the individual worker in the Employment Tribunal.

Employers have a duty to take all reasonable steps to ensure that the limits contained in the Working Time Regulations are complied with. This includes a maximum 48 hour average working week (which the employee can voluntarily contract out of) and limits on night working. The Regulations also provide entitlements to daily and weekly rest breaks and paid annual leave, which the employer is under a duty to ensure workers can take but is not obliged to force workers to take.

A failure by an employer to take reasonable steps to comply with the maximum 48 hour average working week is a criminal offence punishable by a potentially unlimited fine. The HSE is responsible for monitoring compliance and expects employers to maintain records going back at least two years to show that the 48 hour maximum has been complied with in respect of all employees who have not opted out. Employers should bear in mind that the maximum includes time the worker spends working for other employers.

The ability of workers to opt-out of the maximum 48 hour average working week has been the subject of lengthy debate at a European level, with proposals put forward for amendments to be made to the Working Time Directive, which would result in the opt-out being removed. These proposals have, for now, been rejected, and it remains to be seen whether further proposals will be put forward to amend the Directive. (See '*Working time*,' p.423.)

Common law duties

There is a duty implied into all contracts of employment that the employer will take reasonable care for the health and safety of its employees. If an employer breaches this duty and the employee has suffered psychiatric injury as a result, an employee may be entitled to bring a negligence claim against the employer (also known as a claim for personal injury). To do this, the employee must be able to demonstrate that his psychiatric injury was a *reasonably foreseeable* consequence of the employer's breach of duty. Much of the case law has dealt with the issue of whether an individual's psychiatric

Mental health

injury was reasonably foreseeable, as a consequence of bullying suffered by that individual and/or pressures of work.

Cases

Reasonable forseeability

Guidance on the issue of reasonable forseeability was given by the Court of Appeal in its landmark judgment in four conjoined stress cases; *Sutherland (Chairman of the Governors of St Thomas Beckett RC High School) v. Hatton and others* (2002). The main points of the guidance are as follows:

- The key question is whether this kind of harm (psychiatric injury) to this particular employee was reasonably foreseeable.
- Forseeability depends upon what the employer knows, or ought reasonably to know, about the individual employee. An employer is usually entitled to assume that an employee can withstand the usual pressures of the job unless he knows of a particular problem or vulnerability.
- No occupation should be regarded as intrinsically dangerous to mental health.
- An employer is generally entitled to take what he is told by his employee at face value, unless he has a good reason to think to the contrary.
- To trigger a duty on the employer to take steps, the indications of impending harm to health arising from stress at work must be plain enough for any reasonable employer to realise that he should do something about it.
- The employer will only breach the duty of care if he has failed to take the steps that are reasonable in the circumstances, bearing in mind the magnitude of the risk of harm occurring, the gravity of the harm that may occur, the costs and practicability of preventing it, and the justifications for running the risk.

- The size resources and scope of the employer's operation, and the need to treat other employees fairly, can all be taken into account when deciding what is reasonable.
- An employer can only reasonably be expected to take steps that are likely to do some good.
- An employer who offers a confidential advice service, with referral to appropriate counselling or treatment services, is unlikely to be found in breach of duty.
- If the only reasonable and effective step would have been to dismiss or demote the employee, the employer will not be in breach of duty in allowing a willing employee to continue in the job.

On appeal from the Court of Appeal's decision in *Sutherland v. Hatton* the House of Lords overturned one of the four cases, *Barber v. Somerset County Council* (2004) and in doing so emphasised that the guidelines set out by the Court of Appeal, whilst 'useful practical guidance,' did not have statutory force.

The key point for employers in order to avoid the risk of a potential claim is to take such action as is reasonable to avoid exacerbating an employee's ill health, as soon as they become aware of any underlying vulnerability an individual may have to stress in the workplace. Possible remedial actions might include allowing the employee to take a sabbatical, redistributing work, extra training and counselling. What is reasonable for the employer to do will depend on factors such as the size of the employer, the resources available and the impact on other employees.

Sutherland v. Hatton remains the leading case in the area of workplace stress, but subsequent decisions have taken a slightly different stance in relation to some of the guidance set out in that judgment.

Mental health

Provision of counselling services

In the case of *Intel Corporation (UK) Ltd v. Daw* (2007) the Court of Appeal held that an employee's email to her manager stating that she was 'stressed out' and 'demoralised' and including two references to previous episodes of post-natal depression, was crucial to the issue of reasonable foreseeability. In the circumstances, urgent action should have been taken to reduce the employee's workload. The Court expressly rejected Intel Corporation's submission (following the guidelines in *Sutherland v. Hatton*) that its provision of a counselling and medical assistance service was sufficient to discharge its duty of care. The provision of such services and whether the employer has fulfilled its duty will depend on the facts of the case, and it is for the judge to decide in any particular case which parts of the *Sutherland v. Hatton* guidance are relevant.

This was confirmed by the Court of Appeal in *Dickens v. O2 PLC* (2008), in which the Court held that reference to the employer's counselling service was insufficient in the circumstances of the case. Having explained to her employer the difficulties she was experiencing and the severe effect on her health, the Court was satisfied that management intervention was required and the employee should have been sent home and referred to the employer's occupational health department.

Relevance of the Working Time Regulations

The claimant in *Hone v. Six Continents Retail Ltd* (2006), a pub landlord, claimed that he consistently worked around 90 hours per week despite not opting out of the maximum 48 hour working week under the Working Time Regulations. He successfully used his employer's breach of the Regulations as part of his argument that his psychiatric injury had been reasonably foreseeable.

However, the High Court in *Sayers v. Cambridgeshire County Council* (2006) made it clear that the fact that an employee is working in excess of the 48 hour per week limit will not in itself render any resulting injury reasonably foreseeable.

Intrinsically stressful jobs

One of the conjoined cases in *Hartman v. South Essex Mental Health and Community Care NHS Trust and other cases* (2005) considered by the Court of Appeal was *Melville v. Home Office*. The employee in this case was a prison officer whose duties included the recovery of bodies of prisoners who had committed suicide. After helping to cut down a body and attempting revival in May 1998, Mr Melville developed a stress-related illness and eventually retired in 1999 on ill health grounds.

Before the Court of Appeal, the Home Office argued that since it knew of no particular vulnerability of Mr Melville it was entitled to assume that he was up to the normal pressures of the job. The Home Office was not successful in this argument and the Court of Appeal held that it was foreseeable that such an injury may have occurred to employees exposed to traumatic incidents. Home Office documents noted that persons whose duties involved dealing with suicides might sustain injuries to their health, and procedures were put in place in relation to post-incident care, which had not been properly implemented.

Discriminatory harassment

Discrimination legislation outlaws harassment on the grounds of sex, race, disability, sexual orientation, religion or belief and age. The legislation provides

Mental health

that an employer will be liable for workplace harassment on one of the above grounds, carried out by his employees, unless he has taken reasonable steps to prevent this from occurring. Reasonable steps might include, for example, implementing an equal opportunities and anti-bullying policy and training managers in dealing with complaints of bullying and harassment.

In the case of *Essa v. Laing Ltd* (2004) the Court of Appeal confirmed that personal injury, which includes psychiatric injury, arising from acts of discrimination does not need to be reasonably foreseeable in order for employees to recover damages. The employee only needs to prove that the discrimination caused the injury to occur.

Protection from harassment

The House of Lords confirmed in the case of *Majrowski v. Guy's and St Thomas' NHS Trust* (2006) that employers can be held liable for workplace bullying under the Protection from Harassment Act 1997 (PHA). For this to apply, claimants only need to show they have suffered anxiety or distress as a result of the harassment, rather than a recognisable psychiatric injury in order to bring a negligence claim. It is necessary for claimants to establish a 'course of conduct,' in contrast to a one-off incident of harassment, which can be sufficient to bring a claim under discrimination legislation.

In a subsequent case, *Green v. DB Group Services Limited* (2006), the High Court upheld another claim for workplace bullying under the PHA 1997, but made no separate award of damages, since it had taken into account the anxiety caused by the harassment in assessing the amount of compensation awarded in respect of the employer's negligence (a figure of over £800,000).

More recently, in *Sunderland City Council v. Conn* (2007), the Court of Appeal overturned a County Court decision that a manager's conduct towards an employee amounted to harassment under the PHA 1997. There were only two alleged incidents, the first of which did not 'cross the boundary from the regrettable to the unacceptable' and was not sufficiently serious to be regarded as criminal. There had therefore been no 'course of conduct' necessary to establish a claim under the Act.

Unfair dismissal

Ill health is a potentially fair reason for dismissing an employee, as it relates to their capability to do a job.

In the case of *McAdie v. Royal Bank of Scotland plc* (2007) the employee's stress-related illness was attributed to the conduct of the employer. However, the Court of Appeal agreed with the EAT that the employer could still fairly dismiss the employee for ill health capability in these circumstances. Medical evidence demonstrated that the employee had no prospect of recovery from the illness and she had expressly stated that she would never return to work. There was no real alternative to dismissal.

However, the Court of Appeal accepted that the cause of the employee's incapacity was a relevant factor to take into account and approved of the Employment Appeal Tribunal's suggestion that employers should 'go the extra mile' in finding alternative employment for an employee who is incapacitated by the employer's own conduct, or they should put up with a longer period of absence than they would do in normal circumstances.

Disability discrimination

If an employer is considering dismissing an employee who is suffering from a

Mental health

mental illness they must consider whether the illness may constitute a disability under the Disability Discrimination Act 1995 (DDA). The DDA protects those with physical or mental impairments, provided that impairment satisfies the test for a disability under the Act. Stress itself is not an illness, but a stress-related condition could be an impairment within the meaning of the Act. Since 2005, there is no longer any requirement for a mental impairment to be 'clinically well-recognised' in order to be protected under the DDA, which has made it potentially easier for a claimant to establish that they have a disability.

Employers are under a duty to make reasonable adjustments where any arrangements made by the employer place a disabled person at a substantial disadvantage compared to non-disabled employees. Where an employee is suffering from a mental impairment, reasonable adjustments might include a phased return to work after sickness absence, a reallocation of duties, reduced working hours, mentoring or counselling.

Disabled employees are not generally entitled to additional sick pay, unless the employer has caused sickness absence to be prolonged as a result of its failure to make reasonable adjustments. This was the case in *Nottinghamshire County Council v. Meikle* (2004), which was not a case dealing with an employee's mental health but could be applied equally to those with stress-related illness whose employer does not take the necessary steps to enable the individual to return to work.

If an employer dismisses an employee for a reason related to their disability they may be guilty of disability discrimination unless they are able to show that the dismissal was justified. A medical report should be obtained in order to establish the employee's likely prognosis and the effectiveness of any potential adjustments before any decision is taken to terminate an individual's employment.

Pre-employment checks

In view of the potential liabilities faced by employers in relation to employees suffering from mental health problems, it might appear prudent to carry out pre-employment checks to establish whether an individual has any pre-disposition to such impairments. This should be done with caution, since a refusal to employ individuals with previous mental health issues is likely to result in successful claims for disability discrimination.

However, pre-employment questionnaires can assist employers in discovering whether further medical investigations are required in order to establish whether an individual is capable of undertaking the role or will require any reasonable adjustments in order to do so. Provided it is carefully drafted, a questionnaire may alert the employer to whether the individual has, for example, any particular vulnerability in relation to workplace stress.

In *Cheltenham Borough Council v. Laird* (2009), the former managing director of the Council had been granted ill health retirement following a depressive illness. The Council subsequently brought proceedings for negligent and fraudulent misrepresentation against Mrs Laird, on the grounds that she had not disclosed her previous episodes of stress-related depression on her pre-employment medical questionnaire. The High Court rejected the Council's claims, on the basis that the answers provided by Mrs Laird had not been false or misleading. The questionnaire was poorly drafted

Mental health

and the wording did not expressly require Mrs Laird to disclose information about her previous history of stress and depression.

Conclusion
To protect themselves against HSE enforcement action and potential claims by employees, employers should consider the following practical steps:

- Organise and conduct suitable risk assessments of potential stressors.
- Make counselling facilities available to employees.
- Show a receptive and flexible response to complaints.
- Comply with the HSE Management Standards / Guidance.
- Consider pre-employment health checks.
- Provide a written health and safety policy to employees, which includes a section on how to deal with stress.
- Put a bullying and harassment policy in place and ensure employees are aware of their obligations under the policy.
- Provide training to managers in dealing appropriately with employees suffering from stress and mental health issues, including the requirement to consider reasonable adjustments.
- Ensure sickness absence procedures take into account potential disabilities arising from mental impairments.
- Obtain an up-to-date and detailed medical report before considering dismissing an employee with a mental impairment.

See also: Bullying and harassment, p.49; Discrimination, p.110; Medical records, p.257; Occupational health, p.304; Stress, p.381; Working time, p.423.

Sources of further information

HSE (work-related stress): www.hse.gov.uk/stress

MIND: www.mind.org.uk

Mental health foundation: www.mentalhealth.org.uk

The Shaw Trust: www.tacklementalhealth.org.uk

Sainsbury Centre for Mental Health: www.scmh.org.uk

Migrant workers

David Browne, Martineau Solicitors

Key points
- Under the Asylum and Immigration Act 1996, it has been an offence since January 1997 for employers to employ any person who is not entitled to work in the UK.
- There is a distinction between the rights to work in the UK of individuals of Member States of the European Economic Area (EEA) (and Switzerland), the new 'A8' EU Member States (Czech Republic, Estonia, Hungary, Latvia, Lithuania, Poland, Slovakia, Slovenia) and countries outside the EEA.
- Employers must be conscious of the Race Relations Act 1976 in considering employing migrant workers to ensure they do not discriminate against them.
- The Government has introduced an 'Australian style' points-based system, which consolidates more than 80 existing work and study routes into the UK into a five tier system. The first tier, for Highly Skilled Migrant Workers, was introduced in June 2008. Tiers 2 and 5 were implemented in November 2008, and Tier 4 in March 2009. At this time Tier 3 has been suspended indefinitely, largely due to the fact that these jobs are currently filled by EEA nationals.
- The new law on the prevention of illegal migrant working is set out in the Immigration, Asylum and Nationality Act 2006, which came into force on 29 February 2008.

Legislation
- Race Relations Act 1976.
- Asylum and Immigration Act 1996.
- Nationality, Immigration and Asylum Act 2002.
- Immigration (Restrictions on Employment) Order 2004.
- Immigration, Asylum and Nationality Act 2006.
- Immigration (European Economic Area) Regulations 2006.

The law
Sections 15-25 of the Immigration, Asylum and Nationality Act 2006 (the 'Act') detail the law preventing illegal migrant working. In particular, employers must be aware of the following:

- Employing someone who has no right to work in the UK (or to do the work an employer is offering) is a criminal offence.
- Employers have a statutory defence for employing an illegal worker by checking and copying certain original documentation belonging to the employee. What documents are required depends on the individual circumstances of each worker. Guidance for this is available on the Home Office website.
- Employers are obliged to ensure that recruitment practices do not discriminate against individuals on racial grounds.

Under Section 15 of the Act, employers found to be employing migrant workers illegally will be subject to a fine, payable for each person found to have been employed illegally. There is a sliding scale of penalties, principally determined by the number of times an employer has been found to be employing illegal migrants.

Migrant workers

> **Facts**
>
> - In the 12 months to October-December 2008, employment of UK-born workers fell by 278,000 to 25.6 million. In the same period, employment of non-UK-born workers rose by 214,000 to 3.8 million.
> - Analysis by nationality shows a fall in employment of UK nationals by 234,000 to 27.0 million; employment of non-UK nationals rose by 175,000 to 2.4 million.
> - In the first 80 days of the new migrant workers regime, 137 businesses were issued with notices of potential liability worth almost half a million pounds in fines – contrasted with only 11 successful (criminal) prosecutions in 2008.

The Border and Immigration Agency has published a Code of Practice on these civil penalties, and this can be found at www.ukba.homeoffice.gov.uk.

Under Section 21 of the Act there is a specific offence of knowingly employing an illegal migrant worker, which carries a maximum penalty of a two-year custodial sentence and an unlimited fine.

Nationals of the EEA

Article 39 of the Treaty of Rome introduced the principle of free movement of labour and this now applies to all members of the EEA (and Switzerland). Under the legislation, the family of an EEA worker may also move to the UK without restrictions on their right of entry. In particular, EEA nationals are entitled to the same treatment as UK nationals on:

- pay;
- working conditions;
- housing;
- training;
- social security; and
- trade union representation.

Furthermore, under the Immigration (European Economic Area) Regulations 2006, EEA Nationals (together with their Swiss counterparts) may reside in the UK for an initial period of three months, provided they have a valid passport or identity card. Once this period has expired the individual may continue to reside in the UK, provided they continue to be a 'qualified person', namely:

- a job seeker;
- a worker;
- a self-employed person;
- a self-sufficient person; or
- a student.

If an EEA / Swiss National has worked and resided in this country for more than five years they will acquire a permanent right of residence.

'A8' Nationals

Workers from these new Member States must register with the Home Office under the 'Worker Registration Scheme' as soon as they find work. They are not, however, subject to worker registration if they are self employed or provide services in the UK on behalf of an employer who is not established in the UK. Romanian and Bulgarian Nationals require authorisation from the Home Office *before* commencing employment in the UK.

Employers may continue to employ an unregistered worker whilst their application is processed, provided copies of their registration application are retained for

Migrant workers

the duration of the application process. If, however, an unregistered A8 worker is employed after one month and a copy of the Home Office application form has not been retained by the employer (or a certificate of registration has not been received), an employer may commit a criminal offence, facing a maximum penalty on conviction of £5,000. Employing a worker whose application has been refused may also constitute a criminal offence.

The law determining whether a worker is an employee or self employed is complex and outside the scope of this chapter (see 'Self-employment', p.357 and 'Employment status', p.154). Guidance on A8 nationals is available at the Border and Immigration Agency website.

Non-EEA Nationals

Non-EEA Nationals who are subject to immigration control must obtain work permits prior to taking up employment in the UK. There are, however, certain persons who do not require permits, including business visitors, Gibraltarians, Commonwealth citizens given leave to reside in the UK because at least one of their grandparents was born in the UK, and persons wishing to engage in certain specified occupations, for example ministers of religion.

A points-based system for immigration

The Act introduces a new points based system whereby more than 80 pre-existing work and study routes into the UK are combined into five tiers. Each tier has different points requirements and applicants need to score enough points to gain entry clearance or leave to remain in the UK. The Home Office defines these immigration routes as follows:

- *Tier 1 – designed to bring into the UK those migrants with 'the very highest skills'.* They do not need a job offer and will have unrestricted access to the labour market. A migrant who enters under Tier 1 will not need a sponsor under the new system.
- *Tier 2 – for those skilled workers who have received a job offer from a UK employer.* Their attractiveness to the UK is demonstrated by the fact that a UK employer wants to take them on.
- *Tier 3 – for low-skilled migration.* The expectation is that low-skilled migration from outside the EU will be phased out following the enlargement of the EU. The only low-skilled routes that remain will be quota-based, operator-led, time-limited, subject to review, and only from countries that have effective return arrangements. Any new routes will be based on identifications of temporary shortages by the Skills Advisory Body.
- *Tier 4 – for students.* There will be more objectivity and transparency to the decision-making process and a greater role for sponsors in vouching for the students they want the Home Office to allow into the UK.
- *Tier 5 – for youth mobility and temporary workers.* People coming to the UK under this tier are principally here to satisfy non-economic objectives. Youth mobility schemes can play an important role in promoting the UK abroad, as Nationals return home and encourage further trade and tourism.

Tiers 3 and 5 are temporary routes, and migrant workers in these tiers are not able to switch out of them once they are in the UK.

Under this system it is now the responsibility of the employee to lodge and complete the application. Consequently, employers with experience of the requirements of immigration applications will be limited as to the influence they can

Migrant workers

exercise. That said, for all tiers except Tier 1, the most important part of the points based system application for entry clearance or leave to remain is the part over which the applicant has least control, the certificate of sponsorship, or certificate of acceptance of studies. The certificate is issued by an applicant's sponsor, who must first secure a sponsor's licence covering the particular points based system category.

It remains unclear as to whether the Border and Immigration Agency (which operates in the same time zone as the employer) will become obsolete, to be replaced by an entry clearance officer who could potentially be on a 12-hour time difference to them.

Migrant workers and race discrimination

Whilst employers should be aware of the potential pitfalls in employing illegal immigrants, they must not discriminate against migrant workers when seeking to avoid conviction under Section 8. Under the Race Relations Act 1976, it is unlawful for an employer to discriminate on grounds of race, colour, ethnic or national origin or nationality.

The Home Office advises that the best way for employers to ensure they do not discriminate in considering migrant workers is to treat all applicants the same at each stage of the recruitment process. Particularly, employers should not ask people who look or sound foreign for their passports in the first instance if, in other circumstances, they would ask people who look and sound British for a document that includes their National Insurance number.

Similarly, if employers only carry out checks on potential employees who by their appearance or accent seem to be other than British this may also constitute unlawful racial discrimination. Employers are advised to remember that the population of the UK is ethnically diverse and that most people in the UK from ethnic minorities are British citizens. Moreover, most non-British citizens from ethnic minorities are entitled to work in the UK.

Note: The new system for immigration is not completely finalised and the above is accurate at the time of writing (September 2009). For more on this subject, see 'Foreign nationals,' p.194.

> *See also*: Discrimination, p.110; Dress codes, p.129; Employment status, p.154; Foreign nationals, p.194; Human rights, p.226; Self employment, p.357.

Sources of further information

Detailed explanation of the new points based system and the various tiers is available at the Border and Immigration Agency: www.ukba.homeoffice.gov.uk

Minimum wage

Pinsent Masons Employment Group

Key points
- The National Minimum Wage Act 1998 came into force on 1 April 1999. It provides for a single national minimum wage with no variations by region, occupation or size of company. It covers all relevant workers employed under a contract of employment or any other contract.
- The detailed rules of the national minimum wage (NMW) are contained in the National Minimum Wage Regulations 1999. These are updated annually with new minimum rates.
- All relevant workers must be paid the minimum hourly wage averaged across a 'relevant pay period'. The hourly rate was increased for workers aged 22 and over to £5.80 from October 2009.
- Rules exist to say what is relevant pay, and how relevant hours are calculated for different types of workers.
- The NMW applies to gross earnings and is calculated before tax, National Insurance contributions and any other deductions.
- Employers must keep records.
- Employment Tribunals and HM Revenue and Customs inspectors can enforce the duties of employers.
- Not all workers qualify for the NMW. For example, workers attending work experience as part of a course of higher education are excluded.

Legislation
- National Minimum Wage Act 1998.
- National Minimum Wage Regulations 1999.
- Employment Act 2008.

Both the Act and the Regulations came into force on 1 April 1999. They introduced the concept of a national minimum wage, together with employers' obligations and the mechanisms by which workers can enforce these obligations.

Hourly rates
The present hourly rate (which has been effective from October 2009) is £5.80 per hour for workers aged 22 and over. The rate is reviewed annually. However:

- From October 2009, there is a minimum rate of £3.57 per hour for those under 18 but above the school minimum leaving age;
- There is no minimum wage for apprentices under the age of 19 and for apprentices between 19 and 25 in the first 12 months of an apprenticeship contract. Apprentices aged 26 or over are entitled to the national minimum wage; and
- The minimum wage for workers between the ages of 18 and 21 inclusive is (from October 2009) £4.83 per hour.

Entitlement to the minimum wage
According to the Act, the term 'worker' has a specific meaning. It is wider than the term 'employee' and covers a contractor carrying out services personally, unless the employer is the client or customer of

Minimum wage

the person involved. Truly self-employed people are not 'workers'.

Whether a worker has been paid the requisite minimum wage is determined by reference to his total pay over a relevant period. It is necessary to determine a worker's average minimum pay over a 'pay reference period'. This period is specified in the Act as one month unless the worker is specifically paid by reference to a shorter period (e.g. weekly or fortnightly).

In basic terms, the calculation to determine if the minimum wage has been paid is the total relevant remuneration divided by hours worked in the pay reference period.

The Regulations contain detailed and complicated rules relating to pay reference periods, as well as how to calculate what remuneration actually counts towards assessing whether a worker is being paid the required amount. Further, only certain time will count in the calculation of hours worked – only 'working time' counts.

For example:

- travelling to and from home is not working time, but travelling for the purposes of duties during work is;
- time spent training at a different location from a worker's normal place of work is working time; and
- deductions from wages due to an advance or overpayment of wages are not subtracted from the total remuneration.

Tips and gratuities
From 1 October 2009, commission, bonuses and tips paid through payroll systems can no longer be included in relevant pay to calculate the hourly pay. Tips, gratuities and service charges can no longer be taken into account when calculating a worker's remuneration.

Benefits in kind such as uniforms, meals and private health insurance do not count. The only benefit in kind that counts is accommodation. Gross pay figures should be used. Also, different types of workers will demand different consideration, particularly where hours vary from week to week. Those types of workers are:

- time workers (paid by reference to the time that a worker works, e.g. hourly paid workers);
- salaried hours (paid an annual salary in instalments for a set number of hours each year);
- output workers (paid according to the productivity of the worker); and
- unmeasured work (no specified hours – all hours worked should be paid for, but the employer and worker can enter into a 'daily average agreement' to clarify the position, although sometimes as with agricultural workers there are specific legal requirements as to what must be included).

Records
Employers are obliged to keep records that are sufficient to show that they have paid their workers the appropriate minimum wage. It is important that employers maintain sufficient records as they may be asked to prove that they are paying the NMW. A worker has the right to inspect these records if he believes he is being paid less than the required amount. An employer must respond to this request within 14 days (or a later date if one has been agreed between the employer and the worker).

Enforcement
If the employer fails to produce the relevant records, the worker is entitled to complain to an Employment Tribunal, which can impose a fine on the employer up to 80 times the relevant hourly national minimum wage.

Minimum wage

The Act implies a right to the NMW into contracts of employment, so a worker who has been underpaid can commence proceedings in an Employment Tribunal to recover the difference between the wages paid and the NMW. It is presumed that the worker has been underpaid unless the employer can prove otherwise.

The Home Secretary can appoint public officers, who have a variety of enforcement powers. These include powers to require employers to produce records to evidence compliance with the NMW, to require any relevant person to furnish them with additional information, and to gain access to premises for the carrying out of these powers.

Inspections and enforcement can be carried out by HM Revenue and Customs inspectors.

The Act also creates a number of criminal offences, based on obligations under the Act. These include:

- refusing to pay the required minimum wage;
- failing to keep records proving that the minimum wage has been paid for three years;
- entering false information into these records;
- obstructing a public officer; and
- refusing to answer questions or provide information to a public officer.

The Employment Act 2008 has introduced a new method of enforcement, effective from 6 April 2009. The previous separate enforcement and penalty notices are replaced by a single notice of underpayment. Notices of underpayment require the employer to pay a financial penalty to the Secretary of State within 28 days of service. The penalty is now set at 50% of the total underpayment of the minimum wage; the minimum penalty is £500 and the maximum is £5,000.

See also: Discrimination, p.110; Employment contracts, p.146; Equal pay, p.167; Expenses, p.177; Ten years of the national minimum wage, p.276; Young persons, p.430.

Sources of further information

Guidance on minimum wage: www.berr.gov.uk/employment/pay/national-minimum-wage/index.html

Low Pay Commission: www.lowpay.gov.uk

National Minimum Wage helpline: 0845 6000 678.

Comment...

Ten years of the National Minimum Wage

Founder of Loch Associates, Pam Loch is a dual qualified lawyer with extensive experience in contentious and non-contentious employment matters, having acted for employers and employees, advising on all aspects of employment law.

The National Minimum Wage was introduced in 1999. Welcomed by the trade unions and greeted with concern by employers, the national minimum wage for workers in the UK has evolved dramatically over the last ten years.

The background

The National Minimum Wage Act 1998 (NMWA) introduced a basic hourly wage rate for different categories of workers. Reviewed on an annual basis since it was introduced, it applies to workers in all sizes of organisations without any exemptions for smaller organisations.

The three categories of workers' rates are:

1. *Standard (adult) rate*: workers aged 22 or over (there is no upper age limit).
2. *Development rate*: workers aged between 18 and 21 inclusive. Prior to 1 October 2006 this also applied to certain workers aged 22 or over.
3. *Young workers rate*: workers aged under 18 but above the compulsory school age who are not apprentices.

Since the NMW came into force, the Employment Equality (Age) Regulations 2006 have been introduced. In their current form the categories would have been discriminatory and therefore an exemption was introduced to ensure the use of the bandings could remain in place.

The changing face of who is covered by the NMWA

The NMWA applies to workers working in the UK who are over school leaving age. A worker is an individual who works under:

- a contract of employment; or
- a contract (which may be express, implied, oral or in writing) to personally do or perform work or services for another, provided that the other is not a customer or client of a profession or business undertaking carried on by the individual.

Special rules apply to who is regarded as a worker for the purposes of the NMWA and over the years changes in legislation and case law have established that the following benefit from the NMWA applying to them.

Agency workers and agricultural workers (who are entitled to a higher rate set by the Agricultural Wages Board).

Comment: Ten years of the National Minimum Wage

Apprentices – Those aged 16 to 18 years old and those over 19 years working in the first 12 months of the apprenticeship are excluded. The Apprenticeship Bill 2008/09 is likely to change the situation with the introduction of an apprenticeship agreement, which would be treated as a contract of employment. Apprentices would then become entitled to the NMW from outset.

Directors – Non-executive directors are not entitled to NMW, but directors who are also employees are, and HMRC has been monitoring the situation over the years as concerns have grown that directors have not been paying themselves the NMW. With revenue recovery even more important when unemployment increases, HMRC are likely to target Directors who are not paying NMW to enforce payment.

Family and homeworkers – Those who live in their family home or their employer's family home and are treated as a member of the family with no deductions for food or accommodation are not entitled to the NMW.

Overseas workers – NMWA 1998 applies to all workers working in the UK while they work in the UK, however short the period spent in the UK and irrespective of the fact the employer may be based overseas. Workers who usually work in the UK but are temporarily working overseas still qualify for the NMW while they are abroad.

Piece workers – All workers who are paid on the basis of what they produce must be paid NMW as a minimum.

Trainees – Before 2006, workers aged 22 or over who had agreed in writing to participate in an accredited training scheme were entitled to the NMW for the first six months of employment. This was abolished on 1 October 2006.

Voluntary workers – Those employed by charities and voluntary organisations are not entitled to the NMW if the workers:

- receive no remuneration and are not entitled to any remuneration;
- receive only reasonable expenses or benefits in the form of accommodation or subsistence; or
- are placed by a charity or similar organisation with another similar organisation and receive only money for subsistence.

Following a review of voluntary workers and the NMWA, changes were brought into force. Since January 2009, when Section 14 of the Employment Act 2008 became effective, the types of expenses that can be paid to voluntary workers without triggering the entitlement to the NMW now includes reasonable expenses (including accommodation expenses) incurred in order to enable voluntary workers to perform their duties.

The same review concluded that Cadet Force Adult Volunteers should be exempt from entitlement to the NMW. Since January 2009, when Section 13 of the Employment Act 2008 came into force, Cadet Force Adult Volunteers have been explicitly excluded from qualifying for NMW.

Young workers – Workers under the compulsory school age of 16 years are exempt from NMW.

What's the NMW rate?
The banding approach has remained in place since 1999, but what has changed is the approach to what employers can include to calculate the NMW payment. Since the NMWA has come into force,

Comment: Ten years of the National Minimum Wage

some employers have relied on various mechanisms to avoid paying the full NMW from their own funds.

What has become a popular practice is the use of tips left by clients or customers to top up wages to ensure they are least the NMW rate. These practices have been challenged over the years most recently in the Court of Appeal decision in *Annabel's (Berkeley Square), George (Mount Street) and Harry's Bar Limited v. HMRC* in 2009. The Government has been consulting on this as well and has reached the conclusion that, with effect from 1 October 2009, the law will change so that tips, gratuities and service charges can no longer be taken into account when deciding if a worker has received the NMW.

Other payments or benefits have also been deemed to be excluded for the purpose of calculating NMW. Examples of these include meals, fuel, employer's pension contributions, medical insurance and the value of any accommodation in excess of the value given to the benefit, redundancy payments and any premium paid for overtime or shift work.

Certain deductions are permitted and continue to be permitted. Taxes and national insurance are excluded as are payments made in relation to share option or saving schemes.

Enforcing times

Concerns have been growing over the years about the enforcement of the NMWA. The Government has taken steps to increase the HMRC's enforcement rights and from 6 April 2009 employers can receive an automatic penalty if HMRC find National Minimum Wage (NMW) arrears.

Concerned about the failure to pay NMW, employers who are caught face penalties ranging from £100 to £5,000 in addition to the arrears of pay owed to their workers. Employers who settle within 14 days of notification of enforcement, will receive a 50% discount of the penalty for prompt payment. A serious offence could lead to a criminal sentence or an unlimited fine.

Investigating officers have also been given increased powers, including powers to remove the NMW records from an employer's premises. They are also now able to remove complete records rather than having to determine which part relates to NMW.

No standing still

There is no doubt the NMWA has changed its face over the last ten years and will continue to evolve. With the Government again focusing on how to protect vulnerable workers in this millennium, enforcing the NMWA is likely to be a key tool in 2009 achieving their objective.

Money laundering

Anna Odby, Peters and Peters

Key points

- The UK has been identified as one of the major money laundering countries by the US Department of State's Bureau of International Narcotics and Law Enforcement Affairs in its latest International Narcotics Control Strategy Report, released in March 2009. The Home Office has estimated that the total revenue generated by UK organised crime is in the region of £15bn per year. Similarly, the updated National Security Strategy for the UK issued by the Cabinet Office on 25 June 2009 warned that the threat to the UK and the UK's interests overseas from international terrorism remains severe.
- The Serious Organised Crime Agency (SOCA) in its threat assessment for 2009/10 warned that businesses with a high cash turnover and those involved in overseas trading are particularly attractive to criminals, and noted that a significant amount of criminal proceeds generated in the UK is laundered abroad. The United Arab Emirates, the Far East and South East Asia (Hong Kong, Singapore and Shanghai) were particularly popular destinations for the proceeds of crime.
- Between October 2007 and September 2008, SOCA received a total of 210,524 suspicious activity reports (SARs). This figure included 13,223 requests for consent to proceed with a proposed transaction, 58% of which were dealt with within two days. Also included were 956 SARs related to terrorist financing, which were disseminated to the National Terrorist Financing Investigation Unit.
- In October 2008 the Financial Services Authority, for the first time, fined the Money Laundering Reporting Officer (MLRO) of a regulated financial services company in connection with the company's systemic due diligence failings.
- Over £500m has been recovered since the Proceeds of Crime Act 2002 came into force, with a five-fold increase in the value of assets recovered between 2003 and 2007. On 1 April 2008 the Assets Recovery Agency (ARA) merged into the Serious Organised Crime Agency (SOCA). Since the merger, SOCA has recovered over £175m by means of cash seizures and forfeitures, restraint and confiscation orders and civil recovery. Civil asset recovery powers previously only exercised by the ARA have now been extended by the Serious Crown Act 2007 to Revenue and Customs Prosecution Office, the Crown Prosecution Service, the Serious Fraud Office and the Public Prosecution Service for Northern Ireland.

Legislation

- Terrorism Act 2000.
- Proceeds of Crime Act 2002.
- Serious Organised Crime and Police Act 2005.
- Money Laundering Regulations 2007.
- Proceeds of Crime Act 2002 (Amendment) Regulations 2007.
- Proceeds of Crime Act 2002 (Business in the Regulated Sector and Supervisory Authorities) Order 2007.
- Counter Terrorism Act 2008.

Money laundering

Introduction
It remains necessary to exercise caution when consulting the provisions governing your obligations in this area. The regime set up to prevent money laundering and terrorist financing in the UK changes at regular intervals, reflecting corresponding amendments to the relevant international standards developed by the EU and the Financial Action Task Force (FATF).

It is now also necessary to take into account the interaction of efforts to prevent money laundering and terrorist financing with recent efforts to prevent breaches of financial sanctions administered by HM Treasury and its Asset Freezing Unit.

The Proceeds of Crime Act 2002
Whereas the main money laundering offences have remained the same since Part 7 of the Proceeds of Crime Act 2002 (POCA) came into force on 24 February 2003, the available defences have been altered on several occasions. The most recent amendments were introduced on 26 December 2007, by the Terrorism Act 2000 and Proceeds of Crime Act 2002 (Amendment) Regulations 2007.

POCA consolidated and strengthened the previously fragmented UK anti-money laundering regime, and introduced three primary money laundering offences. A money laundering offence punishable by up to 14 years' imprisonment may be committed by dealing with the known or suspected proceeds of any criminal conduct ('criminal property'), however small the amount and in whatever form, in one of the following ways:

1. Concealing, disguising, converting, transferring or removing the criminal property (Section 327 POCA).
2. Entering into, or becoming concerned with, an arrangement known or suspected to facilitate the acquisition, retention, use or control of the criminal property (Section 328 POCA).
3. Acquiring, using or possessing the criminal property, other than in return for adequate consideration (Section 329 POCA).

The Court of Appeal has, however, clarified that no money laundering offence will be committed by any act undertaken by legal advisers in the ordinary course of legal proceedings, notwithstanding any suspicion that may have arisen on the basis of information derived from the conduct of the proceedings. This was the interpretation adopted by the Court of Appeal in its judgment on 8 March 2005 in *Bowman v. Fels* (2005).

Two further exceptions have subsequently been added by the Serious Organised Crime and Police Act 2005. As from 1 July 2005, there is a limited defence available to deposit-taking bodies in respect of any act undertaken in operating an account maintained with it, where the value of the criminal property in question is less than £250 or such higher threshold amount as is specified by an officer of HM Revenue and Customs or by a constable in the course of giving or refusing consent to proceed with an act (Sections 327(2c), 328(5) and 329(2c) and 339a POCA).

The second exception applies as from 15 May 2006, in respect of the proceeds of any conduct committed abroad. These proceeds are not to be considered 'criminal property' if the conduct in question is known, or is believed on reasonable grounds, to be lawful in the place where it occurred; unless it has been specifically excluded by Order of the Secretary of State. To date, the excluded offences are any offences punishable in the UK (had they occurred in the UK) by imprisonment for over 12 months, other

Money laundering

than offences under the Gaming Act 1968, the Lotteries and Amusements Act 1976 or Sections 23 or 25 of the Financial Services and Markets Act 2000.

A further, more general, defence to one of the three money laundering offences may be obtained by disclosing the relevant knowledge or suspicion, and the information on which it is based, to the MLRO in accordance with an organisation's internal compliance systems or, in other cases, directly to SOCA (which on 1 April 2006 took over the function of receiving disclosures from the National Criminal Intelligence Service) and requesting consent to proceed with an act that would otherwise amount to money laundering (Section 335 POCA).

The disclosure, known as a 'SAR,' can be made either before or, where necessary, during, the act in question. In exceptional circumstances the SAR can even be postponed until after the act has occurred, provided that it is made voluntarily as soon as reasonably practicable thereafter. If SOCA does not respond to a request within seven working days, consent can be presumed. If SOCA refuses permission to proceed, a 'moratorium' period of 31 working days (from the date of receipt of the refusal) is imposed, during which time no action can be taken in relation to the criminal property.

In the absence of consent to proceed, the only remaining defence in circumstances where none of the exceptions apply is a 'reasonable excuse'. There is as of yet no guidance from the courts on what may amount to such an excuse, although specific examples have been suggested in industry-specific guidance.

Failure to disclose

A criminal offence punishable by up to five years' imprisonment will be committed by failing to make a SAR as soon as is practicable when one is required (Section 333 POCA). The obligation to disclose arises wherever information acquired as a result of carrying on a business in the 'regulated sector' gives rise to knowledge or suspicion, or reasonable grounds for such knowledge or suspicion, that another is engaged in money laundering. A separate failure to disclose offence will be committed by an MLRO who fails to pass on to SOCA any SAR received when required to do so (S.331 and 332 POCA).

'Suspicion' for the purposes of POCA has been widely interpreted by the courts and will be found to exist where someone thinks that there is a possibility, which is more than fanciful, that another person is, or has been, engaged in or has benefited from a crime (*R v. Da Silva* (2006)). There must be some possible facts on which a suspicion can be based, but whether such possible facts are sufficient to ground suspicion is irrelevant as long as the suspicion is genuinely held and there is no bad faith (*Shah and Anor v. HSBC Private Bank (UK) Ltd* (2009)).

The activities considered to amount to 'business in the regulated sector' have gradually been expanded since POCA first came into force, and are currently set out in the Proceeds of Crime Act 2002 (Business in the Regulated Sector and Supervisory Authorities) Order 2007. They include acts undertaken in the course of business by:

- credit and financial institutions;
- auditors, insolvency practitioners, external accountants and tax advisers;
- legal professionals and notaries, when participating in financial or real property transactions;
- trust or company service providers;
- estate agents;
- high value dealers, when receiving total cash payments in excess of €15,000; and
- casinos.

Money laundering

As of 1 July 2005 the information in question will only need to be disclosed, however, if it includes either the identity of the money launderer or the location of the laundered property; unless it is reasonable to expect that it will assist in revealing the same (Section 330(3a) POCA). Nor does an obligation to disclose arise if the activity in question would not amount to a money laundering offence due to the exception for overseas conduct discussed above (Section 330(7a)).

The disclosure obligation has caused some concern in its application to legal professionals and other relevant professional advisers, who may owe duties of confidentiality to their clients. For this reason SOCA has undertaken to preserve the confidentiality of reports as far as possible, and concerns about breaches of confidentiality by both the person making the disclosure and the end user of the disclosure can be reported to SOCA's SAR Confidentiality Hotline on 0800 234 6657. In its latest report on the SAR regime, SOCA revealed that only two such breaches were found during the period October 2007 – September 2008.

Whereas confidential information may often be required to be disclosed, information protected by legal professional privilege is expressly excluded from the disclosure obligation (Section 330(6)(b) POCA). The protection applies to any information passing between an independent legal professional and their clients for the purpose of seeking or providing legal advice ('advice privilege'), as well as to the wider category of information passing between legal advisers and third parties in connection with legal proceedings ('litigation privilege').

As of 21 February 2006 the privilege exception extends also to other 'relevant professional advisers' (appropriately regulated accountants, auditors or tax advisers) and persons employed by, or in partnership with, legal advisers or other relevant professional advisers to provide that adviser with assistance or support. Nor is an MLRO obliged to pass on to SOCA any privileged information he receives through an organisation's internal reporting system. By contrast, a constable or an officer of HM Revenue and Customs must forward to SOCA as soon as practicable any disclosures made to them, in full, regardless of whether such disclosures contain privileged information (new Section 339Za POCA).

A general, as yet untested, defence of a 'reasonable excuse' for failing to report is available (Section 330(6)(a) POCA). A further, more limited, defence applies to employees who have not received appropriate anti-money laundering training from their employer; such persons will only be liable if they fail to disclose in circumstances when they actually knew or suspected money laundering, as opposed to when there are merely reasonable grounds for such knowledge or suspicion (Section 330(7) POCA).

These 'required' disclosures make up the majority of the SARs received by SOCA. Although a failure to use any prescribed form for disclosures to be punishable by a criminal fine (Section 339 POCA), subject to a defence of reasonable excuse (Section 339(1b) POCA), the Home Office has decided against prescribing any form for the time being. In the meantime, SOCA encourages electronic disclosure.

Tipping off

Until 26 December 2007 it was an offence to inform anyone of the fact that a SAR had been made, or that an investigation was likely to be conducted as a result of a SAR, if doing so was known or suspected to prejudice any investigation (old

Money laundering

Section 333 POCA, now repealed and replaced by new Section 333a POCA). This was the old offence of 'tipping off,' punishable by up to five years' imprisonment. Still in force is the similar but separate offence under Section 342 POCA of prejudicing an investigation, committed by informing anyone that a money laundering investigation is about to be commenced or underway, to the prejudice of that investigation.

The restrictions on 'tipping off' caused problems in practice, as regulated persons and institutions found it difficult to provide their customers and clients with a credible reason for any delay in executing their instructions. In effect, a customer or client could not be told that a transaction was being delayed because of the need to await consent, or that consent to transact had been denied.

These concerns have gradually been alleviated by the courts' confirmation that delay in performing a client's or customer's instructions, caused by the making of a SAR, will not expose the maker of the SAR to any risk of legal action for breach of contract in circumstances where it would be a criminal offence to honour a customer's mandate (see *K Ltd v. National Westminster Bank Plc* (2006)).

The courts have also confirmed that SOCA is obliged to reconsider any refusal of consent to proceed with a transaction, not only at the insistence of the requesting party but also of the affected customer or client (see *R (on the application of UMBS Online Ltd) v. Serious Organised Crime Agency & HM Revenue and Customs* (2007)).

Concern has further been alleviated by the new 'tipping off' offence, which only applies where knowledge of a SAR or a money laundering investigation has been acquired in the course of a business in the regulated sector (Section 333a POCA). A range of exemptions have also been introduced (Section 333b POCA), to permit discussions about SARs or money laundering investigations in the following circumstances:

- Disclosures as between employees, officers or partners who are members of the same undertaking or group.
- Disclosures by credit or financial institutions to credit or financial institutions belonging to the same group situated in an EEA State, or a non-EEA State subject to equivalent anti-money laundering obligations.
- Disclosures by professional legal advisers or relevant professional advisers to professional legal advisers or relevant professional advisers who perform their professional activities within different undertakings that share common ownership, management or control in an EEA State or a non-EEA State, subject to equivalent anti-money laundering obligations.
- Disclosures as between credit institutions, financial institutions, professional legal advisers and relevant legal advisers and their counterparties of the same kind, which relate to common clients, transactions or services, if the disclosure is made exclusively for the purpose of preventing an offence under Part 7 POCA (i.e. a money laundering, failure to report or 'tipping off' offence) and if both institutions or advisers in question are situated in an EEA State or a non-EEA State, subject to equivalent anti-money laundering obligations and equivalent duties of professional confidentiality and the protection of personal data, if situated in an EEA State or a non-EEA State, subject to equivalent anti-money laundering obligations.
- Disclosures to the relevant supervisory authorities for the purpose

Money laundering

of the detection, investigation or prosecution of a criminal offence, a POCA money laundering investigation or the enforcement of a court order relating to POCA.

For the purpose of applying these provisions, as well as the risk-based elements of the Money Laundering Regulations 2007 (set out below), in May 2008 HM Treasury published a 'statement on equivalence' based on a common understanding on third country equivalence agreed by the EU Member States a month previously.

As noted in a July 2009 report by the House of Lords European Union Committee on money laundering and the financing of terrorism, none of the UK overseas territories appear on this list. Furthermore, the statement is issued for guidance only and reliance on it will not provide a defence.

There is a further defence available to professional legal advisers or relevant professional advisers who discuss actual or proposed SARs with their clients for the purpose of dissuading the client from engaging in conduct amounting to an offence (Section 333D(2) POCA). This defence is much narrower than that previously available to the now repealed Section 330 POCA tipping off offence, which permitted professional legal advisers or relevant professional advisers to 'tip off' their clients in privileged circumstances.

Finally, the punishment for breaching the prohibition on tipping off has been reduced from a maximum of five to two years' imprisonment. The maximum punishment for the separate offence of prejudicing an investigation remains five years' imprisonment.

The Terrorism Act 2000

A terrorist financing offence punishable by up to 14 years' imprisonment may be committed by dealing with property likely to be used for the purposes of terrorism, property representing the proceeds of terrorism, or the proceeds of other acts carried out for the purposes of terrorism ('terrorist property') in one of the three following ways (Sections 15-17 TA):

1. Receipt or provision of, or inviting another to provide, property which is intended to be used for the purposes of terrorism or in respect of which reasonable cause exists to suspect that it may be used for the purposes of terrorism.
2. Use or possession of property intended for the purposes of terrorism or in respect of which reasonable cause exists to suspect that it may be used for the purposes of terrorism.
3. Entering into or becoming concerned in an arrangement which makes available to another property when it is known that the property will, or may, be used for the purposes of terrorism, or in respect of which reasonable cause exists to suspect that it may be used for the purposes of terrorism.

A separate offence of laundering terrorist property ('terrorist laundering'), also punishable by up to 14 years' imprisonment, may be committed by entering into, or becoming concerned in, an arrangement which facilitates the retention or control of terrorist property by or on behalf of another (whether by concealment, removal from the jurisdiction, transfer to nominees or in any other way) (Section 18 TA).

As of 26 December 2007, a defence to any of the terrorist financing or terrorist laundering offences will be obtained by voluntarily disclosing any suspicion or belief that property is terrorist property as soon as

Money laundering

reasonably practicable and obtaining consent to proceed from SOCA. Consent may be sought either before or after undertaking an act that would otherwise amount to terrorist financing or terrorist laundering (new Sections 21Za and 21Zb TA). The defence will also be available where the intention was to disclose, but there is a reasonable excuse for the failure to do so (new Section 21Zc TA). The new consent defence is distinct from the pre-existing defence of acting with the express consent of a constable, or intending to obtain such consent but having a reasonable excuse for failing to do so (Section 21 TA).

A belief or suspicion that a terrorist financing or terrorist laundering offence has been committed must in any event be disclosed as soon as reasonably practicable where it is based on information gained in the course of a trade, profession, business or employment (Section 19 TA). This disclosure obligation is potentially wider in scope than the separate obligation under Section 21a TA to make a SAR, which applies only to knowledge or belief of an offence involving terrorist property which is based on information acquired in the course of business in the regulated sector (defined by Schedule 3a TA for this purpose in the same way as it is for POCA).

However, unlike the disclosure obligation in Section 19 TA, the disclosure obligation in Section 21a TA is triggered not only by actual belief or suspicion but also by reasonable grounds for knowledge or suspicion (amended Section 21a TA) and extends to attempted as well as actual incidents (new Section 21Zc(2) TA). Both offences of failing to disclose are punishable by a maximum of five years' imprisonment.

The available defences to the failure to disclose offences under Sections 19 and 21a TA are broadly the same as those available for the corresponding failure to disclose offences under Section 330 POCA. An offence of failing to disclose will not be committed if the information in question is protected by legal professional privilege, which for the purposes of Section 21a only is extended to other relevant professional advisers and persons employed by, or in partnership with, professional legal advisers or relevant professional advisers to provide assistance or support (Section 21a(5) TA). A defence will also be available where there was a 'reasonable excuse' for the failure to disclose. There is, however, no corresponding defence of lack of training.

As under POCA, it is an offence punishable by up to two years' imprisonment to 'tip off' anyone about a SAR relating to, or an actual or potential investigation into, terrorist financing or terrorist laundering, where such information has been obtained in the course of a business in the regulated sector (new Section 21d TA). The same exceptions and defences apply as to the offence under Section 333a POCA, discussed above.

The Money Laundering Regulations 2007

The recent amendments to POCA and TA follow in the wake of the more substantial structural amendments already introduced in the Money Laundering Regulations 2007.

The Money Laundering Regulations ('the Regulations') give effect in the UK to the EU Money Laundering Directives, which in turn seek to give effect in the EU to the FATF's Recommendations. The first Regulations came into force in 1993, and were amended in 2001 and again in 2003. They were replaced in full on 15 December 2007, following the adoption by the EU

Money laundering

institutions of the third Money Laundering Directive in October 2005.

The 2007 Regulations apply only to persons and institutions when conducting 'business in the regulated sector,' as defined for the purpose of the POCA and the TA above, with the exception of persons who engage in financial activity only on an occasional or very limited basis. As the scope of the regulated sector now includes also businesses which were previously unregulated, such business must register with the relevant supervisory authority; consumer credit institutions and estate agents must register with the Office of Fair Trading (OFT), and high value dealers, money service businesses and trust or company service providers must register with HM Revenue and Customs.

A 'fit and proper' test has also been introduced for money service businesses and for trust and company service providers, whereby registration is contingent on the regulator being satisfied that the applicant, any person who effectively directs or will effectively direct the business or service provider, any beneficial owner of the business or service provider and the MLRO are all fit and proper persons with regard to the risk of money laundering or terrorist financing (determined specifically by reference to any convictions or court orders relating to money laundering, terrorist financing, fraud, tax evasion and insolvency).

The Regulations aim to make money laundering and terrorist financing more difficult to carry out, and easier to detect, by requiring the regulated sector to be more vigilant. For this purpose they require regulated persons and entities to 'know' their customers and clients by obtaining and verifying information about their identities, and to obtain information about the stated purpose and intended nature of a proposed business relationship. One of the new requirements introduced in the 2007 Regulations is the need to identify also any beneficial owners of a customer or client; and context-specific definitions of beneficial ownership in respect of body corporates, partnerships, trusts or any other legal entity or arrangement are provided for this purpose. In high risk cases, further information must now also be sought about the source of funds for a particular transaction or about the customer or client's general source of wealth.

If due diligence cannot be performed properly, a business relationship cannot be entered into or continued; subject to a limited exception in respect of lawyers or other professional advisers (defined in the same way as 'relevant professional advisers' under POCA and TA) in the course of ascertaining the legal position for a client or defending or representing a client in, or concerning, legal proceedings (including advice on the institution or avoidance of proceedings). Failure to perform due diligence may also result in sufficient knowledge or suspicion to trigger a disclosure obligations under Section 330 POCA or Section 21a TA.

A further change to previous due diligence requirements is the introduction of a 'risk based' approach, whereby due diligence would be applied on a 'simplified' basis to low risk customers or clients and on an 'enhanced' basis where the risk was higher. The extent of the due diligence required will therefore vary according to the level of risk presented by the nature of the client and the transaction in question.

Specific examples of 'high risk' business relationships include customers or clients who are not physically present for identification purposes ('non face-to-face'), and customers or clients who are

Money laundering

'Politically Exposed Persons' ('PEPs') or close business associates or family members of such persons. The risk level may also be increased as a result of the particular jurisdiction(s) involved, if such jurisdictions have been identified by HM Treasury as having deficiencies in their anti money laundering and counter terrorist financing systems. In October 2008, HM Treasury, for the first time, identified Iran and Uzbekistan as such 'higher risk' jurisdictions following the FATF's identification of deficiencies in the same countries (as well as in Turkmenistan, Pakistan, São Tomé and Príncipe and the northern part of Cyprus).

Transactions associated with these countries should, therefore, attract enhanced due diligence. Where the FATF has applied counter-measures to a non-EEA State, HM Treasury may direct any person not to enter into a business relationship or carry out an occasional transaction, or to proceed further with a business relationship or occasional transaction already in existence, with a person situated or incorporated in such a State.

A further aspect of the new risk-based approach adopted in the 2007 Regulations is the ability in certain circumstances to rely on due diligence performed by other regulated persons or institutions, including persons in another EEA State or a non-EEA State subject to equivalent anti-money laundering obligations; provided that they consent to being relied on. It is also possible to outsource due diligence to third parties. However, in both cases, ultimate responsibility for compliance remains and can never be delegated.

Customer and client relationships must be continuously monitored throughout their duration to ensure that instructions conform to the available information, and contain no suspicious features. Enhanced due diligence is required in high risk situations, and specifically where the customer or client is a PEP. For this purpose, the 2007 Regulations require organisations to adopt appropriate compliance systems; including the appointment of an MLRO and the establishment of internal reporting procedures to enable compliance with the disclosure requirements under POCA and TA discussed above. A SAR should in the first instance be made internally within an organisation to the MLRO, and will not necessarily result in an external SAR to SOCA.

A range of further internal procedures and policies are required to ensure compliance with the 2007 Regulations, and more broadly to prevent money laundering and terrorist financing. Such internal systems must ensure that employees are regularly provided with appropriate training. They must also ensure that any records generated as a result of compliance, which may potentially be of assistance to law enforcement in the investigation and prosecution of money laundering and terrorist financing offences, are retained for at least five years from the end of the business relationship or conclusion of a one-off transaction.

The regulatory authorities supervise compliance with the Regulations, and have for this purpose been provided with powers to request information and to enter and search premises. A breach of the Regulations is a criminal offence punishable by a maximum of two years' imprisonment, regardless of whether any money laundering or terrorist financing has actually taken place. However, the regulators also have the ability to punish breaches instead by means of civil penalties or de-registration. A defence

Money laundering

is available to a person who took all reasonable steps and exercised all due diligence to avoid committing the offence.

Financial sanctions

An interface between financial sanctions and the anti money laundering and counter terrorist financing regime is provided by the 2007 Regulations and the Counter Terrorism Act 2008. In addition to HM Treasury's power under the 2007 Regulations to direct any person not to deal with persons situated or incorporated in a non-EEA State subject to FATF counter-measures, Schedule 7 of the Counter Terrorism Act 2008 confers broader powers on HM Treasury to issue directions to persons in 'the financial sector' – defined as UK credit or financial institutions, or non-UK credit or financial institutions acting in the course of a business carried on by them in the UK.

Such directions may require a credit or financial institution to:

1. Undertake enhanced customer due diligence, either before entering into or during a transaction or business relationship. In addition to identification information and any further specific measures identified in the direction, enhanced due diligence involves obtaining information about the designated person and their business and the source of their funds; as well as assessing the risk of the designated person being involved in activities relating to money laundering, terrorist financing or the development or production of nuclear, radiological, biological or chemical weapons or the facilitation of that development or production.
2. Undertake enhanced ongoing monitoring of a business relationship. In addition to any specific measures included in the direction, this consists of updating due diligence information and documents as well as ensuring that any transactions undertaken, and the source of funds used for such transactions, are consistent with the available knowledge about the designated person and their business.
3. Engage in systematic reporting; providing such information and documents as may be specified in the direction, within the period and in the manner specified therein.
4. Limit or cease business with a designated person. The direction may require a relevant person not to enter into, or continue to participate in, either a specified transaction or business relationship, or a specified description of such transactions or relationships, or any transactions or business relationships with a designated person.

HM Treasury can, however, only issue such directions if a non-EEA State is the subject of FATF counter-measures or if it reasonably believes that the UK's national interests are significantly put at risk by reason of the risk of terrorist financing or money laundering activities carried on in that State, by its government or by resident or incorporated persons.

HM Treasury may also issue directions if it reasonably believes that the UK's national interests are significantly put at risk by the development or production of nuclear, radiological, biological or chemical weapons, or anything that facilitates such development or production, in a non-EEA State.

HM Treasury is empowered to grant licences to exempt acts that would otherwise breach a direction. In the absence of such a licence, a failure to comply with any HM Treasury direction under the Counter-Terrorism Act 2008 is a criminal offence punishable by up to two years' imprisonment. The relevant

Money laundering

Enforcement Authorities have a discretion to impose civil penalties instead.

Similar but distinct requirements are also imposed under separate legal instruments enforcing breaches of EC Regulations which give effect to UN Security Council Regulations on applying financial sanctions to terrorists (under the Terrorism (United Nations Measures) Order 2009 (SI 2009/1747)), and to persons or entities connected with Al-Qaida and the Taliban (under the Al-Qaida and Taliban (United Nations Measures) Order 2006 (SI 2006/2952)).

The requirements in relation to financial sanctions have a much wider scope than HM Treasury directions under the Money Laundering Regulations 2007 (limited to persons and entities conducting business in the regulated sector) or under the Counter Terrorism Act 2008 (limited to credit and financial institutions in the financial sector), applying to any person in the UK, or any overseas person who is a British citizen or a UK body.

Breaches of financial sanctions are also more severely punished, by up to seven years' imprisonment. Such a breach will be committed, in the absence of a relevant licence granted by HM Treasury, by:

- any dealings with funds or economic resources belonging to, owned or held by a restricted person or entity; or
- making funds or economic resources available to, or for the significant financial benefit of, a restricted person or entity; or
- knowingly participating in the circumvention of any prohibitions relating to restricted persons or entities, or otherwise enabling or facilitating their contravention.

Restricted' persons or entities are those subject to a designation by HM Treasury. HM Treasury may designate persons whom it reasonably suspects are, or may be, Osama bin Laden; persons or entities designated by the UN Sanctions Committee. HM Treasury is also empowered to issue directions if it considers it necessary to do so for purposes connected with protecting the public from a risk of terrorism, in respect of persons whom it reasonably suspects are persons who commit, or attempt to commit, participate in or facilitate the commission of acts of terrorism, or are persons identified as such in an EC Regulation. It may also issue directions in the same circumstances in respect of persons owned or controlled, directly or indirectly, by such designated persons, or persons acting on their behalf or at their direction.

As part of the due diligence process under the 2007 Regulations, clients and parties involved in transactions should therefore be cross-checked against the consolidated list of financial sanctions targets maintained by HM Treasury. In the case of a match, a transaction cannot proceed in the absence of a licence from HM Treasury's Asset Freezing Unit.

A match may also give rise to suspicion of money laundering or terrorist financing. However, the Law Society warns against the making of SARs merely on the basis that a customer or client has a similar name to someone on the consolidated list.

Practical guidance

The combined effect of the POCA, the TA, the Regulations and the financial sanctions regime is to impose extensive and often onerous obligations on the private financial sector, breaches of which are severely punished.

Financial institutions in particular have raised concerns that the delay caused by

Money laundering

the need to await consent, and the inability to tell customers the reason for the delay, may not only undermine their customers' goodwill but also expose them to civil liability for breach of contract. These concerns have been addressed, in part, by a series of judicial decisions. In an early case, the Court of Appeal suggested that directions could be sought from the court in cases of difficulty (*C v. S and others* (1999)).

Institutions would, however, have to take a commercial decision as to whether to contest any proceedings brought by customers (*Bank of Scotland v. A Ltd* (2001)). Commercial or other considerations will not excuse non-compliance with POCA (*Squirrel Ltd v. National Westminster Bank Plc and HM Customs and Excise* (2005)). Nor can customers obtain orders to compel institutions to act otherwise than in accordance with their legal obligations. There can be no breach of contract to refuse to honour a customer's mandate, when it would be a criminal offence to do so (*K Ltd v. National Westminster Bank Plc* (2006)).

A further problem is the need to repeat a SAR for every proposed act, even when its contents are largely identical to a previous report. The only concession in recognition of the repetitive nature of much of financial services work therefore remains limited to the exemption of deposit-taking from the need to make multiple requests for consent in respect of the same accounts wherever transactions do not exceed £250.

Despite the recognition of these failings of the consent regime as a result of a Home Office consultation in late 2007, no changes have resulted. Instead the Home Office issued a circular to law enforcement agencies, containing formal guidance on how to operate the consent regime in order to ensure consistency in decisions on the grant or refusal of consent.

The new risk-based approach adopted in the Regulations will require considerable attention to be spent on identifying and assessing money laundering and terrorist financing risk specific to individual businesses. As a result, obligations and compliance procedures are likely to vary considerably as between different industries, sizes of business and types of clientele. Careful notes should be made of any compliance-related decisions and the reasons for them. These records can be relied on to demonstrate compliance if necessary. Businesses should undertake risk assessments on a regular basis and should revise their anti-money laundering policies and training materials accordingly.

The role played by the MLRO in securing compliance within an organisation is crucial. The MLRO must not be impeded in his functions by reason of a lack of independence, failure to cooperate or inability to access information. For firms authorised by the FSA, the position of MLRO is a 'controlled function' for which FSA approval must be sought. Firms regulated by the FSA should also be aware of the responsibility imposed by the FSA Handbook on senior management to ensure that appropriate anti-money laundering policies and procedures are in place.

A range of industry bodies have produced 'best practice' guidance to help with compliance, which should be incorporated into internal compliance policies. Courts and regulators alike may take compliance with any relevant guidance that exists into account when deciding whether an offence has been committed under POCA, the TA, the 2007 Regulations or any of the financial sanctions instruments discussed above; and are obliged to do so where the guidance has been approved

Money laundering

by HM Treasury. To date, HM Treasury has only approved the two-part guidance for the financial sector produced by the Joint Money Laundering Steering Group (JMLSG) (13 November 2007 edition, approved on 18 December 2007) and the anti-money laundering guidance produced by the Consultative Committee of Accountancy Bodies (CCAB) for the tax and accountancy sector (August 2008 edition).

See also: Criminal records, p.78; Whistleblowing, p.414.

Sources of further information

HM Treasury website: www.hm-treasury.gov.uk/fin_money_index.htm

JMLSG: Prevention of money laundering/combating the financing of terrorism: *Guidance for the UK Financial Sector*, Part I (generic) and Part II (sector-specific).

CCAB: *Anti-Money Laundering Guidance for the Accountancy Sector*.

FSA Handbook: Senior Management Arrangements, Systems and Controls (SYSC) Sourcebook, chapter 6.3 Financial Crime.

HM Revenue and Customs: Notice MLR8 – *Preventing money laundering and terrorist financing*; MLR8 *At a glance – a quick guide to the prevention of money laundering and terrorist financing*; and MLR9 – *Guide to Registration*.

Office of Fair Trading: Money Laundering Regulations 2007 – *Core guidance* and *Money Laundering Regulations 2007: Information for estate agents and consumer credit licence holders*.

Monitoring employees

Elizabeth Upton, Bird and Bird

Key points

The monitoring of emails, internet use and telephone calls by both public and private organisations has become a highly discussed topic. Many organisations have a legitimate need to record commercial transactions, to monitor the quality of service being provided, and in some circumstances to monitor their employees' activities. Increasingly, organisations have at their disposal a range of technologies and methods for carrying out employee monitoring. These technologies enable organisations to log their employees' keystrokes, sent and received emails, internet usage, use of software applications and access to documents. There are also a range of technologies with application outside the office. For example, businesses in the transport or services sectors (e.g. delivery or plumbing companies) may be using Global Satellite Positioning (GPS) technologies to track their vehicles and drivers.

Organisations that undertake such monitoring should be aware of the rights of monitored employees and of any third party (e.g. customers) who might be caught by such monitoring. Organisations should also be aware of their obligations under the law and any best practice guidance available. The consequences of implementing monitoring incorrectly include:

- breaches of human rights and other legislation;
- damage to employment and public relations;
- complaints to the Information Commissioner's Office; and
- claims by employees in court or in the Employment Tribunal.

This chapter should be read in conjunction with those on '*CCTV monitoring,*' p.59 and '*Data protection*,' p.84.

Legislation
- Data Protection Act 1998.
- Human Rights Act 1998.
- Regulation of Investigatory Powers Act 2000.
- Telecommunications (Lawful Business Practice) (Interception of Communication) Regulations 2000.
- The Enterprise Act 2002.

Human Rights Act 1998
The Human Rights Act 1998 (HRA) requires UK Courts and Tribunals to give effect to the rights of individuals under the European Convention for the Protection of Human Rights and Fundamental Freedoms. Under the HRA, it is unlawful for a Public Authority to act in a way that is incompatible with a Convention right, and therefore actions can certainly be brought against Public Authorities for Convention violations.

However, case law since its implementation has shown that the HRA may also be used in a dispute between

Monitoring employees

private parties. Although the Human Rights Act cannot be enforced directly against private individuals or companies, it may still be relevant. Since a Court or Tribunal falls within the definition of a 'Public Authority,' it has a duty to apply Convention principles when adjudicating a dispute. As long as a private individual or company can establish an existing cause of action they may bring in a human rights argument. Therefore, when considering any monitoring activity, organisations should be aware of and understand the impact of Article 8 of the HRA, which provides that "everyone has the right to respect for his private and family life, his home and correspondence". The right of an employee to keep personal matters personal, even when these intrude into the workplace, has been confirmed before the European Court of Human Rights (Copland v. United Kingdom, 3 April 2007), in which it was held that Ms Copland's email traffic, internet activity and telephone usage were all monitored by her employer in a manner that did not comply with the law.

Regulation of Investigatory Powers Act 2000

The Regulation of Investigatory Powers Act 2000 (RIPA) lays down the legal basis for monitoring. RIPA sets out provisions for authorising surveillance and specifically addressing the legality of surveillance over some private networks.

RIPA makes it an offence to intercept a communication in the course of its transmission by means of a public telecommunications system or postal service. Therefore, in the same way as it is an offence to open an individual's letter before it is delivered to them, an email sent from an internet service provider cannot be intercepted.

RIPA also makes it a criminal offence to intercept a communication made over certain private telecommunications systems that are attached to a public telecommunications system. For the interception to be caught by this provision, it must be intentional, made without lawful authority and made without the authority of the person who controls the operation or use of the system. As an organisation will have the right to control the use of its own private telecommunications system, its subsequent decisions to intercept communications would clearly not amount to a criminal offence. This provision will not therefore restrict organisations from carrying out monitoring over their own networks.

Section 1(3) of RIPA does, however, restrict monitoring by organisations. This provides that anyone who intercepts a communication over a private network may be liable to the sender or the recipient, or intended recipient, of the communication that is intercepted. However, as there are many legitimate occasions in which an organisation would wish to monitor communications, RIPA sets out some broad exceptions to this principle.

Section 4(2) of RIPA also gives the Secretary of State the power to implement Regulations to authorise conduct which appears to him to constitute a legitimate practice required by a business in order to monitor or keep a record of business communications. It is under this authority that the Telecommunications (Lawful Business Practice) (Interception of Communication) Regulations 2000 (LBP Regulations) were introduced.

The LBP Regulations only authorise the interception of communications wholly or partly in connection with an organisation's business, and only if such interception is effected solely for the purpose of monitoring or keeping a record of communications relevant to

Monitoring employees

> **Facts**
>
> - 65% of organisations monitor usage of the internet, rising to 86% in local government and 88% in the police.
> - 65% of employers use software to block connections to websites during working hours and to block access to sites deemed irrelevant to the job.
> - 18% of employers limit internet access to certain times of the day.
>
> *Source: Chartered Management Institute Survey 2008.*

the organisation's business. This would mean, for example, that if an organisation makes available an internet terminal or a telephone in the staff canteen solely for employees' private use and not in connection with the employer's business, then the organisation would not be entitled to intercept any such communications under the LBP Regulations.

The LBP Regulations do authorise employers to intercept communication without consent in order to:

- establish the existence of facts relevant to the business;
- ascertain compliance with relevant regulatory or self-regulatory practices and procedures;
- ascertain the standards achieved by employees (i.e. quality checking);
- prevent or detect crime;
- investigate or detect unauthorised use of the telecommunications system; and
- ensure the system's security and effective operation.

In order to obtain the benefit of the LBP Regulations, the organisation must also make all reasonable efforts to inform users of the system that communications may be intercepted. 'Users' has been interpreted to mean employees and others using the organisation's system for the purposes of receiving and making outbound calls (but not people calling into the system).

For employers who are Public Authorities, RIPA also imposes supplemental restrictions on their ability to carry out covert monitoring. Surveillance is covert if it is carried out in a manner that is calculated to ensure that persons who are subject to the surveillance are unaware that it is or may be taking place.

Data Protection Act 1998

Where monitoring of employees involves the processing of personal data, the Data Protection Act 1998 (DPA) also applies (see 'Data protection,' p.84) and employers will need to comply with any relevant obligations under the DPA. This will be the case particularly where monitoring is automatic (e.g. the automatic recording and monitoring of telephone calls, emails and internet access), but may also apply where staff are recorded on CCTV or where their GPS position is monitored. Monitoring that is not done automatically but which creates paper records that are then entered into a computer system or are filed in a structured filing system will also be covered. However, if an organisation arranges for a supervisor to listen into a call but no record of the call is made, then the DPA is not relevant – although other legislation such as RIPA may still need to be considered.

Monitoring employees

There are two key provisions in the DPA that affect monitoring:

1. Transparency; and
2. Proportionality / necessity.

In order to establish transparency, the fair processing code in the DPA obliges organisations to inform individuals about whom they collect personal data as to the purpose of the processing – including, in this case, monitoring. The individuals should not be misled as to the purposes for which the information was obtained and are also entitled to know the identity of the party controlling the information.

The data protection principles further provide that personal data may only be collected where it is necessary for one of the lawful bases for processing, and where it is relevant and not excessive for the purpose for which it is collected. It must not be retained longer than is necessary.

These tests of transparency, necessity and proportionality are, in broad terms, consistent with the principle stated at a high level in Article 8(2) of the European Convention of Human Rights.

It is important to remember that the Information Commissioner, as a Public Authority, is bound to act in a way that is consistent with Convention rights. This will extend to interpreting the DPA so as to promote these principles.

Organisations should be particularly careful if it is possible that sensitive personal data, such as information about an individual's health, could be captured by monitoring as there are stricter requirements for the processing of such data.

The DPA grants the individual's rights to compensation and rectification, blocking, erasure and destruction of personal data. A monitored individual will also have the right to be provided with copies of all information held about him. The Information Commissioner may be able to take action against organisations that do not comply with their obligations under the DPA.

Employment Practices Code

The Information Commissioner has issued an Employment Practices Code for the use of personal data in employer–employee relationships. The Code has no specific legal status and there are no specific sanctions for failing to comply with this Code. However, it provides an indication as to how the Commissioner will apply the DPA and it is possible that Employment Tribunals may have regard to the Code.

It is in the interests of both the employer and employees to comply with the Code. The Code encourages transparency about monitoring, which increases trust in the workplace, and it helps the employer to meet its legal requirements under the DPA and RIPA, protecting it from legal action.

Part 3 of the Code is concerned with processing, which the Information Commissioner classifies as 'monitoring'. The Code suggests that this means:

'Activities that set out to collect information about workers by keeping them under some form of observation, normally with a view to checking their performance or conduct. This could be done either directly, indirectly, perhaps by examining their work output, or by electronic means.'

Some of the examples of monitoring are exactly the kinds of activity that one would expect to be covered. For example:

- using automated software to check whether a worker is sending or receiving inappropriate emails;

Monitoring employees

- randomly checking emails to detect evidence of malpractice;
- examining logs of websites or telephone numbers to check for inappropriate use; and
- use of CCTV cameras – to ensure compliance with health and safety rules, for example.

The Code also covers some activities that one may not have expected to be covered. So, for example, it would also apply to electronic point of sale information gathered through checkout terminals used to monitor the efficiency of checkout operators, and videoing workers to collect evidence of malingering. The Code is also intended to cover information obtained through credit reference agencies to check that workers are not in financial difficulty.

The key message in the Code is that monitoring must be proportionate. In the Commissioner's view, monitoring is an interference with workers' privacy, which is permissible only where 'any adverse impact of monitoring on workers (can) be justified by its benefit to the employer and/or others'.

The Code provides employers with detailed guidance to help organisations ensure that monitoring is proportionate. Employers are encouraged to carry out impact assessments. This involves considering:

- what is the purpose of the monitoring arrangement and the benefit likely to result;
- whether it would have an adverse impact;
- whether there are any alternatives to achieve the identified purpose;
- the obligations arising from the monitoring; and
- whether the monitoring can be justified.

Other recommendations cover:

- notifying employees with a sufficient level of detail that monitoring is being carried out;
- ensuring that information collected through monitoring is only used for the purpose for which it was collected;
- ensuring that information collected through monitoring is stored in a secure way and access is limited;
- ensuring that individuals can gain access to monitoring information if requested in a subject access request;
- providing monitored individuals with an opportunity to make representations; and
- having a person responsible for checking that the organisation's policies and procedures comply with the DPA.

It is important to remember that different people in a company will have a role in monitoring, and they should all be given training. These people include management at different levels, IT staff and human resources.

The Code contains guidance concerning specific types of monitoring, such as the monitoring of electronic communications, video and audio monitoring, and covert monitoring. The Code suggests that organisations should adopt a policy in relation to electronic communications, setting out acceptable and unacceptable use of email, internet and telephone and the monitoring that will be carried out of such use.

The Advisory Conciliation Arbitration Service (ACAS) is an independent statutory body that provides guidelines on good practice in developing effective workplaces with good employment relations. By following the recommendations of ACAS, an employer can show that it has followed reasonable

Monitoring employees

guidelines to help it stay within the law, and this would be taken into account in any subsequent Court or Tribunal hearing. ACAS has produced an advice leaflet on internet and email policies, which is available in printed form and on the internet, setting out the advantages of adopting a policy and providing guidance as to the content of a policy.

The Code also provides guidance on how an organisation can meet the requirements of, and come within the exemptions of, RIPA and the LBP Regulations. It should be noted that, if an organisation is making use of an exemption under RIPA and the LBP Regulations, it still needs to comply with the requirements of the DPA regarding the collection, storage and use of the information involved in the monitoring.

Regulation of Investigatory Powers Orders

The Enterprise Act 2002 gave new powers of surveillance to the Office of Fair Trading (OFT) for the purposes of investigating cartel activities. Sections 199 and 200 of the Enterprise Act 2002 amended the Regulation of Investigatory Powers Act 2000 to grant the OFT the powers of intrusive surveillance and property interference.

In addition to the Enterprise Act powers, the Regulation of Investigatory Powers (Directed Surveillance and Covert Human Intelligence Sources) Order 2003 has added the OFT to a list of bodies given certain powers under RIPA.

The legislation allows:

- authorised OFT officers access to communications data such as telephone records;
- authorised OFT officers to conduct directed surveillance (e.g. watching a person's office); and
- the use of covert human intelligence sources (i.e. the use of informants).

The OFT can only exercise these powers after authorisation by a senior OFT official (currently the chairman) and following the Home Office Codes of Practice. It has also published its own Code of Practice setting out how it will exercise its powers. The OFT is subject to regular inspection by the Interception of Communications Commissioner and the Surveillance Commissioners to ensure the powers are used appropriately.

The power of access to communications data is only available to the OFT in the investigation of criminal cartel cases under the Enterprise Act 2002. The powers do not enable the OFT to obtain details about the content of the calls or other communications, but only details of the times, duration and recipients of communications.

Authorisations to use the power can only be given when they are necessary and proportionate in order to investigate a cartel.

The OFT officers can also carry out directed surveillance, i.e. to observe a person with the objective of gathering private information to obtain a detailed picture of the person's life, activities and associations.

Conclusion

The recording and monitoring of phone calls, emails and internet access is legally and politically sensitive. If organisations intend to record or monitor communications, they should first establish a coherent policy that meets all relevant legislative requirements. Part 3 of the Employment Practices Code should assist organisations to adopt monitoring policies that are likely to be successful and that avoid the legal pitfalls outlined above.

Monitoring employees

See also: CCTV monitoring, p.59; Data protection, p.84; Human rights, p.226; Internet and email policies, p.236; IT security, p.244; Personnel files, p.317.

Sources of further information

The Employment Practices Code can be found at www.informationcommissioner.gov.uk

Information about the OFT's powers can be found at www.oft.gov.uk

Information about RIPA can be found at www.homeoffice.gov.uk

The ACAS advice leaflet on internet and email policies can be found at www.acas.org.uk/media/pdf/d/b/AL06_1.pdf

Workplace Law's *IT and Email Policy and Management Guide v.3.0* has been designed to alert employers of the potential problems associated with using computer systems, the internet and email systems within the workplace and to provide certain safeguards. For more information visit www.workplacelaw.net/Bookshop/PoliciesAndProcedures.

Night working

Pinsent Masons Employment Group

Key points
Employers should ascertain whether they employ workers who would be classified as night workers. If so, they should check:

- how much working time night workers normally work;
- if night workers work more than eight hours per day on average, whether the amount of hours can be reduced and if any exceptions apply;
- how to conduct a health assessment and how often health checks should be carried out;
- that proper records of night workers are maintained, including details of health assessments; and
- that night workers are not involved in work that is particularly hazardous.

Legislation
- Working Time Regulations 1998.
- Management of Health and Safety at Work Regulations 1999.

The Working Time Regulations provide basic rights for workers in terms of maximum hours of work, rest periods and holidays. Night workers are afforded special protection by the Regulations. Depending on when they work, workers can be labelled 'night workers'.

Once that label is applied, an employer must take all reasonable steps to ensure that the normal hours of a night worker do not exceed an average of eight hours for each 24 hours over a 17-week reference period (which can be extended in certain circumstances). In addition, an employer must offer night workers a free health assessment before they start working nights and on a regular basis thereafter. The other provisions in the Regulations relating to rest breaks and holidays apply equally to night workers.

What is night-time?
In the absence of any contrary agreement, night-time is defined as the period between 11 p.m. and six a.m. Night-time hours can be determined through particular forms of agreement, provided it lasts at least seven hours and includes hours between midnight and five a.m. A 'night worker' is any worker whose daily working time includes at least three hours of night-time:

- on the majority of days he works;
- on such a proportion of days he works as is agreed between employers and workers in a collective or workforce agreement; or
- sufficiently often that he may be said to work such hours as a normal course, i.e. on a regular basis.

If workers work fewer than 48 hours on average per week, they will not exceed the night work limits.

Special hazards
Where a night worker's work involves special hazards or heavy physical or

Night working

mental strain, there is an absolute limit of eight hours on any of the worker's working days. No average is allowed. Work involves a 'special hazard' if either:

- it is identified as such between an employer and workers in a collective agreement or workforce agreement; or
- it poses a significant risk as identified by a risk assessment that an employer has conducted under the Management of Health and Safety at Work Regulations 1999.

Health assessment

All employers must offer night workers a free health assessment before they begin working nights and thereafter on a regular basis. Workers do not have to undergo a health assessment, but they must be offered one.

All employers should maintain up-to-date records of health assessments. A health assessment can comprise two parts – a medical questionnaire and a medical examination. It should take into account the type of work that the worker will do and any restrictions on the worker's working time under the Working Time Regulations. Employers are advised to take medical advice on the contents of a medical questionnaire.

New and expectant mothers

New and expectant mothers have certain special rights in relation to night work. See 'Pregnancy,' p.324.

See also: Occupational health, p.304; Pregnancy, p.324; Working time, p.423.

Sources of further information

Guidance on night working is available from the DirectGov site: www.direct.gov.uk/en/Employment/Employees/WorkingHoursAndTimeOff/DG_10028519

Notice periods

Vanessa di Cuffa, Freeth Cartwright

Key points
- In an employment law context, a contract (whether express of implied) will have a period of notice to end the relationship.
- There is a statutory minimum level of notice that has to be given but the parties can contract to give greater period of notice.
- The notice period will be determined either by law or by the terms of the contract, but it can be varied in some circumstances.
- Employees intending to take maternity, paternity, adoption or parental leave must give notice to the employer.
- An employee wishing to take adoption leave will also need to give notice.
- Employees close to retirement have legal rights to notice.

Legislation
- Section 86, Employment Rights Act 1996.
- Section 4, Section 11, Maternity and Parental Leave Regulations 1999.
- Schedule 2, Regulation 16(2) Maternity and Parental Leave Regulations 1999.
- Maternity and Parental Leave Regulations 1999 and the Paternity and Adoption Leave (Amendment) Regulations 2006.
- Employment Equality (Age) Regulations 2006.
- Work and Families Act 2006.

Contractual and statutory notice

In employment law, when the parties to an employment relationship want to bring the relationship to an end, they will have to serve notice.

Section 86 of the Employment Rights Act 1996 provides that employees with between one month and two years' continuous service are entitled to at least one week's statutory notice and, thereafter, to a further one week's notice for each complete year of continuous employment, up to a maximum of 12 weeks' notice after 12 years. The minimum period of notice given by an employee after one month's employment is one week. A longer period of notice may be expressly agreed.

Garden leave

Many contracts of employment provide an employer with the option of not allowing an employee to attend the workplace during the notice period. The employee is paid and receives the same benefits. This is known as 'garden leave'. It means that an employee is unable to commence any new role.

The reason behind such a clause is clear. It allows an employer to keep an employee on notice, out of circulation and away from confidential information and/or trade secrets in the business. The clause has to be inserted into the contract in order that the employer is not acting in breach of the contract. See *'Restrictive covenants and garden leave'*, p.350 for more information.

Payment in lieu of notice (PILON)

A PILON clause gives the employer the right to terminate an employee's contract of employment with immediate effect and to

Notice periods

pay in lieu of the notice period that would have been worked. This means that the employer is not terminating the employee's contract in breach of contract and can still enforce post-termination restrictive covenants if applicable.

The inclusion of PILON in a contract of employment means that the payment will be fully taxable.

If a PILON clause is included in the contract and is not discretionary, an employee does not have an obligation to mitigate their loss in the event that they are dismissed without notice or pay in lieu in the circumstances where the employer is not entitled summarily to terminate the contract. Therefore the employee will have a claim as a debt for pay in lieu of notice in relation to the notice period, even if the employee succeeds in finding another job on identical terms and conditions of employment immediately.

Fixed term contracts (FTC)

Statutory notice periods do not apply to a contract of employment for a specific task that is not expected to last more than 13 weeks unless, due to circumstances, the employment extends to 13 weeks or more. You can, however, include a notice period that allows for earlier termination.

If an FTC is for a period of four weeks or less, but owing to circumstances the employer allows the employee to continue in post for 13 weeks or more, the contract stops being an FTC and in a sense becomes a permanent contract with statutory notice periods applying.

If an employee has been employed on an FTC that has expired and then enters into a further FTC with the same employer, provided the gap between the two contracts is not more than 26 weeks, the interval between the two contracts will not break the continuity of the contract.

Subject to the above, statutory notice periods do not apply to an FTC. There is nothing to prevent an employer from including a notice period in an FTC that allows earlier termination of employment as a contractual term, if the employer wishes to have this facility. It is actually considered sensible to do this as, without an early termination clause, an employer may be committed to pay for the full term of the FTC, even if circumstances change such that the employee is no longer required. The reason why the employer ends a contract early should, in any event, be a fair reason and be reasonable in all the circumstances.

Notice periods of maternity, paternity, adoption or parental leave

An employee intending to take maternity or paternity leave must give notice before the end of the 15th week before the expected date of birth. They must state the expected week of childbirth and the date of the start of the leave. An employee taking paternity leave should also state how much leave is being taken. An employee taking maternity or paternity leave is able to change their mind about when they want to start maternity / paternity leave providing they inform the employer at least 28 days in advance.

For an employee intending to take adoption leave, employees must notify the employer within seven days of confirmation that they have been matched for adoption, the date the child is expected and the date leave will commence.

Employees, unless it is otherwise collectively agreed, must provide their employer within 21 days' notice of when they will take parental leave.

Notice periods

Employees returning from maternity or adoption leave do not have to give any notice to their employer if they are returning at the end of their entitled leave. The employer is responsible for informing the employee of when the leave expires.

In the event that an employee wants to return early, eight weeks' notice must be given to the employer. Failure to do this means an employer can postpone the return until this has run out or until the date when the leave would have ended. Should the employee not wish to return at the end of a period of leave, normal contractual notice must be given to the employer. There is no requirement for an employee to state in advance whether she intends to return after maternity or adoption leave.

Retirement

If an employer wishes to compulsory retire an employee, the starting point is that the employer will need to formally notify the employee in writing of their intended retirement date, and of their statutory right to request not to retire, at least six months, but not more than 12 months, before their intended retirement date.

Once an employer has properly notified an employee of their intended retirement date and of their right to request to continue working beyond that date, if they wish to make a request they must do so in writing at least three months, but not more than six months, before their intended retirement date.

Where an employer has failed to comply (either at all or within the prescribed time limits) with their duty to notify the employee of their intended retirement date and of their right to request, the employee can still make their request at any time in the six months up to the intended retirement date. Where an employer has completely failed to notify, the employee's request should identify what they believe to be their intended retirement date.

See also: Dismissal, p.124; Employment contracts, p.146; Fixed-term workers, p.187; Leave, p.252; Pregnancy, p.324; Restrictive covenants and garden leave, p.350; Retirement, p.353.

Sources of further information

Workplace Law Network provides premium members with unrestricted access to a comprehensive range of online information – factsheets, case reports and daily news items – on employment, health and safety and premises management. Members also benefit from an online advice service and a free subscription to the *Workplace Law Magazine*. For more information email membership@workplacelaw.net or call our membership services team on 0871 777 8881.

Occupational health

Greta Thornbory, Occupational Health Consultant

Key points
'Work is generally good for your health and wellbeing.' The authors of this statement, Waddell and Burton, added several provisos in that there are various physical and psychological aspects of work that are hazardous and can pose a risk to health, and work should do the worker no harm. Conversely, employers want to employ people who will give them good service, who have the knowledge, skills and understanding to take on the roles and tasks required of them. Occupational health (OH) services are designed to support and help employers meet these requirements.

This chapter will cover:

- What is Occupational health (OH)?
- How OH can help employers to fulfil their legal requirements.
- The financial implications of health and safety at work, whilst ensuring business viability.

Legislation
- Health and Safety at Work etc. Act 1974.
- Management of Health and Safety at Work Regulations.

What is OH?
In 1950 the Joint ILO (International Labour Organisation) / WHO (World Health Organisation) issued the first definition of OH, which was updated in 1995 to these three objectives:

1. The maintenance and promotion of workers' health and working capacity;
2. The improvement of working environment and work to become conducive to health and safety; and
3. The development of work organisation and working cultures in a direction that supports health and safety at work and in doing so promotes a positive social climate and smooth operation and may enhance the productivity of the undertaking.

Defining 'health'
The most accepted definition is from the World Health Organisation, which defines health as 'a state of complete physical, mental and social wellbeing and not merely the absence of disease or infirmity'.

Why occupational health?
OH has been and is promoted on all levels; the international perspective is supported by the WHO / ILO. In turn, OH has been, and is, supported at a national level by all UK governments to a greater or lesser extent. Although to date there is no legal requirement for employers or employees to have access to OH, it is strongly recommended in much of the guidance issued from government departments.

OH also figures clearly in the Government strategies for health at the beginning of the 21st Century. Various government departments, together with the HSE, have

Occupational health

produced a plethora of strategies and plans. The first of these was 'Securing health together' as a long-term strategy for Great Britain. 'Securing health together' is the Government's ten-year occupational health strategy. It aims to tackle the high levels of work-related ill heath and to reduce the personal suffering, family hardship and costs to individuals, employers and society.

With the motto 'Healthy work; healthy at work and healthy for life,' the strategy encompasses all aspects of health and work combined. The 'Securing Health Together' document states in its introduction that better occupational health will benefit everyone; that if an individual's health at work is improved they will have more fulfilled lives and that the benefits to organisations are that people will work more effectively.

Since then there have been a number of new initiatives, the most significant of which can be found at www.workingforhealth.gov.uk. Dame Carole Black presented her report in March 2008 and the Government response was published in November that year. The response, available on the Working For Health website, entitled 'Improving health and work: changing lives,' indicates a number of changes including a Business Health check tool (available at the website), occupational health telephone help lines and modification of the sicknote scheme to a 'fit note' scheme.

At the moment, 'Investors in People' are incorporating a 'Wellbeing at Work' Framework and a free online assessment is available; there are many health promotion programmes ongoing such as Well@Work managed by the British Heart Foundation and funded by Sport England and the Big Lottery Fund, as well as tax breaks for companies providing bikes for cycling to work

In 2000, the Government and the HSC launched their 'Revitalising Health and Safety' initiative, 26 years after the Health and Safety at Work etc. Act 1974 became law. The aim of the strategy was to inject new impetus into the health and safety agenda, and to gain maximum benefit from links between OH, safety and other government programmes. The programme highlighted the importance of promoting better working environments. In 2004, the White Paper 'Choosing health; making healthy choices easier,' concluded in its executive summary that this was the start, not the end, of a journey, and that the Government was serious about engaging everyone in choosing health.

The Working for Health website also offers employers the chance to undertake a business health check to help employers assess the cost of ill health to their business and the impact of wellness programmes on these costs.

All together, there are a number of government initiatives that promote the use of occupational health services, but at this time of economic recession, employers are more interested in where to save money than spend it on new services for employees. Where access to an occupational health service exists, it is important to remember that it can help to save the company money.

Legal aspects

There is a great deal of legislation that employers are required to consider and comply with regarding the health, safety and welfare of employees; not only health and safety legislation but also the legislation that comes under

Occupational health

employment law, all of which affects the health of the employee.

The Health and Safety at Work etc. Act 1974 (HSWA) is an overarching piece of legislation in that it sets out the duty of the employer to take care of the health, safety and welfare of their employees, and of others who may be affected by his work undertaking – so far as is reasonably practicable. It is from this main Act that most secondary health and safety legislation is derived and singularly the most important Regulation is the Management of Health and Safety at Work Regulations, which charge employers with the duty to undertake a risk assessment in relation to the health and safety of employees.

Employers will take a calculated risk of not getting caught by the enforcing bodies, be they the HSE or local councils, by not complying with the law. However, if they want to attract business then they may be compelled to do so. Comments have also been made that to be profitable means that companies have to operate very closely to what is legally acceptable, otherwise they would not remain in business, and to succeed in business you have to be prepared to take risks – this is particularly so for small and medium-sized enterprises (i.e. enterprises with fewer than 250 employees).

One legal requirement for employers is Employer Liability Compulsory Insurance (ELCI) and this is often quoted when challenging employers about their health, safety and wellbeing provision for employees. However, there are many costs not covered by the insurance. The issue here is that it is the cost of the insurance that is the problem, not that it is a compulsory legal requirement.

OH professionals offer sound advice on how to comply with applicable legislation to reduce the adverse effects of work on health, and to reduce the risk of prosecution and legal liability. This is particularly relevant where health surveillance is required or where health is likely to be affected, resulting in costly long-term sickness absence. It is known that work-related stress-related conditions and MSDs are the two main causes of long-term sickness absence.

At an Employment Tribunal, when Dundee City Council was found in breach of the Management of Health and Safety Regulations, the personnel manager admitted that he did not understand the meaning of OH and the Tribunal itself struggled to define it during the course of the hearing. It would probably have been better if they had asked for an OH expert from one of the OH bodies to give an explanation and to demonstrate the business case. According to reports, the HSE has said that the appropriate use of OH expertise and resources is necessary to comply with statutory duties and will help with reducing work-related sickness absence.

Financial aspects

If employers want 'maximum output for minimum outlay,' they need to appreciate the financial benefits of considering the health and wellbeing of employees, particularly the occupational health or the ill health that is caused or made worse by work. OH advises organisations on pre-employment health assessment, health surveillance and monitoring, managing absence and general health and lifestyle issues.

Every employer pays a premium for ELCI. This is to cover injuries and ill heath experienced by employees whilst at work.

Occupational health

It does not cover the whole scenario. For every £1 of insured costs of an accident or ill health, there will be another £10 of uninsured costs. The HSE describes ELCI as the tip of the iceberg. As the founder of easyJet said after being cleared of the death of five people in a tanker accident and a subsequent 11-year lawsuit: "If you think safety is expensive, try an accident".

See also: Absence management, p.30; Health surveillance, p.212; HIV and AIDS, p.215; Mental health, p.261; Pregnancy, p.324; Smoking, p.369; Stress, p.381.

Sources of further information

Working for Health: www.workingforhealth.gov.uk

World Health Organisation (WHO): www.who.int/en

HSE: *Securing health together* (2000): www.hse.gov.uk/sh2/sh2strategy.pdf

Health and wellbeing at work project: www.investorsinpeople.co.uk/mediaresearch/tools/pages/healthandwellbeingatwork.aspx

Tax breaks for employers by cycling to work: www.dft.gov.uk/pgr/sustainable/cycling/cycletoworkschemeimplementat5732

Workplace Law Group's ***Occupational Health 2008: Making the business case – Special Report*** addresses the issues of health at work, discusses the influence of work on health and highlights the business case for occupational health services at work.

Using case studies, examples from professional experience and the findings of the many Government reports and surveys on the subject, the Special Report focuses on the advantages of occupational health services, and the benefits they can provide to a company, in terms of financial savings, increased employee morale, and improved corporate image. For more information visit www.workplacelaw.net/Bookshop/SpecialReports.

Part-time workers
Pinsent Masons Employment Group

Key points
- It has always been risky to treat part-time workers less favourably than comparable full-time workers, owing to the potential for a claim of sex discrimination.
- Regulations introduced in 2000 now provide protection for part-time 'workers' (wider than the term 'employees'), irrespective of sex discrimination.
- Part-time workers can request a written statement from their employers if they suspect discrimination requiring their employer to provide an explanation for their treatment.
- Employers should review their practices and procedures to ensure that they are compliant with current legislation.
- There is no exemption for small businesses.

Legislation
- Part-time Workers (Prevention of Less Favourable Treatment) Regulations 2000.
- Part-time Workers (Prevention of Less Favourable Treatment) Regulations 2000 (Amendment) Regulations 2002.

Overview
The Part-time Workers (Prevention of Less Favourable Treatment) Regulations 2000 (the Regulations) came into force on 1 July 2000 to provide a basic right for part-time workers not to be treated less favourably on the grounds of their part-time status than comparable full-time workers unless this can be justified on objective grounds. This means part-time workers are entitled, for example, to:

- the same hourly rate of pay;
- the same access to company pension schemes;
- the same entitlements to annual leave and to maternity and parental leave on a pro rata basis;
- the same entitlement to contractual sick pay; and
- no less favourable treatment in access to training.

Definitions
The Regulations apply to 'workers' and not just to 'employees'. The wider definition will include part-time workers who may not be employees, such as homeworkers and agency workers.

A part-time worker is someone who is 'paid wholly or partly by reference to the time he works and, having regard to the custom and practice of the employer in relation to workers employed by the worker's employer under the same type of contract, is not identifiable as a full-time worker'.

A part-time worker must therefore be identified by reference to the particular circumstances of each employer.

'Less favourable treatment'
To assert less favourable treatment, a comparison must be made with a particular full-time worker. However, the Regulations only allow part-time workers to compare themselves with full-time workers working for the same employer in the same or similar work and with a similar level of qualifications and experience. They must

Part-time workers

also be employed under the same type of contract.

By virtue of the Amendment Regulations, which came into force on 1 October 2002, a part-time worker can compare himself to a full-time worker regardless of whether either of the contracts is permanent or for a fixed term.

Where they believe they are being treated less favourably than comparable full-timers, part-time workers may request a written statement of the reasons for their treatment from their employer, to be provided within 21 days.

Discrimination at all stages of employment – recruitment, promotion, terms of employment and dismissal – is potentially unlawful. Promotion is an area where employers have often in the past favoured full-time staff over part-timers.

Previous or current part-time status should now not form a barrier to promotion to a post, whether the post itself is full-time or part-time.

Part-time employees must not receive a lower basic rate of pay than comparable full-time employees, unless this can be 'objectively justified' (e.g. by a performance-related pay scheme).

The same hourly rate of overtime pay should be paid to part-timers as to comparable full-time employees, once they have worked more than the normal full-time hours. The Regulations do not provide part-time workers with an automatic right to overtime payments once they work beyond their normal hours. However, part-timers working beyond their contracted hours should be paid the same as a full-timer would be paid for working the same number of hours,

Facts

- Women who work full-time earn, on average, 17% less per hour than men working full-time. For women who work part-time, the gap in pay relative to full-time men is a huge 38% per hour.
- Just over one million women who are currently not working would like to work and 15% of the 5.1 million women working part-time would like to increase their hours.
- 79% of women who work part-time state that they do not want a full-time job, and of these, 74% say that children or domestic family responsibilities are their reason for working part-time.
- According to Women and Work Commissioners reports, 45% of women working part-time are under-utilising their skills compared to 35% of women (and men) working full-time.
- According to Women and Work Commissioners reports, 20% of women intended to do no paid work at the end of their maternity leave, 54% intended to work part-time and 26% to work full-time.
- Only 7% of managers and senior officials work part-time, compared to 33% of those in administrative and secretarial occupations.
- Only 8% of those in skilled trades occupations work part-time, compared to 52% of those in personal service jobs and 57% in sales and customer service jobs.

Part-time workers

otherwise there is a risk of an equal pay claim.

The Regulations allow part-time workers to participate in the full range of benefits available to full-timers such as profit-sharing schemes, unless there are objective grounds for excluding them. Any benefits should be pro rata to those received by comparable full-time workers.

Employers must not exclude part-time workers from training schemes as a matter of principle. They should take great care to ensure that part-timers get the same access to training as full-time workers.

Part-time workers must be given the same treatment in relation to maternity leave, parental leave and time off for dependants as their full-time colleagues, on a pro rata basis where this is appropriate. Similarly, career break schemes should be made available to part-time workers in the same way, unless their exclusion is objectively justified.

Less favourable treatment will only be justified on objective grounds if it can be shown that the less favourable treatment is to achieve a legitimate objective (e.g. a genuine business objective), that it is necessary to achieve that objective and that it is an appropriate way to achieve the objective.

Dismissal

There are certain situations in which a dismissal by an employer for a specific reason will be treated as being automatically unfair. For example, where someone is dismissed for bringing proceedings against the employer under the Regulations, this will be deemed automatically unfair. No qualifying period of employment is required for such a claim. Where someone is dismissed as a result of his part-time status and a comparable full-time worker was not dismissed, this will be a form of less favourable treatment and the employee may make a complaint to a Tribunal under the Regulations, as well as bringing an ordinary unfair dismissal claim.

If there is a redundancy situation, then part-time workers should be treated just as favourably as full-timers, unless this difference in treatment can be objectively justified. Part-time status should not be a criterion for selection for redundancy.

Practical points

Government guidance has been published with the Regulations and may be accessed at www.berr.gov.uk/employment/workandfamilies/part-time/page12080.html.

Employers will find it useful to take note of the following points:

- They should review periodically when they can offer posts on a part-time basis. If an applicant wishes to work part-time, the employer should ascertain whether a part-time worker could fulfil the requirements of the job.
- Employers should look seriously at requests to change to part-time working and, where possible, explore how this can be carried out.
- They should review how individuals are provided with information on the availability of part-time and full-time positions.
- Employers are encouraged to keep representative bodies informed about certain aspects of the business' use of part-time workers.
- Managers should amend their handbooks to include a section on part-time workers and the consequences of breaching the Regulations.

Part-time workers

- Disciplinary procedures should be amended to make it a disciplinary offence to discriminate against part-time workers.
- Awareness of the rights of part-time workers may need to be raised and training provided on the subject.

Enforcement

Employees are able to present a claim to an Employment Tribunal within three months seeking compensation if they believe that their rights have been infringed.

See also: Discrimination, p.110; Employee benefits, p.138; Family-friendly rights, p.182; Fixed-term workers, p.187.

Sources of further information

Workplace Law Group's **Guide to Flexible Working 2008** provides information on the formal legislative right to request flexible working, but also considers flexible working patterns in a wider sense. It covers the reasons why some employers are looking to introduce flexible working into their workplace, explores different flexible working patterns, including their benefits and disadvantages, and provides detail on the formal legislative right to request.

It also looks at the employment and non-employment legal issues that surround flexible working and the necessary amendments that need to be made to an employee's contractual terms and conditions if a flexible working pattern is agreed. Finally, it gives practical advice in relation to drafting and implementing a flexible working policy. For more information visit www.workplacelaw.net/Bookshop/GuidesTo.

Pensions

Dana Shunmoogum and Emma Tracey, Taylor Wessing

Key points
- Pension provision in the UK falls into two categories – state benefits and private arrangements.
- State pensions comprise of basic state pensions and state second pensions (S2P). Contributions are collected from employees and employers via National Insurance Contributions (NICs). The amount of state pension that an individual will receive will depend on the NICs paid or credited over an individual's working life.
- Private pension arrangements may take the form of either occupational pension schemes or personal pensions.
- Occupational pensions schemes are schemes established by an employer, for the benefit of the employees. Different occupational pension schemes operate different arrangements. These are commonly known as defined benefit schemes or defined contribution schemes.
- Employers with more than five relevant employees who do not offer an occupational or personal pension scheme that meets certain criteria must provide employees with access to a stakeholder pension. This is a type of personal pension to which both employers and employees may contribute.

Legislation
- Income and Corporation Taxes Act 1988 (as amended by the Income Tax (Earnings and Pensions) Act 2003).
- Social Security Contributions and Benefits Act 1992.
- Pension Schemes Act 1993.
- Pensions Act 1995.
- Welfare Reform and Pensions Act 1999.
- Child Support, Pensions and Social Security Act 2000.
- Civil Partnership Act 2004.
- Finance Act 2004.
- Pensions Act 2004.

Overview
This chapter provides a brief overview of the two types of pension provision in the UK – state benefits and private pension arrangements. The chapter is aimed at helping those involved with workplace pension provision.

State benefits
State pensions are provided by the Government on the basis of contributions made or credited to the National Insurance Fund over an individual's working life. These contributions are compulsory and are effectively part of the general taxation and benefits system.

There are two tiers of state benefits – the Basic State Pension and the State Second Pension (S2P).

Basic State Pension
An individual is entitled to receive the Basic State Pension if they meet the following criteria:

- they are aged 60 for females (this is gradually being increased to age 65 between April 2010 and 2020) or 65 years for men; and

Pensions

- they (or their husband, wife or civil partner) have enough qualifying years employment based on NICs.

If NICs have been paid for less than 25% of an individual's working life, they may not be entitled to a State Pension. The Government has recently sought to overhaul this system to the extent that from 6 April 2010 the number of years that will be required in order to qualify for a full State Pension will be reduced to 30 years and any number of qualifying years will give entitlement to at least some Basic State Pension.

There will also be NIC credits available for individuals who care for children or severely disabled people. An employee with a full NIC record is currently (2009/10) entitled to receive £95.25 a week if they are a single person and £152.30 a week if part of a pensioner couple.

State Second Pension (S2P)
Until April 2002, the additional state pension for employees was called the State Earnings-Related Pension Scheme (SERPS). The amount of SERPS pension that an employee received was based on a combination of the amount of NICs that they had paid and their salary.

In April 2002, SERPS was reformed and the additional state pension is now known as the State Second Pension (S2P). This provides a more generous additional pension than SERPS for low and moderate earners, and certain carers and people with long-term illness or disability.

Employees may choose to 'contract-out' of S2P. This means that employees can divert their NIC payments to a private pension scheme but will receive a smaller benefit from the State as a result.

Private pension arrangements
Private pension provision in the UK is highly regulated, both by the Government and other regulatory bodies. In recent years there has been much reform of the pensions industry and this has served to increase the powers of regulatory authorities, including the Pensions Regulator.

Facts
- Since 1997, the employment rate of those aged between 50 and State Pension age has increased from 65% to over 70%, and there are now more than a million individuals over State Pension age who are still in work.
- According to the Equal Opportunities Commission, under the current UK State Pension system, just 25% of women are entitled to a full Basic State Pension, compared to 95% of men.
- The General Household Survey (GHS) estimated in 2007 that 53% of full-time men and 58% of full-time women employees in Great Britain were members of their employer's pension scheme.
- In 2007, the average employer contribution rate for private sector-defined benefit schemes was 15.6% of salary, compared with 6.5% for defined contribution schemes.
- In 2006/07, 61% of single pensioner households had a total pension income (including state and related benefits plus private pension benefits) of less than £10,000.

Pensions

Other than in respect of stakeholder pensions (*see below*) employers and employees are not compelled to set up or contribute to private pensions. The Government is aware that this is likely to result in long-term problems for individuals who have failed to provide sufficiently for their retirement. They have therefore proposed to introduce a new regime whereby employees who are not already enrolled with a recognised occupational pension scheme will automatically be enrolled into the Personal Accounts scheme (although they will have the option to opt out) and employers will be compelled to contribute to the scheme. The proposal is in the first stages of consultation and, if implemented, will not be established before 2012.

Although there is currently no element of compulsion for employers or employees to contribute to a private pension there are significant tax benefits if they choose to do so. In return for complying with specific requirements laid down by legislation, private schemes registered with HMRC can enjoy generous tax relief, both for employees and employers.

Under the current pensions regime, implemented from 6 April 2006, an individual contributing to a private pension scheme is only able to accumulate tax-advantaged benefits from pension saving up to £1.75m (the 'Lifetime Allowance'). This Lifetime Allowance was capped at £1.75m for the year 2009/10 but is subject to change.

Tax relief is further restricted by reference to the amount by which pensions savings increase in any one year (other than the year of retirement). This is known as the 'Annual Allowance' and is limited to £245,000. Again, this sum was set for the year 2009/10 and is subject to review.

The amount of contributions that can be made by an individual, whether employed or self-employed, is restricted to the greater of 100% of UK earnings (subject to the £245,000 limit mentioned above) or £3,600 per annum.

A number of further tax limits were imposed under the new pensions regime but these are outside the scope of this chapter.

There are two types of private pension arrangement – occupational pension schemes and personal pension schemes.

Occupational pensions schemes

Occupational pension schemes are established under trust and operated in accordance with the scheme's trust deed and rules. A group of people will be appointed as trustees of the scheme and are responsible for running the scheme. Legislation requires that at least one third of the scheme's trustee board must be nominated by the members (and pensioners) but it is possible that this fraction may be increased to one half in the future. Previously employers were able to suggest alternative arrangements, which meant they could opt-out of the member-nominated trustee requirements, but this is no longer possible. The trustee board must also consult advisers such as actuaries, administrators and solicitors when reaching its decisions.

Traditionally, most occupational pension schemes were established on a defined benefit (DB) basis, meaning that the pension payable at retirement was calculated by reference to a salary-related formula set out in the scheme's rules. DB schemes involve employees making contributions during their working life and the employer guaranteeing that the final pension will be at a specific level. The advantage of this type of arrangement

Pensions

for employees is that, in the absence of employer insolvency, it provides certainty. The problem for employers is that they bear the risk of poor investment returns and expensive annuity rates.

Owing to the risks outlined above, many employers have chosen to close their DB schemes and now offer employees admission to a defined contribution scheme (DC). DC schemes do not guarantee members a specific level of final pension but instead provide a promise to contribute a given percentage of employee salary and invest this, together with any employee contributions. The actual pension payable at retirement is dependent upon the investment return achieved during the period of membership of the scheme and the cost of securing a pension on the annuity market on retirement.

When an employee leaves a company that operates an occupational pension scheme they may leave their benefits in the scheme until they reach retirement age (during this time they will be referred to as 'deferred members') or they may transfer the benefits they have built up under the scheme to:

- a new pension scheme operated by their new employer;
- a personal pension scheme; or
- an insurance company by way of a deferred annuity (i.e. a promise to pay a pension when the employer reaches a specific age).

Personal pension schemes
Personal pensions are a contract between an individual and a provider other than the employer, usually an insurance company or a bank. All personal pensions operate on a DC basis. Personal pensions are often used by individuals without access to an occupational scheme, employees who do not wish to join their occupational scheme, the self-employed, or employees who have access to an employer's group personal pension scheme (GPP).

Employers frequently offer GPPs as an alternative to an occupational pension scheme. GPPs are simply a collection of personal pension schemes provided by one provider, with each employee having his own personal pension operating within this arrangement. The employer is not obliged to make contributions, although most do. If an employer contributes less than 3% of an employee's salary to a GPP or a personal pension scheme, they must ensure that they also designate a stakeholder pension scheme (*see below*).

Because a personal pension scheme is provided by an organisation other than the employer, an employee's ability to continue to contribute to his or her pension should not be affected if the employee leaves service (although any reduced commissions / charges negotiated by the employer may not continue).

Stakeholder pensions
The stakeholder pension is a particular type of personal pension scheme and was an initiative introduced by the Government in 2001. The Government realised that the basic state pension and S2P was unlikely to provide sufficient benefits for people who were not also contributing to an occupational or personal pension. There is no compulsion on employees to join a stakeholder pension, but employers are obliged to make it available in certain circumstances.

Employers' obligations are:

- to designate a stakeholder pension for their staff (having consulted with employees about the introduction of the stakeholder); and
- to allow employees to have their contributions to the stakeholder

Pensions

deducted from their salaries and passed directly to the insurance company operating the stakeholder.

There is no obligation upon employers to contribute anything towards employees' stakeholder pensions, although this option is available to them. Employers who fail to comply with their obligations risk civil penalties of up to £50,000 from the Pensions Regulator.

Some employers are exempt from the legislation governing stakeholder pensions. In particular it does not apply to:

- employers with fewer than five 'relevant' employees (this is broadly dependent on the number of employees and whether the employer is based in the UK or overseas); or

- employers who operate an alternative occupational or personal pension scheme for their employees that meets certain criteria.

Life assurance

Both occupational pension schemes and GPPs are often linked to a life assurance scheme providing a tax-free lump sum defined as a multiple of salary in respect of employees who die while in the employer's service.

See also: Discrimination, p.110; Employee benefits, p.138; Retirement, p.353.

Sources of further information

HMR&C pension schemes: www.hmrc.gov.uk/pensionschemes

HMR&C stakeholder pensions: www.hmrc.gov.uk/stakepension

The Pensions Regulator: www.thepensionsregulator.gov.uk

Personnel files

Amy Bird, CMS Cameron McKenna

Key points

Accurate and easily accessible personnel records assist employers in many ways. They improve the efficiency of recruitment, training and promotion of staff, help identify problems such as performance, sickness absence or labour turnover, provide information for the purposes of equal opportunity monitoring and assist in compliance with legal requirements.

Data protection principles are likely to apply to information recorded in personnel files.

Legislation
- Disability Discrimination Act 1995.
- Data Protection Act 1998.
- National Minimum Wage Act 1998.
- Working Time Regulations 1998.
- Immigration, Asylum and Nationality Act 2006.

What information should be held in personnel files?

Operating a business involves keeping information about each of the organisation's workers. Employers collect, record and maintain information about their workers during every stage of the employment relationship; for example, during recruitment and through appraisals, training records, sick notes, disciplinary records and the administering of benefits. There is no definitive list of what information should be contained in a personnel file. However, examples of information that are likely to be held in personnel files are:

- Personal details, such as name; date of birth; address; telephone number; emergency contact details; qualifications; national insurance number; details of any disability.
- Details of employment within the organisation, such as job description(s); job application(s); date employment commenced; job title; promotions; shift allocations; pay reviews; secondments.
- Terms and conditions of employment, such as statement of employment particulars; remuneration; notice period; hours of work; holiday entitlement.
- Benefits, such as insurances; private medical cover; share options; company cars; loans; nursery care schemes.
- Training and development activities.
- Performance reviews or appraisals.
- Sickness or injury records.
- Absences, such as holiday; lateness; maternity / paternity / adoption / dependents' leave; compassionate leave; sabbatical.
- Work-related accidents.
- Disciplinary action.
- Grievances raised.
- Record of termination of employment, such as garden leave; post-termination restrictive covenants; payments made on termination; reasons for leaving.

Personnel files

Why do employers keep personnel files?

Some information is required to fulfil legal requirements. For example, employers need to keep records of:

- their workers' pay (including payments of Statutory Sick Pay, statutory maternity, paternity and adoption pay) for the purposes of complying with tax and national insurance obligations and to meet the requirements of the National Minimum Wage Act 1998;
- hours worked by most workers and holidays taken, to comply with the requirements of the Working Time Regulations 1998;
- accidents, injuries and diseases, to comply with health and safety rules and regulations; and
- disciplinary action taken and grievances raised, to provide evidence of compliance with the Acas Code on Disciplinary and Grievance Procedures and any relevant company procedures; and
- proof of identity and other documents obtained to comply with the Immigration, Asylum and Nationality Act 2006, to show an employee has the right to work in the UK.

Keeping accurate personnel files also helps organisations to operate efficiently and remain competitive. Good personnel records can help organisations:

- treat staff fairly and properly, for example in accordance with legislation (*see above*);
- use their staff resources effectively, for example, appraisals or details of a worker's qualifications and experience can help an employer to assess whether a worker would be suitable for promotion;
- develop or amend employment policies and procedures and implement such policies and procedures fairly and consistently. For example, records of disciplinary action can help employers to ensure consistency in the application of the disciplinary procedure;
- improve the efficiency of their recruitment, training and development of staff. For example, a record of a worker's qualifications and experience can help an employer to assess whether a worker has any training needs. Performance reviews or appraisals can help to assess a worker's performance and decide whether there are needs for training;
- more accurately detect, monitor and control problems, such as in relation to performance, discipline, sickness, lateness, absenteeism and high turnover of staff. For example, individual absence records can be used to monitor an individual's absence levels. Statistics on absence levels across the organisation may help employers to detect and monitor problems across the workforce and take corrective action. Exit interviews can provide information to help employers deal with high labour turnover;
- reduce the risk of discrimination on the grounds of, for example, sex, race, disability or age, by providing the information necessary to implement and monitor equal opportunity policies. For example, sickness records can be useful when considering making reasonable adjustments to the job or the workplace for the purpose of complying with the Disability Discrimination Act 1995;
- provide important evidence if an employee makes a claim to an Employment Tribunal. For example, Employment Tribunals would expect organisations to hold records of an employee's termination to show what payments have been made to the employee (e.g. notice pay, redundancy pay, outstanding holiday

Personnel files

> **Facts**
> - The Data Protection Act 1998 sets out principles to which employees need to have regard in keeping personnel files.
> - The Information Commissioner's office publishes an 'Employer's Practices Code,' which has a specific section on record-keeping.
> - According to a survey carried out for Navigant Consulting by YouGov, one million employees have admitted to losing confidential data.
> - In June 2009, the Information Commissioner's Office found Manchester City Council in breach of the Data Protection Act after the theft of two unencrypted laptops containing personal details of 1,754 employees.

pay, etc.). Records of disciplinary action and dismissal are vital if an organisation is faced with complaints about, for example, unfair dismissal or discrimination; and

- provide information that may be required in the context of corporate transactions; e.g. making it easier to comply with requirements to provide 'employee liability information' under Regulation 11 of TUPE.

What considerations do employers need to think about when recording information?

Employers need to understand that the personnel files they keep contain information that is personal and can be sensitive. The Data Protection Act 1998 (DPA) lays down both legal obligations and standards that aim to balance an employer's need to keep information about its workers against a worker's right to respect for his or her private life.

The DPA places legal responsibilities on organisations to register under the DPA and process (e.g. obtain, record, retain, use, disclose or dispose of) personal data in a fair and proper way. The DPA is concerned with personal data that can be processed by equipment operating automatically or which is recorded, or intended to be recorded, in a 'relevant filing system' (*see below*). Everything from workers' personnel files to customer lists may be covered by the DPA. The DPA gives special protection to personal data that is 'sensitive'. Sensitive personal data is information concerning an individual's racial or ethnic origin, political opinions, religious or other beliefs, trade union membership, health, sexual life and any actual or alleged criminal offence. Sensitive data can only be processed under strict conditions.

The Data Protection Act

Personal data

Personal data is any information that relates to an identified or identifiable living individual. An individual's name and address can be personal data, and other information about an individual – for example, an individual's employment history or job title – would also be personal data if the individual could be identified from that information and/or from other information in the possession of the person controlling the processing of that information. Personal data also includes any expression of opinion about an individual and any indication of the intentions of the person controlling the processing of the information, or any other person, in respect of that individual. In August 2007 the Information Commissioner, who is responsible for

Personnel files

the enforcement of the DPA, issued a guidance note on what constitutes personal data for the purposes of the DPA. The guidance includes a flowchart, comprising a series of questions together with illustrative examples, to assist in determining what is personal data.

Relevant filing systems

A relevant filing system contains information within a system that is structured and/or indexed by reference to either individuals, or to criteria relating to individuals, that is readily accessible (i.e. the information is stored in a similar way to a computerised filing system). The Information Commissioner has given guidance on when manual files will be deemed to be a relevant filing system and has indicated that such files will only be covered if they are sufficiently structured so the searcher can retrieve the personal information without leafing through the contents. To help identify whether a relevant filing system is in place, the Commissioner has devised the 'temp test':

"If you employed a temporary administrative assistant (a temp), would they be able to extract specific information about an individual without any particular knowledge of your type of work or the documents you hold?"

If the temp could easily locate the relevant information, the information will be held in a relevant filing system.

A paper personnel file, relating to an individual and indexed internally by subject matter, for example, by reference to personal details, sickness, absence, disciplinary record, etc. is likely to be organised in a relevant filing system for the purposes of the DPA. Similarly, name dividers within a file on a particular topic are likely to be deemed to be a relevant filing system. However, files that are organised chronologically are unlikely to be covered by the DPA.

Data protection principles

Anyone who processes personal information must comply with the eight data protection principles. In summary, these principles state that data must be:

1. fairly and lawfully processed;
2. processed for limited purposes;
3. adequate, relevant and not excessive;
4. accurate and up to date;
5. not kept for longer than is necessary;
6. processed in accordance with the data subject's (e.g. the employee's) rights;
7. secure; and
8. not transferred to other countries without adequate protection.

In June 2009, the British Computer Society and Information Security Awareness launched the Personal Data Guardianship Code, aimed at promoting best practice in following these principles. It also sets out five principles of good data governance: accountability; visibility; consent; access; and stewardship. For more information about the DPA, see *'Data protection,'* p.84.

How to establish and operate an effective personnel records system

It is important to ensure that the system operates effectively for the needs of the organisation, and, where relevant, complies with the DPA. The employer should take into account the following points when setting up and managing a personnel records system:

- *Be clear about the purpose(s) for which any personal information is collected about workers.* The information collected should meet the needs of the organisation.
- *Keep staff informed.* It is not necessary to seek workers' prior consent to keep most employment records about them; however, employers should explain to staff the

Personnel files

purposes for which they intend to process personal data. Employers could include this information in a staff handbook, intranet site or employment contract, or draft a separate data protection policy, to inform workers about the records that are being or are likely to be kept about them and why, the uses to which they are likely to be put, where the records will be kept and for how long, who will have access to the records and the circumstances in which they might be disclosed.

- *Keep personal information stored securely.* Employers are responsible for the security of personal information collected and must take appropriate measures to prevent unauthorised access or unlawful processing, accidental loss, destruction or damage to the employment records. Records may be kept:
  - electronically (on a computer) – there are a number of advantages to storing records electronically; for example, the speed of the provision of information and the flexibility of the information available makes updating and analysing data easier. Password protection, or similar security measures, should be implemented to limit unauthorised access to computerised records.
  - manually – a simple and effective approach for smaller organisations might be to keep paper personnel records using a card index system. Manual files that contain personal information should be securely locked and only those who should have access retain the key.
  - in a combination of the above systems. Employers should restrict information that is taken outside the workplace to what is necessary and put in place rules and procedures that deal with, for example, the information that may be taken off site, and keeping that information secure. In November 2007, following the loss of child benefit records by HM Revenue and Customs, the Information Commissioner's Office issued a recommendation that, amongst other things, portable and mobile devices used to store or transmit personal information, should be protected by encryption software designed to safeguard against unauthorised access to the information stored on the device. In April 2008 the Information Commissioner published two Good Practice Notes on management and notification of breaches of data security, which give guidance on some of the things that an organisation needs to consider where a security breach occurs and on the notification of breaches to the Information Commissioner's Office. The Coroners and Justice Bill was published on 14 January 2009, and, if passed, would increase the Information Commissioner's powers to deal with potential breaches of the DPA, including its inspection powers.
- *Consider which staff should have access to which records.* In July 2008 the European Court of Human Rights ruled that the European Convention on Human Rights imposes an obligation on public bodies and governments to implement measures to keep private data confidential.
- *Ensure that information is easily accessible.* It is useful if the system (whether computerised or manual) is designed so that important information on each subject is easily accessible (e.g. visible on one screen or one side of a card) as this makes locating and updating information easier. However,

Personnel files

structuring personnel files in this way is likely to be deemed to be a relevant filing system and thus within the scope of the DPA.

- *Differentiate between sickness or injury records and absence records.* Because sickness and injury records contain sensitive personal data (details of the illness, condition or injury responsible for a worker's absence) they should be kept separately from absence records (which note the incidence of absence but do not include details of the illness or specific medical condition), where possible. For example, sickness and injury records could be kept in a sealed envelope or subject to additional password protection on an electronic system. This helps to ensure that information on workers' health is not accessed when only information regarding a worker's absence is required. For more information about health information, see '*Medical records*,' p.257.
- *Keep personal data accurate and up to date.* Workers should be asked to check for accuracy and to update information held on their personnel files that is likely to be subject to change, such as their home address, for example, on a yearly basis. It is important that the personnel records system is set up to limit access to individuals' records, so that each worker can only access his or her own record, before asking workers to check and update their records. It is also useful for organisations to review personnel records regularly to check that all the information stored is useful and necessary and that there is no unnecessary duplication of records. Information that is not relevant, out of date or for which there is no genuine business need or legal duty to keep, should be destroyed.
- *Comply with the provisions of the DPA when passing data to third parties or across national borders.* Unless certain conditions are satisfied, personal data should not be transferred to a third party outside the European Economic Area unless contractual or other guarantees have been put in place to ensure an adequate level of data protection for workers.
- *Check the effectiveness of the personnel records system regularly.* It is useful for organisations to know whether the system is providing the information it requires quickly and accurately and to determine whether any improvements can be made.

How long should records be retained for?

It is up to each employer to decide how long to retain their personnel records, as there are no specific document retention periods specified in the DPA. Employers should decide how long to retain information based on:

- the business needs of the organisation; and
- any relevant professional guidelines or statutory requirements (for example, three to six months for Employment Tribunal claims and six years for County Court claims; six years for wage / salary records).

Employers must therefore strike a balance between ensuring that employment records are not kept for longer than is necessary but are not destroyed where there are business needs to retain them.

When deciding which records should be retained, it is advisable to:

- treat pieces of information individually, or in logical groupings, to prevent all the information in a record being retained just because there is a need to keep part of it; and

Personnel files

- consider the principle of proportionality; i.e. records about many workers should not be kept for a long time on the basis that one of the workers might possibly query some aspect of his employment in the future.

Where records are to be disposed of, they should be effectively destroyed; for example, by shredding information recorded on paper and completely and permanently deleting information stored in a computerised format. See '*Confidential waste,*' p.410.

> *See also*: Data protection, p.84; Medical records, p.257; Unlawfully procuring information, p.403; Confidential waste, p.410.

Sources of further information

It is vital that employers familiarise themselves with their obligations under the Date Protection Act and ensure that the appropriate procedures are put in place to ensure compliance. Workplace Law Group's ***Data Protection Policy and Management Guide v.4.0*** has been published to help employers understand and meet those obligations and to provide clear guidance for employees on their responsibilities when handling sensitive personal data. For more information visit www.workplacelaw.net/bookshop/policiesAndProcedures.

Acas publishes an advisory booklet entitled 'Personnel data and record keeping,' which is available at www.acas.org.uk/index.aspx?articleid=717.

The Information Commissioner's Office has published 'Technical Guidance – Determining what is Personal Data,' the 'Employment Practices Code,' and 'Quick Guide to the Employment Practices Code,' available at www.ico.gov.uk.

Pregnancy

Mandy Laurie, Dundas & Wilson

Key points
- Employment legislation provides new and expectant mothers with special rights and protection, including the right to take time off for antenatal care; maternity leave and pay; return to work to the same job; request flexible working; and protection from suffering a detriment or dismissal on pregnancy grounds.

Legislation
- Employment Rights Act 1996.
- Maternity and Parental Leave etc. Regulations 1999.
- The Maternity and Parental Leave etc. and Paternity and Adoption Leave (Amendment) Regulations 2006.
- The Statutory Pay, Social Security (Maternity Allowance) and Security (Overlapping Benefits) (Amendment) Regulations 2006.
- Work and Families Act 2006.
- The Maternity and Parental Leave etc. and Paternity and Adoption Leave (Amendment) Regulations 2008.

Key employment issues

Time off for antenatal care
Expectant mothers are entitled to paid time off to attend antenatal appointments (where the appointment has been made by their doctor, midwife or a registered nurse).

The right to time off:

- is during working hours;
- includes not just the appointment time but travelling and waiting time; and
- should be paid.

If an employer unreasonably refuses time off, or allows time off but does not pay for it (either in whole or in part), the employee can make a complaint to an Employment Tribunal within three months of the date of the antenatal appointment concerned. If the complaint is justified, the Employment Tribunal must make a declaration to that effect and if the refusal to allow time off is unreasonable, the employer will be ordered to pay the expectant mother an amount of pay equal to the pay she would have received for the period of time off requested.

Maternity leave
There are three different types of maternity leave, which are as follows:

1. *Compulsory*. All new mothers (irrespective of length of service) must take two weeks' maternity leave (four if they work in a factory) after the birth of their baby. It is prohibited to deduct the two week period of compulsory maternity leave from any calculation of a discretionary bonus.
2. *Ordinary*. All new mothers may take 26 weeks' maternity leave, providing they inform their employer in writing (no later than the end of the 15th week before their expected week of childbirth (EWC)) that they are pregnant, the date of their EWC and the date they intend their ordinary maternity leave (OML) to start.

Pregnancy

> **Facts**
> - According to the HSE, every year around 350,000 women continue to work during their pregnancy, and of these 69% return to work soon after giving birth.
> - In 2007, the Equalities Review, commissioned by the Government, found that mothers face more discrimination in the workplace than any other group. A woman with a child under 11 is 45% less likely to be employed than a man.
> - According to *The Guardian*, around £15bn is lost to the economy as a result of discrimination against women who are, or may become, pregnant.

3. *Additional.* New mothers, irrespective of how long they have worked for their employer, are entitled to a further 26 weeks' additional maternity leave (AML), which begins at the end of OML. Mothers on AML are entitled to the same benefits available to mothers on OML, with the exception of remuneration.

Maternity pay

A new mother is entitled to Statutory Maternity Pay (SMP) if, by the end of the 15th week before the EWC:

- she has been continuously employed for 26 weeks; and
- her normal weekly earnings for the previous eight weeks were not less than the lower earnings limit for the payment of primary class I National Insurance contributions.

New mothers are entitled to SMP during all of their OML and for 13 weeks of their AML, meaning that they are entitled to 39 weeks' statutory maternity pay in total. The Government has noted its intentions to extend SMP from 39 weeks to 52 weeks for babies due on or after April 2010.

SMP will start on any day of the week, concurrently with OML.

Keeping in Touch Days

New mothers can return to work for up to ten days during their maternity leave without losing their right to leave or SMP, provided both parties agree.

Return to work

Following OML and AML, new mothers are entitled to return to the same job as if they had not been absent. If this is not reasonably practicable, following return from AML, the new mother should return to another suitable and appropriate job within the employer's organisation. If a new mother wants to return early from either OML or AML she must notify her employer eight weeks in advance.

Right to request flexible working

A mother who has been continuously employed for 26 weeks has the right to formally apply in writing to her employer to request a change in hours, times or location of work for the purpose of enabling her to care for her child. An employer may refuse such a request, but only if they are justified by certain business reasons. Any request should follow the formal statutory flexible working process (see *'Flexible working'*, p.190).

Unfair dismissal

Dismissals relating to the right to take time off for antenatal care, maternity leave and

Pregnancy

pay, return to work, detrimental treatment and pregnancy-related dismissals will be automatically unfair, irrespective of the new or expectant mother's length of service. These are covered in *'Family-friendly rights,'* p.182.

Fertility treatment

In February 2008, the ECJ ruled that women who have had their ova fertilised but not yet implanted will not be considered pregnant and thus are not protected from dismissal by the EC Pregnant Workers Directive. However, dismissal of a woman, if related to her IVF Treatment, may amount to discrimination on the grounds of sex, as IVF Treatment is for women only.

> *See also*: Childcare provisions, p.65; Dismissal, p.124; Family-friendly rights, p.182; Flexible working, p.190; Leave, p.252.

Sources of further information

Electronic template maternity, paternity and adoption policies and management guides are downloadable from www.workplacelaw.net/bookshop/PoliciesAndProcedures.

HSE – Expectant mothers: www.hse.gov.uk/mothers/faqs.htm

Workplace Law Group's **Guide to Flexible Working 2008** provides information on the formal legislative right to request flexible working, but also considers flexible working patterns in a wider sense. It covers the reasons why some employers are looking to introduce flexible working into their workplace, explores different flexible working patterns, including their benefits and disadvantages, and provides detail on the formal legislative right to request. For further details visit www.workplacelaw.net/bookshop/guidesTo.

Private life

Mark Kaye, Berwin Leighton Paisner

Key points
- It is reasonable for workers to have a legitimate expectation that they can keep their personal lives private and workers are entitled to a degree of privacy in the workplace.
- Interference in a worker's private life is justifiable in certain circumstances. However, disciplining or dismissing without proper justification could give rise to an unfair dismissal claim and special protections are in place to ensure that workers are not discriminated against because of issues in their home life.
- Employers have an obligation to take into account a worker's human rights. The use of personal data by an employer, in particular 'sensitive data', is strictly regulated in the UK, principally under the Data Protection Act 1998.

Legislation
- Access to Medical Reports Act 1988.
- Employment Rights Act 1996.
- Data Protection Act 1998.
- Human Rights Act 1998, Schedule 1.
- Employment Equality (Religion or Belief) Regulations 2003.
- Employment Equality (Sexual Orientation) Regulations 2003.

General rules
Most employees have an expectation that what they do in private or in their own time is their own affair. It is reasonable for workers to assume that they can keep their personal lives private, and workers are entitled to a degree of privacy in the workplace.

However, the right to respect for privacy is not absolute. Sometimes it is fair and reasonable, because of the impact that the individual's private activities have on either his work or the workplace, for the employer to interfere.

Generally, dismissal for outside conduct will only be fair if it has a material impact on either the employee's suitability to continue in his role, or the employee's business (e.g. reputation or adverse customer reaction etc.). Before dismissal, alternative positions might have to be considered (e.g. an employee-driver facing a temporary driving ban might be able to undertake alternative work in the short-term or perform his driving duties by alternative means).

Where an employer is, in principle, justified in probing into an employee's private life, the law protects an employee in a number of respects. The employer must ensure that it is not contravening these protections if any disciplinary action or dismissal is going to be fair.

Where disciplinary action or dismissal for outside conduct is contemplated, general principles of fairness require an investigation, and a proper disciplinary process should be followed.

Relying on a criminal conviction to justify dismissal will not necessarily be fair. The employer must generally conduct its

Private life

own investigation and satisfy itself that dismissal is reasonable and appropriate.

Care needs to be taken with regards to respect for private life, not just during employment but at the recruitment stage as well.

Principal protections for workers are given in the legislation discussed below.

Human Rights Act 1998
The relevant parts of the Human Rights Act 1998 (HRA) for these purposes are the right to respect for private and family life (Article Eight) and the right to freedom of expression (Article Ten). It is possible to interfere with a worker's human rights where this can be justified in a work context.

While the rights of employees under the HRA are only directly enforceable against a public sector employer, all employers must be aware of these rights to ensure that their treatment of employees is fair. As Tribunals have to take account of the HRA, if an employee's human rights have been disregarded in a disciplinary investigation leading to dismissal, for example, it could result in the Tribunal finding the dismissal unfair.

Data Protection Act 1998
Information about a worker's private life will involve personal data and, in many cases, sensitive personal data. The Data Protection Act 1998 (DPA) regulates the use of personal data by an employer and covers data contained in some manual records as well as all computerised records.

The Employment Practices Code issued by the regulatory body, the Information Commissioner, assists employers in complying with the DPA. It emphasises the need, when intruding into a worker's privacy, to carry out an impact assessment, which balances the employer's objectives against any adverse impact of the intrusion for the employee. An area where impact assessments are especially relevant is workplace monitoring.

Sensitive personal data includes information about a person's ethnic or racial origins, political opinions, religious or other beliefs, trade union membership, health, and criminal record. Before using 'sensitive personal data', it may be necessary to obtain explicit consent from the employee. Consent is not necessary where the data is to be used for, among other things:

- ensuring a safe system at work or otherwise to comply with health and safety rules; or
- preventing or detecting crime.

Therefore, where an employer suspects that an employee has been involved in

---

Facts

During the past year, almost 25% of all complaints made to the Data Protection Information Commissioner related to subject access requests not being complied with, whilst more than 10% of all complaints arose out of the disclosure of personal data. Claims in the Employment Tribunal for both sexual orientation and religious discrimination have risen more than 45% during the period 2006-08 and the data available for 2009 indicates that this trend is set to continue.

Private life

a criminal offence outside work, which is relevant to the job that he performs, or within the workplace, intrusion into the employee's privacy may well be justified under the DPA.

Discrimination legislation

The rules governing discrimination most likely to be relevant to a worker's private life are the Employment Equality (Sexual Orientation) Regulations 2003 and the Employment Equality (Religion or Belief) Regulations 2003. They make it unlawful for employers to discriminate on grounds of actual or perceived sexual orientation, religion or belief.

Sexual orientation covers orientation towards persons of the same sex, of the opposite sex, and of the same sex and the opposite sex. Religion or belief covers religion, religious belief or similar philosophical belief.

The Regulations prohibit:

- direct discrimination – e.g. dismissing someone because he frequents gay clubs or bars;
- indirect discrimination – e.g. inviting only spouses of employees to a work social event, or holding all social events on a Friday, or catering only for employees of a Christian belief;
- victimisation – e.g. not promoting someone because he has made (or intends to make) a complaint about being discriminated against on sexual orientation or religious grounds; and
- harassment – being unwanted conduct that has the purpose or effect of violating a person's dignity or creating an intimidating, hostile, degrading or offensive environment.

Care needs to be taken at the recruitment stage as well as during employment. Questions about the prospective worker's private life during the recruitment stage could give rise to other forms of discrimination, notably discrimination on the grounds of sex or disability. For example, asking a job applicant or existing employee about their plans to have children could give rise to a sex discrimination claim, or asking about serious medical ailments during an interview could create exposure to a disability discrimination claim.

Tribunal cases

As noted above, the general rule is that off-duty conduct can be a valid reason for dismissal if it is relevant to the person's employment and makes that employee unsuitable for the job, or risks damaging the employer's business.

Examples of past Tribunal cases include the following:

- A teacher of teenaged pupils was fairly dismissed after having allowed others to grow cannabis in his garden, in view of the position of responsibility and influence that he held.
- A manager was fairly dismissed after having smoked cannabis in front of subordinates at a work party, because the employer decided that her conduct had undermined her authority at work.
- A teacher was fairly dismissed after his conviction for an offence of gross indecency with a man.
- An air traffic controller was fairly dismissed for use of drugs outside work, because of a need to maintain public confidence in the safety of the air traffic control system. While there were no signs of the employee being anything other than fully capable at work, dismissal was a proportionate response in the circumstances.
- A probation officer (whose duties included supervising sex offenders) was fairly dismissed for participation outside work in activities involving bondage and sado-masochism.

Private life

The Court decided that the individual's human right to respect for his private life had not been infringed because his activities were public knowledge (via a website on the internet), and although his right to freedom of expression was infringed, the employer was entitled to protect its reputation and maintain public confidence in the probation service.

- An employee was unfairly dismissed when banned from driving, because he had offered to perform his duties using public transport, at his own expense, which was, in the circumstances, a workable alternative.
- A postman was unfairly dismissed after a conviction for football hooliganism, because the Post Office could not show that its reputation had been damaged by the conduct.
- An employee was fairly dismissed after his employer discovered he had been cautioned by the police for engaging in sexual activity with another man in a public toilet. The Court of Appeal found that as the activity had taken place in a public place, the employee's right to respect for his private life had not been engaged.
- An employee was fairly dismissed for falsifying timesheets where the employer had obtained evidence through covert surveillance of the employee's home. The employer was found not to be in breach of Article Eight and its actions were justified as it was investigating criminal activity.

Social networking

The recent increase in social networking sites, business or non-business related, are having an impact on blurring the boundaries between employees' private and working lives. The recent case of a teenaged girl who was sacked from her job for describing it as 'boring' is an example, as is the case of *Hays Specialist Recruitment (Holdings) Ltd and Another v.* *Ions and Another*, an interesting example of how the use of social networking websites can lead to potential issues for employers and employees. Mr Ions was encouraged by his employer, Hays, to join LinkedIn (a business-oriented social networking website). Hays alleged that he had deliberately transferred details of Hays' contacts from its confidential database to his personal account at LinkedIn. Despite Mr Ions' argument that this was done with Hays' consent and that, once the business contact has accepted the invitation to join his network, the information ceased to be confidential as it could be seen by all his contacts, the High Court held that Hays had reasonable grounds for considering that it might have a claim against Mr Ions in relation to the transfer of confidential information to his LinkedIn account while still employed by Hays.

Recruitment considerations

Employers often ask prospective workers questions that relate to their private life, particularly during the interview process. Recording the answers gives rise to data protection principles. Employers do not have complete freedom to ask any question they like about a job applicant's private life, as this could result in potentially damaging evidence against them (e.g. asking a woman about whether she is pregnant or has children).

Drug / alcohol testing

The extent to which employers have the right to require workers to undertake random drug or alcohol testing is limited, as such testing is likely to entail an invasion of personal privacy that breaches Article Eight. However, testing is justified where it is in the interests of, among other things, ensuring safety at work and public safety. The Information Commissioner's Employment Practices Code provides helpful guidance on alcohol and drug testing.

Private life

Workplace relationships

Although workplace relationships are commonplace, many employers are uneasy about relationships formed between work colleagues – especially if one is the direct report of the other. The risks include claims by other employees of favouritism and fallout when the relationship ends (e.g. sexual harassment claims).

Some employers require the employees to make a 'relationship declaration' (at the beginning and the end of the relationship). Others introduce a complete ban or a ban on relationships between a supervisor and his/her direct or indirect report. Such bans can risk infringing the right to privacy under Article Eight.

An employer needs to be very careful if it seeks to resolve the issue by dismissing an employee for breaking a rule on workplace relationships, or asking one of the employees to leave. Such action carries a high risk of exposure to unfair dismissal, and possibly discrimination, claims.

Practical steps for employers

- Have clear rules on what amounts to acceptable conduct both in and outside work.
- Communicate the rules to employees.
- Ensure that the rules are followed, consistently, in practice.
- Ensure that any allegations of inappropriate off-duty conduct are properly investigated and that, where relevant, the requirements of the HRA and the DPA are taken into account.
- Be satisfied that the off-duty conduct makes the employee unsuitable for the job.
- Check whether there is any alternative to dismissal.
- Do not automatically assume that a criminal conviction will justify an employee being dismissed.

See also: CCTV monitoring, p.59; Data protection, p.84; Discrimination, p.110; Believe it or not, p.121; Dismissal, p.124; Human rights, p.226; Monitoring employees, p.292; Personnel files, p.317.

Sources of further information

The Employment Practices Data Protection Code can be found at the Information Commissioner's Office: www.ico.gov.uk

Probationary periods

Gemma Cawthray, Veale Wasbrough

Key points
- A probationary period is a trial period at the beginning of a new employment relationship, which usually lasts for a few months.
- The employee should be subject to assessments and reviews throughout the probationary period, in order to assess whether he/she is capable of undertaking the role to which he/she was appointed.
- At the end of the probationary period, the employee may be confirmed as a permanent employee if he/she has successfully completed the period, or if his/her performance is considered unsatisfactory he/she may then be dismissed, or if his/her employment is unsatisfactory but there is hope of some improvement the probationary period may be extended for a short period to continue to assess suitability.

Legislation
- Employment Rights Act 1996.
- Employment Rights Act 2002.

Introduction
A probationary period is a trial period of normally about three to six months, sometimes longer, at the beginning of an employment relationship. During the probationary period the employer will assess the employee's suitability for the position and at the end of the period decide whether or not the individual should be confirmed as a permanent employee.

When should a probationary period be used?
It is usually sensible and advisable for employers to use a probationary period when appointing a new employee. Although interviews and assessments are a useful way of assessing applicants, they cannot fully reveal whether an employee is suitable for the position. Usually this can only be done by observing the employee in the role. Accordingly, a probationary period allows an employer to assess whether the employee is capable of performing the job and whether he/she fits into the team.

However, there may, of course, be circumstances where a probationary period may not be appropriate – for example, if an employee is going to be employed on a short, temporary contract, or if the employee is an existing employee who has simply moved to a different post.

Length of period
Normally, a probationary period will last for between three and six months. However, the length of the period should be determined by the industry sector and how long the employer needs to assess the employee's suitability for the specific role. Some roles may require a longer probationary period in order to properly assess an employee's capabilities. However, it should be borne in mind that, generally speaking, an employee cannot bring a claim for unfair dismissal until he/she has 12 months' continuous service. This is the reason why most employers choose to set probationary periods of fewer than 12 months, as it enables them to dismiss the employee during or at the end of the probationary period without the risk of the employee bringing a claim for

Probationary periods

unfair dismissal. There is persuasive case law that implies that a failure to confirm an appointment at the end of a probationary period, even if it is over 12 months, is not a dismissal, but this is untested in England and Wales and is uncharted waters, which most employers would prefer to avoid.

It is usually prudent to include a provision allowing for the extension of the probationary period if the employer considers that this is appropriate in the circumstances. However, before deciding whether or not to extend the probationary period, consideration should be given to whether an extension is likely to lead to an improvement in performance or whether there are specific issues to be addressed.

If performance has generally been poor and there is no further training or guidance that could be offered which would be of benefit and lead to a significant improvement, then it may not be worthwhile extending the period. Consideration should also be given to whether the employee has been unable to work during some of the period, for example due to sickness. As mentioned above, when considering extending the period, the employer should bear in mind the date upon which the employee will acquire one year's service.

During the probationary period

During the probationary period employees have the same statutory entitlements as permanent employees, such as entitlements to minimum wage and holiday pay and the benefit of health and safety regulations and working time regulations. However, during the probationary period most employees only have limited contractual rights. In particular there is usually a reduced notice period. The terms of the probationary period should be set out in the employee's contract of employment. It is also prudent for employers to have a probationary policy that clearly sets out the purpose of the period and the details relating to the governance of the employment relationship during the probationary period.

The main purpose of the probationary period is to assess the employee's suitability by monitoring and reviewing performance regularly. Such reviews allow the employer to assess the employee's performance to date and consider if further supervision or training is required, or whether steps should be taken to dismiss the employee prior to the end of the probationary period.

Any concerns with the employee's performance or capability should be brought to the attention of the employee as soon as possible, in order to give him/her the opportunity to rectify the situation. Employers should ensure that all employees who have similar roles, or who undertake substantially the same role, are subject to the same length of probationary period and the same rules.

Expiration of the probationary period

At the end of the period (whether or not extended) the employer must decide whether to dismiss the employee, or confirm the employee in post. If it is the latter situation, the employer should clearly notify the employee that he/she has successfully passed the probationary period and that he/she is now a permanent employee on permanent contractual terms.

If the employee is dismissed, it is good practice for the dismissal to be in accordance with the ACAS Code. Although many employees will not have one year's service at the end of their probationary period and therefore will be unable to bring a claim for unfair dismissal, they may still be able to bring claims that do not require a year's service, such as unlawful discrimination.

Probationary periods

Best practice, regardless of length of service, would be for the employer to set out in writing that it is considering dismissal and inviting the employee to a meeting to which he/she has the right to be accompanied by a work colleague or trade union representative. The meeting should be held and the employee given the opportunity to make representations. The employee should be informed of his/her right to appeal.

See also: Disciplinary and grievance procedures, p.106; Dismissal, p.124; Employment disputes, p.150; Interviewing, p.244; Recruitment and selection, p.335.

Sources of further information

Workplace Law Network provides premium members with unrestricted access to a comprehensive range of online information – factsheets, case reports and daily news items – on employment, health and safety and premises management. Members also benefit from an online advice service and a free subscription to the Workplace Law Magazine. For more information email membership@workplacelaw.net or call our membership services team on 0871 777 8881.

Recruitment and selection

Anna Youngs, Mills & Reeve

Key points
- Carefully and clearly define the job description of the vacant post(s).
- Carefully draft the advertisement for the job vacancy and consider where the advertisement is to be placed.
- Limit the information requested on the application form to information relevant to the post.
- Prepare questions to be asked at interview in advance and keep score sheets to record answers given during the interview.
- Data collected during the recruitment process must be used in accordance with the Data Protection Act 1998.
- Confirm any offer of employment in writing and clearly set out any attached conditions.

Legislation
- Equal Pay Act 1970.
- Rehabilitation of Offenders Act 1974.
- Sex Discrimination Act 1975.
- Race Relations Act 1976.
- Disability Discrimination Act 1995.
- Data Protection Act 1998.
- Employment Equality (Religion or Belief) Regulations 2003.
- Employment Equality (Sexual Orientation) Regulations 2003.
- Employment Equality (Age) Regulations 2006.

Some employment rights start on the first day of employment. However, all discrimination legislation offers protection throughout the recruitment process, starting when the job advertisement is placed. Equally, an employer must ensure that all documentation relating to a job is accurate to ensure that misrepresentations are not made.

Job description
Once a vacancy has arisen and there is a need to recruit, the initial step should be to clarify the role and the employer's requirements within a job description. The vacancy may be a new role within an organisation or a vacancy caused by a person leaving or reducing their working hours (for example working part-time). In any case, careful consideration should be given to the job description, including necessary skills, expertise and qualifications.

The job description will become an important contractual document because it will define the job and be useful if there are any disputes over the nature and requirements of the job. Also, it will give focus to those involved in the recruitment process, making them aware of the requirements of the organisation.

It is not necessary to list every task the employee would be required to carry out within the job description, as maintaining some flexibility can be beneficial to both an employer and an employee. The job description should instead contain the main duties and responsibilities, reporting structure, place of work, and objectives. Other details such as pay and working hours do not need to be included as these

Recruitment and selection

will be contained within the contract of employment.

In addition to the job description, a person specification can be used to detail the type of person and competencies required to perform the job. The document would list those qualifications, training, skills, experience, knowledge and personal skills that are either essential or desirable criteria. Like the job description, these should be relevant to the job, such as the ability to manage a team. Consideration should be given to how necessary these criteria are and whether any alternatives are equally as acceptable, such as equivalent qualifications to GCSEs.

Advertising

The next step in the recruitment process is to advertise the vacant post. Not only must the advert be accurately drafted so as to not misrepresent the job vacancy, but also an employer must be aware of discrimination legislation. When drafting the advertisement, certain phrases should be avoided that may be perceived as discriminatory, such as gender-specific words like 'salesman' and the use of phrases such as 'young and dynamic' or 'fit and healthy'. It is advisable to state within the advert that the organisation is an Equal Opportunities Employer.

Not only must care be taken over the wording of the advert but also where the advert is placed. If adverts are publicised in limited places, it could be argued that it limits the types of people who will be aware of the vacancy; for example, only placing the advert on the internet could be considered to discriminate against older people who are less likely to have access to the internet, or if a job is only advertised internally or by word of mouth, there is a risk that an employer will continue to recruit people of a certain race, sex, religion etc.

Application forms

Certain questions should be avoided on the application form and placed on a separate equal opportunities monitoring form, which should then only be used by Human Resources / Senior Management and not those directly involved in selecting applicants.

The following questions should not be placed on the application form:

- The applicant's marital status or previous names;
- The applicant's race or religion;
- The applicant's national insurance number or passport number;
- The applicant's nationality;
- The applicant's sexual orientation;
- The applicant's date of birth;
- The level of sickness absence taken by the applicant; and
- Whether the applicant has a particular health condition.

It is legitimate to ask questions about the applicant's health, but again these should be kept to a document other than the application form. If questions are asked about an applicant's health, reasons for such questions should be given; for

---

Facts

- Prospective employees / workers can bring claims against a prospective employer regarding the recruitment process, including advertising, short listing and what happened at interview.

Recruitment and selection

example, asking whether any adjustments need to be made to the recruitment process or to assist the applicant when they attend interview. A blanket request for answers to health-related questions may lead to an inference of discrimination (for example on the grounds of age or discrimination), so you must have a good reason for asking.

It is legitimate for an employer to ask whether or not an applicant requires a work permit.

It is also permissible to ask about past criminal convictions. However, an applicant is not required and should not be asked to provide details of spent convictions unless an exemption applies under the Rehabilitation of Offenders Act 1974. In certain cases, such as where an employee will be working with a vulnerable group of people, an employer is entitled to information about spent convictions.

Shortlisting

When considering which applicants to shortlist for interview, only the information provided on the application forms should be considered (as well as any accompanying documents provided by the applicant such as their CV). The equal opportunities monitoring form should not be considered by those carrying out the shortlisting exercise.

Applicants should be selected for the next stage of the recruitment process after a comparison of the details provided on the application form with the job description and person specification. If an applicant is to be rejected, the reason should be recorded and kept for at least six months to assist in providing feedback to unsuccessful applicants and to explain any decisions should a claim be brought at an Employment Tribunal.

Some employers may choose to use selection and aptitude tests as part of their selection process. Any such tests should be carefully considered to ensure that the tests are evaluating skills relevant to the post. Adjustments should be made to any such tests if an employer is aware that an applicant has a certain condition(s) that may hinder their ability to perform in the test.

Interviews

It is important that those employees who are to carry out interviews should be trained in equal opportunities and aware of their employer's equal opportunities policy.

At the interview, questions should centre around the job description and person specification. To ensure consistency, questions should be prepared prior to the interview and a score sheet used during each interview.

If, during the interview, the applicant discloses information about themselves, such as they have children under the age of five or require certain adjustments to be made to their workplace, the information should be noted as well as the response given by those conducting the interview. Notes of the interview should be kept for at least six months after the interview, again to provide feedback and to allow any decision not to offer the job to be justified.

There are certain questions that should not be asked of an applicant during the interview and are the same as set out above in the section on Application Forms. It is legitimate to ask during the interview if an applicant has a disability, and discuss any adjustments that need to be made to the role.

Retention of recruitment records

Throughout the recruitment process an organisation will collect a great deal

Recruitment and selection

of personal data about an applicant and the Data Protection Act 1998 will apply to these records. The Information Commissioner has issued the Employment Practices Code. Part One of the Code provides guidance on how to remain within the remit of the Data Protection Act during recruitment and selection.

The Code does not specify how long an organisation should retain information obtained during the recruitment process, but states that it should only be retained for such periods as are necessary to complete the recruitment process and suggests that any data obtained during a recruitment process should be retained for no more than six months, although as the time limits for bringing claims can be extended by three months under the Statutory Dispute Resolution Procedures, a period of nine to 12 months may be justifiable. Any information obtained during the recruitment process must be stored securely until it is destroyed.

In relation to the successful applicant, an employer should only retain information that is relevant to the continuing employment relationship.

Making a job offer

Once the successful applicant has been identified, an offer of employment should be made in writing and should set out comprehensively the terms of employment to avoid any uncertainty at a later stage, such as salary, job description and start date.

The letter should state a date by which the offer of employment is to be accepted and whether or not there are any conditions that must be fulfilled, such as pre-employment checks. Employers are entitled to make an offer of employment, subject to receiving a health report, criminal records bureau report, proof of qualifications and satisfactory references.

See also: Criminal records, p.78; Data protection, p.84; Disability legislation, p.98; Discrimination, p.110; Equal pay, p.167; Foreign nationals, p.194; Interviewing, p.240; Personnel files, p.317; Unlawfully procuring information, p.403.

Sources of further information

ACAS: Advisory booklet – *Recruitment and induction*: www.acas.org.uk/index.aspx?articleid=744

Information Commissioner: The Employment Practices Code – Part 1: www.ico.gov.uk/Home/what_we_cover/data_protection/guidance/codes_of_practice.aspx

Age Concern: www.ageconcern.org.uk

Equality and Human Rights Commission: www.equalityhumanrights.com

Redundancy

Sarah Lee and Lisa Norman, BPE Solicitors

> **Key points**
>
> Section 139 of the Employment Rights Act 1996 defines redundancy as the dismissal of an employee from employment wholly or mainly due to:
>
> - his employer ceasing or intending to cease carrying on business for the purposes for which the employee was employed, either completely or in the place that the employee was employed (known as the place of work redundancy); or
> - the requirements of the employer's business to carry out work of a particular kind having ceased or diminished or are expected to cease or diminish whether that is across the business or where the employee is employed (known as type of work redundancy).
>
> Section 195 of the Trade Union and Labour Relations (Consolidation) Act 1992 (TULRCA) also includes a definition of redundancy when used for assessing eligibility for redundancy payments. Section 195 defines redundancy as a dismissal for a reason not related to the individual concerned.
>
> Collective consultation must take place where an employee intends to make 20 or more employees redundant in any 90-day period. As a result of the Dispute Resolution Regulations 2004 employers should follow a basic procedure for consultation regardless of the number of employees involved.

Legislation
- Trade Union and Labour Relations (Consolidation) Act 1992 (TULRCA).
- Employment Rights Act 1996 (ERA).
- Employment Act 2002.
- Employment Act 2002 (Dispute Resolution Regulations 2004).

Redundancy payments
To be eligible for a statutory redundancy payment an employee must have at least two years' continuous service. The lower and upper age limits (18 and 65) on the right to claim redundancy payments no longer apply as a result of age discrimination legislation which came into force on 1 October 2006. Statutory redundancy payments are calculated in accordance with the employee's age, length of service and the rate of the employee's weekly pay (subject to a statutory cap which is currently £330 per week but traditionally increases on 1 February each year). The employee's weekly pay is multiplied by their complete year's service and age multiplies as follows:

- By 1.5 for every year in which the employee was 41 years old or older;
- By 1 for every year in which the employee was aged between 22 and 40; and
- By 0.5 for every year in which the employee was between 18 and 21.

The maximum payment is 30 weeks' pay or £9,900. A redundancy ready reckoner is

Redundancy

available on the BIS website to calculate statutory redundancy payments due.

Penalties
Failure to carry out a proper procedure (whether the statutory dispute resolution procedure or collective consultation procedure) may result in substantial claims. Getting the collective consultation wrong can result in claims for protective awards in the value of 90 days' pay per employee.

Claims for unfair dismissal in relation to any aspect of the redundancy process can also be brought if there is a fault in the process. Employees usually need one year's continuous employment to make such a claim unless they link it to discrimination. The current statutory maximum compensatory award for unfair dismissal is £63,000. There is also potential liability for a basic award, which is calculated on the same basis as the redundancy payments. Therefore, if they are paid the redundancy pay, only the compensatory award will be made. Failure to follow the statutory Dispute Resolution procedures will allow an Employment Tribunal to increase a compensatory award by between 10% and 50% depending on the circumstances and will also make the dismissal automatically unfair. Any uplift will not take an award beyond the statutory maximum.

Redundancy process checklist
Below is a checklist of the most important issues to be considered in a redundancy process. Please note it is not a comprehensive guide and individual circumstances may vary. It is not intended to be a substitute for legal advice, which should be sought regarding individual circumstances.

Step 1 – Planning
As soon as the possibility of redundancy has been identified as an option, document the reason for the proposed redundancies and plan the redundancy process.

Step 2 – Redundancy policy
Does your company have a redundancy policy in place, which has been communicated to the employees, or is there an implied policy in place through custom or practice? If so, check that those policies are compatible with the statutory procedures and then follow your own policy. If you have no policy or it does not follow the Statutory Dispute Resolution Procedures the following steps should be taken.

Step 3 – Collective consultation
If you are proposing to dismiss 20 or more employees from one establishment over a 90-day period, you are required to enter into collective consultation with appropriate representatives. This may be a Trade Union representative or an elected employee representative. Your collective consultation should set out the framework for redundancy selection and who will be in the pool of selection. You will also have to carry out individual consultation after the collective consultation.

If you are proposing to make 100 or more employees redundant at one establishment within a 90-day period, consultation must take place in 'good time' and at least 90 days before the first of the dismissals.

If you are proposing to dismiss at least 20 but fewer than 100 employees at one establishment within a 90-day period, collective consultations must begin in 'good time' and at least 30 days before the first dismissal.

Collective consultation should start as soon as redundancies are proposed. The employee representatives can assist in the planning stage of the selection process and reduce the risk of claims

Redundancy

being brought for failure to follow proper procedure.

There is an obligation for employers to inform the Secretary of State for Trade and Industry of proposed large-scale redundancies using form HR1. A copy of the form should be sent to the appropriate representatives.

Collective consultations should include discussions about avoiding dismissals, reducing the number of employees to be dismissed and mitigating the consequences of dismissal. Consultation should also be undertaken with a view to reaching agreement. Regardless of whether or not agreement is possible, the next step is individual consultation.

Step 4 – Individual consultation

To follow a fair procedure in accordance with the Statutory Dispute Resolution Procedures, all employees should be invited to a meeting in writing informing them of the potential redundancy situation.

Employees are entitled to attend meetings with a fellow employee or a Trade Union representative of their choice.

Inform each employee of the reason for the redundancy and the selection process that is going to take place. Inform them of the reason why they are potentially at risk of redundancy and ask them to consider whether they are in the correct pool for selection. If they do not consider they are in the correct pool, consider their reasons for this.

After the meeting confirm whether or not the employee is in the pool of selection and provide them with details of the redundancy selection criteria (e.g. length of service, skills and qualifications, disciplinary record) taking care not to unlawfully discriminate against the affected employees.

Hold a second meeting where you discuss the selection criteria and any alternatives to redundancy you or the employee may have, including alternative employment or job sharing.

Confirm the options in writing

If appropriate, apply the selection criteria and provisionally select the redundant employees. Write to those selected employees to confirm this. Do not state that they will be made redundant but do inform them that a possibility of the full and final meeting will be their dismissal.

Inform the employee at the final meeting the reason why they have been selected for redundancy and explain the consequences of this. Invite the employee to comment on the selection. After the meeting consider any points raised by the employee and then confirm to them in writing their selection for redundancy. Be sure to offer the employees the opportunity to appeal to a higher level of management.

Consider whether there is any suitable alternative employment within the company or group of companies that can be offered to the employees, and if they accept it decide whether a trial period should be given in their new role.

Redundant employees will be entitled to notice payments, redundancy payments and payment of accrued but untaken holiday pay.

Statutory dismissal procedure (SDP)

These procedures have now been repealed; however, there is an ongoing transitory period during which time the procedures will remain valid. The SDP

Redundancy

required the employer to write to the affected employees and invite them to a final meeting, inform them of their dismissal and then write to them offering them an appeal against their dismissal on grounds by reason of redundancy. It is still good practice and compliant with the new ACAS Code of Practice to carry out this step. For more information, see '*Dismissal*,' p.124.

See also: Disciplinary and grievance procedures, p.106; Discrimination, p.110; Dismissal, p.124; Employee consultation; p.142; Employment disputes, p.150; Employment Tribunals, p.158; Notice periods, p.301; There's no other way – alternatives to redundancy, p.344.

Sources of further information

BIS's Redundancy Ready Reckoner: www.berr.gov.uk/employment/employment-legislation/employment-guidance/page33157.html

Workplace Law Group's **Redundancy Policy and Management Guide v.4.0** can help employers in England and Wales ensure that they comply with their requirements under law, and to provide a clear record of the policy and procedure. For more information visit www.workplacelaw.net/bookshop/policiesAndProcedures.

Redundancy support from Workplace Law

0871 777 8881
Redundancy | Downsizing | Consultancy

If you are concerned at the current slowdown of the economy and its impact on your organisation, one of the first questions to consider is how you can manage your human resources capital – your people – to match the immediate and future needs of your business. Any decisions taken could have a long-standing impact on recruitment in the future.

Redundancy or restructuring is part of the everyday working world, as we constantly have to react to changing business needs. Although redundancy is a fair reason for dismissal there are a number of steps employers need to take before terminating a contract and failure to follow the correct procedures can prove to be a costly error and result in unnecessary Employment Tribunal claims.

Our redundancy specialists

Gayn Bond FCIPD
Head of HR
Workplace Law Group

Ali Moran MCIPD
HR Consultant
Workplace Law Group

How we can help

Workplace Law's team of HR and employment relations specialists have years of experience in handling redundancies and downsizing programmes and can provide cost-effective support to help you plan and implement any decision to downsize your workforce. Our expert team can help you with:

- Redundancy planning
- Assistance with consultations
- Implementing a redundancy programme
- Confidential advice
- In-house training courses

Workplace Law Network

Workplace Law Network premium members have access to telephone support and online advice 24 hours a day, seven days a week. If you are an employer who is not a premium member but would like to discuss your organisation's needs please contact us in total confidence.

Call us today on **0871 777 8881** to find out more about our redundancy support services

Comment...

There's no other way – alternatives to redundancy

> Joanna Downes is an Associate in the Employment Team at Clarion Solicitors LLP. Joanna deals with all areas of employment law and frequently assists Clarion Solicitors LLP's Corporate Team on the employment related issues involved in corporate transactions. Joanna has a particular expertise with employee information and data protection and recently presented to a Marketing industry summit in London.

In many businesses, employee costs are the highest single item of expenditure. Accordingly, in difficult times the temptation to cut headcount can be hard to resist. However, compulsory redundancies are not always the 'quick fix' or the complete solution. In reality, such short-term measures can affect the long-term prospects of the business. In losing key staff, not only will morale be seriously damaged but the business may be less able to get back on its feet when there is an upturn in the market. Certainly, in larger businesses, the loss of revenue arising from the bad publicity generated by high-profile job losses could outweigh any cost-saving in the long-term.

Employers who are contemplating a redundancy procedure would be wise to consider the business alternatives, prior to making any firm decisions.

Reducing headcount

A **recruitment freeze** is probably the tool most commonly-used by employers in order to contain rising employment costs. Over time, a recruitment freeze, combined with natural attrition, is an easy cost-effective mechanism to reduce costs (with few potential employment implications).

Withdrawing employment offers before new employees join is also an attractive way to reduce employee headcount. An employer may withdraw an offer of employment at any point before it is accepted, without being in breach of contract. However, once the offer is accepted by the potential recruit, an employment contract comes into existence, and an employer will have to terminate the contract by giving the employee notice (or making a payment in lieu of notice) to avoid legal ramifications.

Many employers will look to use **softer alternatives** to withdrawing job offers, such as asking graduate recruits or apprentices to delay starting work for a period of time. Before doing so, employers should be alive to the fact that such techniques can have an adverse effect on the reputation of the business, especially in the market for future employees.

Another swift and cost effective means of reducing staff costs is to **reduce the number of agency, temporary or casual staff**. This is often cheaper

Comment: Alternatives to redundancy

and legally simpler than dismissing permanent employees, provided the employer complies with any contractual arrangements (for example, length of notice) which might be in place with the relevant provider or agency. However, this strategy may not be suitable where temporary staff form a large part of the organisation's workforce. In such a case, cutting staff could lead to poor motivation levels and reduced ability to meet customer demand.

Secondments can offer another headcount reduction option to a struggling business. The secondment may be internal within the employer group or to an external client needing additional resources. In either case, it is important that the scope of the secondment is recorded in an agreement between the original employer, the 'host' organisation, and the employee. The secondment agreement should detail, amongst other matters, how quickly the employee can be required to return to work – in case there is an upsurge in work or demands.

Another option for employers is to offer **early retirement** to volunteers. Employers contemplating this option would be well advised to retain discretion as to whether or not they accept the volunteers' decision to retire early. By failing to retain such discretion, the business could risk losing its most experienced and skilled staff. Employers should also consider the effect that early retirement might have on pension entitlements, particularly where there are final salary schemes where the financial impact may be significant.

Reducing hours

Hours of work are a fundamental part of a contract of employment, and therefore can only be changed with the relevant employee's agreement. An employer seeking to adopt **shorter working hours**, such as four-day weeks, would be advised to explain to employees the impact on them personally (i.e. a reduction in pay) and also on the organisation as a whole (for example, the avoidance of compulsory redundancies). Recent difficult economic conditions may have made previously resistant employees more willing to consider a reduction in their hours, rather than risk losing their job.

Alternatively, or in addition to reducing core working hours, employers may wish to consider a **ban on overtime**. This is relatively straightforward if the employees have no contractual entitlement to overtime work. Where there is a contractual entitlement, however, the employer must obtain the employees' consent (as above) before ceasing to offer it. Any business that is considering changing an employees' contract of employment should seek specific legal advice to avoid breach of contract and/or constructive dismissal claims.

Reducing remuneration

Like the hours of work, pay is a fundamental part of a contract of employment and reducing remuneration is likely to be the most problematic alternative to redundancy. Unless an employee consents to a **pay cut** (after proper consultation), an employer who pays less than is required under the contract of employment would be in breach of contract and also at risk of constructive dismissal. Again, it is advisable for the employer to inform the workforce of the proposals in advance and explain the impact on the individual and the costs-benefits to the organisation as a whole.

Where an employee is not contractually entitled to a salary increase (for example, on an annual basis), another option would be to **freeze pay**. This is likely to

Comment: Alternatives to redundancy

be viewed by employees as a pay cut, and may have a consequent effect on employee motivation levels, as well as potentially limiting the business' ability to attract new talent. As a result, employers should consider imposing salary freezes for only a limited period, as permanent freezes could lead to an exodus of employees.

Likewise, where the employer offers **non-contractual benefits** such as Christmas functions and team 'away days', it may consider withdrawing these. Where the entitlement to the benefit is set out in the contract of employment, however, the employer will need to obtain the employees' consent to the change.

If a **bonus** is entirely discretionary, employers may decide not to pay any bonus to employees. The legal position is that discretion should not be exercised '*capriciously, in bad faith or in a way calculated to or likely to destroy the relationship of trust and confidence*'. If a bonus is assessed at nil, but the employee has met all of the necessary performance conditions to achieve a bonus, the employer's decision is likely to be challenged. Further, if bonuses make up a large percentage of employees' remuneration, there is a significant risk of employee dissatisfaction. Communication of the rationale behind the lower (or nil) bonus may well help to improve relations with employees.

Summary

The Chartered Institute of Personnel and Development has estimated that the cost of a single employee's redundancy is more than £16,000. Whilst redundancies might seem the cheap and simple option, the reality is that redundancies are not only costly but can have detrimental long-term effects on a business (most notably the loss of experienced staff). The alternatives set out above are just some of the options employers should consider with a view to cutting costs, whilst avoiding compulsory redundancies.

It is worth remembering that in a difficult economic climate employees may be more willing to discuss pay cuts and hour reductions if it means that job security is preserved. By explaining the savings that will be made by the proposed measure, and what the alternatives are, consent should be more readily achieved and good employee relationships may be preserved.

References

Pinsent Masons Employment Group

Key points

The subject of employee references will usually arise when offering a prospective employee a contract of employment or when providing a reference for a current or former employee.

An employer is under no obligation to provide a reference for a current or former employee, unless a term in the contract of employment compels it, or, as in some regulated industries such as financial services, it is obliged to provide a reference under the regulations of a relevant body.

If a reference is given, the referee must take great care in compiling it and must use all reasonable skill and care to ensure the accuracy of the facts contained in the reference and the reasonableness of the opinions contained within the reference as the referee may be liable as a consequence of a defective reference.

Employers should be aware that if the reference results in the former employee suffering a loss or failing to be employed by the new employer then the content of the reference will be made known to the individual.

Legislation

There is no legislation that sets out what must be included in references or the form they should take. There are, however, data protection issues, and employers should have regard to the Data Protection Act 1998 when giving references and responding to employees' requests for access to information (including references) that the employer holds.

Offering a prospective employee a contract of employment

When recruiting new staff it is common for a prospective employer to make a job offer expressly conditional on receiving satisfactory references from the prospective employee's previous employer.

If the prospective employer's decision to employ is conditional upon receipt of a satisfactory reference, this must be made clear in the offer letter. To avoid dispute, it should be made clear that it is for the employer to determine what is satisfactory.

Providing a reference for a current or former employee

An employer is under no obligation to provide a reference for a current or former employee, unless a term in the contract of employment compels it, or, as in some regulated industries such as financial services, it is obliged to provide a reference under the regulations of a relevant body.

However, if a reference is given, the referee must take great care in compiling it, for he may be liable as a consequence of a defective reference.

Duties are owed by the employer to recipients of references and to the subject of those references.

References

When giving a reference about an existing employee who is seeking employment with another employer, there are a number of points that an employer must consider:

- An employer must use all reasonable skill and care to ensure the accuracy of the facts contained in the reference and the reasonableness of the opinions contained within the reference. Failure to do so may amount to a breach of the implied term of trust and confidence, entitling the employee to resign and claim constructive dismissal.
- Even if the reference is factually accurate, the employer must be careful not to give an unfair impression of the employee concerned. Therefore the employer should not include a disproportionate amount of negative facts and exclude those that are to the credit of the employee (e.g. stating that he always took long lunches, but not stating that he always worked late in the evening).
- Where an employee has been the subject of disciplinary action, this should only be referred to in the reference being provided where the employer:
    - genuinely believes the statement being made to be true;
    - has reasonable grounds for believing that the statement is true; and
    - has carried out as much investigation into the matters referred to in the statement as is reasonable in the circumstances.
- It would accordingly not be appropriate for an employer to refer to a disciplinary incident where the employment is terminated before a full investigation was conducted.
- Other than in certain circumstances (e.g. where industry rules or practice require full and frank references), references do not have to be full and comprehensive. The employer's obligation is to provide a true, accurate and fair reference that does not give a misleading impression overall. Some employers will limit the reference to basic facts such as the dates of employment and the position held. Employers are entitled to set parameters within which the reference is given, e.g. by stressing their limited knowledge of the individual employee.

A practical danger

References could be used in evidence where the dismissal of an employee is the subject of litigation, so employers should take care in giving a reference in such circumstances. It is not unusual for employers to give positive references to employees who have been sacked for poor performance, as part of a negotiated settlement in such circumstances. Should they choose to do so in terms that are misleadingly favourable to the employee, the referee may find himself liable to a subsequent employer who relies on the references.

Employees' claims

The most common action for an employee who is the subject of an inaccurate reference is a damages action in respect of any economic loss which may flow from a carelessly or negligently prepared reference.

In order to establish that an employer is in breach of its duty to take reasonable care in the preparation of a reference, the employee must show that:

- the information contained in the reference was misleading;
- by virtue of the misleading information the reference was likely to have a material effect upon the mind of a

References

reasonable recipient of the reference to the detriment of the employee;
- the employee suffered loss as a result; and
- the employer was negligent in providing such a reference.

See also: Employment contracts, p.146; Interviewing, p.240; Recruitment and selection, p.335.

Sources of further information

Workplace Law Network provides premium members with unrestricted access to a comprehensive range of online information – factsheets, case reports and daily news items – on employment, health and safety and premises management. Members also benefit from an online advice service and a free subscription to the *Workplace Law Magazine*. For more information email membership@workplacelaw.net or call our membership services team on 0871 777 8881.

Restrictive covenants and garden leave

Anna Youngs, Mills & Reeve

Key points
- Restrictive covenants operate to protect the employer's business after an employee has left employment.
- They are prima facie void as a restraint of trade.
- To enforce a covenant, the terms must be no wider than necessary to protect a legitimate business interest.
- Restrictive covenants are enforced by the Courts.

Introduction
An employee must observe certain restrictions that are implied by law into a contract of employment (e.g. fidelity, obedience, working with due diligence and care, not to use or disclose the employer's trade secrets or confidential information during employment). However, these implied terms are of a limited nature and, save in respect of highly confidential information, do not apply after termination of the contract.

Restrictions that apply to employees after the employment relationship ends either take the form of a garden leave clause or a restrictive covenant.

What are restrictive covenants and when do employers need them?
Restrictive covenants are contractual post-termination obligations (commonly incorporated into an employee's contract of employment) that seek to prevent employees from doing certain things that may be damaging to the employer's business when they leave the employment.

The main types of restrictive covenants are:

- Non-solicitation of staff (to prevent ex-employees from recruiting key employees of the business).
- Non-solicitation of customers and non-dealing covenants (to protect the client base of the business by preventing employees from dealing with and soliciting customers).
- Non-competition (to prevent the ex-employee from taking up employment in competition with the business).
- Protecting confidential information acquired by the ex-employee during the course of employment.

These covenants can be used in isolation, or together in order to bolster the protection provided to the employer.

However, the employer's need to protect its business must be balanced against the employee's right to earn a living and take up work in their area of expertise.

The legal approach to restrictive covenants
The starting point in law is that restrictive covenants are void as being a restraint of trade and are therefore unenforceable unless the employer can show that it is a justifiable covenant, which will only be the case where:

- the employer has a legitimate interest to protect, which will vary

Restrictive covenants and garden leave

depending on the nature of the business (examples include business connections, stability of the workforce, confidential information etc.); and
- the covenant goes no further than is reasonably necessary for the protection of the legitimate interest.

There can never be any certainty as to the enforceability of restrictive covenants because to enforce any restriction the employer has to obtain a court order, which is granted at the discretion of the court by reference to what it regards as reasonable in the circumstances.

When will a restrictive covenant be enforceable?

Even if there is a legitimate interest to protect, the restriction can be no wider than reasonably necessary to protect that interest. This is achieved by limiting the scope of the covenant by reference to the restricted activities, the length of the period of restraint and, where appropriate, the geographical area to which it applies (e.g. the duration of the restricted period should be no longer than necessary to protect the business interest). The following factors are useful pointers:

- *Non-solicitation of staff.* Consider which groups of employees need to be protected and the time period necessary for the influence over these staff to diminish.
- *Non-solicitation of customers.* In respect of current customers, the covenant should be limited to customers with whom the employee had contact, and the time period should be limited by considering the amount of time it would take for the employee's successor to build up a relationship with these customers. The general customer base and prospective customers can also be protected in certain circumstances.
- *Non-dealing covenants.* A blanket ban on dealing with any customer should be avoided, and therefore consideration should be given to which key contacts are at risk because of the relationship with the employee.
- *Non-competition.* The restriction must be for a limited time and may need to be limited in terms of geographical area. Consider how long it will be until competitive activities by the individual are no longer a material threat to the legitimate business interest, as well as the area of activities of the employee and the size of the restricted area.
- *Protecting confidential information.* The key to confidentiality clauses is to carefully define what is 'confidential information'.

As well as considering what the legitimate business interest is, the employer must consider what level of protection is reasonably necessary in respect of any given employee. What is enforceable against one employee may not be against another. For example, a senior employee would have very different contacts to someone at a trainee level, and even employees at the same level may have different access to customers and confidential information.

In almost all cases, the length of the restrictive period will be a key factor.

What if the clause is too wide-ranging?

If a clause is too wide-ranging, it will not be enforceable. The court will not re-write the clause, but they may sever unenforceable clauses and 'blue pencil' restrictions, leaving enforceable restrictions intact.

The court, in deciding whether unlawful provisions may be severed from the rest of the terms, will consider whether:

- the provisions can be removed without needing to amend the remaining wording;

Restrictive covenants and garden leave

- the remaining terms are supported by adequate consideration; and
- deleting the unenforceable wording changes the character of the contract.

Note: If an employer commits a repudiatory breach of contract, or terminates the employment in breach of contract, it is highly unlikely that any restrictive covenants will be enforced.

Garden leave

The need for garden leave normally arises where employees hand in their notice in order to work for a competitor, although they can still work where the employer gives the employee notice of termination. The aim of garden leave is to keep the employee away from confidential information long enough for the information to become out of date, and from customers long enough to enable customer relationships to be forged with an alternative contact. This can be done either by changing the employee's duties during their notice period, or by requiring the employee to stay at home (whilst enjoying normal pay and benefits) on 'garden leave' during all or part of their notice period.

Putting an employee on garden leave is still a restraint of trade, and therefore the same principles as with restrictive covenants apply, such as having a period no longer than is reasonably necessary to protect a legitimate business interest. Therefore, even where, for example, 12 months' notice is required, in the first six months the employee could be assigned alternative duties (provided the contract allows for this) and then only the latter six months would be garden leave.

Enforcing restrictive covenants

Restrictive covenants are enforced by the courts. An employer may seek an injunction to prevent an employee from breaching the terms of the covenant. If this is not possible, there is a claim against the employee for damages for breach of the covenants, provided that the covenant is enforceable (i.e. not an illegal restraint of trade) and provided that any breach of the covenant has caused the employer loss.

Enforcing breaches of restrictive covenants is difficult and expensive, so employers need to think carefully about whether their 'legitimate business interest' warrants the time and expense of litigation. Perhaps negotiation and persuasion is a sensible first step, but bear in mind that litigation must be commenced swiftly if there is to be any hope of enforcing a restrictive covenant.

See also: Dismissal, p.124; Employment contracts, p.146; Leave, p.252; Redundancy, p.339.

Sources of further information

Workplace Law Network provides premium members with unrestricted access to a comprehensive range of online information – factsheets, case reports and daily news items – on employment, health and safety and premises management. Members also benefit from an online advice service and a free subscription to the *Workplace Law Magazine*. For more information email membership@workplacelaw.net or call our membership services team on 0871 777 8881.

Retirement

Lizzie Mead, Berwin Leighton Paisner

Key points
- The law on retirement in the UK has been revised radically by the implementation of legislation preventing age discrimination.
- The Employment Equality (Age) Regulations 2006 (the Regulations) provide that retirement at the age of 65 or over is not unlawful, provided that the correct statutory retirement procedure is adhered to.
- Retirement ages of less than 65 are directly discriminatory on the grounds of age unless they can be justified. However, in most industries, lower retirement ages are unlikely to be justifiable.

Legislation
- The Employment Rights Act 1996.
- The Employment Equality (Age) Regulations 2006.

The position pre-October 2006
Prior to 1 October 2006, it was lawful to retire an employee at normal retirement age. Employees who were over the employer's normal retirement age (or 65 if there was no default age) were not entitled to bring an unfair dismissal claim if their employment was terminated for any reason. The entitlement to a statutory redundancy payment also ceased at the age of 65 (or at normal retirement age if this was lower).

The impact of the Age Discrimination Regulations
This position has been changed by the introduction of the Regulations. The Regulations give effect in the UK to the EU Employment Directive 2000/78/EC. Less favourable treatment on the grounds of age, whether direct or indirect, is now unlawful unless it can be justified. This applies throughout the sphere of employment, from recruitment through to retirement. One of the most significant consequences is that it is now potentially unlawful for an employer to seek to enforce a retirement age for its employees.

Seeking to force an employee to stop working merely because they have reached a certain age is less favourable treatment on the grounds of age. Before the implementation of the Regulations, there was a significant amount of discussion and consultation as to whether enforced retirement ages would become entirely unlawful or, if not, at what age they should be permitted. Although it is perhaps the clearest example of age discrimination, the counter arguments are that preventing employers from retiring employees at all would hinder legitimate business succession planning and put an added strain on pensions arrangements.

Eventually, the legislation has settled on a default retirement age of 65. This means that the Regulations allow employers to retire employees once they reach the age of 65 (or another default retirement age set by the employer if it is higher than 65). There is, however, a proviso. Retirement at the default retirement age is only exempted from being age discrimination if the employer follows the statutory retirement procedure. The obligation to follow the

Retirement

procedure applies notwithstanding any express term in the employee's contract of employment.

If an employer seeks to apply a retirement age of less than 65, they will need to show that this can be objectively justified and then follow the statutory retirement procedure. Justification means showing that the employer had a legitimate aim for introducing a lower retirement age and also showing that the policy was a proportionate means of achieving this aim. In reality, it will seldom be possible to do so. For example, in a safety-critical industry, it may be legitimate not to employ individuals over the age of 60 if there is a concern about their physical ability to do the job. However, it may be possible to address this concern by asking employees over the age of 60 to undergo medical examinations to confirm their continued fitness. If a medical would address the issue, a blanket retirement age of 60 will not be proportionate and will not therefore be justifiable.

The statutory retirement procedure

The Regulations amend the Employment Rights Act 1996 (the Act) so that retirement is now a potentially fair reason for dismissal. Instead of employees over normal retirement age or 65 being exempted, however, the crucial issue is whether the statutory procedure as set out in the Act has been followed. This process is as follows:

- *Stage One.* The employer must notify the employee of the date on which it is intended that they will retire and of their right to request not to be retired. This notification must be given no fewer than six and no more than 12 months before the retirement date. If the employer fails to give this notice within six months of retirement, the employee may be awarded up to eight weeks' capped pay. The employer still has an ongoing duty to give this notification up to two weeks before the retirement date. Whether or not this is complied with is important when considering unfair dismissal issues.
- *Stage Two.* The employee may make a written request not to be retired. The request may be made between three and six months before the retirement age (or at any time less than six months if the employer has not complied with stage one). The request must be in writing, set out the details of how the employee wishes their employment to be extended (whether indefinitely, for a set period or until a set date) and should state that it is made under paragraph five of Schedule Six of the Regulations.
- *Stage Three.* The employer must hold a meeting to consider the request

Facts

- By 2011, the mean age of the UK population will exceed 40 for the first time; by about 2017/18, there will be more people over the age of 40 than below the age of 40.
- Government estimates for the UK show that life expectancy for people aged 65 in 2007 will be around 86 for men and around 88 for women.
- Around one third of employers have a compulsory retirement age. The rest either have no retirement age or work on a more flexible basis.

Sources: Age Concern, ONS, Government's Actuary Department.

Retirement

within a reasonable period (unless the request is agreed to immediately) at which the employee has the right to be accompanied and respond in writing as soon as is reasonably practicable. The response must set out details of the outcome. If it is refused or granted for a shorter period, the employee must be given the right to appeal. There is no duty for the employer to give reasons.
- *Stage Four.* If the employee appeals, the appeal meeting takes the same form as the initial meeting. An appeal does not extend the employee's employment, which will terminate no later than the date that the original decision is notified in accordance with Stage Three.

Employers should ensure that any requests to work beyond the normal retirement age (NRA) are considered on a case by case basis. If the employer has a blanket policy of allowing all employees to work beyond its contractual retirement age (to the same later age) this may have the effect of raising the NRA.

In what circumstances will a retirement amount to an unfair dismissal or age discrimination?

The Regulations have significantly amended the unfair dismissal provisions in the Act. There is no longer an age cap for unfair dismissal claims but, if the above procedure is followed correctly, the employee cannot challenge the reason for dismissal. It is deemed to be on the grounds of retirement and to be fair. The employee could potentially raise another discrimination claim; for example, sex discrimination, if only women are not permitted to work past retirement.

If the retirement takes place at or after a retirement age of 65 or over and notice was given in accordance with Stage One, the retirement is deemed to be fair and cannot be challenged by the employee. If the employer has not given notice in accordance with Stage One and/or the retirement is before the normal retirement age, retirement shall not be the reason for dismissal. Although the employer can seek to rely on another reason, it is unlikely to be able to demonstrate a fair dismissal in these circumstances and so it is likely to be both unfair dismissal and age discrimination.

Alternatively, in cases where the employer has failed to give the appropriate Stage One notification within six months of the retirement date, but there is an intended date of retirement and the employee's employment terminates on or after that date, retirement may be the reason for dismissal and this is to be determined by a Tribunal, giving consideration to the extent that the employer did comply with the ongoing duty to give notice and with Stage Three of the duty to consider procedure.

While this process is technical, the crucial issue is that it is extremely important for employers to follow the correct procedure. Failing to do so leaves companies vulnerable to findings of unfair dismissal, age discrimination and potentially an uplift for breach of the statutory dismissal procedure (this does not apply to retirement dismissals but if the dismissal was not on the grounds of retirement, there is a risk that the procedure applied and was not followed).

Future developments

The Government has pledged to review the concept of retirement ages again in 2010. There is a possibility that the default age of 65 may be raised or it may be removed altogether, meaning that all retirements will need to be capable of justification. At the time of writing, the retirement age is also potentially

Retirement

the subject of a judicial review, as there is an argument being raised by age charities that it does not comply with the EU Directive and is therefore unlawful. In March 2009 the ECJ confirmed that the provisions allowing employers to compulsorily retire employees at age 65 are potentially lawful. However, since the compulsory retirement law discriminates on grounds of age, it must still be objectively justified. This question will now be determined by the High Court. Employers should be alive to the possibility that employees who bring age discrimination tribunal proceedings in the UK may request a stay of the proceedings until a decision is made on this subject by the High Court.

> *See also*: Discrimination, p.110; Dismissal, p.124; Health surveillance, p.212; Redundancy, p.339.

Sources of further information

BIS: www.berr.gov.uk/employment/discrimination/age-discrimination/index.html

Age and the workplace: Putting the Employment Equality (Age) Regulations 2006 into Practice: www.acas.org.uk/media/pdf/r/j/Age_and_the_Workplace.pdf

Self-employment

Sarah Lee and Lisa Norman, BPE Solicitors

> **Key points**
>
> The purpose of this chapter is to help direct the minds of those who are considering 'jumping ship' and setting up their own business.
>
> We look first at the legal differences between employed and self-employed status. We then look at the issues to be addressed in starting up and running a business of your own successfully. Finally, we look at the implications for existing businesses in engaging the services of a self-employed individual.

Employed versus self employed – what is the difference?

The chapter on Employment Status (p.154) sets out the necessary considerations in addressing the question of 'Who is employed and who is self-employed?' This chapter also sets out the legal consequences of such a distinction. In short, where:

- an individual is obliged to provide services personally; and
- there is mutuality of obligation between the two parties; and
- the individual is subject to 'sufficient' control at the hands of the person for whom he works,

the individual is likely to be an employee and thus benefit from unfair dismissal protection, redundancy payments, statutory notice, equal pay, maternity rights and sick pay, to name but a few. Assuming, however, that an individual is not or would rather not be an employee what are the considerations / implications for them?

Why might you want to become self-employed?

There are many reasons why an individual may consider becoming self-employed. For example, they may have been made redundant recently or indeed some time ago and are struggling to find work. Alternatively, an individual may be seeking more flexibility or control in terms of their work and, in particular, in terms of their working hours. This is often the case for individuals, both male and female, who wish to spend more time with their family.

What are the immediate and obvious concerns to being self-employed?

Although there are many benefits to being self-employed there are also a number of risks. For example, you will have to accept that:

- you will not necessarily earn a regular income;
- in practice, it is likely you will end up working long hours;
- you won't get paid when you are on holiday;
- you will have to make your own arrangements in terms of pension; and
- you will have to arrange adequate cover for sick leave.

From a personal perspective, you will also have to accept the lack of social contact with other employees, a transition that some people find very difficult.

Practical issues

There are a number of issues to address in establishing your own business.

Self-employment

What kind of business will you operate and how will you trade?
You will need to decide whether you are going to trade as a sole trader, a partnership or indeed, as a limited company. There are pros and cons to each option as well as financial considerations. Consequently, it is worth taking advice as to which format best suits your needs.

What about the finances?
You will need to register with HM Revenue and Customs on a self-employed basis. From this, your income tax and national insurance position will become clearer. A reputable accountant will help you through the registration process and the daunting regime of self assessment and payments on account (if relevant). Your accountant will also help with VAT registration as and when your turnover reaches (currently) £64,000. If you need funding you will need to devise a strategy dealing with who you will ask, when, and produce relevant presentations for each potential investor.

Depending on the nature of the business, you may have to address the issue of money laundering. You will have to consider suitable processes to address money laundering at the outset of any relationships and have suitable documentary evidence of compliance with the necessary regime. Once you are up and running you will need to establish a credible system for record keeping and decide how you will invoice clients e.g. weekly; monthly; at the end of a project. You will need to produce budgets, cash flows and so forth and ensure that you can pay your invoices and liabilities as and when they fall due for payment.

Where will you trade?
It may be that you intend to operate your business from your premises at home. Alternatively, you will need to find appropriate premises from which to operate. This may be an outright purchase or a rental property. Whichever option you choose you will have to establish whether you are required to pay business rates. You may also have to consider whether planning permission is required in terms of the use of the building or indeed whether any permits are necessary.

Marketing
To be successful, people will need to know about your business. You will, therefore, have to give serious consideration to how you will advertise your business. Options vary from flyers through the door to adverts in newspapers and appropriate trade journals or indeed on television. Much will depend on what you can afford and your target area. In any event, you may wish to utilise the expertise of external marketing / PR experts.

Insurance
This is an important area and you should obtain quotes before making the decision to set up on your own – for some, this cost will be prohibitive! You will need public liability insurance and probably occupier's liability insurance. Depending on the circumstances, you may also need employer's liability insurance. Whatever the situation, you are likely to need insurance for your premises both in terms of the building itself and the contents. If you have vehicles for use in connection with the business, they will have to be insured for business use.

Licences
Once again, your needs will depend on the nature of the business you are operating but you will need to check no licences are needed.

Health and safety
Your business premises will have to comply with all aspects of health and safety legislation. The Environmental

Self-employment

Health department of your Local Authority will be able to provide all of the information you require and external health and safety consultants will conduct the necessary risk assessments for you and implement the necessary policies and procedures. Breach of health and safety law carries punitive penalties including, in some cases, imprisonment. It is a vast area of the law in which you should not seek to compromise.

Data protection

The Data Protection Act applies to all organisations, no matter how small or large. Its purpose is to prevent the abuse of an individual's personal data. If you hold or use personal data, which includes information about any staff on your books, customers or client, you must comply with the eight principles contained within the Data Protection Act. As a rule of thumb, you should appoint an individual with responsibility for ensuring that your business adheres to the Data Protection Act. In addition, you may be required to register ('notify' if you adopt the language of the Act) with the Data Protection Commissioner, for which a small fee is payable.

Employing others

It may well be that you need to employ or engage other staff from the outset. Alternatively, this may become a necessity as and when your business expands. If so, you need to consider the capacity in which you wish to engage others, e.g. as employees, as consultants, as casuals and, whatever their status, you need to look at the implications of it. For example, are they lawfully entitled to work in the UK and do you have the necessary paperwork to back up what you have been told in this respect? If they are consultants, who is responsible for what? Have they got adequate insurance? How will you pay them? What if the relationship evolves and they are more akin to employees than consultants? If they are employees, once again you will have to consider whether they are allowed to work in the UK. You will also need the necessary paperwork to back this up. You will have to distribute contracts of employment and consider implementing appropriate policies and procedures. You will have to address health and safety issues in the workplace, even if the workplace happens to be the individual's home. You will have to be familiar with all aspects of employment law and consider your obligations in respect of holidays, sickness, maternity, paternity to name but a few. You will also have to consider the lawfulness of any decisions to dismiss!

Implications for other business of having self-employed individuals on the premises

The concerns here are numerous. Set out below, however, are a couple of common misconceptions. A common 'nuisance value' Employment Tribunal claim relates to alleged 'self-employed' consultants who, on termination of their contract for services, argue that they were actually an employee of the organisation to whom they provided their services. This is an extremely common claim in the IT sector but can happen in any sector of the working world. In light of this potential claim, steps have to be taken to ensure parties are clear from the outset as to what the nature of the relationship will be. Thereafter, the contract must reflect this intention and the practices adopted must do nothing to compromise this situation. Also, as a business you will be responsible for certain actions of consultants, contractors and indeed some visitors whilst they are on your premises. It should be made clear at the outset, therefore, what your policy is in relation to discrimination, for example. You will also have to consider health and safety.

Self-employment

Conclusion

This chapter gives a flavour of the considerations to be addressed in relation to self-employed status. It can, by no means, address all of the issues but should help address your mind to the various concerns / implications that you will need to consider before launching on your own.

See also: Employment contracts, p.146; Employment status, p.154; Fixed-term workers, p.187; Part-time workers, p.308.

Sources of further information

HMRC: www.hmrc.gov.uk/selfemployed/

Workplace Law Network provides premium members with unrestricted access to a comprehensive range of online information – factsheets, case reports and daily news items – on employment, health and safety and premises management. Members also benefit from an online advice service and a free subscription to the *Workplace Law Magazine*. For more information email membership@workplacelaw.net or call our membership services team on 0871 777 8881.

Sickness benefits

Nicole Hallegua, Berwin Leighton Paisner

Key points
- Contracts of employment and statements of terms must state whether or not the employer makes payments for periods of absence due to sickness and, if so, upon what terms.
- Certain qualifying employees are entitled to statutory sick pay (SSP), in respect of which, for a specified period, employers are responsible.
- When terminating the employment of those who are absent due to sickness (whether for conduct, capability or some other substantial reason), consideration must be given to (a) the fairness of the decision and the procedure followed; (b) the existence of permanent health insurance schemes; and (c) the question of disability discrimination.

Legislation
- Health and Safety at Work Act 1974.
- Social Security Contributions and Benefits Act 1992 (as amended).
- Disability Discrimination Act 1995 (as amended).
- Employment Rights Act 1996.
- Working Time Regulations 1998.
- The Disability Discrimination Act 2005.
- EC Working Time Directive (93/104/EC).

Guidance
- Disability Rights Commission Disability Discrimination Act 1995 Code of Practice Employment and Occupation (8 September 2004).
- BIS Guidance on matters to be taken into account in determining questions relating to the definition of disability (2006).
- *HM Revenue and Customs v. Stringer* (2006).
- ACAS Code of Practice on Disciplinary and Grievance Procedures (in force from 6 April 2009).
- Discipline and grievances at work: The Acas Guide (6 April 2009).

Entitlement to sick pay
Most employees have an entitlement (either contractual or statutory) to be paid sick pay from their employer while absent from work due to ill health.

Contractual sick pay
In practice, most employers operate company sick pay schemes that expressly outline each employee's contractual entitlement. Provided the employer pays to the employee the minimum level of remuneration he would be entitled to under the Social Security Contributions and Benefits Act 1992 (as amended) (SSCBA), the employer can opt out of the SSP scheme.

Statutory Sick Pay (SSP)
The legislative provisions dealing with payment of SSP are lengthy and technical. Broadly speaking, the SSCBA provides that all employees, subject to certain specified exceptions, are entitled to receive SSP from their employer. This entitlement is limited to 28 weeks in a three-year period. The weekly rate of Statutory Sick Pay for days of sickness from 6 April 2009 is £79.15.

Sickness benefits

To qualify for SSP, certain prerequisite conditions must be satisfied. Essentially these are as follows:

- The individual must be an 'employee', not a worker, during 'the period of incapacity for work' (PIW);
- The employee must have four or more consecutive days of sickness (including weekends and holidays) during which he is too ill to be capable of doing his work;
- The employee must have had an average weekly earnings of not less than the current Lower Earnings Limit (LEL) within the previous eight weeks. The current LEL 2009/10 is £95 per week;
- The employee must notify his employer of his sickness leave (subject to certain statutory requirements and any agreement between them); and
- The employee must provide evidence of his inability to do his normal job. This is usually done by self-certification (days one to seven inclusive) and a doctor's certificate (day eight onwards).

Those who do not, or no longer, qualify for SSP may be entitled to other social security benefits, e.g. incapacity benefit, statutory (and/or contractual) maternity pay, etc.

All employers have a statutory obligation to keep (and retain for at least three years) records for SSP purposes. As a minimum, for each employee, an employer must record the dates of any PIWs over the four or more consecutive days of absence and details of payments made (or not made) in respect of the PIWs.

Sickness leave

When dealing with sickness leave, a distinction should always be made between absences on grounds of longer periods of medically certificated illness (capability issues) and those bouts of persistent short absences caused by unconnected minor illnesses that may call for disciplinary action if no valid reason is given for the absence or there is a failure to comply with the attendance procedure (conduct issues). In both dismissal scenarios, a potentially fair reason must exist and the employer must act reasonably in all the circumstances, and adopt a fair procedure before taking the decision to dismiss as a consequence of the reason. Further, what may be considered fair and reasonable will vary according to the particular circumstances of each individual case.

Conduct

A dismissal on the grounds of conduct owing to persistent periods of absences

---

Facts

- According to a 2005 CIPD annual absence survey, employees take on average 8.4 sick days leave a year, with public sector employees taking an average of 10.3 days.
- In March 2008, Dame Carol Black published a report into the health of the working population which made a number of recommendations involving close cooperation between the Government and employers and in particular the replacement of sick notes with electronic 'fit notes' which emphasise what the employee is able to do at work. At the date of writing, it is not known when these recommendations will be implemented.

Sickness benefits

from work should be fair, provided the employer:

- believed the employee to be guilty of misconduct;
- has reasonable grounds to believe the employee is guilty of misconduct;
- before any disciplinary meeting, investigates the extent of and reasons for the employee's absences (thereby allowing the employee an opportunity to explain);
- informs the employee of the level of attendance he is expected to attain, of the time within which he should achieve it, and that he may be dismissed if there is insufficient improvement;
- thereafter monitors the situation, and offers support or assistance if appropriate, for a reasonable period prior to dismissal; and
- follows a fair dismissal procedure which is compliant with the Acas Code of Practice (where appropriate).

Capability

A dismissal on the grounds of incapability due to ill health should be fair where the employer can demonstrate it acted reasonably in treating the employee's absence or attendance record as a sufficient reason for dismissal.

The employer should:

- investigate the employee's true medical position and prognosis for recovery (e.g. by obtaining a medical report with the employee's consent);
- after considering the requirements of the business, the possibility of alternative employment and the likelihood of the employee returning to work in the foreseeable future, conclude there is no alternative but to dismiss;
- consult with the employee about the possibility of his employment being terminated prior to dismissal; and

- follow a fair dismissal procedure which is compliant with the principles established by case law.

Following the repeal of the Statutory Dismissal and Disciplinary Procedures on 6 April 2009, the only principles governing procedural fairness in respect of capability dismissals will be those set out in case law. These largely reflect the pre-6 April 2009 position including writing to the employee to explain the issues, meeting with the employee to consult prior to any decision to dismiss, and providing a right of appeal if the employee is dismissed.

Only when an employer obtains a clear prognosis of the employee's state of health will it be able to adequately assess the requirements of the business and what other alternative positions may be offered to the particular employee.

Dismissals and permanent health insurance (PHI) schemes

Where an employee has a right to receive permanent health benefits, the grounds on which an employer can dismiss are considerably restricted. In short, an employer will act unlawfully when it dismisses an employee who is in receipt of benefit under a PHI scheme. This is because there is an overriding implied term that an employer should not dismiss the employee while he is incapacitated and thereby deprive him of the very disability benefit that it is the primary purpose of PHI schemes to provide.

An employer can, however, include provisions in the contract of employment to enable it to fairly dismiss, notwithstanding the PHI cover.

Further, in such circumstances, an employer may be able to dismiss for good cause such as gross misconduct or for some other form of fundamental breach

Sickness benefits

by the employee. Potentially, dismissal for capability or a genuine redundancy situation could also be a good cause for dismissal in these circumstances. What is crucial is that the 'good cause' must be something other than the ill health.

Dismissals and disability discrimination

Any worker who is dismissed in the light of his illness could potentially bring a claim under the Disability Discrimination Act 1995. To do this he would need to show that, by reason of the dismissal, the employer treated him less favourably because of his illness and that the illness constitutes a disability as defined by the legislation, i.e. 'a physical or mental impairment which has a substantial and long-term adverse effect upon a person's ability to carry out normal day-to-day activities'. The conditions that this includes were extended by the Disability Discrimination Act 2005 to cover HIV, cancer and MS from the point of diagnosis. Whether an employee is 'disabled' for the purposes of the Disability Discrimination Act 2005 may be straightforward, but where it is not the employer may need a medical report to establish disability and what 'reasonable adjustments' will then be required. If proven, the ultimate question then becomes whether the employer can be expected to wait any longer for the employee. To avoid a finding of discrimination and unfair dismissal, the employer will need to justify the reason for dismissing the employee and show that it made all reasonable adjustments as are practicable in the circumstances.

Notice rights

Where an employee who is incapable of work because of sickness or injury has his employment terminated with the statutory minimum period of notice and his contract of employment or statement of terms specifies normal working hours, he is entitled to receive a minimum hourly rate of pay during that notice period for any period during normal working hours in which he is too ill to be capable of doing his work.

Where an employee who is incapable of work because of sickness or injury has his employment terminated with the statutory minimum period of notice and his contract of employment or statement of terms does not specify normal working hours, he is entitled to a week's pay for each week during that notice period when he is too ill to be capable of doing his work.

Where an employee who is incapable of work because of sickness or injury has his employment terminated by contractual notice of at least a week more than the statutory notice period, then there are statutory provisions in place which disapply the employee's (otherwise protected) right to be paid statutory notice pay. In such circumstances, no notice pay in addition to any statutory sick pay is required to be paid by the employer.

Accrual of holiday

For some time, there has been a controversial issue as to whether workers on indefinite sick leave are entitled to accrue paid holiday under the Working Time Directive. The long-awaited decision in *Stringer and Schultz-Hoff* has now been heard in the European Court of Justice and the House of Lords. The Courts have held that employees will continue to accrue the four weeks' statutory minimum holiday entitlement under the Working Time Directive (but not the additional 1.6 weeks provided for under the UK law) whilst on sick leave.

The practical implications of this decision are as follows:

- Employees accrue annual leave whilst on sick leave and employers must allow employees to take such leave;

Sickness benefits

- Employees may not carry over accrued holiday from one holiday year to the next whilst still in employment;
- On termination of employment, employees are entitled to payment for annual leave accrued in their final year;
- On termination of employment, in some circumstances where the employer has repeatedly failed to pay, employees can also claim for unpaid holiday pay from previous holiday years; and
- Additional issues arise for consideration where an employee has the benefit of PHI cover. In particular, whether employees who take annual leave whilst receiving PHI benefit will be treated by the PHI insurer as returning to work.

See also: Absence management, p.30; Discrimination, p.110; Dismissal, p.124; Leave, p.252.

Sources of further information

ACAS: www.acas.org.uk

What to do if your employee is sick: www.hmrc.gov.uk/employers/employee_sick.htm#3a

Comment...

Going the whole hog – coping with swine flu

Founder of Loch Associates, Pam Loch is a dual qualified lawyer with extensive experience in contentious and non-contentious employment matters, having acted for employers and employees, advising on all aspects of employment law.

As swine flu continues to hog the headlines, the global pandemic has spawned a new wave of personal injury claims and sickness absence, costing employers thousands of pounds, and irreparable damage to business reputation. Although there is no approved vaccine to protect against the virus in the UK at the moment, employers can take steps to protect their businesses from the risk of exposure.

Data protection

This might sound fairly straightforward on the face of things; however, employers should be aware that steps which require employees to go into quarantine or imposing vaccinations at work could expose them to claims of breach of confidentiality and privacy.

It is important to remember before an employer announces another employee has fallen victim to the virus that information about the health of an employee is personal. As such, an employer cannot disclose any details relating to the health of an employee unless they have the employee's explicit consent. Of course, one way to achieve that is to ask the employee to give their consent at the time.

Some employees may be reluctant to consent to the nature of their illness being disclosed, for fear of being stigmatised on their return to work. Consequently, an employer may be restricted on the amount of information that can be disclosed. Employees should also be reminded that they must keep information relating to the health of their colleagues confidential.

Prevention and risk assessment

In some cases, panic measures have been taken to prevent the spread of the virus, such as asking staff to maintain a distance of one metre from each other at all times in the workplace. There are many ways to reduce the spread of the disease without having to resort to such drastic measures in the hope it may prevent the spread of the disease.

Needless to say, employers should restrain themselves from making immediate changes that are unnecessary. For example, changing their dress code policies to force employees (and visitors) to wear all-in-one protection suits in the workplace or indeed face masks is a step too far at the moment.

The first sensible step for an employer to take is to review their sickness absence procedures, update their health and safety

Comment: Coping with swine flu

policy, and keep up to date with the latest advice from the Government.

Another is to conduct a risk assessment in the workplace to carry out a range of social and organisational checks to assess the risk of swine flu spreading. When carrying out this assessment, the employer would be assessing whether or not there is a genuine belief that an employee is at risk of contracting the virus and how that can be prevented.

It is worth bearing in mind that just because an employee may be frightened of contracting the virus, that would not be evidence that they are in any way at risk, regardless of how dramatic their reaction.

Vulnerable employees

Employers should be aware that once they know an employee is pregnant, they have a duty to carry out a risk assessment and make arrangements to protect the employee's (and the unborn baby's) safety whilst at work.

With conflicting information and advice being given by the Authorities, there has been increasing concern about the impact of swine flu on pregnant women. Some pregnant women have become extremely anxious over the effects the flu may have on them, due to the higher risk of developing complications from contracting the virus. It is important, therefore, that employers issue information that is measured and addresses all the concerns their employment population may have on the swine flu.

Employers could be exposed to claims being pursued by vulnerable employees (including those employees with a disability) who may contract the illness and be more adversely affected than other employees. It is essential therefore that the employer can show risk assessments were undertaken, adequate hygiene precautions put in place, and, if appropriate, that flexible working options were available to defend their position.

Sickness absence

Sickness absence policies and procedures should clearly require the affected employee to report the nature of their illness (confidentially) as soon as symptoms appear. The employee should of course then remain at home until the symptoms disappear or they are no longer infectious.

In terms of minimising the risk of the illness spreading, employers should try to make sure healthy workers reduce or avoid contact with individuals who may be showing symptoms of the virus. Encouraging employees to work from home if there is an outbreak in a department would be one measure.

An affected employee may of course be able to carry out work from home and if that can be achieved then the period of leave could still be fully paid, regardless of their sick pay entitlement. For employees whose earnings are dependent on commission which can only be earned while at work, the position could be more complex. Remaining away from the workplace could have serious consequences in terms of their livelihoods and as a result they may be more reluctant to remain at home if they are unwell. Each situation would have to be considered taking into account the applicable facts, but it may have to be necessary to consider taking disciplinary action if employees are not carrying out lawful and reasonable instructions to remain at home.

Employers may also have to consider a back-up plan if significant numbers of their

Comment: Coping with swine flu

employees are affected. It would wise to prepare for this possibility by putting in place arrangements to hire additional temporary staff to supplement departments where employee numbers have fallen below the minimum level required to run efficiently. Employers may also want to consider training other employees to cover absences in other departments as a further protective measure.

So far, the general approach to swine flu in the UK has been fairly proactive. The Government has taken reasonable steps to try and deal with the pandemic and has been trying to accelerate the availability of a vaccine. One measure the Government is contemplating as part of this approach is to change the period of self-certification of sickness absence from seven to 14 days.

Currently, employees can self-certify their absence for up to seven days and then they must produce a certificate from their GP to cover any further periods of sickness absence. The Government is contemplating this change on the basis that GPs are overwhelmed due to the numbers affected by the illness. A temporary change to the self-certification periods should reduce their workload to some extent.

Critics have already voiced their concerns over these new plans. Although considered a mild flu, with sufferers only experiencing symptoms for seven days or fewer, the virus is being seen by some as a free pass to a fortnight's holiday away from work. It seems that swine flu has become the latest fashion accessory, being affordable enough to ensure everyone gets their ration of the disease, regardless of whether it's genuine or not. Employers should have a return to work interview process as part of their sickness absence policy and make sure the process is followed each time. By doing this, it should help to ensure only those employees who are genuinely unwell are absent from work.

Redundancies
Many businesses will be more susceptible to the impact of increased absence levels due to the difficult economic climate. Despite taking all the necessary steps to minimise damage and costs to the business caused by the virus, the survival rate of many businesses may hang in the balance, forcing many to consider making redundancies.

Although this may appear to be an extreme reaction to the pandemic, for some businesses, it may be the only solution left as a result of the impact on their business. Whatever the reason, employers should ensure that they consider the alternatives to redundancies first and carry out a fair procedure, using an objective selection process and properly consulting with the employees to avoid successful claims for unfair dismissal.

Conclusion
Ultimately, an employer is exposed to risks if they do not take active steps to reduce the possibility of swine flu having a negative impact on their business. It is essential that plans are put in place to deal with issues such as running the business with a skeleton staff, updating health and safety and sickness absence policies and keeping employees well informed of any changes to the business. It would be unwise for any employer to bury their head in the sand in the hope that this will pass them by.

Smoking

Hayley Overshott, Kennedys

Key points

Smoking in prescribed places is now against the law throughout the British Isles. Since 2004, Regulations have been phased in for each country within the UK, with the ban slowly taking effect at different dates across the different countries. The Republic of Ireland was the first to introduce the ban in 2004, whilst England was the last to follow suit, and has now been 'smoke-free' since July 2007.

For all of the UK, it is therefore now against the law to smoke in virtually all 'enclosed' and 'substantially enclosed' public places and workplaces, meaning that previously designated indoor 'smoking rooms' have now been outlawed. The ban also applies to public transport and work vehicles used by more than one person.

Employers and managers of smoke-free premises and vehicles have legal responsibilities to prevent people from smoking, namely to:

- take reasonable steps to ensure staff, customers, members and visitors are aware that the premises and vehicles are legally required to be smoke-free;
- display 'no smoking' signs in smoke-free premises; and
- ensure that no one smokes in smoke-free premises or vehicles.

In January 2009, the Department of Health presented its Health Bill 2009 to Parliament, which contains provisions to ban the display of tobacco products and regulate tobacco vending machines. The Bill has negotiated its committee stage and should complete its journey through Parliament in October 2009.

Legislation

The Health Act 2006 requires workplaces to be smoke-free. At the present time, the nuts and bolts of the 'smoke-free' legislation in England is set out in the following Regulations:

- The Smoke-free (Premises and Enforcement) Regulations 2006 set out definitions of 'enclosed' and 'substantially enclosed' places and the bodies responsible for enforcing smoke-free legislation.
- The Smoke-free (Exemptions and Vehicles) Regulations 2007 set out the exemptions to smoke-free legislation and vehicles required to be smoke-free.
- The Smoke-free (Penalties and Discounted Amounts) Regulations 2007 set out the levels of penalties for offences under smoke-free legislation.
- The Smoke-free (Vehicle Operators and Penalty Notices) Regulations 2007 set out the responsibility on vehicle operators to prevent smoking in smoke-free vehicles and the form for fixed penalty notices.
- The Smoke-free (Signs) Regulations 2007 set out the requirements for no-smoking signs required under smoke-free legislation.

Smoking

> **Facts**
> - Smoking in a smoke-free premises or vehicle can attract a fixed penalty notice of £50 or a fine up to £200.
> - Failure to display no-smoking signs in smoke-free premises and vehicles can attract a fixed penalty notice of £200 or a fine up to £1,000.
> - Failure to prevent smoking in a smoke-free premises or vehicle can lead to a fine up to £2,500.
> - Company Director, Martin Lenehan, was caught smoking when the Council's enforcement team paid a visit to Metric Scaffolding UK Ltd, in January 2009. Leyland Magistrates found Mr Lenehan guilty of smoking in a smoke-free place, contrary to Section 7 of the Health Act 2006. He was ordered to pay a fine of £175, along with £75 costs and a £15 victim surcharge.

Similar legislation exists for Scotland, Wales and Northern Ireland. The Scottish position is set out briefly below, but the focus of this chapter is on the application of the smoke-free legislation as it applies in England and Wales.

Scotland

On 30 June 2005, the Scottish Parliament passed the Smoking, Health and Social Care (Scotland) Act 2005, which introduced a complete ban on tobacco smoking in enclosed public places in Scotland from 26 March 2006. The Act makes it an offence for those in charge of 'no-smoking premises' to knowingly permit others to smoke there. It is also an offence to fail to display 'no-smoking' signs in such premises. The Act provides that culpable managers may also be prosecuted, as well as their employer companies.

The Prohibition of Smoking in Certain Premises (Scotland) Regulations 2006 add flesh to the Act's bones and contain provisions relating to the provision and display of no-smoking signage, giving effect to Schedule 1 of the Act, which lists the types of premises that are prescribed to be no-smoking premises, defining key expressions such as 'premises' and 'wholly enclosed,' and setting out the levels of the relevant fixed penalties and other administrative matters.

In February 2009, the Scottish Parliament introduced a further Bill relating to smoking and public health. The Tobacco and Primary Medical Services (Scotland) Bill seeks to:

- ban cigarette vending machines as well as tobacco displays in shops;
- introduce a registration scheme for tobacco retailers;
- give Trading Standards officers powers to issue fixed penalty notices for retailers who sell cigarettes to under 18s; and
- introduce banning orders to prevent retailers selling cigarettes if they continually break the law.

Common law

Prior to the ban, in an employment law context, the Courts and Tribunals had tended to imply a right to protection for employees in the workplace, stating that there was a term implied into employment contracts that the employer would provide and monitor for his employees, so far

Smoking

as is reasonably practicable, a working environment that was reasonably suitable for the performance by them of their contractual duties. Applying this formula, it was held that a non-smoker was constructively dismissed (i.e. there was a fundamental breach of her employment contract) as a result of being required to work in a smoke-affected atmosphere, despite her protests. The smoking ban has reinforced this implied right.

Having said this, employers who choose to introduce anti-smoking measures that go beyond the requirements set out in the smoke-free legislation, for example by banning smoking anywhere on the premises, whether inside or out, must take care that by doing so they are not seen to be victimising smokers who may for many years have enjoyed an unfettered right to smoke in the workplace, in order to avoid the possibility of antagonism and ill feeling.

The best way to avoid this problem is to have introduced a reasonable and carefully considered smoking policy, with the smoke-free legislation at its heart, and to have consulted employees on its introduction. This is discussed in further detail below.

What is the effect of the smoke-free legislation in England?

Overview
As indicated above, employers and managers in charge of premises and vehicles to which the legislation applies should:

- take reasonable steps to ensure staff, customers, members and visitors are aware that the premises and vehicles are legally required to be smoke-free;
- display 'no-smoking' signs in smoke-free premises; and
- ensure that no one smokes in smoke-free premises or vehicles.

Which premises does the ban apply to?
Premises:

- that are open to the public;
- that are used as a place of work by more than one person; or
- where members of the public might attend to receive or provide goods or services,

are to be smoke-free in areas that are enclosed or substantially enclosed.

Premises are 'enclosed' if they have a ceiling or roof and, except for doors, windows and passageways, are wholly enclosed either permanently or temporarily. Premises are 'substantially enclosed' if they have a ceiling or roof but there is an opening in the walls or an aggregate area of openings in the walls that is less than half the area of the walls.

The ban, therefore, includes offices, factories, shops, pubs, bars, restaurants, private members clubs and workplace smoking rooms. A 'roof' also includes any fixed or movable structure, such as canvas awnings. Tents, marquees or similar are also classified as enclosed premises if they fall within the definition.

Which vehicles does the ban apply to?
'Enclosed vehicles' are to be smoke-free at all times if they are used 'by members of the public or a section of the public (whether or not for reward or hire)'; or 'in the course of paid or voluntary work by more than one person, even if those people use the vehicle at different times, or only intermittently'.

For example, a delivery van used by more than one driver, or which has a driver

Smoking

and passenger, must be smoke-free at all times. It should be noted that the Regulations do not extend to vehicles used for non-business purposes.

What signs should be displayed?

All smoke-free premises must display a no-smoking sign in a prominent position at each entrance that:

- is the equivalent of A5 in area;
- displays the international no-smoking symbol in colour, a minimum of 70mm in diameter; and
- carries the words, 'No smoking. It is against the law to smoke in these premises,' in characters that can be easily read.

In addition, any person with management responsibilities for a smoke-free vehicle has legal duties to display a no-smoking sign in each enclosed compartment that can accommodate people.

What penalties can be imposed?

Smoking in a smoke-free premises or vehicle can attract a fixed penalty notice of £50 or a fine up to £200. Failure to display no-smoking signs in smoke-free premises and vehicles can attract a fixed penalty notice of £200 or a fine up to £1,000.

Failing to prevent smoking in a smoke-free premises or vehicle can lead to a fine up to £2,500.

The smoke-free legislation is enforced by a number of bodies, but primarily by district councils.

Are there are exemptions from the smoke-free legislation?

There are some limited exemptions, including the following:

- Private dwellings (with particular exceptions such as a communal stairwell);
- Designated bedrooms in hotels, guest houses, inns, hostels and members clubs (if they meet conditions set out in the Regulations); and
- designated bedrooms / rooms used only for smoking in care homes, hospices and prisons (if they meet conditions set out in the Regulations).

Employment issues

Introducing a smoking policy

All employers should by now have taken action to comply with the statutory smoking ban. In terms of the introduction of new or revised smoking policies to supplement or reinforce such action, an employer should consider both the form of the policy and the manner of its introduction. Whether a policy is reasonable or not will be a question of fact. However, as well as considering the implications of smoking bans, a prudent employer should take account of:

- the practicalities of the workplace;
- the nature of the business, including whether clients will be regularly visiting the building and whether employees are visiting clients at their homes;
- workplace opinion;
- assistance to smokers in adapting to the new policy;
- consultation with individuals and/or their representatives;
- ensuring that employees are fully aware of the possible sanctions for breach of the policy, including cross-references to the disciplinary procedure; and
- regular reviews of the policy for ongoing effectiveness.

A smoking policy could be incorporated into an existing employee handbook or a health and safety policy. It is advisable that the policy be in writing; however, a verbal understanding could also be implemented.

Smoking

When introducing a smoking policy it is advisable for employers to give employees plenty of notice and to train managers on the operation of the policy. The policy, including the consequences of breaching it, should be notified to staff perhaps via a staff intranet or by letter, and reference should be made to where the policy can be found.

Once a policy is in place it must be consistently enforced. It would, however, be sensible to support smokers during the early period of the policy and perhaps to avoid overly harsh sanctions during those early stages.

Disciplining employees who breach the ban

Disciplinary procedures should be updated to include a breach of a no-smoking policy as an act of misconduct and possibly gross misconduct. Having publicised the alterations, employers should make good on the promise to use them when there are reasonable grounds for doing so.

When considering sanctions for breach of a no-smoking policy, dismissal will not always be an appropriate sanction. For a first time breach, a more reasonable response would be to issue a written warning. The nature of the sanction will depend on the facts of the individual case. While in most cases dismissal would not be an appropriate sanction, in one case in 2007, where the employee breached a no-smoking policy in a factory using highly flammable materials, an Employment Tribunal found the dismissal to be within the reasonable range of responses due to the danger attached to such an action.

Smoking areas and breaks

Employers may wish to designate specific areas outside their premises as smoking areas. This may be appropriate to prevent employees from smoking too close to the premises' windows and entrances. It would be advisable to set out in the smoking policy where employees can and cannot smoke.

Employers could consider imposing limits on the amount of time or number of breaks that employees are allowed to take, in order to prevent resentment arising on the part of non-smoking employees. While employees are entitled to smoke during any lunch break or other break permitted under the Working Time Regulations 1998, employers are not, however, required by law to give employees who smoke additional breaks. If an employer does decide additional breaks should be provided to smokers, the details of this should be set out clearly in the smoking policy.

Assisting employees in giving up smoking

It is advisable when implementing a no-smoking policy to consider offering support to employees to give up smoking. NICE has provided guidance – *Workplace smoking: what you can do to encourage your employees to stop smoking* – which can be found at www.nice.org.uk/PHI005.

This guidance is not legally binding, but is provides some practical suggestions for employers to consider. It suggests that employers should publicise information on local stop-smoking support services. It also recommends that consideration should be given to providing on-site stop-smoking support for employees or to allow employees to attend smoking cessation services during working hours without loss of pay.

See also: Discrimination, p.110; Driving at work, p.133; Occupational health, p.304; Staff handbooks, p.375.

Smoking

> **Sources of further information**
>
> Helpful guidance, including downloadable signage, can be accessed at the following websites:
>
> England – www.smokefreeengland.co.uk
>
> Wales – www.smokingbanwales.co.uk
>
> Scotland – www.clearingtheairscotland.com
>
> Northern Ireland – www.spacetobreathe.org.uk
>
> If you employ any staff or offer services to any members of the public, Workplace Law Group's *Guide to Smoking Ban 2007* will prove essential reading to ensure compliance.
>
> This guide is designed to explain the many complex aspects of the smoking ban, and suggest ways in which employers, premises managers and service providers can keep in line with the legislation. Written in Workplace Law Group's jargon-free, plain-English style, this downloadable publication is an indispensable resource for all those affected by the ban. For more information visit www.workplacelaw.net/Bookshop/GuidesTo.

Staff handbooks

Jo Bradbury, Martineau Solicitors

Key points
- Ensure that staff handbooks are easy to read.
- Use a format that is easy to update.
- Reduce printing costs by publishing on your company intranet site.
- Ensure that all staff have access to the staff handbook.
- Ask new starters to sign to confirm they have read and understood the contents of the staff handbook.
- Build time into induction training to read the staff handbook.
- Clarify whether or not the contents are contractual.
- Review and amend policies regularly to reflect legislative changes and best practice.

Legislation
- Equal Pay Act 1970.
- Sex Discrimination Act 1975.
- Race Relations Act 1976.
- Employment Act 1989.
- Trade Union and Labour Relations (Consolidation) Act 1992.
- Disability Discrimination Act 1995.
- Employment Rights Act 1996.
- National Minimum Wage Act 1998.
- Working Time Regulations 1998.
- Employment Relations Act 1999.
- Part-time Workers (Prevention of Less Favourable Treatment) Regulations 2000.
- Employment Rights Act 2002.
- Fixed-term Employees (Prevention of Less Favourable Treatment) Regulations 2002.
- Information and Consultation of Employees Regulations 2004.
- Employment Equality (Age) Regulations 2006.

Purpose

Employers increasingly issue their staff with staff handbooks. Staff handbooks are an essential employee management tool, which can be adapted to suit all organisations. They provide an essential element of good communication and can put in place a system of best practice for the employer and employee to follow throughout the course of an employment relationship.

Staff handbooks can vary considerably in terms of scope and length and, to this extent, can be tailored to suit the employment circumstances.

Once a staff handbook is assembled, employees can refer to one central source in order to clarify the employer's position with regards to any number of policies (including, for example, pay structures, holidays and absences, training, equal opportunities, disciplinary and grievance matters, redundancy, health and safety and so on).

Staff handbooks are also a very convenient way of inducting new members of staff to the structure and culture of an organisation.

Importantly, they can also be instrumental to employers in successfully defending Employment Tribunal claims.

Staff handbooks

Legal position

There is no legal requirement for an employer to publish a staff handbook. A Contract of Employment and/or a Section 1 Statement can adequately set out an employee's terms and conditions. However, certain terms and conditions are often too lengthy and cumbersome to include in the Contract / Section 1 Statement. Staff handbooks therefore provide an ideal solution to set out additional contractual information, together with other, non-contractual information, which may be of key importance to both the employer and the employee.

Broadly speaking, a staff handbook will be made up of four sub-categories:

1. *Contractual issues*. These may include, for example, individual pay rates or enhanced redundancy provisions (over and above the statutory position) which are deemed to form part of an employee's terms and conditions of employment.
2. *Non-contractual issues*. These will encompass provisions that fall within the general statutory entitlement (such as statutory sick pay or maternity leave), together with more general company policies that are not considered to be part of the terms and conditions of employment (for example, use of the internet at work).
3. *Company-specific information*. Including the hierarchy of the management structure, mission statements or a company history.
4. *Industry data*. This might include information about money laundering policies or quality standards within that field of work.

Crucially, employers must be careful when drafting Contracts of Employment / Section 1 Statements and staff handbooks to be absolutely clear about which parts of the staff handbook are contractual (by explicitly saying so in the Contract/ Section 1 Statement) and which are not. For example, if a contract makes reference to the disciplinary and grievance procedures being set out in the staff handbook, wording should also be inserted in the contract to clarify that, for the avoidance of doubt, these policies do not form part of the employee's terms and conditions of employment. This means an employer will be free to raise and update policies and procedures.

This method also offers greater protection to the employer. For example, an employee should be prevented from successfully claiming breach of contract where the employer fails to complete a grievance investigation within the desired timeframe set out in its policy, provided that policy expressly states that the contents of the policy do not form part of the employee's Contract of Employment.

That said, recent developments in case law have shown that Tribunals are prepared to interpret disputed handbook provisions as creating contractual rights in favour of the employee, particularly where those provisions relate to remuneration (such as enhanced redundancy payments). It is therefore advisable for employers to separate contractual from non-contractual rights, or to expressly state the position (including a denial where provisions do not have contractual force) in order to eliminate any scope for ambiguity or dispute.

At various times, an employer may seek to rely on the policies set out in a staff handbook, for example during an Employment Tribunal claim. In order to do so successfully, it will be vital that the employer can demonstrate that the employee had access to, and full knowledge of, the contents of the staff handbook / relevant policy (including the

Staff handbooks

latest version). One way to achieve this would be to ensure that all staff sign a document acknowledging that they have seen and/or have access to the staff handbook as amended from time to time.

Format

For staff handbooks to be effective, they must be easily accessible to all employees. The format in which the staff handbook is published will therefore depend on the type of organisation.

Some employers prefer to issue all staff with a hard copy of the staff handbook. This way, it is easy to monitor who has or has not received a copy. Employees can be asked to sign a document to acknowledge receipt of the hard copy as evidence of this. It is advisable for hard copies to be produced in binders so that out-of-date sections can be removed and replaced as and when required. However, hard copy staff handbooks can be costly for the employer to produce, particularly where there are a large number of employees. Updating the sections can also be more onerous as new hard copy sections will need to be distributed, clearly identifying that they replace the previous section in order to avoid confusion.

Alternatively, employers are more often favouring intranet-based staff handbooks, which are particularly useful in large organisations provided that all employees have unlimited access to the information they contain, as and when required. Internet policies can be updated more easily and the information is available to employees instantaneously, without the need for costly or onerous distribution. However, employers must be careful to ensure that their employees are informed as and when changes are made to the staff handbook. Intranet-based staff handbooks are also preferred in paper-free office environments, although it is helpful to provide a facility whereby relevant sections of the staff handbook can be printed off if an employee prefers to refer to a paper-based format. As above, it is also worth ensuring that members of staff sign a document to acknowledge that they are aware of the contents of the staff handbook and that they have access to this (as amended).

Employers should also be aware of their obligations under the Disability Discrimination Act 1995 and be ready to provide employees with the contents of the staff handbook in formats such as large type, Braille or audio, where it is reasonable to do so.

Updates

Given the fact that employment legislation is in a constant state of flux, staff handbooks and the policies within them can easily become out-of-date, reflecting bad practice or, at worst, unlawful provisions. It is therefore essential that each employer has in place a system that monitors and reviews the policies contained within their staff handbook. In this way, any necessary amendments can be made ahead of/at the time of changes to the law.

To the extent that staff handbooks incorporate terms and conditions for employees, any changes made to these terms and conditions should not be undertaken until consultation and agreement has been reached with the employees (or, where appropriate, employee representatives) as unilaterally imposed changes to terms and conditions are not enforceable.

Similarly, it is also considered best practice to consult with recognised trade unions/ employee representatives whenever significant changes are made to any (non-contractual) policies set out by

Staff handbooks

employers. This helps to maintain good employment relationships and can also support an employer in defending an Employment Tribunal claim if it can show that the employee was not only aware of the change but was consulted about, and agreed to, the change in a particular policy.

Key advantages

Staff handbooks can be crucial in ensuring that a consistent approach is taken across the board in dealing with any number of employees. This can avoid feelings of unequal treatment or discontent, and can also significantly limit the likelihood of Employment Tribunal claims being brought. For the employer, staff handbooks can bring harmonisation to a workforce that, previously, may have worked under different terms, conditions and policies.

Similarly, employees find staff handbooks user-friendly and know where to look in order to obtain specific information relating to their employment. In turn, this provides an additional advantage to the employer, who is not left to deal with queries that would otherwise crop up time and time again.

Drafting the Handbook

Some employers will produce their staff handbooks internally, within the human resources / personnel department. The same internal department would also then be responsible for updating the staff handbook as and when required. Alternatively, some employers seek legal advice in drafting and/or reviewing existing staff handbooks, in order to ensure that the policies are compliant with the latest legislative changes and views on best practice.

There is also widespread use of external guidance sources available to assist with the drafting of staff handbooks. Certain industries publish model documents and contracts as precedents. Advice can also be sought from the BIS (previously BERR) website and the ACAS code of practice. Various policies can also be viewed and downloaded from the internet, although employers should be cautious of adopting such general-purpose policies without at least considering whether they meet the needs of the individual employer and are consistent with any terms contained within the contracts of employment, as well as the extent to which they are compliant with current legislation.

Content checklist:

- Absence / sick leave and pay;
- Collective agreements (if any);
- Deductions from wages (including recovery of overpayments);
- Disciplinary and grievance procedure;
- Equal opportunities / equality and diversity;
- Family-friendly policies including maternity, paternity and adoption leave, emergency time off for dependants and parental leave;
- Health and safety policy (this could be published as a separate document or handbook);
- Holiday leave and pay;
- Hours of work;
- Information and consultation arrangements (if any);
- Notice periods; and
- Pay and benefits (including overtime pay).

Optional:

- Bank holiday working;
- Bereavement / compassionate leave;
- Bullying and harassment;
- Communications;
- Company car;
- Company equipment (mobile phones, laptops, tools, etc.);
- Dress code;
- Drugs and alcohol;

Staff handbooks

- DSE eyesight policy (could be included in the health and safety handbook);
- Expenses procedure;
- Flexible working arrangements;
- Forms for in-house use;
- Gifts and hospitality;
- Housekeeping;
- Incapacity and capability;
- Induction;
- Internet and email policy;
- Introduction to the organisation;
- Jury service;
- Organisation chart / management structure;
- Organisation products and services;
- Performance management/appraisals;
- Redundancy;
- Reference policy;
- Retirement and pension benefits;
- Smoking;
- Stress;
- Termination of Employment;
- Time off for trade union representatives (if applicable);
- Training and promotion; and
- Whistleblowing.

Checklist of dos and don'ts

Do:

- ensure that you are familiar with current employment legislation and how this affects your policies and procedures;
- use bullet points, short sentences and paragraph subheadings;
- write confidently, concisely and directly;
- write formally;
- choose a format that is easy to update – loose-leaf or ring binders are helpful;
- try to make your handbook attractive to encourage staff to read it;
- think about including a frequently asked questions section (FAQS);
- consult senior managers and staff representatives (if applicable) when drafting new policies and procedures;
- get the contents checked from a legal perspective before publishing; and
- get it proofread to reduce errors or typing mistakes.

Don't:

- use scene-setting, padding or long lead-ins;
- use long paragraphs;
- use foreign phrases or Latin;
- use jargon, clichés or humour;
- be vague – this can lead to misinterpretation resulting in disputes with your employees; or
- ignore current employment legislation or best management practice.

See also: Alcohol and drugs, p.43; Bullying and harassment, p.49; Disciplinary and grievance procedures, p.106; Employment contracts, p.146; Employment Tribunals, p.158; Holiday, p.219; Redundancy, p.339; Restrictive covenants and garden leave, p.350; Smoking, p.369.

Staff handbooks

Sources of further information

ACAS guidelines on drawing up handbooks are available at www.acas.org.uk

Comprehensive, accurate and up-to-date policies and procedures are required by all employers to ensure that they comply with the latest employment law and health and safety legislation. Unfortunately, however, most of us don't have time to keep policies updated, or simply don't have the expertise to know what the policies and procedures should cover.

That's why Workplace Law Network's team of expert editors and advisors has drafted a series of 21 complete and updated policies and procedures templates, covering all the major areas of risk to employers. All documents are issued electronically in MS Word format so that you can customise them for your organisation, and are accompanied by extensive guidance on the subject matter. The templates are written in the plain-English, jargon-free style you will find in all Workplace Law publications. Each template is downloadable, giving you instant access upon purchase. For more information visit www.workplacelaw.net/bookshop/policiesAndProcedures.

Stress

Nicola Cardenas-Blanco, Martineau Solicitors

Key points
- All employers owe a legal duty of care to their employees. Injury to mental health is treated in the same way as injury to physical health.
- Sixteen general propositions for bringing any civil claim for compensation for stress were provided by the Court of Appeal and approved as general guidance by the House of Lords. These are listed below (see '*Criteria for civil cases*').
- A successful claim must show that, on the balance of probabilities, an employer had knowledge or deemed knowledge of the foreseeability of harm to a particular employee, so that the lack of his taking reasonable steps to, as far as is reasonably practicable, alleviate the risk of or prevent that harm occurring constituted a breach of duty of care to the employee, and that this caused the injury or loss.
- The HSE has urged employers to carry out risk assessments and implement measures to eliminate or control workplace stress or risk criminal prosecution. The HSE's Management Standards on stress (a web-based toolkit to help businesses comply with their duties) were published on 3 November 2004. Employers will need to take on board this HSE guidance in order to provide best practice in health and safety.

Legislation
- Health and Safety at Work etc. Act 1974.
- Management of Health and Safety at Work Regulations 1999.

Main cases
- *Stokes v. Guest Keen and Nettlefold (Bolts and Nuts) Limited* (1968).
- *Walker v. Northumberland County Council* (1995).
- *Katfunde v. Abbey National and Dr Daniel* (1998).
- *Sutherland v. Hatton* (2002).
- *Barber v. Somerset County Council* (2004).
- *Hartman v. South Essex Mental Health & Community Care NHS Trust* (2005).
- *Mark Hone v. Six Continents Retail Limited* (2005).
- *Edward Harding v. The Pub Estate Co. Limited* (2005).
- *London Borough of Islington v. University College London Hospital NHS Trust* (2005).

Legal aspects of stress claims
All employers owe a legal duty of care to their employees. Injury to mental health is treated in the same way as injury to physical health.

Criteria for civil cases
A successful civil claim must show that, on the balance of probabilities, an employer had knowledge or deemed knowledge of the foreseeability of harm to a particular employee, so that the lack of his taking reasonable steps to, as far as is reasonably practicable, alleviate the risk of or prevent that harm occurring, constituted a breach of duty of care to the employee, and that this caused the injury or loss.

Stress

> ### Facts
>
> - In 2007/08 an estimated 442,000 individuals in Britain, who worked in the last year, believed that they were experiencing work-related stress at a level that was making them ill.
> - Around 13.6% of all working individuals consider their job very or extremely stressful.
> - The annual incidence of work-related mental health problems in Britain in 2007 was approximately 5,750 new cases per year. However, this almost certainly underestimates the true incidence of these conditions in the British workforce.
> - An estimated 237,000 people, who worked in the last 12 months, first became aware of work-related stress, depression or anxiety in 2007/08, giving an annual incidence rate of 780 cases per 100,000 workers.
> - Self-reported work-related stress, depression or anxiety accounted for an estimated 13.5 million lost working days in Britain in 2007/08.
> - The incidence rate of self-reported work-related stress, depression or anxiety has been broadly level over the years 2001/02 to 2007/08, with the exception of 2005/06 where the incidence rate was lower than all other years.
>
> *Source: HSE.*

A stress injury is not as immediately visible as, for instance, a broken leg, and the 16 propositions put forward by Lady Justice Hale in the Court of Appeal judgment of *Sutherland v. Hatton* (and related cases) are still regarded as the best useful practical guidance as to whether or not a stress claim may be successful. (These propositions are listed in full at the end of this section).

Nonetheless, every case does still depend on its own facts and in the later House of Lords case of *Barber v. Somerset County Council* Lord Walker preferred as a statement of law the statement of Swanwick J in *Stokes v. Guest Keen and Nettlefold (Bolts and Nuts) Ltd* that "the overall test is still the conduct of the reasonable and prudent employer, taking positive thought for the safety of his workers in the light of what he knows or ought to know".

State of knowledge

Knowledge of the employee and the risks they are facing is key in both leading House of Lords cases on workplace stress. Lord Walker went furthest in the *Barber* case and stated that, where there was developing knowledge, a reasonable employer had a duty to keep reasonably abreast of it and not be too slow to apply it. Where the employer has greater than average knowledge of the risks, he may be obliged to take more than the average or standard precautions.

Knowledge is critical in the area of what is or is not 'reasonably foreseeable' in a civil claim. This was reinforced by the Court of Appeal case of *Mark Hone v. Six Continents Retail Limited*. In this case it was brought to the employer's attention that long hours were being worked and the employee was tired. It was held that it did not matter that the employer did not

Stress

accept the level of the recorded hours as accurate as the fact the employee had been recording those hours was sufficient to indicate that he needed help and contributed to the "sufficiently plain indications of impending harm to health".

This may be contrasted with another Court of Appeal case of *Edward Harding v. The Pub Estate Company Ltd* where, as manager, the claimant's hours were within his own control, no reduction in hours was requested, nor additional staff; complaints concentrated on working conditions. In this case, the Court of Appeal overturned judgment at first instance because they found no sufficient message was ever passed to the employers of a risk to the employee's health.

On deciding if a psychological injury was reasonably foreseeable after the event, it has been held that this is "to a large extent a matter of impression" (*London Borough of Islington v. University College London Hospital NHS Trust*). Therefore, all factors that would go to make up such an impression should be monitored, such as working hours, increased workload, time off sick etc. as well as specific indications of stress from employees. This is therefore a matter to be considered on the individual facts of each case.

Part-time workers

However, time actually spent at work may well be a crucial factor in some cases. It was held in the Court of Appeal case of *Hartman v. South Essex Mental Health and Community Care NHS Trust* that it would only be in exceptional circumstances that someone working for two or three days a week with limited hours would make good a claim for injury caused by stress at work.

Confidential advice / health service

There are a number of precautionary measures outlined at the end of this chapter for employers to protect themselves against workplace stress claims and, in particular, the provision of a confidential advice service was thought likely to provide a good defence in the *Sutherland* case.

It was confirmed in *Hartman* that the mere fact that an employer offered an occupational health service should not lead to the conclusion that the employer had foreseen risk of psychiatric injury due to work-related stress to any individual or class of employee. An employer could not be expected to know confidential medical information disclosed by the claimant to occupational health. However, there may be circumstances where an occupational health department's duty of care to an employee requires it to seek his or her consent to disclose information that the employer needs to know, if proper steps are to be taken for the welfare of the employee.

Stress in other civil claims

Stress now raises its head more often in claims involving bullying and harassment, disability, discrimination and constructive dismissal. Failure to recognise and address stress issues in the context of these types of claim could result in significant liability for an employer. For instance, where an employee may establish that he falls within the definition of a disabled person under the Disability Discrimination Act 1995 and an employer fails to make reasonable adjustments to the workplace for this disability, compensation would also be payable for the psychiatric or physical injuries occurring from stress suffered as a result of this.

Sixteen propositions for stress claims

A summary of the 16 propositions stated in *Sutherland v. Hatton* is provided below.

Stress

General
1. The ordinary principles of employers' liability apply.
2. There are no occupations that should be regarded as intrinsically dangerous to mental health.

Reasonable foreseeability
3. The threshold question to be answered in any workplace stress case was stated as: 'whether this kind of harm to this particular employee was reasonably foreseeable'. This has two components: (a) an injury (as distinct from occupational stress) that (b) is attributable to stress at work (as distinct from other factors).
4. Foreseeability depends upon what the employer knows (or ought reasonably to know) about the individual employees.
5. Factors likely to be relevant in answering the threshold question include:
    - the nature and extent of the work done; and
    - signs from the employee of impending harm to health.
6. The employer is generally entitled to take what he is told by his employee at face value, unless he has good reason to think to the contrary.
7. To trigger a duty to take steps, the indications of impending harm to health arising from stress at work must be plain enough for any reasonable employer to realise that he should do something about it.

Duty of employers
8. The employer is in breach of duty only if he has failed to take steps that are reasonable in the circumstances.
9. The size and scope of the employer's operation, its resources and the demands it faces are relevant in deciding what is reasonable; these include the interests of other employees and the need to treat them fairly (e.g. in any redistribution of duties).
10. An employer can only be expected to take steps that are reasonable in the circumstances.

Guidelines for employers
11. An employer who offers a confidential advice service, with referral to appropriate counselling or treatment services, is unlikely to be found in breach of duty.
12. If the only reasonable and effective step would have been to dismiss or demote the employee, the employer will not have been in breach of duty in allowing a willing employee to continue in the job.

(However, in light of the lead judgment of Lord Walker in *Barber* that there is a requirement for 'drastic action' if an employee's health is in danger, it may be said that in the absence of alternative work, where an employee was at risk, ultimately the employer's duty of care would not preclude dismissing or demoting the employee at risk).

13. In all cases, it is necessary to identify the steps that the employer both could and should have taken before finding him in breach of his duty of care.
14. The claimant must show that the breach of duty has caused or materially contributed to the harm suffered. It is not enough to show that occupational stress alone has caused the harm; it must be attributable to a breach of an employer's duty.

Apportionment
15. Where the harm suffered has more than one cause, the employer should pay only for that proportion of the harm suffered that is attributable to hi wrongdoing, unless the harm is truly indivisible. It is for the defendant to raise the question of apportionment.
16. The assessment of damages will take account of pre-existing disorders or vulnerability and of the chance that

Stress

the claimant would have succumbed to a stress-related disorder in any event.

It is not the case that one or other of the tests is more important; all 16 have to be looked at in respect of each individual case.

Criteria for criminal liability

There is no specific statute or other regulation controlling stress levels permitted in the workplace; therefore broad principles of health and safety at work will be applied as set out in the Health and Safety at Work etc. Act 1974 (HSWA) and the Management of Health and Safety at Work Regulations 1999 (MHSWR).

Where no action is taken by an employer on stress, he may be deemed to have fallen short of his duty to take all reasonably practicable measures to ensure the health, safety and welfare of employees and others sharing the workplace and to create safe and healthy working systems (HSWA).

Additionally, there is the requirement to undertake risk assessments of stress and put in place appropriate preventive and protective measures to keep the employees safe from harm (MHSWR).

Any breach of an employer's statutory or regulatory duties under health and safety legislation towards his employees giving rise to criminal liability may also be relied upon by a civil claimant as evidence of the employer's breach of duty in a negligence action and, indeed, in support of a claim for constructive dismissal.

Risk assessments

West Dorset Hospitals NHS Trust was the first organisation to have an improvement notice issued against it with the requirement that it assessed and reduced the stress levels of its doctors or other employees or face court action and a potentially unlimited fine. More recently, Liverpool Hope University has been served with an improvement notice on similar grounds. The HSE has urged employers to carry out risk assessments and implement measures to eliminate or control workplace stress or risk criminal prosecution.

It is therefore important that risk assessments for stress are undertaken, regularly reviewed and recommended actions implemented. Unlike civil litigation, any criminal prosecution carries with it the threat of an unlimited fine and/or imprisonment.

A general risk assessment of potential 'stressors' at work should be sufficient for most businesses but should additionally take into account any discrete categories of employees, such as night workers, the young, and expectant mothers. But if an employer becomes aware of an employee at specific risk or who has raised any concerns, an individual risk assessment should be carried out for them, recommendations implemented and regularly reviewed.

Health and safety policy

It is further recommended that an employer's health and safety policy sets out guidance on how stress should be dealt with and a clear complaints-handling procedure. In this way a company can show that it has followed its own procedures in dealing with any complaints and implementing any actions.

Conclusion

In order to protect themselves against enforcement action as well as employee claims, employers are advised to organise risk assessments of potential stressors, to make facilities such as counselling and grievance procedures available to

Stress

employees, and to show a receptive and flexible response to complaints. In addition, compliance with the HSE Management Standards / Guidance will assist in showing that an employer has met the reasonable standard of duty of care required.

Combating stress: an employer's checklist

- No employer has an absolute duty to prevent all stress, which can be as a result of interests outside work. However, once an employee has raised the issue of stress, an employer is under a duty to investigate properly and protect the employee as far as is reasonably practicable.
- Health monitoring – both through a confidential advice line and/or regular company medicals.
- Counselling – an employer who offers a confidential advice service, with referral to appropriate counselling or treatment services, is unlikely to be found in breach of duty. This is of course relative to the problem and the service provided but is a good indication that a proactive approach by an employer can protect him from stress claims and enforcement action.
- Pre-employment health check – this may allow vulnerable potential employees to be excluded from stressful roles. At a pre-employment health assessment the primary responsibility of the occupational physician is to the employer. (*Katfunde v. Abbey National and Dr Daniel* (1998)). However, employers should be careful not to make stereotypical assumptions or treat applicants with a history of vulnerability less favourably as this could lead to complaints of disability discrimination.
- Regular medicals – these are a useful tool in alerting employers of any risks. However, medical confidentiality has to be observed and express consent given by employees for their clinical information to be shared with employers.
- Dismissal – in the absence of alternative work, the employee deemed at risk should be dismissed or demoted.
- Written health and safety policy – clear guidance in a company's health and safety policy on how stress should be dealt with shows that the company is complying with the health and safety regulations to provide a safe working environment for employees and enables staff to follow a set procedure. It would also stand as a defence where an employee fails to disclose that he is suffering from stress because of ignorance of a company's procedures.
- Equally, a bullying and harassment code should be in force and there should be a clear complaints-handling procedure.
- Risk assessments should cover all workplace risks and should therefore include stress. HSE guidance on risk assessment can be found at www.hse.gov.uk/pubns/indg163.pdf.
- Risk assessments should be regularly reviewed and recommended actions implemented.
- Working time – employers can combat stress by monitoring and recording employees' working time with action being taken if the benchmark set out in the Working Time Regulations 1998 is breached.
- Implementation of HSE Management Standards / Guidance will assist in showing that an employer has met the reasonable standard of duty of care.

See also: Discrimination, p.110; Medical records, p.257; Mental health, p.261; Occupational health, p.304; Working time, p.423.

Stress

Sources of further information

HSE guidance

As part of the general duty to keep abreast of developing knowledge and practice, employers should be aware of the HSE's stress page at www.hse.gov.uk/stress/index.htm. This includes example stress policies and the HSE's Management Standards for workplace stress.

Additional HSE guidance includes an action pack (*Real Solutions, Real People* (ISBN: 0 7176 2767 5 priced at £25.)). The pack includes a guide for employers and employees alike and an introduction to the Management Standards. Other HSE guidance in the form of free leaflets include the following: *Tackling stress: the management standards approach – a short guide*; *Making the Stress Management Standards work: How to apply the Standards in your workplace*; and *Working together to reduce stress at work: A guide for employees*. These are available at the publications section of the HSE stress web page.

The Management Standards look at six key areas (or 'risk factors') that can be causes of work-related stress: 'demands,' 'control,' 'support,' 'relationships,' 'role,' and 'change'. The standard for each area contains simple statements about good management practice that can be applied by employers.

HSE guidelines such as these are voluntary and as such are not legally binding. They do, however, have evidential value. They assist the court in the interpretation of legislation and what the reasonable standard of duty of care owed may be. Therefore, compliance with these Management Standards / Guidance will assist in showing the court that an employer has met the reasonable standard of duty of care required.

Strikes

Howard Lewis-Nunn, Rochman Landau

Key points
- Strike action is perceived as a fundamental right, but there are exceptions.
- Industrial action does not, of itself, incur criminal liability either on the part of the organiser or the participator.
- If the employee was taking part in unofficial industrial action at the time of his or her dismissal, then subject to limited exceptions, he or she has no right to complain of unfair dismissal.
- A person is not entitled to be paid for the period while he or she was on strike.

Legislation
- Trade Union and Labour Relations (Consolidation) Act 1992.
- Trade Union Reform and Employment Rights Act 1993.

Right to strike
The right, or freedom, to strike in civil law is heavily restricted. It is in effect a right to leave after giving due notice. The right to organise is generally limited to a right to organise primary, but not secondary, industrial action; that is action against an employer directly involved in the dispute, about pay and other terms and conditions of employment or about other specified employment-related matters. Article 11 of the European Convention on Human Rights confers no express right to strike – see *Ministry of Justice v. Prison Officers Association* (2008).

Where the industrial action is organised by or in the name of a trade union, then the union must hold a strike ballot and give the employer formal notice of intention to take industrial action.

Criminal law
Industrial action does not, of itself, incur criminal liability either on the part of the organiser or the participator. Criminal offences committed in connection with a strike, such as threatening behaviour, assault etc., are not subject to any special rules as compared with such acts committed otherwise than in connection with a strike.

Contractual liability
Industrial action does not normally incur liability in contract at collective level, but is often a breach of contract at the individual level; that is between employer and worker. The contract-breaker, the worker, leaves him or herself open to an action for breach of contract and this can have the effect of making the organiser, usually a trade union, liable in tort, generally for one or more of the following:

- Inducing a person to break a contract;
- Interfering with business by unlawful means;
- Indirectly interfering with a contract by unlawful means;
- Intimidation; and
- Conspiracy.

In relation to liability in tort there is a statutory defence available under Section 219 of the Trade Union and Labour Relations (Consolidation) Act 1992 that the act was done in 'contemplation or

Strikes

furtherance of a trade dispute'. The issue of whether industrial action is a breach of the contract of employment depends on the terms of the contract, express or implied, upon the nature of the acts done or omitted to be done, and the circumstances in which the industrial action took place. However, in Case C-438/05 *Viking Line* (11 December 2007) and Case C-341/05 *Laval un Partneri* (18 December 2007) the European Court of Justice held that the free movement provisions of the EC Treaty, here Articles 43 (freedom of establishment) and Article 49 (freedom to provide services), impose obligations on trade unions which may make collective action unlawful.

Unfair dismissal

This is probably the most important area of the law relating to strikes. The Trade Union and Labour Relations (Consolidation) Act 1992 differentiates between unofficial industrial action (Section 237) and official industrial action (Section 238) and within official action gives special treatment to 'protected' industrial action (Sections 238(2B) and 238A). If the employee was taking part in unofficial industrial action at the time of his or her dismissal, then subject to limited exceptions, he or she has no right to complain of unfair dismissal.

The exceptions are:

- jury service;
- family case;
- health and safety cases;
- working time cases;
- specified employee representatives;
- whistleblowing;
- flexible working; and
- dependants' emergencies.

Dismissal takes place on the date the employment actually ends unless the contract is terminated by notice, in which case the date of the dismissal is the date when notice is given (Section 237(5)).

Industrial action is unofficial unless:

- the employee is a member of a union and his union has authorised or endorsed the action; or
- he or she is not a member of a union but the industrial action has been authorised or endorsed by at least one of the unions involved; or
- none of the participants is a member of a trade union.

The question of whether a person was a member of a union is to be determined as at the time he or she began to take part in the industrial action, but the union membership is to be disregarded if it is unconnected with the employment in question (Section 237(6)). A union will have authorised or endorsed industrial action if it has done so:

- in accordance with the union's rules; or
- by the union's leadership as defined; or
- by some lesser union official or committee, provided that the union has not disowned the industrial action in accordance with Section 21.

Pay

A person is not entitled to be paid for the period while he or she was on strike. The correct amount to be deducted is the pay for the period of the strike, not the loss to the employer – see *Cooper v. Isle of Wight College* (2007).

Where a person has been involved in non-strike industrial action and given only partial performance of the contract of employment the employer is entitled to make an appropriate deduction from salary – see *Spackman v. London Metropolitan University* (13 July 2007), where a 30% deduction was upheld by the County Court.

Strikes

See also: Dismissal, p.124; Trade unions, p.391.

Sources of further information

Trade Union and Labour Relations (Consolidation) Act 1992: www.opsi.gov.uk/acts/acts1992/ukpga_19920052_en_1

Trade unions
Pinsent Masons Employment Group

Key points
A trade union is an organisation consisting of workers whose main purpose is the regulation of relations between the workers and their employers.

Employers are prevented from offering inducements to their employees not to be a member of a trade union, not to take part in the activities of a trade union, not to make use of the services of a trade union and not to give up the right to have their terms and conditions of employment determined by a collective agreement. Further protection is provided to ensure that employees should not suffer detrimental actions for being a union member or using a union's services.

Legislation
- Trade Union and Labour Relations (Consolidation) Act 1992.
- Trade Union Reform and Employment Rights Act 1993.
- Employment Relations Act 1999.
- Employment Relations Act 2004.

Trade unions and collective agreements
In some industries, negotiated collective agreements exist relating to pay and terms of employment, and in some circumstances those agreements can also form part of the workers' contracts of employment.

A collective agreement may not always be enforceable between the union and the employer. However, the terms of a collective agreement may become incorporated into an individual employee's contract of employment, and so themselves become terms and conditions of employment.

Collective agreements can be incorporated if the employment contract expressly says so, or if the custom and practice in the industry is that the collective agreements are impliedly incorporated. However, some parts of collective agreements are not appropriate for incorporation.

Generally, once the terms of a collective agreement are incorporated into a contract of employment, they become terms of the contract and in some cases can remain in force even if the original collective agreement terminates.

Trade union recognition
The Employment Relations Act 1999 (ERA) created rules for trade unions to be recognised by employers on a statutory basis as long as certain conditions are fulfilled (see '*Statutory recognition*' below).

In general terms, however, 'recognition' of a trade union is important in a number of ways. If a union is recognised, employers will have certain duties, for example:

- to consult with the union and its representatives on collective redundancy situations;
- to disclose information for collective bargaining purposes; and
- to allow time off to employees engaged in trade union activities or duties.

Trade unions

> **Facts**
> - The rate of union membership (union density) for employees in the UK fell by 0.6 percentage points to 27.4% in 2008, down from 28.0% in 2007.
> - Amongst all those in employment, including the self-employed, in the UK, union density fell from 25.3% in 2007 to 24.9% in 2008.
> - Estimates of union membership for UK employees shows membership in 2008 has fallen by 1.8% (125,000) to 6.9 million compared to 2007.
> - Membership for those in employment has fallen by 1.5% (112,000) to 7.2 million, in the same period.

In addition, employers are under a duty to provide information to and consult with recognised trade unions concerning TUPE transfers.

Statutory recognition

In certain circumstances, even outside the provisions of the ERA, trade union recognition can take place voluntarily. An employer can voluntarily recognise a trade union, either expressly by stating so or by clear conduct which shows an implied agreement to recognise that union.

Accordingly, an employer that actually enters into negotiation with a trade union about terms and conditions of employment, conditions of work, employee discipline, trade union membership, etc., may be deemed to recognise the union voluntarily.

However, the statutory procedure also allows the trade union to apply for recognition so that it can conduct collective bargaining regarding pay, hours and holidays. The procedures are complex and are set out in Schedule A1 to the Trade Union and Labour Relations (Consolidation) Act 1992 (TULRA), the legislation containing the recognition machinery introduced by Schedule 1 to ERA. To trigger the statutory procedure, the trade union must apply to the employer in respect of the workers who wish to constitute a bargaining unit (BU). A BU is determined by a number of factors that may result in a sector of the workforce being identified as a BU even though they may not have been the subject of separate negotiations in the past or even where the employer wishes to negotiate with the whole workforce.

The request to the employer must:

- be in writing;
- identify the relevant trade union and the BU; and
- state that the request is made under paragraph eight of Schedule A1 to TULRA.

Further, the trade union must be independent and the employer must employ at least 21 workers.

Negotiation

The employer should, within ten working days of receiving the written request from the trade union, accept the request, reject it, or offer to negotiate.

If the parties agree on the BU and that the trade union should be recognised in respect of the BU, that is the end of the statutory procedure.

However, if the employer rejects the trade union's request outright or fails to respond, the union can apply to the Central Arbitration Committee (CAC).

Trade unions

The employer or the trade union may request the Arbitration, Conciliation and Advisory Service (ACAS) to assist in conducting negotiations. If the employer proposes that ACAS assistance be requested, and the union fails to respond within ten working days of the proposal or rejects such a proposal, no application to the CAC can be made. This is provided that the proposal is made by the employer within ten working days of having informed the union of its willingness to negotiate.

The trade union may approach the CAC if no agreement is reached between the parties, and if the employer fails to respond to the request within the ten-working-day period. If the employer informs the union within ten working days that it does not accept the request but is willing to negotiate, then there is an additional 20 days for negotiation, starting the day after the first ten-day period ends. If no agreement is reached at the end of the additional 20-day period, or if the parties agree a BU, but do not agree that the trade union is to be recognised, the trade union may apply to the CAC. On a practical note, if the employer reaches an agreement with the trade union that a ballot on recognition can take place, it may wish to include an undertaking by the trade union that the latter will not make another request for recognition for a period of time.

The CAC may accept the request if the initial request for recognition was valid and is on the face of it 'admissible'.

The CAC will normally decide within ten working days of it receiving the request whether it may accept the claim. The CAC decides if the application is admissible by asking whether the trade union has 10% membership and whether the majority is likely to be in favour of recognition.

If the CAC accepts an application, but the BU has not been agreed, the employer must, within five working days, supply certain information about his workforce to the union and the CAC. If the BU has not been agreed by the parties, the CAC will try to help the parties to agree a BU within 20 working days of it giving notice of its acceptance. If the claim is not accepted by the CAC, this is an end to the statutory procedure.

If an agreement is reached between the parties, or if the CAC determines the BU, and this BU is different from the one originally proposed, then the validity test must be applied again.

If the CAC is satisfied that more than 50% of the workers constituting the BU are members of the trade union, it must usually issue a declaration that "the trade union is recognised as entitled to conduct collective bargaining on behalf of the workers constituting the BU", but may hold a ballot if any of the following three factors apply:

1. It is in the interests of good industrial relations; or
2. A significant number of the trade union members within the BU informs the CAC that they do not wish the trade union to conduct collective bargaining on their behalf; or
3. Evidence leads the CAC to doubt whether a significant number of trade union members really want the trade union to conduct collective bargaining on their behalf.

If any of these conditions apply, or if the CAC is not satisfied that the majority of the workers in the BU are members of the union, then the CAC must arrange to hold a secret recognition ballot in which the workers constituting the BU are asked whether they want the trade union to conduct collective bargaining on their behalf.

Trade unions

Within ten working days of receiving the CAC notice, the trade union, or the trade union and the employer together, may notify the CAC that they do not want a ballot to be held. If a ballot is held in any event or if no objection is made, the ballot will be conducted by a Qualified Independent Person (QIP), who is appointed by the CAC. A QIP can, for example, be a practicing solicitor.

The ballot must take place within 20 working days from the day the QIP is appointed, or such longer period as the CAC may decide. It may be conducted at a workplace, by post, or by a combination of these two.

The CAC must inform the employer and the trade union of the result of the ballot as soon as it is reasonably practicable after it has itself been so informed by the QIP.

If a majority of the workers voting in the ballot, and at least 40% of the workers constituting the BU, vote in favour of recognition, the CAC must issue a declaration that the trade union is recognised as entitled to conduct collective bargaining on behalf of the BU.

The parties will then have a 30-working-day negotiation period in which they may negotiate with a view to agreeing a method by which they will conduct collective bargaining. If no agreement is reached, the employer or the trade union may apply to the CAC for assistance.

If an agreement still cannot be reached, the CAC must take a decision.

The Code of Practice: *Access and Unfair Practices during Recognition and Derecognition Ballots* gives guidance regarding the union's access to workers during the period of recognition ballots and the avoidance of unfair practices whilst campaigning during that period. Whilst the Code imposes no legal obligations, its provisions are admissible in evidence and will be taken into account by any court, Tribunal or the CAC where relevant.

See also: Employee consultation, p.142; Strikes, p.388; TUPE, p.399.

Sources of further information

Central Arbitration Committee (CAC): www.cac.gov.uk

ACAS: www.acas.org.uk

Training

Lizzy Campbell, Anderson Strathern

Key points
- Well trained staff can help businesses retain a competitive edge.
- Training staff in basic employment law and equality and diversity issues will help reduce risk to the business.
- There is a statutory defence open to employers in discrimination legislation and, although it is a difficult test to meet, training in equality and diversity is one of the things that businesses can do to help them meet their obligations.

Legislation
- Sex Discrimination Act 1975, Section 41(3).
- Race Relations Act 1976, Section 32(3).
- Disability Discrimination Act 1995, Section 58(5).
- Race Relations (Amendment) Act 2000.
- Employment Equality (Religion or Belief) Regulations 2003, Regulation 22(3).
- Employment Equality (Sexual Orientation) Regulations 2003, Regulation 22(3).
- Disability Discrimination Act 2005.
- Employment Equality (Age) Regulations 2006, Regulation 25(3).
- Equality Act 2006.

Why train your staff?
A business' most important resource is its employees. Giving employees the tools to enable them to excel is one way of making sure that they remain highly motivated and committed. Well-trained staff can be key to businesses achieving improved quality and increased productivity. This appears to have been recognised by the Government in the Apprenticeships, Skills, Children and Learning Bill, which is currently being debated in the House of Lords. If this Bill does become law, it will give employees the right to request time to undertake training (subject to meeting certain conditions).

Well trained staff will give a business that competitive edge. Proper staff training will, of course, also help businesses manage risk. So, in terms of workplace law, what are the key areas where training will be of greatest benefit?

Basic employment law for managers
The increasing complexity of employment law can leave employers exposed if managers do not have a basic understanding of the main requirements of current employment legislation. The absence of such knowledge can lead to a decision to discipline or dismiss being made which may not stand up to scrutiny in an Employment Tribunal. There are therefore certain key areas where training for managers is required if a business is going to avoid exposure to possible claims.

In the first instance, managers need to be aware of the importance of the contract of employment and the basic statutory rights of an employee.

The procedures adopted by an employer are vital to the fairness of any decision made to discipline or dismiss an employee so every manager should be trained in the

Training

nature and application of the business' grievance and disciplinary procedures and should understand the basic requirements for conducting a fair and reasonable disciplinary process (see *'Disciplinary and grievance procedures'*, p.106).

Managers should also be aware of the potentially fair reasons for dismissal. They need to know what they can or should take into account when considering an appropriate sanction and what evidence they require to justify the decision that is taken.

It is also useful for managers to be aware of the potential costs to the business – in terms of money, time and damage to reputation – of not complying with current employment law requirements.

Equality and diversity

Increasingly, employers are becoming aware of the benefits of training their staff at all levels in equality and diversity issues. Included in this should be a basic grounding in discrimination law.

A key time of risk for employers can be during recruitment and selection where a lack of sound reasoning or inconsistent practices may leave a business exposed to accusations of bias. As the number of discrimination claims continues to rise, many organisations already make it compulsory for staff to attend recruitment and selection training. Part of this should be to ensure that all staff – not just managers – have a general awareness of the six prohibited grounds of unlawful discrimination.

In each piece of discrimination legislation (see *'Legislation', above*) there is a statutory defence open to an employer accused of discrimination. However, in order to establish such a defence, the employer has to be able to say that it took 'such steps as were reasonably practicable' to prevent its employee doing whatever discriminatory act is being complained of. The bar for this test is set high. To have any prospect of being able to clear it, the employer will, at the very least, require to:

- have well drafted Policies and Procedures, which are clearly communicated to its staff;
- ensure that staff are trained in the application of those Policies and Procedures; and that managers know how to spot potential problems as they develop and take appropriate action to remedy these; and
- train in equality and diversity issues more generally.

This training should include the provision of update sessions to ensure that knowledge and understanding is kept current.

All of this needs to be in place and operating consistently before an employer has any prospect of successfully making out a statutory defence.

Public sector duties

All Public Authorities have duties under the Race Relations (Amendment) Act 2000, the Disability Discrimination Act 2005 and the Equality Act 2006 to eliminate discrimination and promote equality of opportunity. There is a proposal in the Equality Bill to extend these duties to the other protected characteristics. However, under the existing duties, many organisations have made training of their staff a key element in meeting their obligations under these Acts in their supporting Equality Schemes. Having committed themselves to such a course of action, it is vitally important that those in the public sector meet their obligations. A failure to do so may lead to an Employment Tribunal being invited, in

Training

any discrimination claim, to consider that a lack of regard for equal opportunities has been shown. This could then lead to the establishment of an evidential basis for inferring discrimination.

Many public sector organisations are also using their procurement processes to meet their statutory duties to promote equality of opportunity. Those who have expressed an interest in providing services to such organisations may now be asked to demonstrate their own anti-discrimination practices and policies. It is therefore not unusual to be asked, for example, if all managers undergo compulsory training in equality and diversity. Apart from the obvious downside to the business of not providing such training, a negative answer can now also mean a lost business opportunity. It is therefore becoming increasingly important for businesses looking for new opportunities to make sure they retain the competitive edge by putting such training in place.

See also: Absence management, p.30; Bullying and harassment, p.49; Disability legislation, p.98; Discrimination, p.110; Recruitment and selection, p.335; Stress, p.381.

Sources of further information

Workplace Law Training specialises in providing training and development in the areas of HR and employment law, health and safety, and premises management. We provide training in our own right, but are also approved by a number of leading professional institutes to teach accredited training programmes under their syllabus – notably the CIPD, IOSH, and NEBOSH. We run courses throughout the UK for a wide range of clients both in the public and private sectors. Our team of highly qualified trainers and consultants all have practical experience in the workplace as well as sound legal knowledge. We pride ourselves on our friendly, professional teaching style. For more information visit www.workplacelaw.net/training/traininghome.

Total HR support, all year round

Employment law is more complex than ever and the number of Employment Tribunal claims being made against employers is continuing to rise to record levels. Employment law affects every aspect of running a business, from initial recruitment right through to termination of employment: and the cost of getting it wrong for employers has never been greater. How can you possibly gain the expertise – and find the time – to keep on top of it all?

Workplace Law can help.

The Workplace Law HR support service provides you with total support, 365 days of the year, regardless of how many people you employ. Since every organisation is unique, so is our support. Tailored to meet the specific needs of your business, your people and the sector you operate in.

HR support services: key features

- Our 24 hour HR advice service provides you with telephone and online assistance all day, every day, 365 days a year.
- We produce a customised staff handbook and supporting policies to address the specific challenges and risks your business faces. We come up with workable solutions that can be integrated into your personnel management system.
- We draft customised letters and documentation for any personnel situations that might arise.

Support services: why we are different

High quality: All our HR advisors are members of the Chartered Institute of Personnel and Development (CIPD) and are experienced trainers, consultants and practitioners. Our quality assurance process and CPD programme ensures high standards with regard to both technical knowledge and levels of customer service.

Personal service: We don't impose a standard system on you. Instead we work with you to produce policy documentation and records that are appropriate to your business.

Competitive rates: Because our HR support contract is tailored specifically to your business, we don't charge you for what you don't want. Our rates are transparent and offer great value: we specify a service level agreement with you and deliver against it. As a support service client you can also save 10% on additional consulting services.

Get in touch

Private sector
Call Nicola Cameron
01223 431063
07818 591991
nicola.cameron@workplacelaw.net

Non profit sector
Call Greg Wyatt
01223 431056
07854 357402
greg.wyatt@workplacelaw

TUPE

Pinsent Masons Employment Group

Key points
One of the biggest employment law issues for workplace managers is the impact of the Transfer of Undertakings (Protection of Employment) Regulations 2006 (TUPE 2006) on the sale of a business or on a change of service provider. TUPE 2006 came into force in April 2006 and repealed and replaced the Transfer of Undertakings (Protection of Employment) Regulations 1981 (TUPE 1981). Where TUPE 2006 applies, it provides that contracts of employment and associated liabilities transfer by operation of law from the outgoing employer or service provider to the incoming employer or service provider.

Legislation
- Acquired Rights Directive 2001.
- Pensions Act 2004.
- Transfer of Undertakings (Protection of Employment) Regulations 2006.

Does TUPE apply?
TUPE 2006 applies to 'a transfer of an undertaking, business or part of an undertaking or business situated immediately before the transfer in the UK to another person where there is a transfer of an economic entity which retains its identity (a 'business transfer')'. Whether there has been a business transfer is not always straightforward.

The key questions are:

- Is there any undertaking or entity?
- Does the undertaking retain its identity after the transfer?
- Has there been a change in employer?

The law in this area is notoriously uncertain, but there will ordinarily be a business transfer if there is a transfer of significant assets from the old employer to the new employer, or where a substantial proportion of the workforce transfers in terms of skill and number. Case law suggests that the incoming employer cannot simply refuse to take on staff to avoid the application of TUPE.

In each case a general review of a number of key indicators is necessary to determine whether there has been a business transfer. These include:

- the type of undertaking being transferred;
- whether tangible assets (such as buildings, property, etc.) are transferred;
- whether intangible assets (such as goodwill) are transferred;
- whether the majority of employees are taken on by the new employer;
- whether customers are transferred;
- the degree of similarity between the activities carried on before and after the transfer; and
- the period for which activities cease (if at all).

TUPE also applies in a service provision change. A service provision change covers situations where a contract to provide a client (public or private sector) with a business service, e.g. office cleaning, workplace catering, etc., is:

TUPE

- awarded to a contractor ('contracted out' or 'outsourced');
- re-let to a new contractor on subsequent re-tendering ('reassigned'); or
- ended with the bringing 'in house' of the service activities in question ('contracted in' or 'insourced').

There will not be a service provision change where:

- the contract is wholly or mainly for the supply of goods for the client's use;
- the activities are carried out in connection with a single event or task of short-term duration;
- there is no identifiable grouping of employees providing the service; or
- any organised grouping does not have, as its principal purpose, the provision of services to a particular client e.g. where employees provide services to a number of clients.

The original employer or service provider is known as the 'transferor' whereas the new employer or service provider to whom the business or contract is transferred is known as the 'transferee'.

Implications of TUPE 2006

A summary of the principal implications of TUPE 2006 is as follows:

- Employees who were assigned immediately before the transfer to the relevant business / service become employees of the transferee.
- The terms and conditions of their employment transfer to the transferee. All contractual terms transfer, including certain rights relating to occupational pension schemes.
- In broad terms, liabilities in relation to the transferring employees transfer to the transferee.
- Changes to terms and conditions of the transferring employees will be void if the sole or principal reason for the change is the transfer itself or a reason connected with the transfer which is not an economic, technical or organisational reason (an 'ETO reason') entailing a change in the workforce.
- Any employee dismissals will be automatically unfair where the sole or principal reason for the dismissal is the transfer itself or a reason connected with the transfer which is not an ETO reason entailing a change in the workforce.
- Collective agreements and trade union recognition in respect of transferring employees usually transfer to the transferee.
- Obligations exist for both parties to inform and (in certain circumstances) to consult with employee representatives. Both transferor and transferee are jointly and severally liable for any failure by the transferor to inform and consult.
- There is an obligation on the transferor to provide the transferee with certain specified information about the transferring employees (e.g. their identity and age), known as employee liability information, at least 14 days before completion of the transfer.
- There is the right to make permitted variations to terms and conditions of employment on the transfer of an insolvent business, provided the changes are designed to safeguard employment opportunities by ensuring the survival of the undertaking, and the changes are agreed with appropriate representatives of the employees.

Which employees transfer?

Only those assigned to the business or service that is subject to the relevant transfer will transfer under TUPE 2006. The key questions will be the amount of time they spend working for the business or providing the service, whether they

TUPE

are part of the organisational framework, the nature of their responsibilities and reporting lines. Also, only those employed 'immediately before the transfer' will transfer, or those who would have been employed immediately before the transfer if they had not been otherwise unfairly dismissed for a reason connected to the transfer.

There is nothing to prevent the transferor from inserting employees into the business just before the undertaking is transferred. Only proper investigation and due diligence on the part of the transferee can sort out whether such potentially undesirable employees have been 'dumped' into the business.

Employees have the right to object to transferring to a new employer. However, if they exercise this right, their employment terminates immediately. There will be no dismissal and no resignation and accordingly they will have no right to claim compensation as a result. An exception is that the employee would still have the right to claim constructive dismissal if the employer commits a repudiatory breach of contract or because of actual or planned detrimental changes to his terms and conditions. The worker must be an employee of the transferor (not a self-employed contractor).

Changing terms and conditions

Changes to terms and conditions are void (i.e. ineffective) if the sole or principal reason is the transfer itself or a reason connected with the transfer that is not an ETO reason entailing changes in the workforce.

Changes to terms and conditions are potentially effective (i.e. effective, subject to being agreed between the parties) if the sole or principal reason is not the transfer itself but is a reason connected with the transfer that is an ETO reason entailing changes in the workforce. One of the predominant reasons for changing terms and conditions is to harmonise terms and conditions; in normal circumstances this will not qualify as an ETO reason.

There is no particular time period following which a change will no longer be connected to the transfer. It will simply be a matter of fact as to whether the causal link has been broken.

One way of circumventing this difficulty is to terminate employment and to re-engage on revised terms. If an employee is dismissed for a reason connected to the transfer, that dismissal is automatically unfair. The employee would then have the right to claim unfair dismissal. So this route is only viable with the consent of the employee.

Legal advice should be sought to manage any change to terms and conditions, the reason for which could be considered to relate to the transfer.

Information and consultation

Both the transferor and the transferee must provide information and, if necessary, consult with 'appropriate representatives' (i.e. trade unions if they exist, or elected employee representatives) of any employees affected by the transfer.

The transferor and transferee must provide the following information in writing to the appropriate representatives of their respective affected employees:

- Confirmation that the transfer is to take place;
- When it will take place;
- The reasons for it;
- The 'legal, economic and social implications' of the transfer;
- Any 'measures' that the transferor envisages taking towards the affected employees (if there are no such measures, that should be made clear); and

TUPE

- Any 'measures' that the transferee envisages taking towards the affected employees (again, if there are no such measures, that should be made clear).

The transferee is under a duty to give information to the transferor as to the measures it intends to take in relation to the affected employees.

If there are no 'measures' then there is no need to consult. Given the wide interpretation of 'measures' it is rare that there will be no need to consult. The information must be given sufficiently in advance of the transfer to enable proper consultation to take place if necessary. The consultation must be with a view to seeking agreement.

If either employer fails to inform and consult in compliance with TUPE, the representatives may present a complaint to an Employment Tribunal within three months of the completion of the transfer.

If the Tribunal finds that the complaint is well founded, it may order the employer who has failed to comply with the duty to pay appropriate compensation to affected employees. The amount of compensation will be that which the Tribunal considers just and equitable having regard to the seriousness of the failure of the employer in question to comply with their duties, and will not exceed an amount equal to 13 weeks' gross pay per employee. This is uncapped.

TUPE 2006 differs from TUPE 1981 in that it provides for the transferor and transferee to be jointly and severally liable for any award of compensation made by an Employment Tribunal for failure by the transferor to comply with the information and consultation requirements. The rationale on making the two parties jointly and severally liable is that, if such a liability were to pass wholly to the transferee, there would be little or no incentive for the transferor to comply with the relevant information and consultation requirements.

See also: Contractors, p.74; Dismissal, p.124; Employee consultation, p.142; Employment Tribunals, p.158; Redundancy, p.339; Trade unions, p.391.

Sources of further information

Workplace Law Group's ***TUPE Transfers 2007: Rights and Responsibilities Special Report*** is aimed at people who have to deal with TUPE issues on a regular basis, and sets out what the Transfer of Undertakings (Protection of Employment) Regulations (TUPE) 2006 legislation is intended to do, what it actually does and how the process may be managed. The Report defines exactly what and who is transferred in a TUPE transfer (and what isn't), what the roles and responsibilities are of the transferor and transferee, and how the whole process should be managed.

Using case law examples, the report highlights what can and does go wrong, how TUPE relates to contractors and service providers, whether union membership transfers and is recognised, and other issues ancillary to protecting employees and employers during a business transfer or takeover. For more information visit www.workplacelaw.net/Bookshop/SpecialReports.

Unlawfully procuring information – vetting, blacklisting and social engineering

Leonie Power, Pinsent Masons Employment Group

Key points
- There are legal obligations on employers acting as data controllers under the Data Protection Act 1998 to ensure that they procure personal data about prospective employees in a fair and lawful manner.
- Section 55 of the Data Protection Act 1998 makes it a criminal offence to knowingly or recklessly obtain personal data or the information contained within such data without the consent of the person in lawful control of the relevant database.
- Once in force, Section 56 of the Data Protection Act 1998 will make it a criminal offence for a data controller, in connection with employment or prospective employment, to compel individuals to use their right of subject access to seek access to specified data (e.g. criminal records).

Legislation
- Police Act 1997.
- Data Protection Act 1998.
- Human Rights Act 1998.
- Criminal Justice and Immigration Act 2008.
- Employment Relations Act 1999 (Blacklists) Regulations 2009 (draft).

Background
The topic of unlawfully obtaining the personal data of prospective employees hit the headlines in March 2009 when the media widely reported an investigation by the Information Commissioner's Office into the use of a database run by Mr Ian Kerr, trading as The Consulting Association. It was reported that the database contained details of construction workers' trade union activity and employment history. It had allegedly been used by 40 construction companies, without the knowledge of the individuals, to vet potential employees.

There were subsequent calls to strengthen the law by introducing new Regulations to prohibit blacklisting. Draft Regulations were introduced in 2003 but were never implemented. These draft Regulations have now been revised and the Government intends for them to go before Parliament for approval later this year and to be introduced shortly after that. In the meantime, the key legislation that applies in relation to pre-employment vetting is the Data Protection Act 1998 (DPA).

Notwithstanding the blacklisting controversy, it is important not to lose sight of the fact that vetting can often be an important part of the recruitment process. In some cases, employers are legally obliged to vet, for example, for certain posts that involve working with children/vulnerable adults. In other situations, there may be good reasons to vet, where

Unlawfully procuring information

> **Facts**
> - Under Section 77 of the Criminal Justice and Immigration Act 2008, the Secretary of State may introduce a custodial sentence in respect of knowingly or recklessly obtaining personal data or the information contained within such data without the consent of the data controller (i.e. the person in lawful control of the relevant database).
> - Section 144 of the Criminal Justice and Immigration Act 2008 will give the Information Commissioner (the privacy regulator) a new power to impose monetary fines in respect of breaches of the Data Protection Act 1998. Current indications are that this power will come into force in April 2010.
> - The Government has introduced revised draft Regulations – the Employment Relations Act 1999 (Blacklists) Regulations 2009 – to outlaw the compilation, dissemination and use of employment blacklists. This chapter does not deal with the draft Regulations but looks primarily at the impact of the Data Protection Act 1998 on pre-employment vetting.

there are particular risks to the employer, customers or others if vetting is not undertaken. The crucial point is that vetting should be done lawfully and fairly.

Legal obligations on employers

The DPA sets out eight data protection principles. A number of those principles have an impact on how employers should obtain information about prospective employees. This chapter looks at the relevant principles and what these principles mean in practice for employers who wish to undertake pre-employment vetting in a way that complies with the DPA. For these purposes, vetting involves the employer undertaking investigations about the employee using third party sources.

Some key questions that arise in this context are as follows:

- Do you have a good reason to vet?
- When should you carry out the relevant checks?
- What have you told applicants? Is consent required?
- What have you told the Information Commissioner?
- What sources will you use? Are they reliable?
- Do you use third party recruitment agents? If so, what obligations are imposed on them in relation to obtaining personal data?

First Data Protection Principle

Personal data must be processed fairly and lawfully

Employers have an obligation to process personal data about applicants fairly and lawfully. This obligation means:

- providing applicants with an appropriate data protection notice including:
    - the identity of the employer;
    - the purpose or purposes for which the data are intended to be processed; and
    - any other information that is necessary to make the processing fair (e.g. disclosure to third parties).
- satisfying one of the conditions for processing the personal data, as set out in Schedule 2 of the DPA; and
- if the vetting involves processing sensitive personal data

Unlawfully procuring information

(e.g. conviction data), satisfying a sensitive data condition, as set out in Schedule 3 of the DPA.

In practical terms, the cornerstones of the first data protection principle are transparency and proportionality.

Transparency

The Information Commissioner's Data Protection Employment Practices (the 'Code') is a good source of information about what the data protection principles mean in practice. It is clear from the Code that recruitment forms should set out that vetting will take place and what will be involved in the vetting exercise. In particular, applicants should be told what sources will be used and what information will be revealed to those sources as part of the vetting exercise.

The Code also makes clear that applicants should be told at the outset that their application is likely to be rejected if the vetting exercise reveals particular information about them.

Another aspect of transparency is the notification provided to the Information Commissioner. Under the DPA, except in limited circumstances, a data controller is required to notify the Information Commissioner of the types of processing of personal data undertaken by such data controller. If applicable, it is advisable to check that the notification is up to date and covers use of personal data for vetting purposes.

Proportionality

As indicated above, data controllers who undertake pre-employment vetting must satisfy one of the conditions for processing the personal data collected, as set out in Schedule 2 of the DPA. The condition that is likely to apply is that the processing is necessary for the purposes of legitimate business interests pursued by the employer and is not unwarranted by reason of prejudice to the rights and freedoms or legitimate interests of the applicant. In order to satisfy this condition, employers must be able to demonstrate that they have acted in a way that it is proportionate to the risks that they are seeking to address.

Proportionality demands that employers consider whether the vetting is justified by reference to the advertised job. The Code suggests that vetting is likely to be justified if it is undertaken to reduce particular and significant risks to the employer, to the employer's customers or to others.

However, while certain types of vetting may be justified for employees holding particular positions of trust within the business, comprehensive vetting is unlikely to be justified for all employees. The Code suggests that employers should also consider whether there is a less intrusive way to get the information that they need, for example, by getting the relevant information from the applicant and then verifying it.

Based on the Code, it seems that acting fairly or proportionately is also about carrying out any necessary checks late in the recruitment process and ensuring that detailed checks are only carried out in relation to applicants who are chosen for the job. If the vetting involves processing sensitive personal data (e.g. conviction data), employers must comply with one of the additional conditions set out in Schedule 3 of the DPA for processing such sensitive personal data. In many cases, employers will need the explicit consent of the individual.

While consent is not always necessary to undertake vetting, in practice, it is a good idea to provide a data protection notice

Unlawfully procuring information

in writing and to ask applicants to provide consent at the same time (e.g. in the relevant application form). In any event, as indicated in the Code, it is important to secure the consent of an applicant if it is required to obtain information or documents from a third party.

Third Data Protection Principle

Personal data must be adequate, relevant and not excessive in relation to the purpose or purposes for which they are processed
In order to be fair and lawful, the collection of personal data must comply with the other relevant principles of the DPA, including the third data protection principle.

Even where vetting is justified, a mistake that is often made by employers is that they use the vetting process as a general 'fishing expedition' to gather as much information as possible about applicants. The Code makes clear that, once employers have identified a justifiable objective for vetting, they should seek only such information as is necessary to achieve that objective.

The Code also suggests that employers should only look for information where they are likely to find it and should not ask for information from the applicant's family or close associates unless there are exceptional reasons for doing so.

For these reasons, indiscriminate vetting exercises using social networking sites raise a number of data protection concerns. It is certainly arguable that this type of vetting amounts to general intelligence-gathering and is comparable to approaching the family and friends of the applicant. Obviously, use of information obtained as part of a vetting exercise must also take account of anti-discrimination laws. However, consideration of this issue is outside the scope of this chapter.

Fourth Data Protection Principle

Personal data shall be accurate and, where necessary, kept up to date
The source from which personal data is obtained is often the key to ensuring its accuracy and reliability. Consequently, another principle that is relevant to obtaining personal data is the fourth data protection principle.

So, how does this requirement translate into what employers should do in practice? Clearly, any recruitment decision should be based on accurate data. A key point outlined in the Code is that employers should take into consideration the reliability of the source of the information before deciding what weight to attach to it.

The Code also makes clear that employers must not base a recruitment decision solely on information obtained from an untrustworthy source and should ensure that there is a process by which applicants can comment on information unearthed by the vetting exercise. Such process should also allow the feedback from the applicant to be taken into account in deciding whether the applicant should be selected for the job.

The requirement to ensure accuracy raises further concerns about the practice of referring to social networking sites as a means of vetting prospective employees. There are serious questions about the reliability of information obtained from such sources as the basis for a recruitment decision. In any event, individuals should be given the opportunity to make representations regarding information that will affect such decision.

Unlawfully procuring information

Seventh Data Protection Principle

Appropriate technical and organisational measures shall be taken against unauthorised or unlawful processing of personal data and against accidental loss or destruction of, or damage to, personal data

This data protection principle is likely to have a bearing on the collection of personal data to the extent that employers must put measures in place to ensure the security of personal data submitted by applicants. For example, if applicants are invited to submit personal data via the employer's website, the employer should ensure that security measures such as encryption-based software are in place to protect the personal data while it is in transit.

In addition, security is an important issue if employers will be using a third party to obtain personal data on their behalf. For example, if a recruitment agency is engaged to undertake recruitment checks on behalf of an employer, a robust contract should be put in place to address the specific data protection risks.

Due diligence should also be carried on the third party service provider both prior to appointment and during the term of the contract to ensure that appropriate technical and organisational measures are in place.

Other data protection principles

This chapter focuses in particular on the data protection principles that are likely to have an impact on how personal data is obtained, i.e., the first, third, fourth and seventh data protection principles. Obviously, all of the eight data protection principles outlined in the DPA will be relevant to the ongoing storage and processing of the relevant personal data.

New power to fine

So what happens if employers procure personal data in a way that breaches the DPA? Currently, the enforcement powers available to the Information Commissioner in respect of a breach of the data protection principles are quite limited. However, Section 144 of the Criminal Justice and Immigration Act 2008 introduces a new power whereby the Information Commissioner may impose monetary fines in respect of breaches of the Data Protection Act. The new powers will be contained in Sections 55a-e of the Data Protection Act and are due to come into force in April 2010 (but will not apply retrospectively).

Essentially, the new Section 55a will allow the Information Commissioner to serve a monetary penalty notice on a data controller if satisfied that:

- there is a serious failure to comply with the data protection principles;
- the failure was of a kind likely to cause substantial damage or distress; and
- the failure was either deliberate or the controller knew or ought to have known of the risk of contravening the data protection principles and failed to take reasonable steps to prevent such contravention.

It is not yet clear how the new powers will be exercised and/or how the amount of the penalty will be determined. The Information Commissioner is required to prepare and issue guidance on how he proposes to exercise these functions (to be approved by the Secretary of State). The maximum penalty will be set out in Regulations yet to be published by the Secretary of State.

Section 55 Data Protection Act 1998 – 'Social engineering'

As well as the data protection principles, there are a number of other provisions

Unlawfully procuring information

of the DPA that have a bearing on the procurement of personal data. Section 55 of the DPA (referred to as 'social engineering') makes it a criminal offence knowingly or recklessly to obtain or disclose personal data or the information contained within such data without the consent of the data controller. The example given in the Code is of an employer who misleads another data controller into disclosing information by indicating untruthfully that the applicant had agreed to such information being disclosed.

Consequently, not only must personal data relating to prospective employees be procured by an employer in accordance with the data protection principles, employers may be guilty of a criminal offence if they try to obtain personal data about such prospective employees in an underhand way, i.e. without the consent of the data controller of the relevant personal data.

Under Section 77 of the Criminal Justice and Immigration Act 2008, the Secretary of State may make an order to introduce the following custodial sentences in respect of a breach of Section 55:

- On summary conviction, up to 12 months' imprisonment; and
- On conviction on indictment, up to two years' imprisonment.

Before making such an order, the Secretary of State must consult the Information Commissioner and such media organisations or others as he considers appropriate. Fines can apply in the alternative or together with imprisonment.

Employers should also remember that there is a possibility that a director or officer of a company could be vicariously liable under Section 55 as a result of the actions of one of their employees.

Consequently, it is important to put in place policies and procedures to ensure that employees understand their data protection responsibilities, not only in respect of personal data relating to prospective employees but also in respect of personal data relating to colleagues, customers and other third parties.

Section 56 Data Protection Act 1998 – 'Enforced subject access'

Under the Data Protection Act, individuals can apply for access to information held about them – this right is known as the right of subject access. Enforced subject access occurs where an employer compels an individual to use their right of subject access to obtain personal details to be used by the employer for the purposes of making a recruitment decision.

For example, an individual may be forced to access their medical information by a potential employer as part of the recruitment process.

Section 56 makes it a criminal offence for an employer, in connection with employment or prospective employment, to require an individual to produce 'relevant records'. 'Relevant records' are essentially criminal records and include records showing convictions or cautions where the data controller is a chief officer of police or the Secretary of State.

In general, the practice of enforced subject access in this area is considered to be in conflict with the Rehabilitation of Offenders Act 1974. This is because the information provided in response to a subject access request for 'relevant records' will usually include information about spent convictions and most employers are not entitled to ask for this information under the Rehabilitation of Offenders Act. However, Section 56 has not yet been implemented and is not due to be brought into force until certain

Unlawfully procuring information

provisions of the Police Act 1997 (i.e. those dealing with certificates of criminal records) have been brought into force.

Enforced subject access to health records does not give rise to a criminal offence. However, any term or condition in a contract is void to the extent that it requires an individual to supply or produce to any other person a 'health record' or a part or copy of such 'health record' that has been or is to be obtained by an individual by means of exercising their right of subject access. 'Health record' is defined in Section 68(2) of the Data Protection Act.

Practical guidelines
- Application forms / recruitment materials should set out the information necessary to ensure the fairness of any pre-employment vetting – generally it is a good idea to obtain consent to the relevant vetting at the same time.
- Employers should check that their notification with the Information Commissioner is up to date.
- Vetting must be proportionate to the perceived risks to the employer or to the employer's customers / third parties.
- Information collected should be relevant to the objectives of the vetting exercise.
- When making a recruitment decision, employers should take account of the reliability of the sources from which the relevant information was obtained, should allow the individual to provide feedback and should take that feedback into consideration.
- Employers should ensure that they have a written contract in place with third parties who will be carrying out recruitment checks on their behalf and that they undertake appropriate due diligence in relation to such third parties.
- Employers should have a policy that sets out employees' responsibilities in relation to the handling of personal data.

See also: Criminal records, p.78; Data protection, p.84; Medical records, p.257; Personnel files, p.317; Private life, p.327; Confidential waste, p.410.

Sources of further information

Information Commissioner's Data Protection Employment Practices Code: www.ico.gov.uk

Confidential waste

David Flint, Lynsey Morris and Valerie Surgenor, MacRoberts Solicitors

Key points
- Confidential waste includes any record that contains personal information about a particular living individual or information that is commercially sensitive.
- Examples include correspondence revealing contact details, personnel records, job applications and interview notes, salary records, Income Tax and National Insurance returns, contracts, tenders, purchasing and maintenance records and sensitive industrial relations negotiation material.

Legislation
- Data Protection Act 1998 (DPA 1998).
- Freedom of Information Act 2000 (FOIA 2000).
- Freedom of Information (Scotland) Act 2002 (FOISA 2002).
- Waste Electrical and Electronic Equipment (WEEE) Directive (2002/96/EC).
- Waste Electrical and Electronic Equipment Regulations 2004 (WEEE Regulations).
- Data Retention (EC Directive) Regulations 2009.

Implications of the Data Protection Act 1998

The DPA 1998 does not set out a standard way in which confidential waste should be disposed of. Businesses must ensure that the steps they are taking meet with the intention of the DPA 1998.

The DPA 1998 covers all computer records, information held in a relevant filing system, discs and CDs.

Companies have several responsibilities under the DPA 1998. They must ensure that data is not kept for longer than is necessary and also that when data is finished with it is destroyed in a safe and secure manner. Throwing files away into office bins in the hope that they will be adequately destroyed is not sufficient. Companies must take appropriate technical and organisational measures to prevent against unauthorised or unlawful processing of personal data and against accidental loss or destruction of, or damage to, personal data.
The Act specifically states that in deciding the manner in which to destroy data, consideration must be given to the state of technological development at that time, the cost of the measures, the harm that might result from a breach in security and the nature of the data to be disposed of.

The issues that must be addressed with regards to confidential waste in a paper environment are different to those that must be addressed in an electronic environment. Special care must be taken when destroying electronic records as these can even be reconstructed from deleted information. Erasing or reformatting computer disks (or personal computers with hard drives) which once contained confidential personal information is also insufficient.

Although the DPA 1998 does not prescribe an exact method by which confidential

Waste, confidential

records should be destroyed, employers should consider the following:

- Procedures regarding the storage and disposal of personal data including computer disks and print-outs should be reviewed.
- Waste paper containing personal data should be placed in a separate 'confidential' waste bin and shredded by a reputable contractor, who meets the new BS8470 standard on securely destroying confidential waste and is registered and audited to ISO 9001:2000. It is also advisable to ensure that the contractor's employees are screened in accordance with BS7858.
- If sub-contractors are used as data processors, a sub-contractor who gives guarantees about security measures and takes reasonable steps to ensure compliance with those measures should be chosen. Furthermore, a contract should be drawn up with the data controller and certificates of destruction of documents by the sub-contractor should be issued as proof that the process has been completed.
- A standard risk assessment should be completed in order to identify threats to the system, the vulnerability of the system, and the procedures that can be put in place in order to manage and reduce the risks.

Penalties for non-compliance

Contravention of the DPA 1998 is a criminal offence. At present, the maximum fine is £5,000. However, new legislation, suggested to come into force in April 2010 under the Criminal Justice and Immigration Act 2008, will amend the DPA 1998 to allow the Information Commissioner's Office discretion to impose much higher penalties for any breach of data protection. This will include significantly more substantial fines, dependent on the severity of the breach. Individuals who suffer damage as a direct result of a contravention of the Data Protection Act by a data controller are entitled to be compensated for that damage. Prosecutions under the DPA 1998 are becoming increasingly common and monetary sanctions will soon be considerably more severe for those found to be deliberately or negligently infringing the principles of the Act.

There is also a strong commercial incentive for businesses to protect personal data following the publicity of the TK Maxx scandal in 2007. Financial and personal data obtained from approximately 45.7 million payment cards used by customers in stores of TJ Maxx (the owners of the UK TK Maxx) was accessed by hackers in a comprehensive data security breach. It was believed that hackers had access to the computer system of TJ Maxx and data held over a period of nearly 18 months, although the data held in some instances could have been up to five years old. Whilst the company insisted that the majority of data stolen was out of date, customers were urged to check all bank and credit card statements to ensure no unauthorised use. The TJ Maxx case is just one example of what has since been a long line of security breaches since 2007, including the loss of 25 million child benefit records by HM Revenue and Customs, which saw the head of HMRC having to resign as a result and all families having to be advised in writing of the security breach.

Additional responsibilities for Public Authorities

Section 61 of the FOISA 2002 and Section 46 of the FOIA 2000 place additional responsibilities on Public Authorities regarding the management and disposal of their records. Section 61 and Section 46 respectively state that it is desirable for Public Authorities to follow the

Waste, confidential

Code of Practice on Records Management (the Code). The Code sets out various practices regarding the creation, keeping, management and disposition of their records. The implications of the FOISA 2002 and the FOIA 2000 are very far-reaching as the Code is applicable to all records in all formats, including paper, electronic, video and microfilm. It should be noted that the ambit of this definition is wider than that under the DPA 1998 and extends to all personal data.

The issues discussed in the Code affecting the disposal of confidential information can be summarised as follows:

- The disposition of records must be undertaken in accordance with clearly established policies that have been formally adopted by authorities and are enforced by properly authorised staff. Authorities should establish a selection policy that sets out in broad terms the function for which records are likely to be selected for permanent preservation and the periods for which other records should be retained.
- Disposal schedules should be drawn up for each business area. These schedules should indicate the appropriate disposition action for all records within that area.
- A permanent documentation of any records destroyed showing exactly what records were destroyed, why they were destroyed, when they were destroyed and on whose authority they were destroyed, should be kept. The record should also provide some background information on the records being destroyed, such as legislative provisions, functional context and physical arrangement.
- Records should be destroyed in as secure a manner as is necessary for the level of confidentiality they bear.
- Authorities must have adequate arrangements to ensure that before a record is destroyed they ascertain whether or not the record is the subject of a request for information under the FOISA 2002 or the FOIA 2000. If a record is known to be the subject of a request under either the FOISA 2002 or the FOIA 2000, the destruction of the record should be delayed until either the information is disclosed or the review and appeal provisions have been exhausted.

Disposal of IT equipment

Companies, when disposing of their IT equipment, must act with extreme care in order to ensure that personal data is completely erased. Despite the fact that contravention of the DPA 1998 is a criminal offence, a study published by the University of Glamorgan's Computer Forensics Team revealed that around half of second-hand computers obtained from various sources contained sufficient information to identify organisations and individuals. This clearly illustrates that businesses are failing properly to delete highly sensitive information stored on their computers before they are sold on, and failing to meet the requirements of the DPA 1998.

There are various ways a business may dispose of its IT equipment responsibly. Shredding disks is considered to be the most effective way to destroy a disk and all the personal data that it contains. Where businesses wish to reuse a disk, unless they can adequately delete the files themselves, refurbishers or recyclers should be used.

The European Waste Electrical and Electronic Equipment (WEEE) Directive seeks to regulate the disposal of electronic equipment by requiring that member states of the European Union ensure that approximately 20% of their WEEE (around four kilograms per person in the UK) is collected and recycled. The Directive received effect in the UK on

Waste, confidential

1 July 2007. Manufacturers and importers of electrical and electronic equipment (EEE) are now responsible for financing the producer compliance regimes for the collection, treatment, recycling and recovery of WEEE. Such schemes will be monitored by the relevant environmental agency.

Retailers, on the other hand, must either offer customers a free exchange (or 'take-back') of WEEE for EEE, or help to finance public waste WEEE recycling services. The Regulations are reasonably specific about the sort of equipment that falls under their ambit and the sort of equipment that does not. Replacement peripherals and components, such as hard disk drives, are not considered WEEE under the Regulations except where they are inside equipment that is within their scope at the time of disposal.

Failure to comply with the WEEE Regulations may result in a breach of the DPA 1998 as well as considerable bad publicity.

The Data Retention Regulations

The new Data Retention (EC Directive) Regulations 2009 came into force in April 2009. These Regulations require that public communications providers (defined as providers of a public electronic communications network or service) retain communications data for a specific period, beginning at the date of the communication. This period is 12 months in the UK. The data to be retained includes telephony and internet data stored or logged in the UK, such as who sent the data, where it was sent from and when. For example, telecommunications services will involve retaining data relating to the name and address of the subscriber, the calling telephone number and the date and time of the start and end of the call. This information is subject to data protection and data security. Although the Regulations specify that the data held should be destroyed at the end of the period of retention, there is no specific guidance on how this should be done. The Regulations simply require the data to be deleted 'in such a way as to make access to the data impossible'.

It is therefore important that such public communications providers, and indeed any organisation that processes personal data, create their own successful methods of destruction of confidential waste in order to avoid any loss and any potential security breach.

See also: Data protection, p.84; IT security, p.244; Personnel files, p.317.

Sources of further information

Information Commissioner: www.informationcommissioner.gov.uk

British Security Industry Association: www.bsia.co.uk

Whistleblowing

Pinsent Masons Employment Group

Key points
- The Public Interest Disclosure Act 1998 protects workers from detriment as a consequence of disclosing wrongdoings on the part of their employer.
- To fall within the protection, the employee's disclosure must have been made in a certain way, about certain matters, to certain people.
- The definition of those protected under the Act goes beyond employees and includes contractors.

Legislation
- Employment Rights Act 1996.
- Public Interest Disclosure Act 1998.
- Public Interest Disclosure (Prescribed Persons) Order 1999.
- Public Interest Disclosure (Prescribed Persons) (Amendment) Order 2003 and 2005.

Protection
The Public Interest Disclosure Act 1998 has become known as the 'Whistleblowers' Act' because it protects workers who suffer detriment as a result of 'blowing the whistle' – disclosing wrongdoing – on their employers, provided that the informer goes through the correct channels.

To be protected, the worker must be able to show that:

- in his reasonable belief the disclosure relates to one of a list of specified wrongdoings; and
- the disclosure is made by one of six specified procedures to specified people.

List of wrongdoings
A protected disclosure is a disclosure made by a worker which in the reasonable belief of the worker tends to show that:

- a criminal offence has been, is being or is likely to be committed;
- a person has breached, is breaching or is likely to breach a legal obligation;
- a miscarriage of justice has occurred, is occurring or is likely to occur;
- the health and safety of an individual has been, is being or is likely to be endangered;
- the environment has been, is being or is likely to be endangered; or
- there is an attempt to cover up one of the above.

Procedures for disclosure
In order to be protected, the disclosure must be made only to the category of persons set out in the Act, not any person.

Any one of six methods of disclosing will be protected so long as the worker can show that he was justified in choosing that method.

1. Disclosure to employer / third party
The disclosure must be in 'good faith' (i.e. honestly, even if it is careless or negligent) and can be to the employer (e.g. telling the chairman that a director is fiddling expenses) or to a third party if one is involved (e.g. a supplier). A policy may also exist allowing workers to complain

Whistleblowing

to a particular person (e.g. an external accountant).

2. Disclosure to legal advisor
A disclosure made 'in the course of obtaining legal advice' will be protected even if it is not made in good faith.

3. Disclosure to ministers
A disclosure can be made 'in good faith to a Minister of the Crown' if the employer is one appointed by an Act of Parliament (e.g. an NHS trust and statutory tribunals). The worker is not required to first make a disclosure to the employer.

4. Disclosure to prescribed persons
The current list of 'prescribed persons' (see Employment Rights Act 1996, Section 43F) is given in the Public Interest Disclosure (Prescribed Persons) (Amendment) Order 1999.

Specific persons are listed for particular purposes or industries including the HSE, Financial Services Authority, HM Revenue and Customs and Serious Fraud Office. The worker must reasonably believe that the information disclosed is substantially true and that it falls within the remit of the prescribed person.

5. Other external disclosure
Wider disclosures are possible to persons such as the media, police and MPs but to remain protected the worker must pass a number of tests.

In such a case, however, the worker must:

- make the disclosure in good faith and not for personal gain;
- reasonably believe that the information disclosed and allegations are substantially true; and
- show it is reasonable to make the disclosure, and that one of the following reasons is true:

  - the worker reasonably believes at the time of making the disclosure that he will be subjected to a detriment by the employer if disclosure is made to the employer or to a prescribed person; or
  - the worker reasonably believes that evidence will be concealed or destroyed if disclosure is made to the employer; or
  - the worker has previously made disclosure of the same information to the employer or to certain prescribed persons.

There is a list of considerations governing whether the disclosure is 'reasonable' or not. These are:

- the identity of the person to whom the disclosure is made;
- the seriousness of the wrongdoing;
- whether the wrongdoing will or is likely to continue or recur;
- whether the disclosure is made in breach of a duty of confidentiality which the employer owes to any other person;
- if the employee has previously disclosed substantially the same information to the employer, or to a prescribed person, whether they have taken action and what action they have taken or might have taken; and
- if a previous disclosure is made to the worker's employer, whether the worker complied with any whistleblowing procedure authorised by the employer.

6. Exceptionally serious failures
Where the wrongdoing is 'exceptionally serious', the other methods of disclosure can be overridden. However, the employee takes clear risks. He must:

- make the disclosure in good faith and not for personal gain;
- reasonably believe that information and allegations are substantially true;

Whistleblowing

- show that the wrongdoing is of an 'exceptionally serious nature': this is a matter of fact (the worker could be mistaken, even if he believes it is serious – if wrong, he loses protection); and
- show it is reasonable for the worker to make the disclosure bearing in mind the identity of the person to whom the disclosure is made.

What can the worker claim?

Legal protection is given to workers who make a protected disclosure in certain specified circumstances (see above). They will have the right not to be subjected to any detriment by their employer on the ground that they have made a protected disclosure, and not to be dismissed and not to be selected for redundancy for this reason.

'Detriment' does not technically include dismissal. However, a dismissal will be regarded as automatically unfair if it is due to the worker making a disclosure, and no qualifying period of service is needed for a worker to bring such a claim of unfair dismissal. There is no limit on the amount of compensation that can be awarded.

Practical issues

Employers should consider introducing a whistleblowing policy, separate from disciplinary and grievance procedures, in order to encourage such matters to be resolved within the organisation and in a regulated manner. Further, any provision in a contract of employment purporting to prevent a worker from making a protected disclosure will be void.

> *See also*: Discrimination, p.110; Dismissal, p.124; Money laundering, p.279.

Sources of further information

ACAS: www.acas.org.uk

Financial Services Authority: www.fsa.gov.uk

Public Concern at Work: www.pcaw.co.uk

Work experience, internships and apprenticeships

Elizabeth Stevens and Louise Westby, Steeles Law

> **Key points**
>
> At a time when the level of unemployment is continuing to increase at an alarming rate, students and recent graduates are finding it much harder to gain a foothold on the first rung of the career ladder. Employers have the pick of a large group of well-qualified potential employees, and will be looking for individuals who stand out from the crowd.
>
> One way of doing this is for students and graduates to gain valuable work experience in industry. A well-prepared and managed work experience placement could also prove to be of great benefit to an employer.

Legislation
- Employment Rights Act 1996.
- National Minimum Wage Act 1998.
- Public Disclosure Act 1998.
- Working Time Regulations 1998.
- Apprenticeships, Skills, Children and Learning Bill.

Introduction
Work experience students could provide the perfect resource of carrying out research, tackling projects placed on the back burner or freeing up permanent staff. The National Council for Work Experience (NCWE) cites typical projects carried out by students as:

- marketing and market research;
- design and implementation of databases;
- research and development; and
- reviewing work processes and efficiency.

Work experience placements, managed and monitored effectively, provide an opportunity to identify the most able candidates as potential recruits; effectively you 'try before you buy,' thus saving on recruitment costs.

The Government has launched an official internship scheme, known as the Graduate Talent Pool, aimed at improving the employability of graduates. It is intended the scheme will support around 5,000 internships of up to three months on a rolling programme.

The Department for Business, Innovation and Skills (BIS) will facilitate applications from graduates and match them with internships placed on the website by employers.

It is intended that most employers will pay their interns, or at least reimburse their expenses, but some will offer unpaid work experience or volunteer schemes. Graduates receiving Jobseekers Allowance for six months or more will be able to do an internship for up to 13 weeks whilst still claiming an allowance.

Work experience, internships and apprenticeships

Good practice
When considering taking on a work placement student, your first steps should include:

- Consider what you are looking for in a work experience student.
- Establish exactly what gaps you have in the organisation that a student may be able to fill. Ensure there is real work for placements to do and offer a variety of tasks to make the work experience more worthwhile for both parties.
- Consider how much time and resources (both human and financial) can be devoted, whether the placement is paid or voluntary and whether you will be paying expenses.
- Allocate responsibility for induction and management. Supervisors need to be clear about their roles and what is expected of them.
- As with any other new recruit, it is important a job description is in place; this ensures that you will get applicants who are right for the job.
- Consider what access (if any) the student will require to the organisation's IT systems and what security measures need to be put in place.
- Decide how long you will need the work placement to last.

The placement should be managed effectively throughout. It would be prudent to provide a short induction during the first day to brief on the ethos of the company, housekeeping issues and what is expected of the work placement.

It is also recommended that if paid work experience is provided, a contract of employment is in place setting out clearly the student's working hours, obligations, responsibilities and what is expected of them during the placement (although not all work experience placements will give rise to an employment relationship – see below).

Towards the end of the placement, gather feedback from the students, so that if necessary you can make any appropriate changes to your work placement scheme. It is also helpful to the student to provide feedback on their performance, in order for them to learn from the experience and to further develop their skills.

Confidentiality
An employer should consider any confidentiality issues associated with a potential work placement. There may be some posts to which it would be preferable not to assign students, or there may be particular aspects of the work with which a student should not be involved. In these circumstances, an employer should try to plan around this. Alternatively, it might be necessary for the student to sign a confidentiality agreement prior to starting the placement.

Supervision
Proper supervision of the work placement is important, to ensure the work is being carried out to the correct standard and to identify potential problems at an early stage. In 2008 it was reported that a teenager on a work placement at a large city law firm was jailed for five months after stealing £13,500 and attempting to steal a further £46,500 while working in the firm's accounts department. This is an extreme example, but mistakes made by a work experience student could prove costly, or at least embarrassing, to the company.

Legal considerations
There are several potential areas of liability to bear in mind when considering offering work experience placements.

Status of work experience staff
An employer may offer individuals workplace experience or, as now more commonly the case, an internship. The latter is a more formalised programme of

Work experience, internships and apprenticeships

work, usually over the summer holidays with candidates being picked after an interview process.

Whichever term is used, it is important to determine whether an individual will fall into the category of a worker, employee or simply a volunteer to determine what, if any, employment rights will follow from their status.

Worker

A work experience student is likely to fall within the wide statutory definition of a 'worker'. A worker is essentially an individual who undertakes to personally perform work or services for another party and is not a client or customer of that party. Thus, if a student is personally obliged to do certain tasks and there is an obligation to work set hours, they will probably be a 'worker' for certain statutory purposes.

A worker has fewer rights than an employee, but will have certain statutory employment rights under the Employment Rights Act 1996 (ERA), including the right to be accompanied at grievance and disciplinary hearings, not to be discriminated against on the grounds of sex, race, disability, etc., and whistleblowing rights. Generally, they will also be subject to the rules under the Working Time Regulations 1998 (WTR) and National Minimum Wage Act 1998 (NMWA).

Employee

If an individual on a work placement has taken on responsibilities normally undertaken by an employee of the organisation, they may be deemed to be 'employed'. This means that they may be entitled to claim unfair dismissal and maternity leave, along with other rights given to employees under the ERA.

In practice, the right to claim unfair dismissal is unlikely to arise, given the requirement for 12 months' continuous service. However, there are exceptions to this general rule. For example, if the dismissal was for a discriminatory reason, no period of service is required to bring a claim. It will also be automatically unfair to dismiss an employee for certain inadmissible reasons, e.g. health and safety reasons, or seeking to enforce rights under the WTR. An employee dismissed in these circumstances does not need any qualifying period of continuous employment in order to bring a claim for unfair dismissal.

There is no single test to determine if an individual is an 'employee'. However, both parties must be under an 'irreducible minimum of obligation'. In other words, the employer is obliged to provide work, usually for remuneration, and exercise sufficient control over the individual, who is obliged to personally perform the work required.

Volunteer

A volunteer will not enjoy any rights under the ERA, provided they are a genuine volunteer. Volunteers on work experience would probably spend all their time work shadowing (i.e. observing employees going about their normal activities) rather than carrying out set tasks independently. It also encompasses those who provide their time and effort without any contractual obligation to do so and individuals engaged by a charity or voluntary organisation, who receive no monetary payment or only money for expenses.

Apprentice

Apprentices undertake specific training usually for a fixed term of years or until a set qualification is achieved. Whilst apprentices are 'employees' under the ERA, they have greater rights.

Workplace Law Network
www.workplacelaw.net

Work experience, internships and apprenticeships

An apprentice cannot be dismissed in the same way as an ordinary employee, nor can they be made redundant unless there has been a fundamental change in the employer's business. If an apprentice is dismissed in breach of contract, any damages awarded may take into account wages and training lost under the fixed term of the contract and loss of future employment prospects.

Government-backed apprenticeships, where there is a tripartite agreement in which the employer provides the opportunity for work experience, and the training is carried out under the auspices of a training provider, can result in apprenticeship contracts.

The Apprenticeships, Skills, Children and Learning Bill was introduced into the House of Commons in February 2009. The Bill creates a new apprenticeships structure which, through apprenticeship frameworks, facilitates the creation of apprenticeship agreements between the employer and apprentice. Such an agreement would be treated as a contract of service, rather than a contract of apprenticeship, which may make the scheme more attractive to employers. The Bill is likely to receive Royal Assent in Autumn 2009.

Working time

The number of hours a work experience placement works will be generally down to agreement. However, the limits on working hours contained in the WTR apply to 'workers' and therefore may apply to those on work experience.

Employers should bear in mind the main provisions of the WTR, namely:

- the 48 hour limit on average weekly working time;
- the right to daily rest breaks of at least 20 minutes when working more than six hours and rest periods of 11 consecutive hours in any 24-hour period; and, if applicable
- the specific provisions relating to night time working,

unless the specific exclusions or derogations contained within the WTR are applicable.

An employer should also note that there are special provisions relating to young workers (those who are over 15 and under 18 and who are over the compulsory school age). In these cases:

- the working time limit must not exceed eight hours a day or 40 hours a week;
- rest breaks of at least 30 minutes must be taken where daily working time is more than four and a half hours, as well as a rest period of at least 12 consecutive hours in any 24-hour period; and
- young workers are prohibited from working between ten p.m. and six a.m. or, where contractually required to work later than ten p.m., 11 p.m. to seven a.m.

Again, the WTR provide for a number of exceptions and derogations.

National minimum wage

Employers should bear in mind that paid work experience staff are likely to be entitled to receive the national minimum wage (NMW). The NMW stipulates all workers are entitled to be paid NMW provided they are of school-leaving age or ordinarily work in the UK.

The current rates (as at 1 October 2009) are £5.80 for workers aged 22 and over, £4.83 for 18-21 year olds and £3.57 for 16-17 year olds. The rates increase on 1 October each year.

Work experience, internships and apprenticeships

Genuine volunteers are not workers and are therefore not entitled to the NMW, but, for this exception to apply, the relationship must be properly voluntary in nature and not merely labelled as such in order to circumvent the requirements of the NMW.

As well as volunteers, there are other circumstances when a work experience placement will not be entitled to the NMW. These include:

- Apprentices under the age of 19 or apprentices over the age of 19 who are in their first year of apprenticeship;
- Individuals who undertake work experience resulting from government work placements and schemes funded by the European Social Fund;
- Students carrying out work experience under the European Union's Leonardo da Vinci programme; and
- Workers on a higher education course where part of the course is work experience, provided this experience does not exceed one year and is required by the course.

Further Guidance on NMW and internships is available from the Department of Business, Innovation and Skills.

HM Revenue and Customs (HMRC) Compliance Officers can carry out inspections at any time to determine entitlement to the NMW and the level of pay received by workers. The Employment Act 2008, which came into force in April 2009, has changed how the NMW is enforced. Notices of underpayment now require an employer to pay a financial penalty within 28 days of service. The penalty is set at 50% of the total underpayment (the minimum penalty is £100, the maximum £5,000). If the employer complies with the notice within 14 days, the financial penalty is reduced by 50%.

The Act has also changed the way that criminal offences under the NMW are enforced. The most serious cases are triable in the Crown Court. This means that employers who deliberately fail to pay the NMW may now face stiffer penalties.

Discrimination

Discrimination legislation, which prohibits both harassment and discrimination on grounds of race, sex, disability, religion or belief, sexual orientation and age applies to workers, prospective workers and also those seeking or undergoing vocational training.

From a practical viewpoint, employers should extend their equal opportunity policies to work placements and make copies accessible to applicants. All applicants for work experience should be considered on an equal basis without reference to any potentially discriminatory factors, and a thorough and transparent selection process should be followed.

Whistleblowing

There are specific provisions within the ERA introduced by the Public Disclosure Act 1998 (PIDA), protecting workers who make disclosures about certain types of malpractice in the workplace, otherwise known as 'whistleblowing'.

Essentially protected disclosures relate to breaches of criminal or civil law, miscarriages of justice, and risks to health and safety or the environment.

Workers who blow the whistle are protected from detriment and dismissal. Employers should be aware that under PIDA the definition of 'worker' is a lot wider than the definition contained within the ERA and will include those who undertake work experience as part of a training course or are provided with training for employment (except in cases

Work experience, internships and apprenticeships

where the course is run by an 'educational establishment'). Thus, most individuals operating within the workplace will fall within the scope of the whistleblowing provisions.

See also: Children at work, p.68; Discrimination, p.110; Employment status, p.154; Minimum wage, p.273; Whistleblowing, p.414; Working time, p.423; Young persons, p.430.

Sources of further information

The NCWE has issued guidelines to help businesses get the most out of work experience placements: www.work-experience.org

Graduate Talent Pool: http://graduatetalentpool.bis.gov.uk

Working time

Pinsent Masons Employment Group

Key points
- The Working Time Regulations 1998 (which implement the EC Working Time Directive into UK law) regulate hours worked, rest breaks and holidays.
- The BERR guidance notes should be read with the Regulations.
- Employees can opt out of the 48-hour week, and other rights can be softened or extended in 'special cases' or by agreement.
- The Regulations do not apply to some sectors, or to time that is not 'working time'.

Legislation
The Working Time Regulations 1998 came into force on 1 October 1998. They have been amended by the Working Time (Amendment) Regulations 2001 and the Working Time (Amendment) Regulations 2003 and the Working Time (Amendment) Regulations 2007.

BERR has issued guidance to assist companies to comply with the Regulations. The Regulations protect workers against working too many hours and not receiving proper rest, and allow them minimum paid holiday rights. Night workers have special rights.

Workers
The Regulations apply to 'workers' – i.e. not only to employees, but also to agency workers, freelance workers and those performing a contract for services. The Regulations do not apply to individuals who are genuinely self-employed. Young workers have special rights.

The Regulations do not apply to workers employed in some industry sectors, including workers in the transport sector and sea fishing, other workers at sea, and certain activities of the armed forces, police or other civil protection services.

The Regulations were amended from 1 August 2003 to extend working time measures in full to all workers in road transport (other than those covered by the Road Transport Directive), non-mobile workers in road, sea, inland waterways or lake transport, to workers in the railway and offshore sectors and to all workers in aviation who are not covered by the Aviation Directive.

Since 1 August 2004 the Regulations have also applied to junior doctors, with some exceptions and special rules.

48-hour week
An employer is expected to take all reasonable steps in keeping with the need to protect health and safety, to ensure that in principle each worker works no more than 48 hours on average in each working week. Young workers may not ordinarily work more than eight hours a day or 40 hours a week.

The average is calculated across a 17-week rolling reference period (which in certain circumstances can be extended).

Work for any employer is included, so care is needed if an employer knows or should know that an employee has more than one job. A worker cannot be forced to

Working time

> **Facts**
>
> - Four million people in the UK work more than 48 hours a week on average; 700,000 more than in 1992 when there was no long hours protection.
> - Nearly two out of three people who claim to regularly work more than 48 hours a week say they have not been asked to opt out of the Working Time Regulations.
> - DTI research found 16% of the workers surveyed were working over 60 hours a week, compared to just 12% of all UK workers in 2000.
> - Full-time employees in the UK work the longest hours in Europe. The average for full-timers in the UK is 43.5 hours, whereas in France it's 38.2 and in Germany 39.9.
>
> *Source: TUC.*

work more than these hours if the hours constitute 'working time'.

'Working time' is defined as any period during which a worker is 'working, at his employer's disposal and carrying out his activity or duties'; any period during which the worker is receiving 'relevant training'; or any additional period which is agreed in a relevant agreement to be 'working time'. This leads to uncertainty, but working time will therefore not usually include, for example, a worker's time spent travelling to and from work or during rest breaks where no work is done. Recent case law has concluded that 'on-call' time constitutes working time if the employee is required to be in the workplace rather than at home.

The Regulations allow a worker to opt out of the 48-hour-week restriction by written agreement in a number of ways, including by way of an amendment to the individual's contract of employment, but it must be in writing and terminable by the worker on a minimum of seven days' (but not more than three months') notice. Even if a worker has agreed to opt out, he cannot be required to work excessively long hours if this creates a reasonably foreseeable risk to health and safety.

Where a worker has contracted out of the 48-hour week, the employer no longer needs to keep records showing the number of hours actually worked by the opted-out individual.

In these circumstances only a list of those who have opted out is necessary.

See *'EC proposals for change'* for amendments to 'on-call' time and the opt-out provision following the political agreement at the meeting of EU employment ministers in June 2008.

Rest periods

The Regulations provide for rest periods to be given to workers.

Employers must provide that rest periods can be taken, but there is no need to ensure they are actually taken. The rest period is in addition to annual leave and can be paid or unpaid.

The provisions can be summarised as follows:

- There should be a minimum rest period of 11 uninterrupted hours between each working day.

Working time

- Young workers are entitled to 12 hours' uninterrupted rest in each 24-hour period.
- There should be a minimum weekly rest period of not less than 24 uninterrupted hours in each seven-day period.
- Days off can be averaged over a two-week period.
- Workers who work for six hours are entitled to a 20-minute break.
- There should be adequate rest breaks where monotonous work places the worker at risk.

Special cases

Workers can be asked to work without breaks in a number of 'special cases'.

Also, where special cases exist, the 17-week average period for the 48-hour week can be extended to 26 weeks. These include:

- where there is a 'foreseeable surge of activity';
- where 'unusual and unforeseeable circumstances beyond the control of the worker's employer' exist;
- where continuity of service or production is needed (e.g. hospital care, prisons, media, refuse and where a need exists to keep machines running);
- where permanent presence is needed (e.g. security and surveillance); and
- where there is great distance between the workplace and an employee's home, or between different places of work.

The basis of the special cases is that, if they exist, there is a reasonable need for work to be carried out quickly in a confined period. If because of one of the 'special cases' a worker is not able to take a rest break when he would ordinarily be entitled to do so, he should be allowed to take an equivalent rest break as soon as reasonably practicable thereafter.

Unmeasured working time

The provisions relating to the 48-hour week, night work, and minimum rest periods will not apply where a worker's work is not measured or predetermined or can otherwise be determined by the worker himself.

Examples are managing executives or other persons who have a discretion over whether to work or not on a given day without needing to consult the employer.

The Working Time Regulations 1999 extended the scope of the unmeasured working time exemption to include the concept of 'partially unmeasured working time', so that where a worker 'voluntarily' chooses to work outside the scope of the hours predetermined by his employer (more likely than not his contractual hours and any contractual overtime), only those hours which were predetermined by his employer will count for the purposes of calculating his working time. This has now been repealed following proceedings being issued by the European Commission against the UK that the exemption was not permitted by the Working Time Directive and was therefore unlawful.

Annual leave

Since 1 October 2007 with the introduction of the Working Time (Amendment) Regulations 2007, statutory holiday entitlement has been increased for full-time workers to 4.8 weeks in each leave year and will increase again to 5.6 weeks on 1 April 2009. A part-time worker is entitled to 4.8 weeks' holiday reduced pro-rata according to the amount of days they work. Where a worker begins employment part-way through a leave year, he is entitled in that leave year to the proportion of the 4.8 weeks' annual leave which is equal to the proportion of the leave year for which he is employed.

Working time

There is no statutory right to take bank holidays but the October 2007 and April 2009 increases in annual leave will give full-time workers a further eight days' holiday to take account of bank holidays, although there is no right for the time off to be taken on bank holidays.

It is not possible to pay a worker instead of allowing annual leave to be made available, save for the additional four days' holiday introduced post-1 October 2007, which can be replaced by payment in lieu during the transitional phase up to 1 April 2009.

Contractual holiday provisions should be checked to ensure enough holiday is given, but can also be used to fill in gaps in the Regulations, including, for example, in relation to the clawback of overpaid holiday pay when an employee leaves.

For the purposes of the statutory leave entitlement, workers are entitled to be paid a 'week's pay' for each week of annual leave. This is calculated in a particular manner. Effectively, where a worker is paid an annual, monthly or weekly amount to which he is contractually entitled, his holiday pay will be the weekly equivalent of that amount. However, where a worker receives a varying amount of pay each week which is not contractually provided for or agreed, a 'week's pay' must be calculated in accordance with the average amount of pay the worker received in the 12-week period prior to the date of payment. Specific pro rata rules apply to untaken holiday when an employee leaves.

The Regulations provide a right to stipulate when a worker can take his leave entitlement, including notice provisions for the employer and the employee.

Agreements
Various parts of the Regulations can be disapplied or softened by specific agreements.

A 'relevant agreement' is usually a contract between an employer and a worker.

A 'workforce agreement' means an agreement between an employer and its workers or their elected representatives.

Records
Employers must keep adequate records to show in particular whether the limits in the Regulations dealing with the 48-hour week and night work are being complied with.

The courts will expect employers to be able to show they are complying with the Regulations and policing working time.

Officers of the HSE are entitled to investigate an employer's working-time practices and can demand to see copies of its records.

Enforcement
The method of enforcing the Regulations depends upon whether the provision relied upon is a limit or an entitlement. The HSE and Local Authorities are responsible for enforcing the limits set out in the Regulations.

Workers may present a complaint to an Employment Tribunal in connection with any failure by their employer to provide them with the relevant protections afforded by the Regulations. Where a worker is also an employee, and is dismissed as a result of exercising a right under the Regulations, his dismissal will be deemed to be automatically unfair.

It is automatically unfair to dismiss an employee for reasons connected with rights and entitlements under the Regulations. Employees may present a claim to an Employment Tribunal regardless of age or length of service.

EC proposals for change
Following the meeting between ministers at the EU Employment, Social Policy, Health

Working time

and Consumer Affairs Council on 9 and 10 June 2008, the EU Council has published its proposed wording for a directive to amend the Working Time Directive. The agreed position is that the opt-out will remain but the following restrictions will apply:

- Workers will have to renew the opt-out in writing annually.
- Workers will be able to opt back in with immediate effect during the first six months of employment or up to three months after the end of any probationary period, whichever is longer. This means that the notice period for opting back in will be two months rather than the current three months.
- An opt-out will be void if signed at the same time as the employment contract.
- An opt-out will be void if signed within four weeks of starting work. (This provision will not apply to workers who work for an employer for fewer than ten weeks in a 12-month period.)
- No worker can work for more than 60 hours a week, averaged over three months, unless permitted in a collective agreement or agreement. (This provision will not apply to workers who work for an employer for fewer than ten weeks in a 12-month period.)
- Working time plus inactive on-call time cannot exceed 65 hours a week averaged over three months, unless permitted in a collective agreement. (This provision will not apply to workers who work for an employer for fewer than ten weeks in a 12-month period.)

In addition:

- The reference period for calculating the 48-hour week may be extended to six months, 'for objective or technical reasons, or reasons concerning the organisation of work'.
- There will be a new category of time called 'inactive part of on-call time', which counts as neither working time not a rest period.
- Compensatory rest may be given after a 'reasonable period' rather than straight after the shift to which it relates.

The amended Directive is not yet in force and once in force the UK Government will need to legislate to implement it here. A number of proposals were put forward by the European Commission (including restricting or abolishing the opt-out system) in 2004; however none of these have yet been implemented and in April 2009 negotiations in Europe came to an end without any agreement been reached on the proposals. The legal framework in this area therefore remains largely unchanged and the opt-out system remains. For more on this subject, see '*UK wins latest battle over 48-hour working week,*' p.428.

See also: Dismissal, p.124; Flexible working, p.190; Night working, p.299; Stress, p.381; Young persons, p.430.

Sources of further information

BERR Working Time Regulations: www.berr.gov.uk/employment/employment-legislation/employment-guidance/page28978.html

Comment...

UK wins latest battle over 48-hour working week

> Andrew Workman is an Employment Law Specialist in the Employment Group at Davies Arnold Cooper. Andrew is an experienced Tribunal advocate. Originally qualifying as a barrister, he has developed particular expertise in representing employers in unfair dismissal and discrimination cases, and has experience at appellate level. Andrew also has substantial experience as an adviser to high net worth individuals and senior executives.

In the UK, employers are entitled to side-step the maximum 48-hour working week imposed by the European Working Time Directive, if a worker agrees to work longer. However, in recent months there have been increasingly worrying developments at European level threatening the continuation of this right to opt-out.

Recently the European Parliament has demanded that there be no exception to the maximum 48-hour working week rule and that the UK be brought into line with those other member states who operate the 48-hour maximum. The key argument has been that workers should not be allowed to opt-out of legislation that was designed to protect their health and safety.

Agreeing to disagree

On 27 April, negotiations between the European Parliament and the European Council of Ministers over both the UK's right to opt out of the maximum 48-hour week, and the change to the definition of 'working time' to exclude the inactive part of on-call time, came to an end – without agreement being reached.

The result is that the opt-out will remain in force for the foreseeable future and employers in the UK will, yet again, breathe a sigh of relief.

What is less welcome is the missed opportunity to clarify whether 'on-call' time is working time within the meaning of the Directive, and whether 'compensatory rest' (required where a worker misses part or all of a minimum daily or weekly rest period) should be taken after a 'reasonable period'.

The Parliament believes that all 'on-call' time, whether the worker is active or inactive (even asleep), should count as working time, while the Council wants only time when a worker is active to count as working time. Disagreement on all of these issues remains, but it is the issue of the opt-out that has caused the most disagreement.

The willingness of employees to work more than 48 hours each week has to an extent been garnered by the ease with which the opt-out, in its current form, can legally be incorporated into a contract upon commencement of employment. If employment contracts do not carefully make provision for the opt-out, it can be

Comment: 48-hour working week

difficult to encourage employees to opt-out at a later date in their employment.

Scrapping the opt-out

For some years now, the European Parliament has been voting to scrap the individual opt-out negotiated by John Major, the then Prime Minister in 1993, and which came into effect in 1998, allowing UK employers to facilitate the benefit of longer working hours from their employees than the 48-hour limit imposed in many other European countries would allow.

As far back as 2005, the European Parliament had voted to remove the opt-out by 2012, being unconvinced by arguments advanced by the CBI and other employer bodies that the competitiveness of UK business would be adversely affected if the opt-out was removed. Since then the issue has been in and out of the headlines as the mechanisms for legislative change in Europe have waxed and waned.

The UK's argument has been that removing the opt-out would damage the competitiveness of UK business and hinder job creation. Indeed, the flexibility of the UK workforce has been a major strength of the UK's labour market.

Flexibility

The Government's backing of the opt-out has wavered over the years, precisely because of the difficult balancing act this issue throws up. Various compromise positions have been suggested but the central difficulty for those opposed to the opt-out has been this: If employees are willing to enter contracts with longer working hours and improve their income accordingly – why not let them?

While employers will point to the lack of coercion involved in agreeing with employees that they work longer hours, unions have argued that the system is open to abuse and that tired, overstretched UK workers, who they argue, work the longest hours in Europe, are putting themselves and others at risk. In the current economic climate, that argument is looking less compelling by the day.

Legally and politically, the outcome of these negotiations at European level is likely to deter the European Commission in the months ahead from seeking a fresh approach to the opt-out issue. Those employers who have already incorporated suitable wording into their employment contracts can now rest easy that, for the time being at least, the opt-outs in their contracts can remain intact.

Young persons

Pinsent Masons Employment Group

Key points
- A young person is a person who has ceased to be a child and who is under the age of 18 years. A child is a person not over compulsory school age, currently 16 years.
- Young workers have particular rights under the Working Time Regulations 1998, particularly relating to rest breaks and night work assessments.
- Particular hourly rates apply to young workers for national minimum wage purposes. General health and safety duties prevent young workers being used for work beyond their capabilities.

Legislation
- Children and Young Persons Act 1933 (as amended).
- Employment Rights Act 1996 (as amended).
- National Minimum Wage Act 1998.
- Working Time Regulations 1998.
- Working Time (Amendment) Regulations 2002.

Working time

Daily rest
Young workers are entitled to a break of at least 12 consecutive hours in any 24-hour period.

Weekly rest
Young workers are entitled to a weekly rest period of at least 48 hours in each period of seven days (i.e. two days off each week). In addition, if owing to the nature of the work and because of technical or organisational reasons a young worker cannot take two days off per week, then the rest can be spread across 36 hours in a week.

Rest breaks while at work
If a young worker is required to work for more than four and a half hours at a stretch, he is entitled to a rest break of at least 30 minutes. A young worker's entitlement to rest breaks can be changed or excluded only in exceptional circumstances. If a young worker is working for more than one employer, the time he is working for each one should be added together to see if he is entitled to a rest break in a total four-and-a-half-hour period of work.

A young person's entitlement to breaks can be changed or not taken in exceptional circumstances only. The circumstances and 'special cases' are narrower than those for older workers and include the situation where no adult is available to do the work. Where this occurs, the worker should receive compensatory rest within three weeks.

Compensatory rest is a period of rest of the same length as the period of rest that a worker has missed.

Annual leave
Young workers have the same entitlements as adult workers in respect of annual leave. Under the Working Time Regulations 1998, all adult employees are entitled to at least 5.6 weeks' paid annual leave in each year.

Young persons

Time off for study and training
Young persons who are not in full-time secondary or further education are entitled to take time off during working hours for the purposes of study or training leading to an external qualification (academic or vocational) which 'enhances the young person's employment prospects'. The length of time that can be taken is that which is reasonable in the circumstances, and the young person should be paid for the time taken off at his normal hourly rate.

National Minimum Wage
The National Minimum Wage Act 1998 came into force on 1 April 1999 and provides for the minimum level of pay to which almost all workers in the UK are entitled. Since 1 October 2004 most workers over 16 years of age have been covered by the Act. The rates are reviewed in October each year. Following the introduction of the Employment Equality (Age) Regulations 2006 on 1 October 2006, minimum wage legislation could be challenged on the basis that it discriminates against people on the grounds of age.

Practical points to remember
Workplace managers should check:

- whether they employ young workers; and
- if they do, how many rest periods and breaks young workers are receiving.

If young workers are not receiving the correct rest periods, managers should consider:

- how these can be given; and
- whether the amount of hours worked can be reduced.

Managers should always ensure that:

- proper records of young workers are maintained, including details of health assessments;
- young workers are not involved in work which is particularly hazardous; and
- young workers are receiving the National Minimum Wage.

See also: Discrimination, p.110; Minimum wage, p.273; Working time, p.423.

Sources of further information

Workplace Law Network provides premium members with unrestricted access to a comprehensive range of online information – factsheets, case reports and daily news items – on employment, health and safety and premises management. Members also benefit from an online advice service and a free subscription to the *Workplace Law Magazine*. For more information email membership@workplacelaw.net or call our membership services team on 0871 777 8881.

Directory of information sources

Access Association
0113 2478102
www.access-association.org.uk

Action on Smoking and Health (ASH)
020 7739 5902
www.ash.org.uk

Advisory, Conciliation and Arbitration Service (ACAS)
08457 474 747
www.acas.org.uk

Age Concern
0800 00 99 66
www.ageconcern.org.uk

Alcohol Concern
020 7264 0510
www.alcoholconcern.org.uk

Association of British Insurers (ABI)
020 7600 3333
www.abi.org.uk

Association of Chief Police Officers (ACPO)
020 7084 8950
www.acpo.police.uk

Association of Sustainability Practitioners
www.asp-online.org

Better Regulation Commission
020 7276 2143
www.brc.gov.uk

Blind in Business
020 7588 1885
www.blindinbusiness.co.uk

British Association of Occupational Therapists (BAOT) / College of Occupational Therapists (COT)
020 7357 6480
www.cot.co.uk

British Automatic Fire Sprinkler Association
British Chambers of Commerce (BCC)
020 7654 5800
www.britishchambers.org.uk

British Institute of Facilities Management (BIFM)
0845 058 1356
www.bifm.org.uk

British Occupational Health Research Foundation (BOHRF)
020 7317 5898
www.bohrf.org.uk

British Occupational Hygiene Society (BOHS)
01332 298101
www.bohs.org

British Retail Consortium (BRC)
020 7854 8900
www.brc.org.uk

British Standards Institution (BSI)
020 8996 9001
www.bsi-global.com

Business in the Community
020 7566 8650
www.bitc.org.uk

Cadw
01443 336 000
www.cadw.wales.gov.uk

Customer Contact Association (CCA)
0141 564 9010
www.cca.org.uk

Central Arbitration Committee (CAC)
020 7904 2300
www.cac.gov.uk

Centre for Accessible Environments (CAE)
020 7840 0125
www.cae.org.uk

Centre for Corporate Accountability (CCA)
020 7490 4494
www.corporateaccountability.org

Centre for Effective Dispute Resolution (CEDR)
020 7536 6000
www.cedr.co.uk

Directory of information sources

Chartered Institute of Arbitrators
020 7421 7444
www.arbitrators.org

Chartered Institute of Personnel and Development (CIPD)
020 8162 6200
www.cipd.co.uk

Chartered Management Institute
020 7497 0580
www.managers.org.uk

CIFAS (the UK's Fraud Prevention Service)
www.cifas.org.uk

Civil Contingencies Secretariat (Cabinet Office)
0207 276 1234
www.cabinetoffice.gov.uk

Commission for Racial Equality (CRE)
see Equality and Human Rights Commission

Criminal Records Bureau (CRB)
0870 9090811
www.crb.gov.uk

Crown Prosecution Service (CPS)
020 7796 8000
www.cps.gov.uk

Department for Business, Innovation and Skills (BIS)
020 7215 5000
www.berr.gov.uk

Department for Communities and Local Government (DCLG)
020 7944 4400
www.communities.gov.uk

Department for Education and Skills (DfES)
See Department for Business, Innovation and Skills (BIS)

Department for Work and Pensions (DWP)
www.dwp.gov.uk

Department of Health (DH)
020 7210 4850
www.dh.gov.uk

Department of Trade and Industry (DTI)
See Department for Business, Innovation and Skills (BIS)

Direct Gov
www.direct.gov.uk

Disability Matters
01794 341 824
www.disabilitymatters.com

Disability Rights Commission (DRC)
See Equality and Human Rights Commission

Employee Assistance Professionals Association
01993 772 765
www.eapa.org.uk

Employers and Work-Life Balance
0207 976 3519
www.theworkfoundation.com

Employers' Forum on Age (EFA)
0845 456 2495
www.efa.org.uk

Employers' Forum on Disability
020 7403 3020
www.efd.org..uk

Employment Appeals Tribunal
020 7273 1041
www.employmentappeals.gov.uk

Employment Lawyers Association
01895 256972
www.elaweb.org.uk

Employment Tribunal
0845 795 9775
www.employmenttribunals.gov.uk

English Heritage
0870 333 1181
www.english-heritage.org.uk

ENTO (formerly Employment NTO)
0116 251 7979
www.ento.co.uk

Equality and Human Rights Commission
0845 604 6610
www.equalityhumanrights.com

Directory of information sources

Equal Opportunities Commission (EOC)
See Equality and Human Rights Commission

Ergonomics Society
01509 234904
www.ergonomics.org.uk

Facilities Management Association (FMA)
07960 428 146
www.fmassociation.org.uk

Federation of Small Businesses (FSB)
01253 336000
www.fsb.org.uk

Financial Services Authority (FSA)
020 7066 1000
www.fsa.gov.uk

Forum of Private Business (FPB)
0845 130 1722
www.fpb.org

Gangmasters Licensing Authority
0845 602 5020
www.gla.gov.uk

Her Majesty's Treasury
020 7270 4558
www.hm-treasury.gov.uk

HM Revenue & Customs
www.hmrc.gov.uk

Home Office
020 7035 4848
www.homeoffice.gov.uk

Information Commissioner's Office
08456 30 60 60
www.ico.gov.uk

Institute of Alcohol Studies (IAS)
01480 466 766
www.ias.org.uk

Institute of Customer Service (ICS)
01206 571716
www.instituteofcustomerservice.com

Institute of Directors (IoD)
020 7766 8866
www.iod.com

Institute of Environmental Management and Assessment (IEMA)
01522 540069
www.iema.net

Institute of Hospitality
020 8661 4900
www.instituteofhospitality.org

International Facilities Management Association (USA)
+1 713 623 4362
www.ifma.org

International Stress Management Association UK (ISMA UK)
01179 697284
www.isma.org.uk

Investors in People
020 7467 1900
www.investorsinpeople.co.uk

Knowledge-Counsel
01344 779438
www.knowledge-counsel.com

Low Pay Commission
020 7215 8459
www.lowpay.gov.uk

Mind
0845 7660163
www.mind.org.uk

National Association for the Care and Resettlement of Offenders (Nacro)
020 7840 7200
www.nacro.org.uk

National Association of Pension Funds (NAPF)
020 7808 1300
www.napf.co.uk

National Register of Access Consultants (NRAC)
020 7735 7845
www.nrac.org.uk

Directory of information sources

Northern Ireland Committee of the Irish Congress of Trade Unions (NIC.ICTU)
028 9024 7940
www.ictuni.org

Office of Communications (Ofcom)
020 7981 3000
www.ofcom.org.uk

Office of Public Sector Information (OPSI)
www.opsi.gov.uk

Patent Office
08459 500 505
www.ipo.gov.uk

The Pensions Regulator
01273 811 800
www.thepensionsregulator.gov.uk

Public Concern at Work
020 7404 6609
www.pcaw.co.uk

Recruitment and Employment Confederation (REC)
020 7009 2100
www.rec.uk.com

Remploy
0800 155 2700
www.remploy.co.uk

Royal Association for Disability and Rehabilitation (RADAR)
020 7250 3222
www.radar.org.uk

Royal National Institute of the Blind (RNIB)
020 7388 1266
www.rnib.org.uk

Royal National Institute for Deaf People (RNID)
020 7296 8000
www.rnid.org.uk

Scottish Centre for Facilities Management
0131 455 2642
www.sbe.napier.ac.uk/scfm

Scottish Trades Union Congress (STUC)
0141 337 8100
www.stuc.org.uk

Sign Design Society
020 8776 8866
www.signdesignsociety.co.uk

Stress Management Society
08701 999 235
www.stress.org.uk

Tailored Interactive Guidance on Employment Rights (TIGER)
See Direct Gov

Telework Association (TCA)
0800 616008
www.tca.org.uk

The Stationery Office
0870 600 5522
www.tso.co.uk

Trades Union Congress (TUC)
020 7636 4030
www.tuc.org.uk

United Kingdom Accreditation Service (UKAS)
020 8917 8400
www.ukas.com

Wales Trades Union Congress (TUC Cymru)
020 7636 4030
www.tuc.org.uk

Work Foundation
0207 976 3500
www.theworkfoundation.com

Working Balance
0161 217 2500
www.workingbalance.co.uk

Working Families
020 7253 7243
www.workingfamilies.org.uk

Working Well Together (WWT)
0845 27 27 500
www.wwt.uk.com

Workplace Law Group
0871 777 8881
www.workplacelaw.net

Index

Absence, 30-34
    disability and, 32
    long-term, 33
    monitoring, 30
    reducing, 30
    short-term, 33
    unauthorised, 33
Access to Medical Reports Act 1988, 30, 217, 257, 327
Addison v. Ashby (2003), 69
adoption leave, 182, 184, 301, 324
age discrimination, 69, 111, 119, 140, 164, 353, 355
Employment Equality (Age) Regulations 2006, 32, 49, 69, 119, 125, 138, 146, 296, 353, 431
agency workers, 35-39, 40-42, 308
alcohol, 43-45, 117, 257, 330
alternative dispute resolution, 72, 152, 153, 234
apprenticeships, 74, 187, 277, 417-422
    Apprenticeships, Skills, Children and Learning Bill, 395, 420
Asylum and Immigration Act 1996, 194, 195, 269
attendance records, 30
Barber v. Somerset County Council (2004), 261, 264, 382, 384
blacklisting, 403-404
    The Consulting Association and Ian Kerr, 87, 88, 403
    Employment Relations Act 1999 (Blacklists) Regulations 2009, 403, 404
Bullying and harassment, 49-53
    definition of, 49
    forms of, 50
    penalties for, 52
    policies to counter, 52

carers, 54-58
    Coleman v. Attridge Law (2008), 57, 116
    flexible working, 54
    parental leave, 56
    National Carers Strategy, 57
CCTV monitoring, 59-64
    British Standard, 63
    Code of Practice, 61
    Data Protection Act 1998 and, 59
    Employment Practices Code and, 62
    Human Rights Act 1998 and, 60
Childcare provisions, 65-67
    employer-supported, 66
    vouchers, 67
Children and Young Persons Act 1933, 68, 69, 430

Children at work, 68-70
    Addison v. Ashby, 69
    age discrimination, 69
    employment restrictions, 68
    time off, 69
Civil Partnerships Act 2004, 138
Contract disputes, 71-73
    adjudication of, 72
    alternative dispute resolution of, 72
    arbitration of, 71
    court proceedings for, 71
    negotiation of, 71
    record keeping and, 73
contracts
    employment, 146-149
    facilities management, 180-181
    fixed-term workers, 187-189
copyright, 229, 230, 236

data controllers, 85-87, 405
Data protection, 59-63, 84-88, 209-211, 224, 258-259, 294, 403-409
    confidential waste and, 410-413
Data Protection Act 1998, 59, 78, 84, 138, 167, 171, 208, 212, 214, 215, 216, 222, 224, 229, 233, 236, 244, 257, 258, 292, 294, 317, 319, 327, 328, 335, 338, 347, 403, 404, 407, 408, 410
Data Protection Employment Practices Code, 258, 409
Department for Business, Innovation and Skills (BIS), 47, 417
Directors' responsibilities, 89-94
    duties to employees, 90
    duty of skill and care, 89
Disability discrimination, 32, 95, 98-102, 110, 115-118, 166, 216, 267, 329, 364
Disability Discrimination Act 1995, 30, 32, 43, 44, 49, 54, 57, 98, 110, 115, 124, 126, 154, 215, 257, 261, 267, 317, 318, 335, 361, 364, 375, 377, 383, 395
    employers' duties under, 99
    service providers' duties under, 100
Disability Discrimination Act 2005, 98, 100, 102, 110, 117, 215, 257, 364, 395, 396
Disciplinary and grievance procedures, 106-109
    after April 2009, 106
Discrimination, 110-120
    age, 119
    Coleman v. Attridge Law (2008), 116
    definition of, 110
    disability, 115-117

Index

Mayor and Burgess of the London Borough of Lewisham v. Malcolm, 116
  on grounds of religion or belief, 118
  on grounds of sexual orientation, 118
  race, 113
  sex, 112
Dismissal, 124-128
  definition of, 122
  unfair, 123, 127
Dress codes, 129-132
driving, 133-137
  mobile phones and, 134-135
  smoking ban, 135
  working time and, 133
drugs, 43-45

Employee benefits, 138-141
  age discrimination and, 140
  healthcare, 140
  pensions, 139
  tax, 139
Employee consultation, 142-145
Employment Act 2002, 54, 106, 107, 124, 146, 154, 182, 190, 339
employment agencies, 37
Employment contracts, 146-149
  altering terms and conditions in, 148
  main terms and conditions in, 146
  statements of particulars and, 146
Employment disputes, 150-153
  ACAS and, 152
  arbitration and, 152
  County Court and, 152
  Employment Tribunals and, 150-151
Employment Equality (Age) Regulations 2006, 32, 49, 69, 119, 125, 138, 146, 148, 276, 353, 356, 431
Employment Equality (Religion or Belief) Regulations 2003, 49, 118, 121, 129, 131, 252, 255, 329
Employment Equality (Sexual Orientation) Regulations 2003, 49, 118, 329
Employment Practices Code, Information Commissioner's, 62, 330
Employment Relations Act 1999, 154, 182, 375, 391, 403
Employment Relations Act 2004, 391
Employment Rights Act 1996, 54, 56, 68, 74, 106, 124, 125, 138, 146, 154, 182, 215, 221, 252, 254, 301, 324, 327, 332, 339, 353, 354, 361, 375, 414, 415, 417, 419, 430
Employment Rights Act 1999, 187, 188
Employment status, 154, 157
Enterprise Act 2002, 292, 297
Equality and Human Rights Commission (EHRC), 7, 101, 120, 175, 227
Equal pay, 167-173
  genuine material factor defence and, 170
  like work and, 167
  North v. Dumfries and Galloway Council and others, 169
  remedies, 171
Equal Pay Act 1970, 138, 146, 167, 172, 335, 375
Equal Pay Act 1970 (Amendment Regulations) 2003, 167
European Convention for the Protection of Human Rights and Fundamental Freedoms, 226, 292
Expenses, 177-179
  East Lancashire Coachbuilders v. Hilton, 179
  Income Tax (Earnings and Pensions) Act 2003, 177
  policies, 177
  Thompson v. Brick Services Limited, 179

Facilities management contracts, 180-181
Family-friendly rights, 182-186
Fixed-term Employees (Prevention of Less Favourable Treatment) Regulations 2002, 37
Fixed-term workers, 187-189
Flexible working, 190-192
Foreign nationals, 194-207
  Asylum and Immigration Act 1996, 194, 195, 269
  Forster v. Cartwright Black, 252, 253

Garden leave, 350-352
grievance procedures: *see* Disciplinary and grievance procedures

hacking, computer, 236, 246
harassment, 49-53
harassment, sexual, 331
Health Act 2006, 133, 135, 137, 369, 370
Health surveillance, 212-214
Holiday, 219-221
Homeworking, 222-225
  Data protection, 224
  insurance and, 223
Human rights, 226-228
  codes of conduct and, 228
  disciplinary and grievance procedures and, 227
  dismissal and, 228
  private employers and, 226
  public authorities and, 226
  semi-public authorities and, 226
Human Rights Act 1998, 59, 60, 110, 111, 129, 226, 234, 236, 257, 292, 327, 328, 403

Immigration, points-based system, 196-200
Immigration (Restrictions on Employment) Order 2004, 194
Income Tax (Earnings and Pensions) Act 2003, 138, 312
Information and Consultation of Employees Regulations 2004, 142

Index

Information Commissioner, 59, 60-64, 82, 84-87, 211, 238, 244, 295, 319-321, 328, 330, 338, 403, 405, 407, 408, 411
Internships, 417-422
insurance, 223-224
Intellectual property, 229-235
Internet and email policies, 236-239
    monitoring, 237
internet domain names, 229
Interviews, 240-243
    diversity, 240
    internal candidates, 242
IT equipment, recycling of, 142
IT security, 244-249

jury service, 250-251

Katfunde v. Abbey National and Dr Daniel (1998), 381, 386

Leave, 252-256
    Compassionate, 252
    Forster v. Cartwright Black (2004), 252-253
    Sabbatical, 255

maternity leave, 65, 67, 112, 169
Medical records, 257-260
Medical Reports Act 1988, 217, 257
medical testing, 216-217
mental health, 261-268
    Stokes v. Guest, Keen and Nettlefold (Bolts and Nuts) Ltd (1968), 381-382
    Sutherland (Chairman of the Governors of St Thomas Beckett RC High School) v. Hatton and others (2002), 261-264
Migrant workers, 269-272
    discrimination, 272
    immigration, points-based system, 271
Minimum wage, 273-275
    enforcement, 274
    hourly rates, 273
    tips and gratuities, 274
misconduct, 53, 106, 363, 373
Misuse of Drugs Act 1971, 43
Money laundering, 279-291
Money Laundering Regulations 2007, 279, 285
Monitoring employees, 292-298
mothers, new and expectant, 300, 324-326

National Minimum Wage Act 1998, 124, 128, 138, 154, 273-275, 417, 419, 430, 431
National Minimum Wage Regulations 1999, 273
Night working, 299-300
    new and expectant mothers and, 300
Notice, 301-303
    garden leave, 301
    fixed-term contracts, 302
    retirement, 303
    pay in lieu of (PILON), 301
nurseries, workplace, 66

Occupational health, 304-307
    'Revitalising health and safety', 305

Part-time workers, 308-311
Part-time Workers (Prevention of Less Favourable Treatment) Regulations 2000, 308
Paternity and Adoption Leave Regulations 2002, 184
paternity leave, 65, 182, 184, 302
Pensions, 312-316
    life assurance and, 316
    occupational, 314
    personal, 315
    stakeholder, 315
    state, 313
Pensions Act 2004, 138, 312, 399
Personnel files, 317-323
    data protection, 320
    relevant filing systems, 320
Pregnancy, 324-326
Private life, 327-331
Probationary periods, 332-334
Public Interest Disclosure Act 1998, 154, 414

race discrimination, 113-114, 131, 166, 198, 272
    dress codes and, 131
Recruitment and selection, 240-243, 335-338
    advertising, 336
    interviews, 240-243, 337
    job descriptions and, 607
    shortlisting, 337
Redundancy, 339-342
    consultation process, 341
    payments, 339
References, 347-349
    employees' claims, 348
Retirement, 353-356

Self-employment, 357-360
sex discrimination, 49, 51, 112-113, 129, 140, 166, 172
    dress codes and, 129
Sex Discrimination Act 1975, 49, 129, 154, 167, 335, 395
Sharp v. Caledonia Group Services (2005), 170
sick pay, 69, 138, 140, 147, 156, 167, 259, 357, 361-365
    contractual, 361
    statutory, 361
sick leave, 361-365
Smoking, 369-374
    ban, 371
    policies, 372
    vehicles, 371
Social Security Contributions and Benefits Act

Index

1992, 138
Staff handbooks, 375-380
Stress, 381-387
 combating, 386
 HSE Management Standards on, 383
Strikes, 388-390
 contractual liability, 388
 unfair dismissal, 389
SureStart Strategy, 65, 66
Sutherland v. Hatton (2002), 261, 264, 265, 381-383

telephone calls, recording, 292, 294
teleworking: *see* homeworking
temporary workers, 35-39
Training, 395-398
TUPE, 399-402
 application, 399
 terms and conditions and, 401
 Transfer of Undertakings (Protection of Employment) Regulations 2006, 399
 which employees transfer, 400

unfair dismissal, 107, 125, 127, 152, 165, 166, 266, 325, 355, 416, 419
Unlawfully procuring information, 403-409
 Section 77, Criminal Justice and Immigration Act 2008, 404, 408

victimisation, 52, 56, 111, 117-119

Walker v. Northumberland County Council (1995), 381, 382, 384
Waste, confidential, 410-413
Whistleblowers, 414-416
Work and Families Act 2006, 54, 138, 182-186, 301, 324
work experience, 417-422
Working time, 423-427
 48-hour week and, 423
 annual leave and, 425
 EC proposals, 426
 rest periods and, 424
Working Time Directive, 40, 164, 166, 263, 364, 425, 427, 428
Working Time Regulations 1998, 68, 69, 124, 128, 146, 154, 423, 430

young persons, 430-431
 annual leave and, 430
 minimum wage and, 431
 rest requirements and, 430
 study leave and, 431